EMPIRE OF COMMERCE

Jeffersonian America

Charlene M. Boyer Lewis, Annette Gordon-Reed, Peter S. Onuf,
Andrew J. O'Shaughnessy, and Robert G. Parkinson, Editors

Empire of Commerce

The Closing of the Mississippi and the Opening of Atlantic Trade

Susan Gaunt Stearns

University of Virginia Press
Charlottesville and London

The University of Virginia Press is situated on the traditional lands of the Monacan Nation, and the Commonwealth of Virginia was and is home to many other Indigenous people. We pay our respect to all of them, past and present. We also honor the enslaved African and African American people who built the University of Virginia, and we recognize their descendants. We commit to fostering voices from these communities through our publications and to deepening our collective understanding of their histories and contributions.

University of Virginia Press
© 2024 by the Rector and Visitors of the University of Virginia
All rights reserved
Printed in the United States of America on acid-free paper

First published 2024

1 3 5 7 9 8 6 4 2

Library of Congress Cataloging-in-Publication Data

Names: Stearns, Susan Gaunt, author.
Title: Empire of commerce : the closing of the Mississippi and the opening of Atlantic trade / Susan Gaunt Stearns.
Description: Charlottesville : University of Virginia Press, 2024. | Series: Jeffersonian America | Includes bibliographical references and index.
Identifiers: LCCN 2023052272 (print) | LCCN 2023052273 (ebook) | ISBN 9780813951232 (hardcover) | ISBN 9780813951249 (paperback) | ISBN 9780813951256 (ebook)
Subjects: LCSH: United States—Economic conditions—To 1865. | Industrial revolution—United States. | United States—Territorial expansion. | West (U.S.)—Discovery and exploration. | Shipping—Missouri River. | BISAC: HISTORY / United States / Revolutionary Period (1775–1800)
Classification: LCC HC105 .S74 2024 (print) | LCC HC105 (ebook) | DDC 330.973/05—dc23/eng/20231212
LC record available at https://lccn.loc.gov/2023052272
LC ebook record available at https://lccn.loc.gov/2023052273

Cover art: "The Jolly Flatboatmen" (detail) by George Caleb Bingham, 1846. (Patrons' Permanent Fund, The National Gallery of Art)

CONTENTS

Acknowledgments	vii
Introduction	1
Part I. Mississippi River Trade to 1783	**11**
1 The Colonial River	17
2 Kentucky Land, Cash, and the Mississippi	31
3 The River at War	47
Part II. The Closure of the River and Sectional Crisis, 1784–1795	**63**
4 An Imperial Problem	67
5 Trading without the River	92
6 Chickasaw Country	112
Part III. Western Trade, Atlantic World, 1796–1803	**129**
7 Cotton and the Americanization of Natchez	136
8 American Trade in a Spanish Port	153
9 The Chickasaw Trace	176
10 Buying the Mississippi	195
Epilogue	215
Notes	221
Bibliography	261
Index	287

ACKNOWLEDGMENTS

This book is the result of more than a decade of labor, and during that time I accrued more than my fair share of debts. As a graduate student at the University of Chicago, I benefited from the guidance of Kathleen Neils Conzen. Only in retrospect have I realized how deliberately she helped shape my graduate experience, providing feedback on my work but more importantly by providing opportunities to discuss how each stage of my education was intended to help me develop my skills as a historian and scholar. I am indebted to her for believing in me and my project, and for teaching me how to identify the cultural background of a region's European American settlers by examining the shape of barns, a lesson that I continue to pass along to both my students and my family on our travels. I also owe a debt of gratitude to Amy Dru Stanley, both for helping me define what type of historian I would like to be and also for assigning the paper that initially brought me to this project. I benefited too from the support of Christine Stansell, who provided a model of professionalism I continue to strive to emulate. I would also like to thank the other members of the faculty and my fellow graduate students, who helped shape this project.

I could not have completed this book without the generous financial support of several institutions. Travel grants from the Filson Historical Society, the Kentucky Historical Society, the Virginia Historical Society, and the University of Chicago made it possible for me to perform the research necessary for completing my dissertation, and a Mellon Humanities Fellowship from the University of Chicago helped support me as I wrote up my findings. After graduating, support from the Economic History Association and the Program in Early American Economy and Society at the Library Company of Philadelphia allowed me to expand on the project's national and international significance. This project could not have been completed without the time and support I received from the Jack Miller Center and the Center for Legal Studies at Northwestern University, where I served as the Alexander Hamilton Postdoctoral Fellow. I am beyond grateful to Pamela Edwards, Joanna Grisinger, Shana Bernstein, Heather Schoenfeld, and Laura Beth Nielsen for their enthusiastic and unending support for me as both a scholar and a human being. I have also benefited enormously from the financial and intellectual support of the Department of History at the University of Mississippi, and especially from my colleagues, who gave me the time I needed to finally see this work through to fruition.

Completing this project took more than fifteen years; as a result, many, many people have read or commented on the project in whole or in part. In particular, I would like to thank Peter Onuf, Kristopher Ray, Kevin Barksdale, and Jonathan Levy for their reading of an earlier version of this text, and Mikaela Adams, Christine Sears, Michelle Orihel, Stephanie Frank, Theresa Rothschadl, Erika Vause, Natalie Inman, Sheila Skemp, and Cathy Matson for providing thoughtful and detailed feedback on more recent drafts. I would also like to thank Nadine Zimmerli, James E. Lewis, and the anonymous reviewer from the University of Virginia Press, whose feedback was invaluable in revising the final manuscript. Finally, I would like to thank my family, especially my parents, for their tireless support. I would also like to thank my children, Jacob and Oscar, without whom this book would have been finished several years earlier. Most importantly, I would like to thank my husband, Dan, whose sacrifices and encouragement have made this book possible.

EMPIRE OF COMMERCE

Introduction

On July 15, 1789, a group of eighteen men from the thirteen American states stood before the governor of Spanish Natchez and vowed their allegiance to King Carlos IV. In Natchez, such an event was a regular occurrence: between 1786 and 1790, over a thousand "Americans" agreed to become loyal vassals of the crown of Spain. Don Manuel Gayoso de Lemos, a graduate of Westminster College and the newly appointed governor of the Natchez district, first read the oath aloud in English. He then read the document aloud in Spanish, with each man placing his hand on the Bible in turn and promising to serve Spain faithfully, to take up arms in its defense, and to alert Spanish officials of any plots against Spanish sovereignty. In the growing riverside community, no one save the Spanish officials charged with noting the community's comings and goings would have taken an interest in the small ceremony. Indeed, there might be little here to concern historians were it not for one name among those pledging fealty to the Spanish crown on that hot July day: Andrew Jackson.[1]

In 1789, Andrew Jackson was twenty-two years old. Already employed as the attorney general of North Carolina's westernmost district, Jackson was a man of huge ambition, searching the western countryside for sufficient land, wealth, and stature to overcome his humble origins. The Natchez district—the region surrounding the riverfront village bearing the same name—had much to offer such a man. A year earlier, Spanish officials had put into place generous land policies in hopes of attracting more American settlers to shore up Spanish defenses against the United States' expansion into trans-Appalachia.[2] Promising land in proportion to the size of a man's "family"—free and enslaved—Spanish policy proved attractive to land-hungry emigrants. In contrast to land almost anywhere within the thirteen states, Spanish land was a true grant: loyalty and labor were the only fees required. For a man like Jackson, with little capital but an abundance of energy and increasing numbers of political and business connections, life as a Spanish subject was undeniably appealing.

In popular memory, Jackson is described as the *American Lion*: the embodiment of a uniquely American mode of political thought, an image that Jackson worked to develop in the decades following the Battle of New Orleans.[3] The fact that thirty years before Jackson was elected president he swore allegiance to the Spanish crown seems antithetical to our view of Old Hickory. But Jackson's presence in Natchez can tell us much about the development of the American West. In 1789, Jackson was not an American and not a Democrat—two terms that would have been relatively meaningless in the contested borderlands of the Mississippi River Valley. Like all residents of the frontier, Jackson's identity shifted and changed as he moved through a region claimed by the United States, Cherokee, Chickamauga, Creek, Chickasaw, Choctaw, and Spanish polities.[4] Wherever he was, Jackson looked out for his own interests, hoping to gain land and a fortune. He adopted the identity, and the loyalties, that he believed would move him closest to this goal.

Two months before Jackson pledged himself a loyal Spanish subject, George Washington stood before a gathered crowd in New York City and took the oath of office as the first president of the United States. Washington's inauguration marked a new start for the new nation, under a constitution that remained contested (Andrew Jackson's North Carolina would not ratify it until November 1789, six months after Washington's swearing-in). Much remained unclear during Washington's inauguration. He swore to protect a nation whose boundaries were unsurveyed and contested, boundaries that—like the new nation itself—existed on parchment but had yet to be given form. Over the next few years, Washington's administration moved to put the precepts of an extended republic into place. Among the president's biggest challenges would be figuring out how to deal with men like Jackson, and the promises and threats posed by the southwestern borderlands.

As Jackson's presence in the Spanish village suggests, areas like Natchez mattered from the nation's start. By becoming a Spanish subject, Jackson was responding to what was by 1789 a major problem for the more than 100,000 settlers who had moved to the West. In 1784, Spain had closed the Mississippi River to American trade. It was geology, far more than geopolitics, which dictated the importance of the Mississippi for western settlers like Jackson. The Appalachian Mountains form a watershed that separates the rivers that flow into the Atlantic from those flowing into the Gulf of Mexico. A drop of rain falling on the eastern side of the mountains would eventually flow into the Atlantic, while a drop of rain that fell west of the Appalachians would find its way first into the Kanawha, Licking, Kentucky, Miami, Wabash, or countless other rivers before flowing into the Ohio and then on to the Mississippi, which would carry it to the Gulf of Mexico. This geological bifurcation had important ramifications for western trade and settlement. Barring inevitable problems with spring floods and summer droughts, travelers heading south and west toward the new settlements in trans-Appalachia found geology worked in their favor: the current of the rivers propelled goods and people inexorably toward the Mississippi and the Gulf, where the port of New Orleans offered a potent lure as both a market for western goods and a transportation hub from which western produce could be shipped throughout the Caribbean or across the Atlantic littoral. In contrast, traveling east along the rivers—from what are now the states of Kentucky, Tennessee, and Ohio back toward the eastern seaboard—necessitated arduous, constant, and backbreaking labor.[5] In 1784, when Spain closed the Mississippi River to American trade, it foreclosed the possibility of western produce reaching eastern markets. Spain's decision both reduced western land values and increased tensions between the United States, then developing along the Atlantic seaboard, and the settlers west of the Appalachians.[6]

The degree of fury created by Spain's decision to close the Mississippi was wildly out of proportion to the size of the United States' share of Mississippi River trade in the early 1780s. In both western settlements and in Congress, outrage over the closure of the Mississippi stemmed not from the immediate curtailment of trade but from two other causes. Settlers in the Ohio Valley, and those in the East who based their wealth on western land, had constructed a vision of western development predicated on market participation. Geographically isolated from markets to the East, and politically cut off from the marketplace of New Orleans, westerners demanded the federal government intervene to provide them with trade. Despite ongoing frontier violence, difficulties claiming and surveying land, and the challenges of establishing a new polity, from 1784 until 1803 gaining access to trade was a central political issue shaping the relationship between the new U.S. government in the East and the trans-Appalachian West.[7]

In western rhetoric and politics, market access equated to land. The legal and economic system imported from east of the Appalachians made market participation a necessity. To obtain legal title to land, settlers needed to be able to pay for it; to retain title, they needed to be able to pay their taxes.[8] In a society that placed landownership at the gateway to both social and political power, the drive to obtain and protect their access to land became westerners' chief demand of both the state and federal governments. The closure of the Mississippi eliminated westerners' access to markets and hence their ability to claim western land, throwing their economy into disarray. As a result, the closure profoundly shaped their beliefs in the role that the government could and should play in protecting and providing them with market access.

Throughout the 1780s and 1790s, the U.S. government, Spanish officials, and the white residents of the Ohio and Mississippi Valleys were preoccupied by what became known as the "Mississippi Question"—the American response to Spanish control of the river.[9] As Americans debated how to react to the river's closure, they also questioned and defined the evolving relationship between trans-Appalachia and the states clustered along the Atlantic seaboard. Spanish control of the Mississippi created a problem negotiated both by high-level government officials such as John Jay and Thomas Jefferson, and by men like Gabriel Bolong, a poor western farmer who was taken captive by the Spanish in 1795 and forced to build the forts meant to prevent Americans from using the river.[10] It inspired some, like Jackson, to seek out opportunities under the authority of different regimes, while others, such as the citizens of Kentucky's Democratic-Republican societies of the 1790s, responded by proclaiming their commitment to the republican principles of the United States—even as they contemplated withdrawing from the American union. With the ratification of the Treaty of San Lorenzo (better known as Pinckney's Treaty) in 1795, the twofold problem of control of the Mississippi River and the role of the West within the emerging United States took on new urgency, as the incorporation of new regions, the development of new crops, and the creation of new commercial ties recast the position of the West within the broader union.

This book examines how western settlers and speculators, eastern and southern politicians, coastal merchants, Mississippi Valley planters, Ohio farmers, and the Chickasaw all helped shape the dimensions of American trade through the continental interior as each of these groups confronted the consequences of Spanish control over the Mississippi. It argues that commercial integration and geographic expansion were linked processes which occupied the core of the development of an American empire. Much like the British empire, the U.S. empire that succeeded it depended on the creation of a system of governance that would allow regions at a distance to become integrated into a centrally focused commercial network.[11] Recognizing the link between commerce and expansion as the heart of empire is key to understanding the progress and development of the early United States. In this view, the task of building an American empire required not only displacing Indigenous peoples, establishing a widely accepted legal regime, and distributing land but also constructing ties of exchange and commerce that could bind the periphery to the center.[12] The development of trade connections, often created in the absence of governmental approval, helped to legitimate the federal government in the trans-Appalachian West, even when the federal government was unable to act to exert western interests. As a result of the robust growth of the trade of the continental interior, the United States became more successful in asserting its interests abroad and secured the loyalty of its western settlers. Rather than radiating outward from a national center like the spokes of a wheel, the trade that would tie the United States together and allow for the continued expansion of an American empire floated along the Mississippi.

This book focuses primarily on the European American farmers, traders, merchants, and politicians who in the last two decades of the eighteenth century debated, contested, and used the Mississippi River to integrate the trans-Appalachian West into the Atlantic world. Not the story of one place, it instead follows the arc of European American colonization of trans-Appalachia between 1775 and 1803. By the time of the Louisiana Purchase, the West had expanded to include a region roughly bordered by the Mississippi to the west, the Appalachians to the east, and the Gulf of Mexico to the south. The northern border was defined by those communities in what are now Ohio and Indiana that lay along the watercourses that emptied into the Ohio River. The book gives the most emphasis to the communities that voiced the greatest concern over access to the Mississippi: the region that in 1792 would become the state of Kentucky, the communities of Natchez and New Orleans along the lower Mississippi River, and the late-arriving but critical settlements north of the Ohio. It also engages with the experiences of the Chickasaw, whose lives were equally affected by Mississippi River trade and the interimperial conflict for control of the river. For the Chickasaw, the European

Americans moving along the river represented both a threat and an opportunity. Most frequently, I refer to the European Americans in trans-Appalachia as "westerners," although occasionally I use that term to refer to all residents of the trans-Appalachian West, whether identified with the United States, Indigenous nations, free or enslaved Africans, or Spanish colonists. Defining white settlers as "westerners" establishes a clear focus for the narrative: these people can only be deemed "western" when considered as a part of the union taking shape east of the Appalachian Mountains. Both the European American colonizers of the trans-Appalachian West and the polity emerging on the eastern seaboard acknowledged a connection between themselves, yet each group was uncertain what form that connection should take.[13] Westerners shared a political heritage and often bonds of family or patronage with the residents of the eastern seaboard, yet experienced being part of the union differently from their cis-Appalachian cousins.

This book faces neither west nor east. Its purpose is broader: to examine the influence exerted by the West over the construction of the American republic.[14] In placing the West at the forefront of the national story, I am nodding to Frederick Jackson Turner, who in 1893 proposed that the American experience emerged out of the milieu of what he called "the frontier."[15] In the decades following the Turnerian moment, several historians applied his concept to revolutionary-era trans-Appalachia. Pinckney's Treaty and the western origins of the Louisiana Purchase both had their moment in the sun, generating works dazzling in scope and detail.[16] There is much to object to in Turner's thesis, from his misrepresentation of Indigenous peoples as part of a "primitive society" to his credulous reliance on an inchoate "American character." Still, many scholars have rightly criticized Turner's conception of "frontiers" as ethnically and racially chauvinistic without undercutting his claim that the West played a larger role than it is usually granted in narratives of American state formation.[17] Any picture of the United States in the 1780s and 1790s that neglects either the trans-Appalachian West or the new nation's capital is incomplete: the West played an integral role in shaping both the form of the American polity and the contours of the developing nation.

In recent years, historians have paid increasing attention to the political economy of the early American republic, examining how issues like taxation, commerce, customs duties, insurance, and accounting reverberated across commercial and political society.[18] The story of the trans-Appalachian West has usually been told as a separate story. *From Furs to Farms*—as one recent account of transformations in Illinois country frames it—delineates how the West's economic activities have largely been regarded.[19] Scholars of the West have tracked time and again the disruptions and creativity spawned by the multicultural world of the fur trade gradually giving way to a world dominated by white commercial agriculture.[20] Land and land speculators played a key role in transforming territory from Indigenous homelands to white property; the largest land speculator was, of course, the American state, which from 1787 onward was committed to selling off the "public domain" to repay the crushing debts incurred by the American Revolution. In partnership with land speculators and the settlers they attracted, the central government played a crucial role in transforming the landscape of the West by creating the apparatus for European Americans to purchase western lands.[21] Neither the economy nor the politics of the West stood apart from those of the rest of the nation. Meanwhile, European American speculators, farmers, and heads of state constructed financial and political models for both the West and the nation based less on the realities of the contested landscape and more on the dimensions of a west they hoped would someday exist. In insisting on its existence, they willed a west of Anglo-American farmers producing for Atlantic world markets into being.

The enactment of Pinckney's Treaty in 1796–97 transformed the relationship between East and West. The treaty redrew the lines around the American polity, bringing the district surrounding Natchez into the American fold, opening American access to New Orleans and the Mississippi, and fully encompassing the Chickasaw homeland. Just as Natchez was becoming part of the United States, the district's plantations pivoted from growing tobacco to producing cotton. Meanwhile, the enactment of the treaty coincided with the end of a decade of interracial violence in the Ohio Country.[22] With peace, the European-American population of the Northwest Territory—and hence its agricultural production—expanded rapidly. Flour as well as corn and its byproducts whiskey and salt pork became increasingly important to the national economy.

Cotton challenged the geopolitical status quo, elevating the importance of Mississippi River trade and of trans-Appalachia more broadly. Cotton heightened the interest of eastern merchants in the Southwest; in turn, these merchants added their voices to those of western farmers agitating for greater federal intervention south of the Ohio River.[23] It might seem ironic to argue that cotton—a crop intrinsically and consequentially associated with the South—played a vital role in linking the West to the rest of the nation. But scholars have repeatedly highlighted the centrality of cotton in the development of the United States. The crop may have been regional but the labor that made mass production possible, the federal laws that safeguarded slavery, and the merchants on both sides of the Atlantic who profited from its sale were not.

Historians taking stock of the relationship between capitalism and slavery have examined the role of cotton production in Tennessee, Mississippi, and Louisiana, three of the regions discussed in this book. Their work has informed my own, as it has yielded profound insights into the role that enslavement played in the construction of not just a regional but a national economy, as well as the role that enslaved people played—no less foundational for being involuntary—as the central engine of American economic development. Cotton and slavery were at the core of U.S. imperial ambitions in the nineteenth century: they dominated American international relations while simultaneously weaving together a new economy that would rapidly span the globe. Slavery, these scholars have shown, was both a labor system and a property regime, creating wealth not only for enslavers but for Americans more broadly, as slaves were insured, mortgaged, and tortured to extract as much money as possible in the unrelenting immoral calculus of the trade in enslaved bodies. In unraveling the role of enslavement as the driving force behind national and international economic and political power, these historians have reoriented how we understand slavery and its relationship to both national development and western expansion. Slavery and the white supremacy that supported it are as American as apple pie and representative democracy.[24] Yet for all these works' considerable explanatory power, they enter the story late—once the lower Mississippi Valley had already ceased being western and begun to be southern. The forces driving the development of the Cotton Belt were in place by the turn of the nineteenth century. By the time of the Louisiana Purchase, American settlements in the lower Mississippi Valley were already importing hundreds if not thousands of enslaved people from Kentucky and North Carolina, inaugurating a domestic slave trade encapsulated in the phrase "sold down the river."

By 1803, Andrew Jackson began to transport enslaved people from the Cumberland to Natchez. Cotton planters from the Mississippi Valley and cotton merchants from the eastern seaboard were already engaged in insuring their shipments in eastern markets and making their voices heard in Congress, a fact embodied in the 1803 congressional decision to send James Monroe to Paris to negotiate for the purchase of New

Orleans. At the same time that cotton was exploding, new avenues for older western produce like flour and salt pork were taking shape on the staple-producing islands of the Caribbean. Western speculators, including the federal government, were dependent on the success of this new Caribbean trade to secure the loyalty and livelihood of western settlers in the Ohio Country and elsewhere. The Louisiana Purchase was thus less the starting point of the cotton juggernaut than it was its first victory, a victory claimed through the collaboration of western farmers, southern planters, and Atlantic merchants.

This book is structured around three key diplomatic decisions with important consequences for the development of trans-Appalachia. The first, Spain's closure of the river in 1784, created a crisis that threatened the unity of the United States. Both westerners and easterners contemplated seceding from the union as each group sought to pursue its own interests, alarming committed nationalists like James Madison and helping to precipitate the drafting of the Constitution. The second crucial moment was the ratification of Pinckney's Treaty in 1795, which changed the role of the West within the political economy of the nation by opening the Mississippi to American trade. Continued Spanish control of the river repeatedly stymied European American visions for the river's trade. As western produce—including cotton—grew increasingly important to the entire American economy, foreign control of the Mississippi became untenable to both western farmers and eastern merchants intent on trading the produce of the trans-Appalachian West throughout the Atlantic world, even as the increased river traffic created by the treaty reoriented the economy of the Chickasaw people toward servicing American traders. Finally, the Louisiana Purchase of 1803 achieved the outcome westerners had been advocating for two decades: the Mississippi became an American river.

Part 1 surveys the relationship between trade and expansion in the era prior to Spain's closure of the Mississippi, tracing the development of European American trade along the river before the closure and the prominent position of the Chickasaw within that trade, before examining the role that westerners hoped the river would play in bolstering the super-heated western land market of the 1770s and 1780s. Part 2 investigates the period following Spain's 1784 closure of the Mississippi, unpacking Congress's reaction to the river's closing and the influence of the so-called Mississippi Question on the drafting and ratification of the Constitution before exploring westerners' anger toward the emerging Federalist administration and the variety of ways that westerners tried to circumvent the river's closure. For the Chickasaw, the decade following the end of the Revolution was one of profound change, as the diplomatic and economic basis of the Southwest shifted in the face of a growing European American presence in the region. The section ends by contrasting the Chickasaw response to Pinckney's Treaty with the response of Kentuckians. For both groups, the passage of the treaty would prove transformative.

Part 3 of the book focuses on the integration of trans-Appalachia into the Atlantic world and the national economy under the terms of Pinckney's Treaty. The year 1795 saw not only the passage of the treaty but also the advent of peace in the contested Northwest Territory. The end of the violence drew a flood of western settlement and investment in western lands; much of that land was purchased on credit, and western farmers needed markets to repay debts to both speculators and the federal government. Meanwhile, in 1797, the village of Natchez transformed from a Spanish outpost invested in tobacco production to a U.S. settlement dedicated to cotton. Getting Natchez cotton and Ohio flour to world markets depended on the cooperation of eastern merchants, whose trade in cotton to Europe and flour to the Caribbean increasingly tied trans-Appalachia within the Atlantic world. These ties then reverberated from the lower Mississippi River Valley north through Chickasaw country, as the Chickasaw reoriented their economy to take advantage of the opportunities created by increased western trade. In 1802, those ties were abruptly cut as Spanish officials once more closed the Mississippi to American trade. Instead of dividing the nation, as the 1784 decision had, the Spanish decision in 1802 united the states of the East and the West, as calls for war against Spain emerged from across the political spectrum. The resulting Louisiana Purchase accomplished westerners' long-term goal: the federal government moved to give them unmitigated access to the Mississippi.

The Mississippi Question helped shape the form that the American empire would take as western land acquisition, along with western loyalty, depended on securing access to markets. Addressing the Mississippi Question is a necessary precursor to understanding the development of the Deep South and Indian removal in the antebellum era. Its consequences reverberated throughout the century that followed, influencing the lives of European American farmers, northern and southern Indigenous peoples, European factory operatives, and enslaved people throughout the United States and the Caribbean. Few things would matter more to the America of Andrew Jackson's presidency than the events unfolding along the Mississippi River of his youth.

PART I

Mississippi River Trade to 1783

———•◆•———

IN THE 1840s, Presbyterian minister John Dabney Shane interviewed a loquacious nonagenarian named Joshua McQueen. Although a minister by training, Shane's true passion lay elsewhere: fascinated by the history of the Ohio River Valley, he spent years crisscrossing Ohio and Kentucky interviewing aging "pioneers."[1] As Shane learned, McQueen had received an impressive education. His travels, first as a member of the Continental Army and later as a hunter and trader in trans-Appalachia, had brought him into contact with people from an astonishing number of backgrounds. Throughout the 1770s and early 1780s, McQueen had navigated his way across the eastern half of a contested American continent. He had crossed the Delaware with George Washington on Christmas Eve 1777 and wintered at Valley Forge. His brother had been held captive first by Shawnee and later by British troops north of the Ohio River. McQueen knew that in New Orleans they served their meat with rice and a bottle of bear's oil; he had spent a season rowing against the current of the Mississippi with a motley crew of French, Spanish, and Native laborers. Although McQueen was no scholar of Latin and Greek, he could communicate in English, French, and some dialects of Algonquian. In 1782, after being discharged from the army, McQueen and two companions floated down the Ohio River bound for the village of Natchez on a boat carrying Pennsylvania flour. They never arrived. Instead, the three men were captured by British Loyalists operating from Chickasaw territory before being rescued by the arrival of Spanish troops.[2]

Eighteenth-century cartographers imbued the Mississippi with many different meanings. On maps drawn by Spanish officials following the Treaty of Paris of 1783, the Mississippi divided the Spanish dominion in the Southeast, a region that included all territory west of the Mississippi, extending north along the river as far as modern-day Kentucky and encompassing the newly won colonies of East and West Florida. Claiming the lower Mississippi Valley by virtue of their conquest of the British during the American Revolution, the Spanish viewed the river as a Spanish asset. By contrast, in penning his map of "the United States of America, as settled by the peace of 1783," London mapmaker John Fielding rendered the Mississippi as less a river than a wall, the western side of which abutted nothing more than blank paper. Throughout the 1780s and 1790s, competing visions of the Mississippi clashed against the realities of life in a borderland. No polity could assert its will for long.[3]

Other maps situated the river differently. In a 1786 meeting among South Carolina officials, Chickasaws, and Choctaws, Chickasaw chief Piominko carefully traced the boundaries of his people's lands on a map he requested from U.S. officials. The Mississippi comprised the Chickasaw's western boundary. For the Chickasaw and Choctaw, two dominant Indigenous polities whose territories bordered the river on its eastern shore, the Mississippi was most commonly known as Balbaha' Ásha' Okhina' ("Foreign speakers are upon it").[4] The name was apt. In the eighteenth century, the river was truly a polyglot locale. Voices could be heard in Mvskokean, Siouan, Algonquian, English, Spanish, and French. However it was the Chickasaw who wielded tremendous power over those who

FIG. 1. Tomás López, *Mapa de América, sujeto a las observaciones astronómicas, con todos los nuevos descubrimientos hasta ahora conocidos*, May 3, 1794. (Bibliothèque Nationale de France, Département Cartes et Plans, Paris, France)

FIG. 2. In the Treaty of Paris of 1783, Americans claimed all of the territory stretching from the Atlantic to the Mississippi River. Although officially Americans claimed territory southward to the 31st parallel, this map shows American claims ending well north of that at the boundary claimed by Spain. John Fielding, *A Map of the United States of America, as Settled by the Peace of 1783*, December 1, 1783. (Library of Congress Geography and Map Division, Washington, DC)

moved along the water. For Piominko, the Mississippi was as much a part of Chickasaw territory as his home at Long Village near the modern-day city of Tupelo, Mississippi. Piominko would carry this map, a statement of Chickasaw sovereignty, until his death in 1799.[5]

Andrew Jackson had a very different mental map of the Mississippi. For the European American colonizers of the trans-Appalachian West, settling in such places as Kentucky, the Cumberland, or the Holston River Valleys, the Mississippi represented the primary pathway for getting the produce of western farms to Atlantic world markets. European American migration to the West, as well as speculation in western lands, exploded in the decades following the American Revolution.[6] Despite endemic violence between European Americans and Indigenous peoples, white settlers and speculators alike believed that the region's rich soil offered a pathway toward prosperity. As Gilbert Imlay, an early Kentucky booster, predicted, from their location "in the centre of the earth" westerners were bound to "become at once the emporium and protectors of the world." The Mississippi was central to that process.[7] Westerners like Imlay imagined a future of agricultural production for world markets, predicated on widespread landownership and participation in a republican form of governance. They envisioned a grand future for both themselves and the region—a future that depended on access to the river.

Although not as successful as Imlay or Jackson, Joshua McQueen shared in their vision of the Mississippi as the gateway to prosperity for the settlers of trans-Appalachia. In the East, book credit and neighborly exchange played crucial roles in the financial lives of eighteenth-century farmers; in contrast, along the western frontier, a vibrant market centered on land created a system that revolved around cash.[8] As McQueen recalled, in Kentucky it was "easy to have plenty of hogs, and great gang of cattle, and plenty of horses.... But capital and labour" were much harder to come by. This was true for all residents of Kentucky, from impoverished veterans like McQueen to their better-off brethren. For McQueen, the lower Mississippi was an El Dorado. As he vividly recalled more than half a century after his first descent of the river, life seemed different in the lower Mississippi Valley. The French he encountered "didn't think a bit more of a dollar there than" Kentuckians did of a few pennies. Along the lower Mississippi, "money was plenty.... Every Jackass had money."[9] Certainly, McQueen was exaggerating. But the proximity of the lower Mississippi to the Atlantic world opened possibilities for obtaining specie that were scarce in Kentucky.

The role of government-sanctioned settlement and violence in the earliest expansion of the United States has been well documented, but the role of money and trade in not only fueling but also enabling westward expansion requires more attention.[10] In the first half of the 1780s, almost no American had the cash necessary to purchase land. Instead, western settlers hoped to use the future produce of their land to gain the cash they needed to secure title. This process, however, required that farm families be able to convert their produce of corn, wheat, pork, and whiskey into cash by carrying it to Atlantic markets. Access to the Mississippi River was key to Anglo-American dreams of profiting from the West—for state authorities in Virginia and North Carolina, for elite speculators, and for western settlers alike. Yet these dreams brought them into direct conflict with the Indigenous powers that controlled the river and the imperial powers vying for territory and trade.

When Joshua McQueen took his first trip down the river in 1782, the Mississippi was home to vibrant markets in fur, flour, and European goods. Empire—and the contest for it—had followed markets, but except for the flour trade between European settlements in Upper Louisiana and

New Orleans, the Mississippi Valley's markets were structured to serve the interests of the Indigenous residents of the continental interior. Because trade was tied to alliances, Choctaw, Chickasaw, Creek, Cherokee, Alabaman, Osage, Caddo, Quapaw, and other Indigenous peoples could use the threat of allying with competing European powers to influence the terms of trade and to demand better and more abundant manufactured goods in exchange for the deerskins on which the Mississippi River's trade was based.[11] Beginning in the 1780s, though, the Ohio and Mississippi Rivers, as well as their tributaries, became the sites of a new market. Anglo-American settlers from Ohio River Valley communities in western Pennsylvania, Virginia's Kentucky district, and North Carolina's Washington district began using these waterways as a means of carrying the produce of newly created western farms to Atlantic world markets. This new market was grafted on top of the older markets in furs, deerskins, and trade goods that had developed over more than a hundred years of colonial contact.

McQueen, like all others who ventured into it, quickly learned that the trade of the Mississippi River operated beyond the control of any single group. Lying between Pittsburgh and Natchez were two thousand miles of river wending their way through a complicated world of alliances and competing sovereignties. European and Indigenous peoples all saw the Mississippi and its tributaries as pathways to both power and prosperity and jockeyed for control over the river's waters—a contest that drove much of the continent's history in the period from 1750 to 1815.[12]

1

The Colonial River

THE MISSISSIPPI RIVER is an ecological marvel. Sitting in a basin carved by the movement of the earth's tectonic plates and the advance and retreat of oceans and glaciers, the river bisects the North American continent, forming a freshwater highway that stretches from the Gulf of Mexico north to the Great Lakes. Today, it drains over 40 percent of the contiguous United States and remains one of the nation's great pathways of commerce.[1] The states and residents that border its waters live in an uneasy tension with the "father of waters." On the one hand, the river serves as a link, connecting distant communities with one another and, via the Gulf of Mexico, with the world beyond. The farmers of Ohio, Illinois, Missouri, Iowa, Louisiana, Mississippi, and even further afield rely on the river for the export of American grain, soybeans, and cotton. The river's waters provide, as they have for a millennium, a mechanism for moving bulky goods cheaply and easily; barge transportation costs a fraction of what it costs to move goods by truck or even train.[2] On the other hand, the river regularly defies human attempts to control it. Record flooding and devastating droughts are occurring more frequently as the river reacts to a changing climate. Nevertheless, the river flows inexorably to the sea, pouring 600,000 cubic feet of fresh water into the ocean every second. Despite changing technologies, economies, and even ecologies, the Mississippi has remained a vital avenue for trade.[3]

The Mississippi begins at Lake Itasca in what is now Minnesota, exiting the lake as a small stream that grows gradually, becoming navigable as it passes the sites of the modern-day Twin Cities. As the rivers that drain the Midwest, most notably the Missouri, which enters the Mississippi at the site of modern-day St. Louis, spill into it, the river gradually changes character, growing ever larger until its merger with the Ohio at Cairo,

Illinois. Here, the ecology of the river valley changes. The river widens; its waters flow shallower, and the current slows. In the era before the river was engineered by the construction of levees, pumps, and dredges, the river annually left its banks; on its retreat, it left rich soil sediment. Unconstrained by hills or mountains, the river changed course often, carving new paths for itself, leaving behind islands and lakes as the river returned to its southward path.

Some 650 years before McQueen first saw the Mississippi, the junction of the Ohio, Mississippi, and Missouri Rivers was the site of Cahokia, the ancient ritual center of the Mississippian peoples. The Mississippians had used their location along the rivers that subdivided the continent to engage in far-afield trade. From the north, river-based trade and tribute networks brought lead from Minnesota; from the south came shells from the Gulf of Mexico. In exchange for pottery produced by the Caddo people of what are now Louisiana and East Texas, the Cahokians bartered "flint-clay ornaments and copper figurines"—themselves evidence of the vast Cahokian trade network that could bring copper from the Great Lakes region to the Arkansas Valley west of the Mississippi.[4]

Around 1200 CE, the Mississippian culture began to decline, but the rivers that had nurtured it remained. So did the peoples who had formed a part of the confederacy. Sometime between 1540, when Hernando de Soto's expedition first brought news of Europeans to the region, and 1682, when René-Robert Cavelier, Sieur de la Salle, directed an expedition from French Canada to the mouth of the Gulf of Mexico, the peoples of the lower Mississippi Valley coalesced into the Creek, Cherokee, Choctaw, and Chickasaw, as well as other less numerous nations. Like their Mississippian ancestors, these new groups tended to practice maize-based agriculture and lived in large communities, building ritual mounds and speaking related languages. To their south lived the proto-historic Plaquemine peoples. Mississippian influences inspired the Plaquemine to adopt mound-building and maize cultivation, and gradually they evolved into the Natchez people.[5] Dispersed across the southern landscape, these matrilineal groups emerged as the dominant people of the lands east of the Mississippi and south of the Ohio River. Two of these groups, the Chickasaw and Natchez, each controlled one of the strategically located highlands along the river's eastern shore. Those who traded on the Mississippi had no choice but to engage—peacefully or otherwise—with both groups.

By the time of the American Revolution, Mississippi River trade had already been shaped by the interactions between the region's diverse peoples, the continent's geography, and changing political and diplomatic relations. Over the near century of European involvement in the lower Mississippi Valley, a complex world of trade, diplomacy, and conflict had taken shape. For the Chickasaw, the Natchez, and newly arrived European colonists, their locations along the river helped to define their roles in this emerging world of river trade.

River People

CHICKASAW HISTORY begins at the Mississippi. Chickasaw migration stories detail the arrival of the proto-Chickasaw people at the river, a sight they had never imagined, and their certainty that the homeland they were seeking lay along its eastern banks. Crossing the river formed the crucial event in their emergence as a new people. Although the Chickasaw placed their largest settlements far away from the river's waters, the Mississippi was nevertheless central to their conception of themselves and their territory. Crossing the river marked the "beginning of Chickasaw history, culture, and language."[6]

In 1700, the Chickasaw lived in dispersed settlements in the northern part of the Black Prairie, a crescent-shaped swathe of fertile, well-watered soil that stretches from what is now central Alabama through Mississippi and up to the modern-day border of Tennessee. The Chickasaw lived in multigenerational house groups, each one occupied by an individual matriline. In summer, Chickasaw families lived in individual homes set off the ground and walled with woven mats; in winter, the entire house group moved into the single, round log winter house that gave the house group its name. Chickasaw children spent their youth helping their mothers and female relatives tend to the fields that the men had prepared in the spring. Chickasaw women grew numerous crops providing a varied diet: corn, melons, beans, squash, and sunflowers were common. Chickasaw men supplemented the family diet through hunting. Social identity was structured around family and clan, with each clan belonging to one of two moieties. The members, clans, and towns of the white moiety were associated with peace and traditionally dwelled in what were known as white towns. Members of the red moiety lived in red towns, associated with war.[7]

Despite their small numbers—in 1700, the Chickasaw numbered only about seven thousand—the Chickasaw played an outsized role in shaping the commerce and diplomacy of the Mississippi Valley.[8] While both historians and historical actors alike have emphasized the Chickasaw's martial prowess in elevating their importance regionally, their geographical position helped to cement their prominence.[9] In 1755, British Indian superintendent Edward Atkin informed his superiors that "it is not possible to cast an Eye ever so lightly over the Map, without being struck with the Importance of" the Chickasaw homeland. While "the Chickasaw Country is in itself a very fine one, being exceeding Fertile, Pleasant & Healthy," he informed his superiors, "without Doubt there is none other in the Western parts of No. America of so much Importance to the English to be possessed of. For it lies in a central place about the middle of the Mississippi, and commands all the water Passages between New Orleans and Canada, and from that River" eastward to the British colonies.[10]

What Atkin was referring to were the Sakti Lhafa', the scored bluffs that line the eastern shore of the Mississippi at the present-day site of Memphis, Tennessee. Called the Chickasaw Bluffs by the English, the Sakti Lhafa' occupy one of the few highlands along the river and the first substantial overlook south of the Mississippi's confluence with the Ohio. The bluffs had tremendous significance for the Chickasaw, who viewed them, as one warrior claimed in negotiations with the Spanish, as "the most precious part of their lands," a place of tremendous strategic and spiritual importance.[11] For the Chickasaw, they demarcated the area of the river that was under Chickasaw control. At the bluffs, the complementary features of land and water collided. The bluffs rising high above the water offered a vantage point from which the Chickasaw could see movements along the river as islands in the river's channel caused the waters of the Mississippi to eddy and swirl. The resulting current forced boats to hug the shore, causing them to come "within a pistol shot of the hill," where they became easy prey for land-based raiding parties.[12] As Atkin noted, control over the bluffs allowed the Chickasaw to control traffic along the river.

From the 1730s to the 1750s, the Chickasaw attacked French boats near the bluffs, killing or ransoming the passengers, appropriating their cargos, and asserting their mastery of the river. Nevertheless, the Chickasaw's control was not absolute. Rising and falling water levels and annual floods constantly carved new geographies into the river's course, allowing a few small boats to slip by without Chickasaw knowledge; after all, the Chickasaw's small numbers made it impossible for them to patrol the bluffs at all times. Even so, control over the bluffs gave the Chickasaw a powerful tool in their diplomacy with other regional powers. The Chickasaw were unquestionably at the heart of Mississippi trade, a reality that everyone engaged in trade along the river—Indigenous, European, and European American—was forced to recognize and consider as they navigated the river.[13]

Snaking south and west of the Chickasaw homeland was an ancient trade and war route—eventually known as the Natchez Trace—that connected the Chickasaw to the Natchez people, who occupied another strategic highland overlooking the Mississippi. Among the low-lying lands of the Mississippi Valley, a little height goes a long way; although the soil along the clifftop lacked the richness provided by the region's river valleys, living on top of the world provided protection from potential foes, both of the human variety and from the frequent flooding that rendered the lower Mississippi Valley a world of half water and half dirt.[14] On the highlands overlooking the Mississippi, the ancestors of the Natchez had practiced corn-based agriculture and built towering ritual mounds. In 1540, they helped to terrify the remnant of de Soto's invasion force as it fled down the Mississippi, demonstrating their superior boatmanship skills as well as the complexity of the interrelated chiefdoms of the lower Mississippi. In 1682, La Salle, at the head of an expedition from French Canada to the mouth of the Gulf of Mexico, became the first European to specifically document the Natchez. Landing near the bluffs on March 26, 1682, La Salle was eventually taken to meet the chief of the Nahy or Natché people, who now occupied a new mound-based ceremonial center that the French would eventually come to know as the Grand Village of the Natchez.[15] Although La Salle was largely unaware to their effects, the presence of Europeans elsewhere on the continent had already deeply affected the Natchez. The disruptions caused by European excursions across the continent had recontoured a world already in flux.

By the early eighteenth century, both the Natchez and the Chickasaw had been drawn into a European contest to wrest control over the trade of North America. Along the Atlantic Coast, increasing British settlement in North and South Carolina set off a chain reaction of events that transformed life in the Mississippi Valley. In the 1670s, English settlers in the Carolinas began encouraging a trade in Indigenous slaves, a process that accelerated in the late 1680s as the Chickasaw became the dominant force within the southeastern slave trade.[16] The Chickasaw economy came to depend on slaving as a way of life with devastating consequences for both them and their neighbors. With increased trade came an increased influx of European diseases. Between 1696 and 1700, smallpox tore through the

Southeast in what historian Paul Kelton has termed the "Great Southeastern Smallpox Epidemic." Thousands died.[17] Smallpox was not the only Old World disease to ravage the interior. In 1700, French colonial official Pierre Le Moyne d'Iberville reported that dysentery was ravaging the Houma, nearly half of whom had died.[18] The Chickasaw and Natchez were similarly affected: decades of warfare and disease took a dramatic toll on their population.[19] Many smaller peoples consolidated for protection. Some, like the Koroa, Tiou, Grigra, and Chitimacha, fled to the Natchez for protection; others, like the Tunica, for instance, sought out a closer alliance with French colonists in New Orleans in order to staunch the demographic collapse.[20] Despite these losses and upheavals, by the 1690s the Chickasaw had become the most successful Indian slavers in the Southeast, preying on the many Indigenous nations of the Mississippi Valley and in the process building strong diplomatic and economic ties with English traders who ventured westward from the Carolinas.[21] In 1715, the Yamasee War more or less brought an end to the southeastern slave trade, but in its aftermath British and French traders continued to compete fiercely for the trade and friendship of Mississippi Valley Indians. The Chickasaw continued their long association with the British. For the Natchez, however, the situation was becoming more complicated.

The Natchez's location along the lower Mississippi brought them into close contact with French colonial officials and Canadian *voyageurs*, French fur traders, for whom the Natchez landing became a popular resting point. *Voyageurs* brought beaver pelts and deerskins downriver to markets at Mobile and, after 1718, at New Orleans. French officials understood the importance of the Natchez's strategic location between French Louisiana and the outposts in French Illinois and worked to build diplomatic alliances. Meanwhile, the Natchez's location along what would become the Natchez Trace also drew them in another direction. The trace tied the Natchez to both the pro-British Chickasaw and to British traders operating out of the Carolinas.[22]

By 1730, the increased presence of Europeans in the region transformed the Natchez's economy. Between 1716 and 1729, the Natchez's involvement in the deerskin trade increased significantly. Rather than focusing solely on their own subsistence needs, the Natchez increasingly expended their energies on supplying British and French traders with deerskins in exchange for trade goods like blankets, guns, and metal tools. Following the establishment of a French trading post in 1713 and the construction of Fort Rosalie on the bluff in 1716, the French increasingly dominated the trade of both the Natchez region and the Natchez people. French traders and soldiers stationed at the post often relied on exchanges with the Natchez to supplement their meager wages. A lively trade in corn, meat, fish, and sex arose as the Natchez adjusted to the permanent presence of the French in their midst.[23]

By 1726, nearly two hundred French colonists had settled at Natchez, and by 1729 the colonial population had doubled to nearly four hundred. Over the previous five years, how the French viewed the village had subtly changed: it had transformed from an outpost of the fur trade to become increasingly oriented toward European-grown staple agriculture. French proprietors coopted the labor of French indentured servants, many of whom the French government had transported as criminals, and nearly two hundred enslaved Africans to grow wheat, indigo, tobacco, and corn.[24] By the fall of 1729, the French colonists had over 25,000 pounds of tobacco in warehouses, awaiting the boats that would ship the tobacco south to New Orleans and then to France, where the colonists hoped the French public would find them more appealing than earlier French efforts at luring the public away from Virginia-grown tobacco.[25] As the number of French colonists grew, it was increasingly Natchez land, instead of the Natchez themselves, that seemed valuable to the French. Meanwhile, repeated bouts with European diseases had severely undermined the Natchez population: between 1715 and 1721, the population of the Natchez had declined from four thousand to only two thousand warriors.[26]

Conflicts over land, as well as French abuse of the Natchez, exacerbated longstanding tensions between the two groups. On November 28, 1729, the Natchez launched a surprise attack on the French settlement. Of the 400 French colonists residing at Natchez, 138 men, 35 women, and 56 children were killed; most of the survivors were pressed into slavery. The French reaction was swift. Acknowledging their own weakness, the French turned to the Choctaw people, the most populous Indigenous group east of the river. Angry that the Natchez had excluded them from a share in the booty the Natchez had obtained from the French, a Choctaw-led force attacked the Natchez villages. When the dust settled, over 200 Natchez lay dead; in May 1731, another 291 were herded onto a ship in New Orleans and sold into slavery in St. Domingue. The remaining Natchez scattered, a substantial number fleeing north to join their old trading partners the Chickasaw, whom the French would eventually come to see as instigators of the violence at Natchez.[27] In 1736, the Choctaw launched a French-inspired war against the Chickasaw. The English-backed

Chickasaw successfully repelled the attacks. Perhaps the remaining Natchez warriors who had found homes among the Chickasaw relished the opportunity to engage once more with their old enemies.[28]

The violence at Natchez marked a new beginning in Mississippi Valley trade, curtailing European expansion northward from the Gulf of Mexico and entrenching new enmities among the various peoples of the lower Mississippi Valley. In the wake of the rebellion, the French were slow to return to the settlement although they did rebuild Fort Rosalie. Ironically, the near-complete destruction of the Natchez people had returned the villages of Natchez to Indian country. Viewed from the Indigenous perspective, the meaning of the land surrounding Natchez had changed as well. The bluffs at Natchez had once been the home of one of the region's most populous and highly stratified societies; now, members of many nations hunted on the land. Politically, the region functioned as a buffer zone between smaller nations to the south and the more militarily and politically powerful Choctaw to the north.[29]

While the violence in the Natchez country slowed the expansion of European settlement in the lower Mississippi Valley, it did little to slow the development of Mississippi River trade. From 1735 until the outbreak of the Seven Years' War, Natchez remained important primarily as a stopping point for the ever-increasing river traffic along the Mississippi. While *voyageurs* transported flour from settlements in French Illinois southward to feed the growing colonial population of New Orleans, and plantations near the mouth of the river produced indigo and tobacco for export to world markets, the Indian trade in deerskins dominated the economic activity of the colony of Louisiana. Warfare too was a common occurrence. The 1736 Choctaw-French war against the Chickasaw was followed by another war in 1740, both of which the Chickasaw won, ensuring their dominance over the region that is now northern Mississippi and increasing their importance as diplomatic and trading partners to Europeans.

Violence, caused in part by competition for access to European trade goods, was a way of life for the Chickasaw in the eighteenth century. From the 1720s to the 1750s, the Chickasaw were engaged in near constant warfare with their southern neighbors, the Choctaw; with the Creek to the east; and with the Quapaw to the west. By 1750, faced with the constant threat of violence, almost the entire population of the Chickasaw nation lived within the fortified walls of Chokkilissa', at the site of modern-day Tupelo, Mississippi. Positioned on a bluff that commanded the surrounding prairie, the Chickasaw town was a veritable fortress that housed a population hollowed out by war. Decades of violence had shrunk the Chickasaw population to only 1,600 individuals. Chokkilissa' was a village of women and children; a 1754 census conducted by British trader John Buckles noted only 350 men capable of bearing arms and estimated there were two or three Chickasaw women for every remaining Chickasaw man.[30] Nevertheless, the British continued to court the still-powerful Chickasaw, who offered them an entrée into the world of the Mississippi River.

A French Port

In 1718, the French founded New Orleans to serve as an entrepôt for Mississippi trade. Previous attempts at creating a French seaport in Louisiana had largely failed; first at Biloxi and later at Mobile, French adventurers had encountered enormous difficulties caused in part by ecological challenges, the remoteness of the region from European trade routes, and a general lack of interest among French officials toward investing in the colony.[31] Inland settlements had been more successful, both at Natchitoches on the Red River and at Natchez. Nevertheless, a port on the Mississippi would help connect France's colonial holdings in New France with its colonies in the Caribbean; it would also serve as a point of exportation for the cotton, sugar, tobacco, indigo, and silk that French promoters imagined Louisiana would soon produce. Yet once more geography made establishing a port along the lower Mississippi challenging. From the mouth of the Mississippi for ninety miles inward, seasonal floods threatened any construction the French might attempt. Ultimately, the French built their port at a curve in the river, where a natural levee had long sheltered a Quinipissa village.[32] While the site eventually selected was marginally dryer than the surrounding wetland, the journey upriver from the Gulf of Mexico could add as much as a month to a ship's journey. This added distance made it impossible for ships to sail directly from Europe or Africa to New Orleans; after the Atlantic crossing, ships needed to stop at a Caribbean port for resupply before venturing up the Mississippi. As a result, New Orleans was only slowly integrated into the Atlantic trade system.[33]

Shortly after the port was founded, the French crown gifted the colony of Louisiana to a new joint stock company—the Company of the West (later, the Company of the Indies), which was closely tied to the French financial reforms instituted by the Scottish financier John Law. Between

1717 and 1721, the stock of the company soared and with it the prospects of Louisiana. Yet that enthusiasm soon flagged when Law's financial schemes failed in 1720; with Law's downfall, the "Mississippi Bubble" burst. Conditions within the colony contributed to the decline in stock values. Over four years, the company had imported six thousand Europeans to the colony; overly rapid immigration, accompanied by a harsh disease environment, caused a subsistence crisis in the colony as earlier colonists were unable to support the new arrivals, and mortality rates rose as high as 60 percent.[34] After 1723, a reorganized Company of the Indies shifted its policies and began importing large numbers of enslaved Africans to the colony, but high death rates continued. By 1731, only about two thousand European colonists and about four thousand enslaved people remained.[35] Economically marginal to the French empire, the colony relied on the labor of enslaved people of African descent to grow tobacco and rice, and to cut and process timber.[36]

Initially, European trade along the Mississippi River grew slowly under the French regime. In 1731, after the Natchez War, the Company of the Indies ceded the colony to the crown. The French in Louisiana consolidated their settlements near New Orleans and began growing tobacco and indigo for export in earnest. French settlements in Illinois at Kaskaskia, St. Genevieve, and Vincennes provided flour that fed the French community at New Orleans, although they seldom could export as much as the port town required.[37] In New Orleans, French merchants imported wine, brandy, cloth, olive oil, and spices for sale to colonists, as well as fabric, guns, and metal goods intended for the deerskin trade. In the 1730s, France attempted to encourage more French merchants to trade in New Orleans by offering a subsidy for goods imported to the colony and guaranteeing the market for Louisianan tobacco.[38] New Orleans traders also began to traffic in lumber, bricks, and tar for sale to the sugar islands of the Caribbean. Despite a near constant demand for enslaved laborers by the white residents of the colony, between 1732 and the end of French colonial rule the Company of the Indies, which held a monopoly on the slave trade, imported only one shipload of enslaved people to the colony, preferring to trade with the more accessible and more lucrative sugar islands over the relatively impoverished colony of Louisiana. Although enslaved people continued to arrive from the Antilles, with labor at a premium staple agricultural production grew slowly.[39]

Unable to produce marketable crops and often barely able to feed itself, Louisiana depended on the deerskin trade, which was conducted both via packhorse and by boat along the many rivers of the lower Mississippi Valley. French traders entered the towns and villages of the lower Mississippi Valley carrying an assortment of manufactured goods; they departed with packs of deerskins that were funneled to either Mobile or New Orleans. The French government of Louisiana was constantly undersupplied, a factor that became a defining characteristic of the region's trade and in the political calculus of the region's French and Indigenous inhabitants. For the Indigenous people of the Southeast, trade was tied to diplomacy. In exchange for fur and deerskins, the French offered guns, gunpowder, and alcohol. West of the Mississippi, the Atakapa and the Opelousa supplied the French colony with "peltries, bear oil, and even horses," while the Quapaw provided the French outpost on the Arkansas River with food and allies for defense.[40] Although the French never profited from their colony, they continued to exchange deerskins and foodstuffs for trade goods—especially brandy and rum—in the decades preceding the Seven Years' War. The reliance on the deerskin trade opened the colony to British competition. With the support of colonial officials in South Carolina and Georgia, British traders ventured west, seeking to extend British influence in the region and offering trade goods to Indigenous peoples that were both more plentiful and of higher quality than those offered by the French.[41] Despite intense imperial rivalry, the deerskin trade of the lower Mississippi River Valley remained relatively circumscribed during the duration of the French colonial presence in Louisiana. From the French perspective, the deerskin trade was a relatively marginal activity pursued by residents of one of its most marginal colonies.[42]

Well before the American Revolution, the presence of European colonists and traders had transformed the lives of the Indigenous people of the vast Mississippi Valley, and with it Mississippi River trade. The Natchez people had been eliminated as an independent entity, but the violence of 1729 had also changed the course of French colonization in the Mississippi Valley. Meanwhile, other Indigenous peoples, such as the lower Mississippi *petite nations*, Cherokee, Choctaw, Creek, and Chickasaw, experienced extensive changes to their economies and lifeways, as traditional subsistence patterns yielded to commercial hunting that shifted their social, cultural, and economic practices. At riverine imperial outposts like Kaskaskia and Vincennes in the Illinois country or St. Louis and New Madrid along the Mississippi, Indigenous hunters encountered European traders who functioned as conduits between the Native and Atlantic worlds.[43] As a result, those worlds grew more interdependent. Thus, when violence began in Europe, it quickly spread to the Mississippi Valley.

In the early eighteenth century, imperial competition, Indigenous politics, and geography all operated in tandem to shape the society of the lower Mississippi. Throughout, the river remained the most significant feature of the landscape, influencing not only how trade developed but also how and where people lived and what economic and subsistence pathways they pursued. Along the river, strategic locations, like the Chickasaw Bluffs, Natchez, and New Orleans, emerged as sites of contact and conflict. While Louisiana produced some crops for export, the colony's economic life was dominated by trade with Indigenous peoples. Within the ongoing eighteenth-century contest for empire, the Mississippi was marginal at best.

Imperial Conflict

The Seven Years' War represented an escalation in the imperial conflict for the continental interior. For the Chickasaw, the war presented an opportunity to fight against the French. Chickasaw war chief Paya Mattaha (Payamataha) described the Chickasaw as "born and bred in a state of war" with the French, and thus natural allies of the English.[44] Yet the war convinced the Chickasaw of the futility of involvement in European conflicts, which they recognized as driving the intertribal violence engulfing the Southeast. Exhausted by decades of warfare, following 1763 the Chickasaw sought peace with the Choctaw, Cherokee, Creek, and Quapaw. By 1768, the Indigenous political landscape of the lower Mississippi had been transformed once more.

The Treaty of Paris of 1763 redrew the imperial boundaries of the Mississippi Valley. A vanquished France ceded the colonies of Canada and New France to Britain, and Spain ceded its longstanding claims to Florida. As a partial compensation for Spain's aid during the war, France agreed to transfer Louisiana and the isle of New Orleans to the Spanish. Lines on a map penned in a drawing room in Versailles did not account for the on-the-ground reality of the Mississippi Valley, which despite European machinations remained very much Indian territory. Indigenous peoples outnumbered Europeans by a factor of at least ten to one in 1763.[45] But the transfer of European claims had several important consequences for life in the lower Mississippi Valley. Although Spanish officials did not arrive in Louisiana until 1769, and the bulk of the European population of Louisiana was culturally French, Indigenous nations nevertheless faced the prospect of establishing diplomatic and trade relationships with a new imperial authority. Meanwhile, the transfer of East and West Florida extended British influence westward. The ongoing presence of two European powers in the lower Mississippi Valley allowed the Indigenous people of the region to continue diplomatic negotiations based in part on their ability to balance Spanish and British aims against one another, but the landscape of their negotiations had changed.[46]

The Chickasaw soon found their territory overrun with British traders willing, in violation of British policy, to trade deerskins for liquor.[47] While both the Spanish and British governments attempted to control trade within their territories, the riverine world of the lower Mississippi defied strict supervision. Many French traders, newly subjects of Spain, continued their longstanding connections with Indigenous communities that now fell within British West Florida, antagonizing British merchants who hoped to dominate the region. Fearing British competition in the fur trade and in the import trade of consumer goods, the Spanish barred British shipping from New Orleans. The settlement of Manchac, located at the junction of the Iberville and Mississippi Rivers, became a critical point of exchange. From Manchac, British traders exported furs and deerskins eastward across Lakes Maurepas and Pontchartrain to Mobile, while English schooners brought in goods that were purchased by colonists in both the British and Spanish settlements, in violation of the mercantilist policies of both empires. Settlers and Indigenous peoples in the region traded with Spanish and British merchants; officials from both empires were unable to enforce control over their colonists.[48] Although many tribes in the region had favored the French over the English as diplomatic and trading partners before Louisiana's transfer to Spain, it was no secret that British merchants had access to more and better supplies of manufactured goods, which became a major factor in the growth of British trade in the region. By 1776, Spanish officials estimated that 98 percent of the river's trade was siphoned off by the English; the merchants of Natchez, now a British settlement, captured much of that trade.[49] Although the imperial officials had changed, the contest for the trade of the Mississippi River remained hotly contested.

Despite the British colonists' willingness to violate imperial directives, when word of the rupture between the eastern colonies and Britain arrived along the lower Mississippi in 1776, few were sympathetic to the Patriot cause. As the war spread, the populations of East and West

Florida swelled due to the arrival of Loyalists fleeing Patriot retaliation. Eager to secure the loyalty of the southeastern Indians, British officials met with delegates from the Choctaw, Creek, and Chickasaw at Mobile in 1777. There, the English urged their longtime allies to aid them in the war against the United States. In particular, they hoped the Chickasaw would agree to patrol the Mississippi in order to disrupt the movement of information and materiel from New Orleans to the American rebels. For their part, the Chickasaw, having just ended decades of warfare with Choctaw and Quapaw enemies, were reluctant to become further entangled in European American affairs.[50]

Throughout the colonial era, no single power, Indigenous or European, was able to control the river's trade. From their homeland on the eastern side of the river, the Chickasaw had come to play a dominant role in the contest for control of the Mississippi River. By the time the Revolution began, the British had recognized that all who traveled along the river were vulnerable to the Chickasaw. Despite being numerically one of the smaller tribes of the lower Mississippi River Valley, Chickasaw military prowess and the strategic location of their territory elevated their importance to the region's politics. The Chickasaw were unquestionably at the heart of Mississippi trade, a reality that everyone engaged in trade along the river—Indigenous and European—were forced to recognize and consider as they navigated the river.

In the 1770s, when Anglo-American settlers began settling in trans-Appalachia, they brought with them a new type of Mississippi River trade. Agricultural products, intended for export to the Atlantic world, joined deerskins as they descended the river. The new arrivals to trans-Appalachia were busily engaged in reshaping the landscape once more, this time by commodifying it. Land became one of the west's most desirable commodities. This new contest for the control of trans-Appalachia would lead to a reimagining of the river as a pathway for creating value for western land. It would also lead to new conflicts and collaborations along the waters of the Mississippi.

2

Kentucky Land, Cash, and the Mississippi

―――•◦•―――

THE OUTBREAK of the American Revolution brought new players into Mississippi River trade. During the Revolution, thousands of European Americans flooded westward, settling in Kentucky, the Washington and Cumberland districts of North Carolina, and western Pennsylvania. These new westerners simultaneously extended the reach of Mississippi River trade and created a new front in the inter-imperial contest for both trans-Appalachia and control of the Mississippi. These changes were driven by the emerging market in western land.

The opening of the Ohio Valley to European American settlement during the American Revolution spawned a speculative bubble in western lands that permeated every level of American society, from the second sons of the poorest backcountry farmer to tidewater grandees. "Every body," speculator John May observed from the Falls of the Ohio in 1781, seemed "determined to monopolize as much [land] as they can."[1] Among the propertied classes, investing in western lands emerged as the national pastime. For the elites of Virginia and North Carolina, the means to speculate in western lands were close at hand, as the unexploited land of the Kentucky district of Virginia and the Washington and Cumberland districts of North Carolina both seemed to offer what George Washington termed "a large field" "where an enterprizing Man with very little M[o]ney may lay the foundation of a Noble Estate in the New Settlemt."[2] In 1780, Virginia merchant Samuel Beall, who speculated in western lands from his home in Richmond, felt that "fifteen or twenty thousand Acres" would be "enough for me & should satisfy any reasonable Man." Ultimately, Beall would claim over 75,000 acres of western land while his partner, John May, claimed over 340,000 acres—an amount exceeding 530 square miles.[3] Although the majority of those who speculated in Kentucky land were southerners, western lands held appeal across regional lines. John Dunlap, editor of the *North American and United States Gazette*, invested in over 130,000 acres of Kentucky land from his home in Philadelphia.[4] These elite speculators hinged their financial futures on a common colonial business model: purchasing underdeveloped land at low prices to sell it after increased western migration raised its value. In other words, they bought low, hoping someday to sell high to imagined swarms of eager buyers—farm families in particular—who wanted to claim a piece of western lands for themselves.

These speculators had good reason to be hopeful. Poor farmers displaced by the war and facing contracting opportunities for land ownership in the East were particularly susceptible to the "mania" for western lands. These poor farmers' desire for western land grew as rumors of the richness of Kentucky soil spread throughout the Atlantic colonies in the second half of the 1770s.[5] Yet the speculators plans were flawed: most of these farmers had no intention of paying for western lands. Once the constraints of the Proclamation of 1763 were lifted, thousands of poor families speculated in western lands by using the only capital available to them—their labor.[6] Settlers' "desire of Securing new Lands" was "so great" that, "notwithstanding the Danger" of the Kentucky frontier and the ongoing war with Britain, thousands of people flooded west.[7] Although these settlers did not command the cash necessary to purchase land in Kentucky or Tennessee, they came west hoping to secure it by some other means. Moses Austin, himself enroute to Kentucky to learn about opportunities to speculate in land, was astonished at the avidity of poor settlers heading west. In his journal, Austin recorded a putative conversation with the ragged travelers he encountered along the Wilderness Trail that led from the Cumberland Gap north to the bluegrass region. "Ask these Pilgrims what they expect when they git to Kentucky," he noted, and "the Answer is Land." Beholding their bare feet and nearly naked state, Austin asked those he encountered, "Have you anything to pay for land[?]" "No," came the quick response, "but I expect I can get it."[8] Both poor settlers and elite speculators assumed that western lands, especially in Kentucky, would prove to be the source of their and their families' wealth.

In Kentucky, obtaining cash took on outsized importance as various claimants jockeyed to secure land. Speculators traded with the state and with one another, often paying a portion of the purchase price in cash up front and promising to make further payments in the future. They were sometimes satisfied to "sell" the land they had effectively mortgaged in exchange for even larger down payments and more favorable repayment plans offered by fellow speculators. Many of the exchanges between speculators were conducted via promissory notes. Speculators' plans hinged on those who would ultimately purchase the lands—western settlers who (they expected) would buy from speculators and pay taxes to the state. This model assumed that farm families would want to move to Kentucky and to pay out the handsome profit that speculators imagined, and further that those farm families would accept the legitimacy of the state's and the speculators' claims to ownership—which it turned out that poor settler-colonizers were more than willing to contest.[9] For its part, the state of Virginia expected to sell its western land in exchange for paper or metal currency and then to tax that land in cash. But the bald fact was that in the first half of the 1780s, almost no American had the cash necessary to purchase land outright. Instead, western settlers hoped to use the future produce of their lands to gain the cash they needed to secure title. The process, however, required farm families to be able to convert their produce of corn, wheat, pork, and whiskey into cash by carrying it to markets. Access to the Mississippi River was key to dreams of profiting from the West—for the state of Virginia, speculators, and western settler-colonists alike.

During the American Revolution, there was no location in the new United States where an individual could gain access to free land. Squatters could, and did, seat themselves across the western landscape. But in order to turn land into a family competency, the legal alchemy that transformed the landscape into property had to be performed. While squatting might enable a family to gain subsistence, legal title was necessary to maintain it—or, as many western settlers hoped, to sell at a profit to a new arrival. Throughout the 1770s, the question of what authority could legally issue title was contentious. Speculators and settlers alternately claimed land based on Native, corporate, and state title; many contended that occupancy and improvement offered better title than that obtained from any other authority.[10] Ultimately, the entity that emerged with the capability to perform the transformation of land into property, and to issue legal title, was the state of Virginia. As Moses Austin's question to the penniless emigrants he found trekking to Kentucky emphasizes, Virginia insisted on being paid.[11]

The 1780s saw a union-wide recession that led to widespread protests against taxation, debt enforcement, and government bonds. In western Massachusetts, farmers under the leadership of Daniel Shays marched on Springfield to close the courts; in Pennsylvania, similarly situated farmers and former soldiers barricaded the roads to prevent the arrival of officials sent to collect a tax that few could pay. Monetary policy was a driving force in the politics of the 1780s. The shortage of specie—gold and silver currency—was at the core of wartime and postwar experiments in paper money that created contention across the thirteen states and ultimately contributed to the writing of the Constitution. In Kentucky the money shortage was particularly acute, as isolation limited westerners' ability to obtain cash from elsewhere. The fact that land had to be paid for played a central role in the political and economic development of the region that would become Kentucky, and in the role that this region would play in the broader experiences of the new nation.

From its inception, western expansion, and especially speculation in western lands, was predicated on trade.[12] In investing in Kentucky, American colonizers imagined a future of agrarian prosperity centered on trade in agricultural produce. They expected to struggle for the first one or two years after their journey west, but after that they imagined that the fertile western soil would be more than able to supply their families' needs and provide them with a surplus that could be shipped to markets in the Caribbean, along the Atlantic Coast, and even as far away as Europe. Some anticipated Kentucky flour traveling even further. Western speculator and promoter Gilbert Imlay, in his popular account of the western country, envisioned a day when western "beef, pork, bacon, butter, cheese, &c. &c" would "furnish the West India islands, and afford relief to the miserable Chinese."[13] Westerners could use the cash they obtained to secure more land, either from the state or from speculators. Both western settlers and speculators viewed the Mississippi River as their best avenue for obtaining the cash they needed to profit from the lands they claimed.

Among those who moved west during the American Revolution was Anne McMeans and her family. The McMeans were of little historic consequence; smallholders from western Pennsylvania, in 1778 they came west to Kentucky hoping to translate their labor into a future as the proprietors of western lands. Anne McMeans's—later Jameson's—1824 account of her life offers a glimpse into the motivations and experiences of thousands of poor families who gambled their families' future prosperity on the hope of obtaining western lands. The McMeans came to Kentucky as part of the first trickle of mass immigration at the height of the Revolution. They soon found that obtaining Kentucky land required cash.[14] Examining the obstacles that settlers like the McMeans faced in attempting to claim western lands reveals how closely trade and western settlement were entwined.

Claiming Land

In 1764, eighteen-year-old Anne Wilson became Anne McMeans. Her husband Andrew was four years older, and both had spent most of their lives on the outermost fringe of European settlement in the river valleys of the backcountry of Pennsylvania and Maryland. As many young couples did, after their marriage the McMeans moved even further west, into the Appalachian foothills, settling at the juncture of the Youghiogheny and Monongahela Rivers, some ten miles south of the recently established Fort Pitt, in a region claimed by both the Virginia and Pennsylvania governments.[15]

Life could not have been easy along the Youghiogheny. Even before the first shots rang out at Lexington and Concord, the people of the Pennsylvania frontier had grown accustomed to endemic violence. One year prior to the McMeans's arrival, George III had issued the Proclamation of 1763, prohibiting British settlement beyond a line stretching down the Appalachian Mountains. Anne and Andrew McMeans chose to settle perilously close to that line. In 1773, violence flared between European Americans and the Indigenous peoples of the Ohio Valley in the conflict known as Lord Dunmore's War, sparked by the increasing presence of American hunters and surveyors west of the Appalachians.[16]

Despite the Proclamation of 1763, by the end of the decade the Appalachians had ceased to be a barrier between Indigenous peoples and the English. Fur was the initial lure that led European Americans to penetrate the king's line. In the 1760s, Kentucky and the rich Ohio River Valley were a hunters' paradise. Intertribal warfare had driven most of Kentucky's Native settlers out of the valley before 1700, but by the 1760s members of various tribes had settled along the Ohio's northern tributaries and depended on Kentucky as a source for game.[17] Large herds of deer, elk, and buffalo, fat bears and flocks of turkeys roamed the fertile soil of the bluegrass region. The presence of European hunters in the region led to escalating conflicts among and with Indigenous peoples over the hunting grounds of the Ohio Valley. Small skirmishes were frequent as each group vied for access to the game of the "great natural park" of Kentucky.[18]

It was European American "long hunters," men like Daniel Boone, who first brought settlers like the McMeans news of Kentucky. These hunters ventured into the Ohio Valley in violation of the king's law and returned east laden with peltry and glowing, near panegyric accounts of the quality of the lands they encountered west of the Appalachians. Their tales were crafted to capture the imagination of colonist-farmers. In early reports, Kentucky was described as a veritable Eden, its soil "rich beyond conception," where even the "wild Oats and Wild Rye, [grow] in such plenty it might be mown and would turn out a good crop."[19] The best land of Kentucky, according to John Filson, author of Kentucky's first guidebook, "[exceeded] the finest low grounds in the settled parts of the continent." Western lands were fertile beyond all imagination, yielding "fifty and sixty bushels per acre," and occasionally "above one hundred bushels of good corn were produced from an acre in one season." All of this could be achieved "without water or manure," wherever a farmer might choose to plant himself.[20] The McMeans likely spent years hearing tales of the storied abundance of Kentucky's soil. To farmers eking out a living on Virginia soil exhausted by tobacco monoculture, or like the McMeans struggling with the rocky soil of the Appalachian foothills, Kentucky came to seem an agricultural paradise, a view summarized by settler Levi Todd, who referred to Kentucky as "the American Canaan."[21]

The outbreak of the Revolution may have made Kentucky seem even more attractive. In fall 1777, Colonel Archibald Lochry, the Continental Army officer responsible for Westmoreland County, which encompassed the McMeans's property, reported that "the whole country . . . from the allegany mountains, is all kept close in forts." These "forts" were often just large cabins, with wooden palisades, where the families in a given area could repair in the event of violence. They did so often, Lochry despaired, as "there [are] very few days there is not some Murder committed in some part of our frontiers. . . . The distressed situation of our country is such that we have no prospect but desolation and destruction."[22] Due to the frequent violence, residents were unable to attend to planting, which threatened their subsistence. Whether violence played a role in Andrew McMeans's decision to move his family westward, the arrival of his sixth child may have impressed upon McMeans that his farm was not large enough to provide for his family. Perhaps he found the lure of the fabled land of Kentucky irresistible. Whatever the cause, McMeans spent the winter of 1777, as George Washington and his troops huddled at Valley Forge, planning yet another move west for himself and his family.[23]

In the spring of 1778, word arrived at the Youghiogheny of a joint expedition of settlers and soldiers traveling westward under the command of Major George Rogers Clark, the ranking military officer west of Pittsburgh. Governor Patrick Henry of Virginia had tasked Clark with establishing a fort, and a community to feed it, at the junction of the Ohio and Mississippi Rivers; Clark used his return journey from Williamsburg as an opportunity to recruit the men and families he would need. The McMeans and several relatives, including Andrew's brothers Robert and Francis, and his sister and her family, decided to join them. In September 1778, McMeans sold his land for $850 of rapidly depreciating Pennsylvania currency and departed with his six children and his wife for a new life along the Ohio River.[24]

Like many western settlers, the McMeans traveled to Kentucky along the Ohio River in one of the flatboats that would become ubiquitous on the river. Easily constructed, Kentucky flatboats were difficult to steer but ideal for traveling through the often drought-depleted currents of the Ohio. Once in Kentucky, the boats could be broken up for firewood or transmuted into the walls or floor of a new home.[25] If the McMeans were lucky, they crowded all their possessions and their children into one boat and their livestock into another; if they were unlucky, they made the journey downriver accompanied by the lowing of frightened and seasick cattle.[26] Likely they joined forces with other families who were headed downriver for both protection and labor to aid in maneuvering the clumsy boats. For Anne McMeans, with six children, one a toddler, and pregnant with her seventh, the journey must have been filled with both trepidation and discomfort. Undoubtedly, she kept a watchful eye for movement along the banks as the family floated down the waters of the Ohio; once underway, boats seldom stopped, hoping to avoid becoming an easy target for the Ohio Indians who opposed the settlers' encroachment on their territory.

The McMeans put to shore just east of the Falls of the Ohio, the future site of Louisville, Kentucky, at a place called Beargrass Creek. Intent on obtaining land of his own, Andrew set out, along with his brothers Francis and Robert and his brother-in-law James Young, to establish a new community between the Falls and the three-year-old community of Harrodsburg in central Kentucky, leaving Anne and the children behind at Beargrass. It would not be until a year later, in fall 1779, that Anne and the family joined Andrew at the lands he hoped to claim along the Salt River.

Andrew and his brothers each claimed four hundred acres by virtue of the right of preemption, or right of first occupancy, a legal doctrine with profound importance in the settlement of the trans-Appalachian West.[27] Preemption was the embodiment of the labor theory of property, the belief that, in the words of political philosopher John Locke, "As *much land as a man tills, plants, improves, cultivates, and can use the product of, so much is his property.*" Preemption depended on the land in question being legally "waste"—land that was not yet property but could become it. For land to be "wasted," no previous title to the land could exist. In 1779, the legislature of Virginia decreed all unclaimed land within Kentucky to be "waste" land, setting itself squarely against the Indigenous nations that claimed previous ownership of the region.[28]

Preemption was not only a denial of Indigenous title but also an acknowledgment that the labor invested in land had a transformative function, that an individual, by applying his hard work in the soil, did "by his labour . . . as it were, inclose it from the common," and as a result was entitled to that land over the competing claims of other prospective purchasers.[29] Poor settlers like the McMeans hoped that this preference for bona fide settlers would translate into free land. Thomas Jefferson had acknowledged the right of "each individual of the society [to] appropriate to himself such lands as he finds vacant, and occupancy will give him title," in his 1774 pamphlet *A Summary View of the Rights of British America*, and the revolutionary government of Virginia reaffirmed the legitimacy of preemption in its land laws of 1776 and 1777, which promised preemption rights to "persons actually settled on any of the said Lands" of Kentucky prior to June 24, 1776.[30] The McMeans, as well as thousands of other ragged settlers, moved west hoping that as a reward for their labor in converting virgin land into productive acreage, they would be granted title to their own piece of the "Promis.d land" of Kentucky.[31]

At first, their hopes seem to have been well-placed. Despite the ongoing war, in May 1779 the Virginia legislature passed a land bill intended to clarify the process for claiming Kentucky land.[32] That summer, emigration to Kentucky surged. Continental Army officials from western Pennsylvania, near the McMeans's former residence, reported that the "emigration down the Ohio from this quarter . . . will Depopulate it altogether. . . . It is thought near one half of what Remains here will go down to Kaintucky, the Falls or to Illenois . . . this spring."[33] Looking back years later, settler Isaac Clinkenbeard remembered that "thousands of people came out" to Kentucky in fall 1779, "more than did for 7 or 8 years after that." Clinkenbeard, himself a new arrival, recalled that the line of emigrants on the overland trail was "strung [from the] Cumberland [Gap north] To Boonsborough."[34]

The 1779 land law created a system—on paper—intended to allow western settlers and speculators to obtain title to western land in an orderly fashion. The system was predicated on cash payments. The law created four distinct types of land "warrants": settlement, preemption, treasury, and military. Each warrant carried distinct characteristics specifying the amount of land the bearer could claim and the price needed to secure that land.[35] The most valuable type of warrants were settlement warrants. Only those who had arrived in Kentucky and worked the land prior to January 1, 1778, were entitled to these, which allowed the bearer to claim up to four hundred acres of land at the low price of ten shillings sterling per one hundred acres.[36] Everyone granted a settlement warrant was also entitled to a preemption warrant—the second most valuable type—which authorized the purchase of a thousand additional acres at the state price of forty pounds per one hundred acres. What gave preemption warrants their value was that holders of the warrants were able to submit their claims to land prior to any other group, enhancing their chances of claiming the best lands. Those settlers, like the McMeans, who had arrived in the West between January 1, 1778, and the passage of the land law in May 1779, received preemption warrants, but they were eligible to claim only four hundred acres of land.[37]

Less valuable than either the preemption or the settlement warrant was the treasury warrant, which anyone could purchase from the Virginia treasury. Purchasers could buy treasury warrants for any amount of land at the rate of forty pounds per one hundred acres, but the treasury warrants carried no privilege of early entry. The fourth type of warrant, the military warrant, could be used to claim lands in designated military ranges. During the Seven Years' War, the colonial government had issued bonds for western lands as a form of payment to soldiers who served in the British Army; the new state governments as well as the cash-strapped Confederation government continued the practice. In October 1779, the government of Virginia spelled out how much land each soldier was entitled to, from one hundred acres for each private who served for at least three years to five thousand acres for a colonel who fought until the end of the war.[38] Adding to the confusion of the marketplace in western lands, all of these warrants were issued in the form of paper securities, which allowed the holder to claim the number of acres denominated on the warrant. They did not refer to a specific tract or parcel of land; moreover, they were all alienable—they remained "good" even as they were passed from hand to hand to settle a debt or pay for goods or services. They were even partible, so that a preemption warrant holder might exchange the right to two hundred acres of his preemption warrant for a month's worth of a new arrival's help in clearing his lands. Both east and west of the Appalachians, secondary markets in all types of land warrants emerged.[39]

No matter which types of warrant were used, obtaining title to land required multiple steps. First, an individual was required to "locate" land, by visiting the land, in person or through an agent, to mark boundaries using stakes driven into the ground or slashes on trees. Often, claimants would also build a cabin or corn patch to prove that they had not only located but also "improved" the land—thereby making themselves eligible to receive a settlement or preemption warrant. Having located the land, claimants—or their agents—had to travel to the state or county land office to register their land claim with the county surveyor. This process was called entering the land: the claimant described the boundaries and adjacent properties to the county land office, which assigned the entry a number. After a waiting period, during which legal protests that the new claim interfered with earlier claims could be submitted to the land office, the government would authorize a county surveyor to survey the claim. The claimant would then hire an official surveyor to ascertain the amount of land contained in the warrant's boundaries and to draw a plat of the area. The plat then had to be reconveyed back to the land office, where two copies of it were entered into the county surveyor's entry book. Once the surveyor, his crew, and any other fees were paid, and assuming no conflicting claims emerged to challenge the legitimacy of the claim, the landowner was granted a certificate denominating the boundaries of their land.[40]

Each stage of this process was complicated, arduous, and often dangerous—especially on the exposed edges of settlement, where most preemptionists had the best chance of finding unoccupied lands. It was also expensive; entering a claim required traveling to Richmond, where the nearest land office was located, a feature of the law that greatly favored the interests of well-connected speculators.[41] Those who completed the process first had the best chance of being able to see their claims through to title, an advantage the law gave to settlement and preemption warrants. Only after those warrants were entered in the surveyor's book would the right to claim western lands be opened up to all.

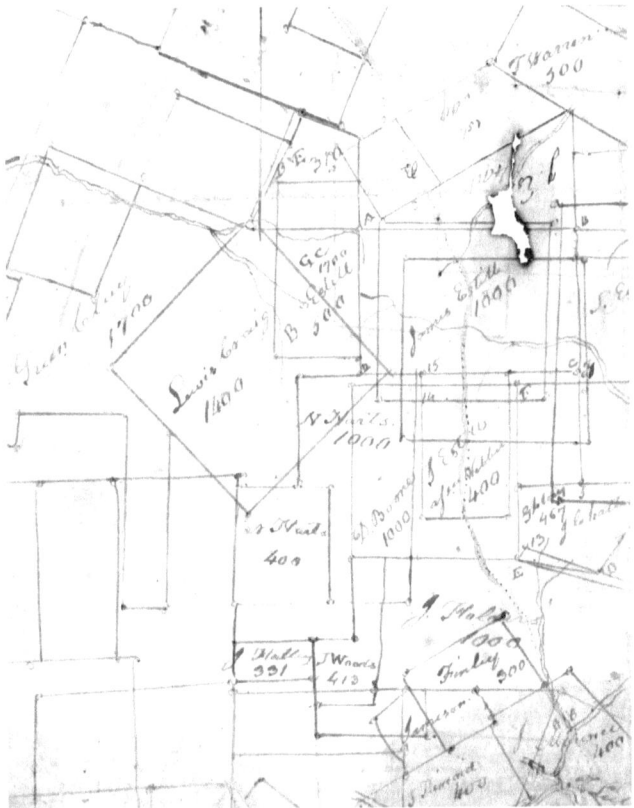

FIG. 3. Much of the best land of Kentucky was surveyed multiple times, resulting in overlapping land claims. (Eastern Kentucky University Special Collections and Archives, Richmond)

Although on paper the law promoted the orderly distribution of lands, in reality it created a morass of competing claims that would persist into the next century. The best lands of Kentucky were claimed multiple times as successive waves of settlers and surveyors scouted the lands of the trans-Appalachian West. Settlers and speculators who moved west gravitated toward regions with the best soil and access to water, or to strategically important sites like the Falls of the Ohio, salt springs, or possible mill sites. Both settlers and surveyors used the "metes and bounds" system to demarcate land, which relied on the features of the natural landscape to describe each parcel of land, compounding the confusion. Surveys defined land that began "a half mile below the Falls at a large Sycamore, Maple and Walnut running Thence North twenty five degrees West two hundred poles to an Elm and four Beeches," or running from "a Black Walnut Hoopash and Hickory on the north bank of Green River about one mile below a remarkable short bend in the Great bend which said bend extends upwards from the mouth of Lewiss Creek."[42] Confusion was inevitable. Boundaries were marked with blazes made on trees that were easily missed while the large size of many western land claims made it possible for a new survey to fall within the bounds of a preexisting claim.

In October 1779, the commissioners appointed by the legislature arrived in Kentucky to begin the process of issuing settlement and preemption warrants and entering the settlers' claims. Andrew McMeans and his brothers set off to meet the commissioners, carrying with them loose descriptions of the land they claimed along the Salt River. Having arrived in Kentucky in 1778, McMeans and his brothers were entitled by law to preemption warrants for four hundred acres apiece. They were just a few of the 1,400 petitioners whom the commissioners interviewed between October 1779 and May 1780. The metes and bounds system of describing land, coupled with the lack of good maps of Kentucky and the clamoring of over a thousand claimants, made it impossible for the commissioners to determine whether land being claimed by each applicant had already been claimed by another. Instead, the commission issued warrants and took locations without making sure that no overlapping claims existed.[43] Ultimately, they granted settlement and preemption certificates that covered over 1,334,050 acres of Kentucky land.[44] Much of the land, including the McMeans's claim along the Salt River, was entered in the books more than once.

Paying for Land

Even if his land had not been entered more than once, Andrew McMeans faced another hurdle in obtaining title. His preemption rights entitled him to claim 400 acres "at the state price" of £40 per hundred acres; thus, he needed £160 to gain title.[45] The McMeans had sold their farm in Pennsylvania in the summer of 1778 in exchange for depreciated Pennsylvania currency; they had used the money to outfit themselves for their journey westward and to sustain them through the winter of 1778–79. By October 1779, the McMeans lacked the money they needed to obtain a clear title. They were certainly not alone in struggling to gather the purchase price for land: obtaining land in Kentucky, even with the doctrine of preemption codified into law, always required cash payment. Westerners lacked the cash they needed to purchase the lands they claimed, a fact that the legislature acknowledged in October 1779 by extending to claimants a year's credit.[46] Despite this concession, Kentuckians faced numerous problems paying for land that would take far more than a year to resolve.

As the winter of 1779 closed in on the West, Kentucky faced an economic disaster. The winter of 1779–80 was bitterly cold; it would live on in legend as the "hard winter." Surveyor John Floyd reported that his "ink froze in the pen." The cold even killed the cane, a ubiquitous native bamboo that provided fodder for both livestock and deer. Poorly supplied new arrivals put additional pressure on strained resources, leading to widespread hunger. When he arrived at the Falls of the Ohio in December 1779, Virginia land commissioner William Fleming found "about 500 people who mostly look like g'osts, daily dying, especially the Young." "No person can conceive the Distress the People in this Country are in for want of Grain, without seeing it," land speculator John May reported of the poverty and privation that he witnessed among the new Kentuckians, "not one Half of them have any [flour], nor can the Rest assist them."[47]

The influx of new settlers and the ongoing grain shortage increased the price of food. In December, a bushel of corn sold at the Falls of the Ohio cost $50, or 15 Virginia pounds; by January 1780, the price had soared to $165 a bushel, or £50. John Floyd begged William Preston to send him flour, even "if it was a dear as gold dust." "Money," he informed Preston, "is of no account here."[48] Rising commodity prices were driven in part by dramatic inflation. "You can have no Conception of the Depochation [depreciation] of Money here, and if no step is taken by the Assembly to prevent it, it will continue to deprchate," John May informed his partner in early 1780, echoing thousands of similar complaints that emerged from across the former colonies. The legislature acknowledged the declining value of the Virginia pound in May 1780, resetting the exchange rate between the Virginia dollar and specie, a move that required claimants to obtain even larger amounts of cash.[49]

Both new and established settlers found that the dire conditions and food shortages brought on by the winter of 1779–80 absorbed what cash they had brought with them. From the Falls of the Ohio in March 1780, May informed his partner that a "very great Profit may now be made by the Purchase of Settlement & Preemption claims, as many of the

Claimants have not Money to clear out their Lands"—that is, to carry the process through to title.⁵⁰ May saw the struggles of families like the McMeans as an opportunity to capitalize on the settlers' misfortune. Many claimants were often willing to sell some portion of the lands designated in their warrants in exchange for the cash they needed to gain clear title to the rest, a practice that further complicated the land market of Kentucky. Those lucky enough to obtain settlement warrants could sell their entire four-hundred-acre claim and use the money they received to clear out a thousand-acre preemption warrant.⁵¹ In the process, though, they would be selling their right to be among the first to claim land.

The lack of cash on the Kentucky frontier was so severe that the government of Virginia acknowledged it in 1781 and again in 1783 by exempting the poorest Kentuckians from the payment of surveyors' fees, although this law did not completely remove the need for eventual payment, in specie, for land. Claimants were required, within a period of two and a half years, to pay twenty shillings in specie, or the equivalent in paper money, per one hundred acres. Under the law, settlers could claim up to four hundred acres, so at the end of the grace period, they owed the state four pounds sterling plus additional office fees. If at the end of two and a half years the settler did not have the cash on hand, the land was forfeited and sold for the state price, effectively allowing individuals with cash to obtain improved land for the same rate they would have needed to pay for virgin land. The original settlers would forfeit their labor and their land. Even though four pounds seems like a small amount, fluctuations in the money supply often placed it out of reach of families like the McMeans. Making matters worse, six months after the act was passed, the legislature once more devalued its paper currency; by December, the scale of depreciation was $1 in specie to $1,000 in paper.⁵²

At every turn, the system created by the land law of 1779 demanded cash. Although intended on its surface to make land more easily accessible to early settlers, in reality the land law resulted in huge windfalls for speculators like May and his partner Samuel Beall, as well as huge lawsuits over competing claims. For their part, speculators could not profit from their lands unless they found someone with cash enough to buy it from them, which few of Kentucky's ragged settlers could manage. Many hopeful land claimants became tenants, paying rent to speculators. As the speculative fervor for Kentucky lands died, some settlers sought to buy smaller tracts of land from speculators. Whether speculator or small farmer, all landowners also faced the prospect of eventually having to pay taxes if they wanted to keep their lands.⁵³

To earn cash to buy and secure land, western settlers needed to find a way to get the produce of the trans-Appalachian West to market. Although for centuries the great waterways of the continental interior—lesser rivers like the Miami, the Wabash, the Kanawha, the Cumberland, and the Tennessee, and the wider and longer Ohio and Mississippi Rivers—had served as pathways by which goods and peoples traversed the continent, the new Anglo-American settlers found themselves frustrated by the geopolitical and geographical context in which they were attempting to gain a foothold. The Appalachians formed a formidable barrier between the West and the established settlements of the Atlantic seaboard, a barrier that could only be crossed with great difficulty. Meanwhile, the Ohio River, the main artery connecting the new trans-Appalachian settlements to the Atlantic Coast, flowed westward with a current that made transporting the bulky produce of the West to eastern markets nearly impossible. Even if goods could successfully be brought upriver to Pittsburgh, at the headwaters of the Ohio, shipping flour to western Pennsylvania was hardly profitable because of high transportation costs and low demand. It was equally impossible for European Americans to travel north up the various tributaries of the Ohio to the Great Lakes. In the two decades following the outbreak of the American Revolution, the lands north of the Ohio were still very much in Indigenous hands, many of them hostile to the encroaching settlers, and the British-held St. Lawrence was not a hospitable place for American farmers.

Western settlers' best chance for getting their products to markets in New York, Philadelphia, and Boston—or to the cash-rich ports of Havana, Bordeaux, and London—lay in traveling down the Ohio to the Mississippi River, before continuing downriver to New Orleans and the Gulf of Mexico, where ships could export the fruits of western soil to the eastern seaboard, the Caribbean, and Europe. When western emigrants like the McMeans imagined what their new lives would be like in the West, they envisioned a flourishing trade down the Mississippi, which would give them access to the cash they needed to secure the land that lay at the heart of their new communities.[54] Thus, westerners' dreams of a profitable future hinged on access to the Mississippi. An anonymous pamphlet writer outlined just how important trade down the Mississippi was to western settlers: "Unless this can be obtained the fertility of their soil will not avail them. The produce which they may raise will be useless on their farms. The doors of Commerce will be shut against them." Most devastatingly, without access to the Mississippi, westerners' "land will . . . decline [rather] than rise in its value."[55] Less frequently did western political philosophers invoke the situation of families like the McMeans, who without Mississippi trade could not obtain land in the first place. Getting land required cash; getting cash to the Kentucky frontier required getting Kentucky produce to a market. But for their land-based economy to thrive, Kentuckians required markets and trade in the Spanish city of New Orleans. The Anglo-Americans who settled in the Ohio Valley structured their economy assuming that someday they would be able to export the produce of their farms down the Mississippi. Virginia's policies, which required cash be paid for land, helped lay the foundation of a western economy that could not function without access to external markets.

During the Revolution, navigating the Ohio and Mississippi Rivers was dangerous. The war had destabilized the politics and trade of trans-Appalachia. From Pittsburgh west to the Ohio's junction with the Mississippi, the river passed through territory contested among American, British, and Indigenous peoples. Passing from the Ohio to the Mississippi, river travelers encountered a different theater of the Revolution. With the outbreak of war, the lower Mississippi Valley had become a site of violent confrontation between the Spanish and British empires. The Chickasaw, Choctaw, Creek, Cherokee, and *petites nations* faced difficult decisions about which party to support or whether they wished to become involved in the conflict at all. War boats patrolled the Mississippi, and forts along its bank were rebuilt as Spanish and British troops, and their Indigenous allies, prepared for confrontation.[56] Even if a boat made it safely to New Orleans, Spain might refuse to allow the boat entry or, more likely, confiscate the cargo and possibly arrest the boatsmen.

Westerners as well as the U.S. government saw not only risk but opportunity in Mississippi River trade. Starved for specie and desperate for allies, the Continental Congress was eager to establish a connection between the American settlements and the Spanish government in New Orleans. For their part, western settlers who had already gambled their—and their families'—safety for the prospect of western lands were willing to undertake the journey in hopes of obtaining the cash they needed to secure those lands. Thus, during the Revolution the first boats loaded with Ohio Valley produce began to arrive in New Orleans, offering western settlers a glimpse of the Mississippi River trade they imagined would one day secure their fortunes.

3

The River at War

With the outbreak of the Revolution, the Mississippi River increased in importance to the United States. As the British blockaded American ports along the eastern seaboard, American merchants and officials began to see the Mississippi as a viable alternative for breaking the stranglehold that Britain had placed on the Confederation's international trade. As early as 1777, Governor Patrick Henry of Virginia wrote to Bernardo de Gálvez, the governor of Spanish Louisiana, requesting immediate Spanish aid for the American war effort and asking Spain to allow Americans to trade in New Orleans. Henry, governor of an impoverished revolutionary state, believed that both measures would help Virginia gain a solid economic footing. "In Exchange for these Advances," Henry offered the governor three things: "the Gratitude of this Free & Independent Country, the Trade in any, or all of its valuable productions, & the Friendship of its warlike Inhabitants." Although Henry was not certain what "at present . . . you set the greatest value . . . they are tendered to you & you will have a Right to chuse that which is most acceptable to . . . the Spanish Nation."[1]

Henry's petitions had an able advocate in Oliver Pollock, a Scottish-born merchant stationed in New Orleans. Even before Spain entered the war, Pollock had persuaded Spanish officials in New Orleans to provide substantial aid to the United States.[2] He also used his personal credit to obtain supplies in New Orleans that were shipped upriver to American troops in the Ohio Valley. As a result, Pollock knew well the difficulties posed by the continued contest for the Mississippi. As early as 1778, he urged American officials to send troops to occupy West Florida, especially at Manchac and Natchez, to secure American supply lines up and down the river. By the end of the war in 1782, Pollock's service to the

United States had led him deeply into debt. To recoup his financial losses, Pollock approached the Spanish governor in New Orleans with a plan to import much-needed flour into the colony. Before the war, New Orleans had occasionally received shipments of flour from Philadelphia, but wartime conditions foreclosed this trade. Along the eastern seaboard, the Continental Army, as well as revived trade with French and Spanish islands in the Caribbean, had increased demand for flour; consequently, eastern flour was extremely dear. Pollock therefore turned to a new source of flour to supply the port of New Orleans: the Ohio Valley.[3]

In the early 1780s, Joshua McQueen and his two companions became part of the first exportations of Ohio Valley produce down the Mississippi.[4] The challenges they encountered as they descended the river foreshadowed the difficulties that would shape postrevolutionary river trade. Before the Revolution, few if any boats carrying Anglo-American produce from the Ohio Valley had arrived in New Orleans, owing partly to the success of the Proclamation of 1763 and partly to the ongoing efforts of the Ohio Valley Indians in preventing western expansion. During the war, western settlement increased dramatically; consequently, so did the amounts of flour available for export as well as western calls for markets to export it to. In the lower Mississippi Valley, Spain's 1779 entry into the American Revolution added new complications to the politics and trade of the river. Spain, Britain, the United States, and Indigenous polities jockeyed for position and control of strategic sites like the Chickasaw Bluffs, Natchez, and the port of New Orleans. They also vied for the loyalty and support of the region's European and Indigenous inhabitants. The war brought significant changes to the lower Mississippi, redrawing the lines of empire while simultaneously reshaping the role that the river could play for an expansive United States.

The Struggle for Mastery

WELL BEFORE Spain officially declared war in 1779, Spanish officials in Louisiana had supported the patriot cause in several ways. Although Spain refused to ally with the rebellious Americans, once the war began Louisiana governor Bernardo de Gálvez acted swiftly to suppress British shipping on the Mississippi. On April 17, 1777, in a surprise raid, Gálvez ordered every British vessel found in the Spanish-controlled part of the river seized and their cargoes forfeited; eleven ships in all, carrying merchandise exceeding $50,000, were seized and auctioned off in New

Orleans. The next day, Gálvez ordered all British merchants to leave the colony and forbade any Spanish subject from sheltering or otherwise aiding the British merchants. At the same time, he offered new concessions to American ships, allowing them to claim Spanish ownership at sea to avoid seizure by the British. Gálvez also offered French merchants expanded trading privileges in New Orleans.[5]

With limited access to the river, British West Florida residents—like those at Natchez and Baton Rouge—were cut off from the rest of the colony and unable to access military aid from British installments in Mobile and Pensacola. Natchez's vulnerability was underscored in February 1778 when a small flotilla of a hundred American soldiers and frontier residents attacked Natchez. The expedition, under the command of James Willing, a member of a prominent commercial Philadelphia family and a former resident of Natchez, sought to bring the region under American control. Without British soldiers in the region, the settlements of Natchez, Baton Rouge, and Manchac fell to Willing. However, he and his men were not satisfied with surrender: instead, they plundered Loyalists' plantations, brutalizing the population, confiscating—or stealing—cash and other valuables, burning several plantations, and capturing 680 enslaved people whom they auctioned in New Orleans. Willing's raid incited the fury of British officials in West Florida, who dispatched two warships to patrol the lower Mississippi. Willing's raid also helped to solidify anti-American sentiment in West Florida. By mid-April, British soldiers, supported by the region's Anglo-American population, had reclaimed the eastern bank of the Mississippi; nevertheless, Willing's success demonstrated how vulnerable West Florida was to attacks arriving from upriver.[6]

In August 1779, Gálvez received word that the Spanish had made their long-awaited decision to enter the conflict as an ally of France. On August 20, Gálvez marched out of New Orleans at the head of 667 men, consisting of a mixture of white and free Black militia as well as Spanish regulars, to attack the British. He was joined a few days later by a force of 600 Acadians and Germans from Louisiana's German Coast and an additional force of 160 Houma, Choctaw, Alabaman, and other Indians.[7] They took the British fort at Manchac, and on September 13 attacked the British fort at Baton Rouge. After an eight-day siege, the British surrendered. As part of the terms, Gálvez demanded the surrender of Fort Panmure, the British fort at Natchez. With little choice, the British commander agreed, and Natchez fell into Spanish hands without a shot fired.[8] Many of the community's most vocal Loyalists fled north and took refuge among the Chickasaw.

By the time of the American Revolution, the Chickasaw were the undisputed authority on the eastern shore of the Mississippi. Although in 1777 they agreed to aid the British by policing the Mississippi, the Chickasaw had no great interest in entangling themselves in a European war, and they patrolled the river on their own terms.[9] The Chickasaw were not watching, for instance, when James Willing and his men traveled down the river. Rather than preventing American passage downriver, as the British had asked, the Chickasaw, and the Loyalists they sheltered, tended to target ships headed upriver. This became a consistent problem for George Rogers Clark, the leader of Virginia's troops in the trans-Appalachian West, who complained that frequent Chickasaw attacks on river traffic were driving up prices for goods in the Illinois country. Clark claimed that the "Checasaws" were working on behalf of the British, who had "instruct[ed them] . . . to block up that River if possible."[10] Clark's reading of the situation was incomplete: such endeavors served Chickasaw interests as much as those of the British, as the Chickasaw kept the majority of the prizes they captured. At the same time, the Chickasaw were strategic in which boats they targeted. Throughout the first four years of the war, most American boats traveling along the river passed up and down the river without interference from the Chickasaw. While a British official reported to his superiors that "the Chickasaws are constantly hunting the Mississippi and Cherokee [Tennessee] Rivers for Virginians, French and Spaniards [and] Every now and then some of each are knocked in the Head," the Chickasaw did so not as allies of the British but rather as defenders of Chickasaw territory.[11]

The Chickasaw's only wartime engagement occurred when Americans attempted to settle on Chickasaw land. In April 1780, a group of about 250 Anglo-American civilians and soldiers set out to establish a fort and town near the junction of the Ohio and Mississippi. Among them were Anne and Andrew McMeans and several members of their extended family; after being unable to secure land in Kentucky on account of being cash poor, they joined this expedition in exchange for a generous land grant.[12] Thomas Jefferson, governor of Virginia, was to be the namesake of the fort. Jefferson had urged Clark, who was to lead the new settlement, to treat with the Cherokee to obtain title to the land, demonstrating a misunderstanding of the lines of power in the Mississippi Valley. The site chosen for the community lay in Chickasaw, not Cherokee, territory.

Had they recognized their error, it is unlikely the Americans would have proceeded.

Almost from the moment of settlement, the Chickasaw laid siege to Fort Jefferson. One settler, recalling the events of that summer years later, described the party of about 150 Chickasaw warriors as "commissioned to destroy" the town.[13] Although the Virginia soldiers were able to repel the Chickasaw, the Chickasaw undermined the viability of the settlement and the fort by cutting down the fort's corn and killing the settlers' cattle. With little prospect of a resupply, the fort was evacuated in June 1781.[14] The Chickasaw's refusal to have Americans settle in their territory marked the end of American attempts to colonize the Mississippi River Valley for over a decade. Although the British could imagine the Chickasaw's actions as the result of allegiance to their longtime allies, Chickasaw refusal to allow American settlement sprang from their own motivations.

Among those evacuated from Fort Jefferson was Anne McMeans. She and her family boarded one of seven boats that remained at the fort and headed downriver to Natchez, hoping from there to find ships that could take them up and around the coast and back to Philadelphia. Traveling with her extended family—in a group consisting of two men, three women, and fourteen children—the McMeans set their boat adrift on the Mississippi River. Within a week, the adults on the boat began to suffer. Anne McMeans herself fell sick, while her husband and two sisters-in-law passed away during the first few days afloat. Desperate, McMeans and her brother-in-law boiled deerskins for the children, but all their efforts to procure enough to eat failed. First her seven-year-old son, then her two-year-old daughter starved to death. She watched helplessly as her brother-in-law became despondent, refusing to hunt to provide the family with food.[15] Certain that the family had no other chance of survival, he suggested they kill and eat one of the children, chosen by lottery, so that the others might survive. McMeans, however, urged her brother-in-law to wait, and less than a day later an Indigenous family who had been hunting by the river offered them some bear meat—testimony perhaps to the difference between Anglo-Americans adrift on the river and Anglo-Americans attempting to coopt Indigenous lands. Fifty years later, McMeans could still recall her feelings at finding salvation from "the hand of a savage who was more likely to murder than relieve us in this time of war."[16]

Providence—assisted by riverine commerce—continued to provide for the desperate family as they floated down the river; in 1781, despite the war, the Mississippi teemed with activity. On their journey downriver the McMeans boat met several parties of Native Americans, an American trader, and two boatloads of Americans in the process of moving to New Orleans, all of whom supplied them with food. While McMeans was too weak to even lift her head, these strangers helped her and her children arrive in Natchez. Although she was desperate to return to Pennsylvania, as she possessed little money or goods, she soon found that "when [she] spoke of it, she was laughed to scorn." Trapped in Natchez, she found work as a housekeeper, supporting herself and her four remaining children from her wages.[17]

While McMeans and her family had been under siege at Fort Jefferson, British Loyalists at Natchez, with the encouragement of British officials, launched a rebellion against the Spanish. In April 1781, they succeeded in taking possession of the fort at Natchez only to receive word a few weeks later that British forces at Mobile and Pensacola had surrendered to Gálvez's troops. The Natchez Loyalists sued for peace, but as they had previously sworn their loyalty to Spain and reneged on their promises, Spanish officials regarded them as rebels. As Spanish troops marched north from New Orleans, many of the Loyalists fled. Thirty or so found refuge with the Choctaw, while another eighty sought shelter with the Chickasaw.[18] The arriving Spanish troops arrested several men who had remained behind in Natchez and sent them to New Orleans for questioning.

Among the Chickasaw, the Loyalists found an ally in trader James Colbert. By 1782, the Scottish-born Colbert had lived with the Chickasaw for more than forty years, and he was a committed British partisan. In 1781, he led a delegation of Chickasaw to Pensacola to help defend the British against a possible Spanish attack. When the eighty Natchez rebels fled to Chickasaw country, he interceded on their behalf, and the Loyalists were allowed to build an encampment near the bluffs. It was from this encampment that Colbert, angered by the Spaniards' arrest of several of the British partisans who had led the resistance at Natchez, decided to take control of the Mississippi. In spring 1782, Colbert and his men attacked Spanish ships traveling along the Mississippi between upriver posts and New Orleans, operating with the help of informants in Natchez who gave them advanced notice of the movement of boats along the river. On May 2, 1782, Colbert and his men scored their greatest success when they captured a boat belonging to St. Louis trader Sylvester L'Abbadie. The boat was carrying an impressive cargo, including six thousand pesos in coin, as well as Señora Nicanora Ramos de Cruzat, wife of the Illinois lieutenant governor, and her four young sons.[19] Colbert and his allies believed they had obtained a powerful tool in securing the release of the British prisoners being held in New Orleans. After holding L'Abbadie and Cruzat captive for several weeks, Colbert dispatched them to New Orleans with a message for the governor.

Following their release, Señora Cruzat and L'Abbadie both reported to the Spanish officials that the Chickasaw were not enthusiastic about the presence of the Loyalists on their territory, tolerating their presence due to the influence of Colbert, who during his long residency with the Chickasaw had married three women and fathered several sons who would ultimately become prominent leaders.[20] Although these raids were conducted from the Chickasaw Bluffs, they likely included almost no Chickasaw. However, the Chickasaw capitalized on the Loyalists' raids: some two hundred Chickasaw shared in bounty captured from the Spanish boats, as a repayment for allowing the Loyalists to use Chickasaw territory; the Chickasaw's share of the six thousand pesos Colbert stole became the first infusion of specie to ever enter Chickasaw territory. In addition to receiving ammunition and liquor from the raiders, Chickasaw leaders took advantage of opportunities to return captured Spanish subjects as a means of opening negotiations with Spanish officials.[21] The Chickasaw were able to use the threat of Colbert and his raiders to strengthen their own bargaining position: they promised the Spanish safe passage through the Chickasaw Bluffs in exchange for trade and military aid. For their part, Spanish officials regarded Colbert and his men as pirates. Interim governor Esteban Miró, who had replaced Gálvez as governor of Louisiana, refused to negotiate with Colbert. Although several of the Loyalist prisoners from Natchez were released, Miró dispatched several others to British Jamaica, thumbing his nose at Colbert's demands for their freedom.[22]

While Colbert was a thorn in the side of the Spanish, it was clear to all observers that it was the Chickasaw who controlled the river. They never allied with the British during the Revolution, preferring to remain as neutral as possible to protect their own interests. By controlling the Chickasaw Bluffs, they were able to police the passage of goods and people along the river, despite Spanish claims to dominance over the Mississippi. As Spanish officials replaced British ones in West Florida, they could neither dislodge nor divert the Chickasaw from their control over the river's trade.

McQueen's Journey

IN THE spring of 1782, as Colbert menaced Spanish shipping and the Chickasaw kept a wary eye on the river, Joshua McQueen floated onto the contested waters of the Mississippi. McQueen was no stranger to either inter-imperial or interracial conflict. In 1777, Joshua McQueen was twenty-one years old and living near Holliday's Cove in present-day West Virginia, then a settlement clinging to the western fringe of the British empire. An unattached young man who seems to have made his living by hunting, McQueen was an ideal recruit for the officers of the Thirteenth Virginia Regiment. Shortly after he enlisted, his regiment marched eastward to help protect Philadelphia; he spent the fall of 1777 fighting in Washington's army at the Battles of Brandywine and Germantown.[23] In the spring of 1778, McQueen was dispatched homeward as the Thirteenth was sent to Fort Pitt to form part of a proposed invasion of Indian country led by General Lachlan McIntosh. McIntosh and his men departed from Fort Pitt in the early autumn, but the invasion was abandoned when more of McIntosh's soldiers departed from military service as their contracts expired and their food supply dwindled. Half-starved, McQueen and his compatriots filtered back into Fort Pitt. A year later, in April 1779, McQueen once more marched out of Fort Pitt as part of Daniel Broadhead's campaign against the Seneca; once more, the expedition ran low on supplies, and McQueen and his companions "had to cut down the wild cherries to get something to eat."[24] Having served for the duration of the war as an infantry soldier, spy, and scout, McQueen received his discharge in spring 1782. Years later, as McQueen recalled the sequence of events that first brought him west of the Appalachian Mountains, he remembered that his friend Nat Tumbleston "had a boat ready, and was going down [the Ohio], just as I was dismissed from the army." Tumbleston had loaded a flatboat with western Pennsylvanian flour, which he intended to sell in Natchez. He had heard that in Natchez, "flour sold at $40 a barrel." Tumbleston's was likely one of the ten boats, each loaded with thirty tons of flour, that departed from Pittsburgh that season. Ten or twelve more of the same size were expected to follow soon after; much of the flour was consigned to Oliver Pollock in New Orleans.[25]

As they departed from Pittsburgh, McQueen, Tumbleston, and their companions were unaware of the dimensions of the turmoil occurring downriver. For his part, William Irvine, the American general commanding U.S. troops in Pittsburgh, worried for the safety of the departing flotilla, fearing that "some of these adventurers may ... fall in to the hands of the enemy." Irvine had heard of British troops' operating in the Illinois country and below the mouth of the Ohio; he supposed that "these boats will be a great object for them."²⁶ Irvine had not yet learned that it was Colbert and the British Loyalists operating out of the Chickasaw Bluffs who were busily molesting traffic along the river, nor could he have known that one month later Colbert and his companions would capture Señora Cruzat. Despite not knowing who posed the greatest danger along the river, McQueen and his companions nevertheless must have weighed the risk of capture against the possibility of high profits. It was a gamble that McQueen would ultimately lose.

While enroute to Natchez, McQueen and his companions were captured by people he identified as British and were imprisoned for three months before, in McQueen's recollection, the "French" freed them. Almost certainly, the "British" forces who captured McQueen's boat were Colbert and the Loyalists operating from the Chickasaw Bluffs. Likewise, the "French" were probably Spanish. Despite his lack of specificity, or maybe because of it, McQueen's recollection acknowledges the complex cultural landscape of the new Spanish colony of West Florida and the contested world of the lower Mississippi. Colbert and his men operated with British consent but were not themselves British soldiers.²⁷ Meanwhile, few of the subjects of Spanish Louisiana were of Spanish descent; many of the colony's officials and officers who attempted to disrupt Colbert and the Loyalists' piracy were former French subjects who had remained following the transfer of the region to Spain in 1763.²⁸ In the lower Mississippi Valley, the conflict over empire had spilled into a conflict over control of trade of the lower Mississippi.

By the early 1780s, the Mississippi River was once more at the heart of a multicultural world of trade. Following his release from British captivity, McQueen was hired on by a fur trader as one of a crew of twenty-seven men who spent their spring and summer months rowing a heavily laden *bateau* up the Mississippi, traveling to St. Genevieve for a season of trade. The crew comprised, as McQueen recollected, "all French and Spaniards" but himself and one other man, who was "of a sort of people that file their teeth [and] Live in some hot country way to the west." This, along with the fact that he spent that year wearing "a handkerchief on my head, same as a Frenchman," dominated his recollections seventy years later.²⁹

The same flour flotilla that led to McQueen's captivity proved the solution to Anne McMeans's exile. Her salvation floated into Natchez in the form of another boat from Fort Pitt. In the boat was Thomas White, an old friend of McMean's from western Pennsylvania, enroute to New Orleans with a cargo of flour being shipped to Pollock. When the flatboats transporting the flour touched in at Natchez, White was overjoyed to find McMeans and some of her children alive. White promised her "that if all the flour he had would serve to pay [her] passage round [to Philadelphia], it should be expended."[30] He brought her and her family to New Orleans, where McMeans encountered another branch of wartime trade linking the Mississippi and the East Coast. As a wartime measure, Gálvez had opened the port to American shipping; with the end of the conflict between the United States and Britain, shipping lanes had reopened. McMeans soon found in port an American captain about to sail from New Orleans to Philadelphia. After she told the captain of her ordeal, the captain was so moved that he allowed her and her children free passage back to the Atlantic Coast.[31] They departed from New Orleans in May 1782.[32] In May 1783, five years after first departing from Pennsylvania, Anne McMeans and her remaining children were reunited with her parents.

The experiences faced by Anne McMeans and her family, as well as Joshua McQueen and his companions, are united by more than timing. Anne McMeans and her trouble finding land in Kentucky and Joshua McQueen's attempt to profit in Spanish Natchez were part of the same imagined political economy of western expansion. The two are linked by Mississippi River trade. Although few western settlers faced the prospect of cannibalism, the experiences of the McMeans family in Kentucky were representative of the confusion over access to land that characterized the 1770s and 1780s. Settlers' mad dash to Kentucky was driven by a common desire for land, and Virginia's demands for cash payment, along with speculators' expectations of profits, linked western expansion to the problem of market access. Everyone who invested in the West, who staked their fortune on the prospect of obtaining or selling western lands, faced the same problems of market isolation and specie deprivation. Getting cash on the Kentucky frontier required getting Kentucky produce to a market. In this, though, the magic of Kentucky soil failed. Without access to markets, securing and profiting from the land that undergirded the western economy was impossible. For his part, Joshua McQueen's captivity embodied the reality of the geopolitical situation of the lower Mississippi Valley. Western settlers might imagine that Mississippi trade would grant them access to markets and enable them to profit from the lands they claimed. But the reality of the Mississippi was that the river lay entirely outside the control of American settlers.

Redrawing the Lines

At the end of the Revolution, the flour trade that had proved Joshua McQueen's downfall and Anne McMeans's salvation unraveled in the face of imperial conflict. In October 1781, British forces surrendered at Yorktown, and in 1783 British, American, French, and Spanish officials met in Paris to discuss the terms of Britain's defeat. Spain had entered the war not as an ally of the United States but as a co-belligerent, necessitating a separate treaty confirming Spain's territorial conquests in the Mississippi Valley.[33] Although they were signed on the same day in September 1783, the British/French/American treaty and the British/Spanish Treaty differed significantly. During the war, Spanish troops had captured Natchez, Pensacola, and Mobile, and had also ventured much further up the Mississippi River, establishing new Spanish positions as far north as the junction of the Ohio and Mississippi Rivers. As a result of these conquests, Spain claimed territory stretching north from the Gulf of Mexico to the current site of Cairo, Illinois, and east all the way to the westernmost settlements of Georgia, yet the treaty between Britain and the United States granted the United States all of the territory north of the 31st parallel—the modern-day border between Florida and Georgia and the traditional northern border of the colonies of East and West Florida.[34] In contrast, the treaty between Spain and Britain was much vaguer. Rather than saying that Spain was granted the territory south of the 31st parallel, the Anglo-Iberian treaty instead stated that "His Britannick Majesty . . . cedes and guaranties, in full right to his Catholick Majesty [the King of Spain], East Florida, as also West Florida," without defining the boundaries of either.[35]

The terms of the Anglo-Franco-American treaty infuriated the Spanish. Britain, they believed, had ceded lands that belonged to Spain by right of conquest. In Paris and Madrid, Spanish officials argued that, based on time-honored traditions of international law and the rules of warfare, Britain had no right to grant to the United States territory that Spain had captured. According to Spain, both the northern and western boundaries designated by the Anglo-American treaty were invalid: thanks to Spain's wartime success, the United States had no legitimate claim to land anywhere along the eastern side of the lower Mississippi River.

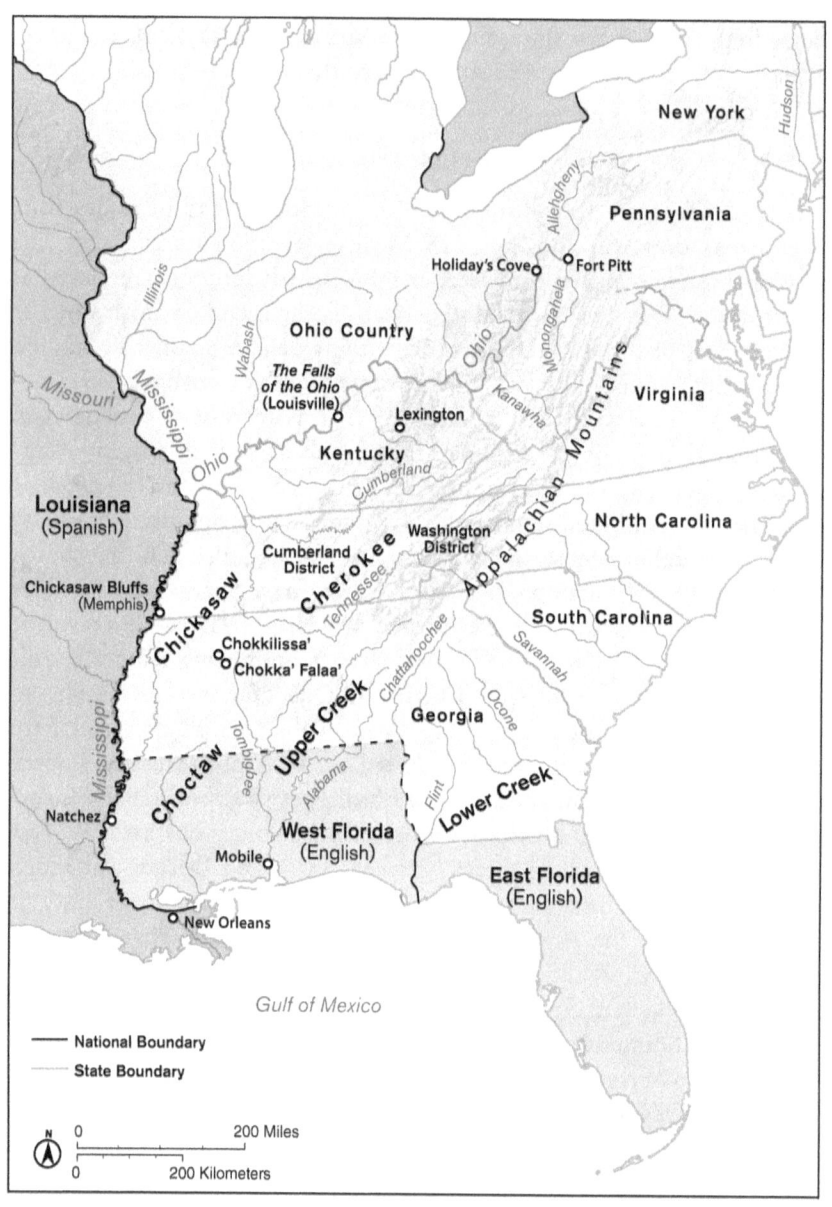

MAP 1. This map, highlighting the area south of the Ohio River, shows the imperial claims of the United States, Spain, and Britain during the American Revolution.

Article 8 of the British-American treaty proved the most divisive. It declared that "the navigation of the river Mississippi, from its source to the ocean, shall forever remain free and open to the subjects of Great Britain and the citizens of the United States."[36] American negotiators had fought for this concession; Britain, which had possessed the right to Mississippi navigation for the previous twenty years, agreed to share it with the United States, which, the United States hoped, would provide settlers in Kentucky and North Carolina's Washington district with much needed market outlets. Both the navigation of the river and the demarcation of a line in the *middle* of the river as the boundary between American and Spanish possessions recycled the territorial terms laid out in the 1763 Treaty of Paris, signed at the end of the Seven Years' War. In 1763, Britain had been in a position of power, victorious in a war fought in arenas across the globe, leaving Spain little option but to concede half the river as well as the right to navigate the river to Britain. By 1783, power in the region had shifted. With both banks of the Mississippi in Spanish control, Spain insisted there was no legitimate rationale by which the United States could claim a right to either Mississippi navigation or the export of American goods through Spanish territory.[37] Britain, Spain argued, had overstepped its bounds: the Mississippi was a Spanish river. Spain alone would decide who would be able to use it.

In 1784, Spain closed the Mississippi to American traffic to shore up its control over the Southwest. That Louisiana and the Floridas had failed to profit their imperial masters in the seven decades of European settlement in the region did not curtail the usefulness of the lower Mississippi Valley to the expansive Spanish empire. Spanish officers envisioned the colony of Louisiana forming a buffer between Spain's holdings in the Gulf of Mexico and its traditional enemy, Britain, which retained its territory in Canada. British forces in Canada could easily use the Mississippi as a pathway into Spanish territory unless the river itself was well-protected.[38] The Spanish also feared American and British interference in their trade with Indigenous peoples in the Southeast and with French and *métis* traders along the upper Mississippi River. The Spanish planned to exclude the United States and British from these markets for both economic and diplomatic reasons. The fur trade of the Upper Midwest and the deer hide trade of the Southeast were central to the economy and diplomacy of Louisiana. Spanish officials knew that maintaining trade networks with Native peoples was synonymous with maintaining political relations. Many Indigenous nations, in particular the Creek, Chickasaw, and Choctaw peoples of what are now Alabama and southern Tennessee, were able to leverage Spanish concern over international rivalries into lower prices and larger annual gifts from the Spanish. In these regions, aggressive Georgian traders competed with Spanish licensed traders, and part of Spain's desire to claim the region arose from the need to exclude these interlopers from Spanish trade.[39]

For the court of Spain, a key military objective during the Revolution had been to drive the British from the Gulf Coast. Spain's newly won control of the coastal territories of North America turned the Gulf of Mexico into a Spanish lake, protecting two of Spain's most lucrative colonies—Cuba and Mexico—from foreign aggression. Furthermore, Spain hoped that the Mississippi Valley could act as a buffer between the silver mines of Mexico and the rapidly expanding Americans. Spanish officials believed that closing the Mississippi would slow American settlement and allow Spain the time it needed to reverse the colonial fortunes of the region. Spanish officials considered the exclusion of rival powers from the region "far more important than the acquisition of Gibraltar," and this thinking structured the Spanish response to American insistence on river access.[40] Opening the Mississippi would, after all, give American traders direct access to Spain's colonies in the Gulf.

During the Revolution, Spain had opened its Caribbean possessions, especially Cuba, to American trade. After it declared war, Spain had used Havana as a staging point for its North American troops, straining local food supplies. Cut off from Spanish resupply by British dominance of the Atlantic, the island turned to American merchants, especially those operating out of Philadelphia, to supply the deficit. In return for Philadelphia flour, the Americans had received valuable sugar and even more valuable specie, amounting, in the estimate of one Spanish official, to more than 3 million pesos over ten months in 1780–81. With the war ending, the Spanish crown resented the role that American importers had come to play in Cuba. Some American merchants had attempted to create new establishments in Cuba, competing with Spanish interests and regularly trafficking in contraband. Excluding Americans and folding the Cuban flour trade back within the mercantilist bonds of empire was Spain's priority after the Revolution. As troops were withdrawn from Havana, the need for copious amounts of flour fell well within the bounds that could be supplied by Spanish colonies in New Spain. Accordingly, in 1783 Spain barred the arrival of American shipping; in 1784, in the months before the court closed the Mississippi, Spain expelled American merchants from Cuba, going so far as to hunt door to door for those who failed to leave voluntarily. Among those expelled was a recently arrived Oliver Pollock, who had hoped to recoup his fortunes on the island. Having been appointed by the Continental Congress to represent American interests in Cuba, Pollock arrived on the island with two boatloads of contraband goods that were immediately confiscated by Spanish officials. By the end of 1784, the only Anglo-Americans remaining on the island were American merchants imprisoned for smuggling. Pollock, although protected from imprisonment by his diplomatic status, was forced into house arrest by his creditors.[41]

By closing the Mississippi, Spain protected both its economic and territorial interests while slowing American expansion. The closure soon became the opening salvo of a Spanish attempt to force the United States to acknowledge Spanish land claims in the Mississippi Valley, giving Spain time to assert the Spanish imperial model over its newly expanded American holdings. The Spanish recognized as clearly as did western settlers the consequences of a closed Mississippi. Don Diego de Gardoqui, the negotiator eventually appointed by Spain to confer with Congress over the future of both nations' interests in the Southwest, summarized the logic of Spain's decision: "The value of the [western] land depends upon the navigation of the river." Closing the river undermined the economic logic behind western expansion.[42] Without Mississippi trade, westerners would lack the cash to translate their dreams of rising land values, either through land ownership or speculation, into reality. Closing the Mississippi dealt a devastating blow to the settlers and speculators of the first American West.

At the same time, Spain's closure of the Mississippi failed to acknowledge that Spain itself lacked control over the Mississippi. From their position at the Chickasaw Bluffs, the Chickasaw made decisions over who was and who was not allowed up or down the river. They had silently acquiesced to Colbert's disruption of Spain's supply lines and seizure of the wife of a Spanish official, and often asserted their own authority over passing vessels. As Anne McMeans's beleaguered family had floated down the Mississippi, they were approached by a group of Chickasaw arrayed along the river's bank. At first, the debilitated occupants of the boats were terrified, but the Chickasaw saw no threat in the half-dead travelers. That evening, they offered the McMeans bear meat and returned the following morning to offer more. Before they departed, the Chickasaw once more proved their control over the trade of the Mississippi. After giving the McMeans the meat, the Chickasaw "took [the McMeans's] pewter, knives, and forks, and everything they could find that suited them."[43]

While Spanish and American officials in Europe could imagine a world in which they controlled Mississippi trade, the Chickasaw's seizure of the McMeans's family goods provides a powerful counterpoint.

For his part, Joshua McQueen made his way back to the Ohio Valley. There, he seems to have turned once more to hunting, traveling through the rivers and forests of the Mississippi watershed gathering meat and furs before returning to Kentucky around 1795, marrying, raising seven children, and living to the ripe old age of 106.[44] Neither Anne McMeans nor Joshua McQueen was particularly remarkable, although remarkable things happened to them. At various points in their travels through Kentucky and along the Mississippi River, both would have benefited from the intervention of a powerful government capable of asserting its will against other colonial powers. But while Virginia was able to provide a mechanism—however inadequate and convoluted—for providing title to land, it lacked the ability to assert itself against either the Spanish or the Chickasaw. Spain's decision to close the Mississippi led westerners to turn to the central government as their best avenue for obtaining access to Atlantic world markets.

When Spain closed the Mississippi to American trade, it created an imperial crisis for the new United States. Obtaining Mississippi trade would require projecting authority over the contested West but also securing the recognition of national claims by foreign and Native powers—obtaining what historian Eliga H. Gould has called "treaty worthiness."[45] In 1784, the United States had not yet become imperial. In the aftermath of the Revolution, establishing domestic authority took precedence over establishing imperial authority. But by making the new American states wrestle over the tension between establishing control at home and asserting its will abroad, the crisis over the Mississippi played a central role in the creation of an American state capable of doing both. Likewise, it revealed the connection between commercial opportunities and territorial expansion. By 1792, three-fourths of the adult white men in Kentucky would own no land, as they were unable to obtain the cash necessary to purchase it.[46] The conflict over how to obtain money erupted not among Kentuckians themselves but between Kentucky and the rest of the union, or even more broadly between Kentucky and all of its imperial neighbors: Britain, Spain, and the United States. The connections between land and cash only heightened the stakes for westerners in need of cash and for the Mississippi River trade. In other words, the market in western lands was tied to the marketplace of the Mississippi. Settlement and trade would expand in lockstep.

PART II

The Closure of the River and Sectional Crisis, 1784–1795

IN NOVEMBER 1792, members of the Chickasaw, Choctaw, Shawnee, and Cherokee gathered in New Orleans to meet with the Francisco Luis Héctor, Baron de Carondelet, the governor of Louisiana. Carondelet had called the meeting to encourage the creation of a "confederation of all the Indian nations that inhabit the region enclosed by the Ohio and Mississippi Rivers, the Appalachian Mountains, and the Gulf of Mexico."[1] Although embraced by Spanish officials, the idea of a pan-tribal alliance had Indigenous origins. In the 1780s, in the face of growing threats from American settlers in Kentucky and north of the Ohio, members of the Wyandot, Shawnee, Chippewa, Odawa, Potawatomi, Lenni Lenape, Miami, Kickapoo, Wea, and Piankashaw had created a military alliance to oppose American intrusions into their territory.[2] Representatives of this Northern Confederacy had visited the Chickasaw, Choctaw, Cherokee, and Creek numerous times. Among the Creek, the prominent leader Alexander McGillivray was a firm proponent of the construction of a similar confederation, under the leadership of the Creek, that would encompass the people of the Southeast, allowing them to present a united front against American efforts to wrest away Indigenous lands.[3]

For their part, the Chickasaw resented Creek attempts at dominance but recognized the need for closer cooperation. In the months prior to the New Orleans conference, Taski Etoka, the "king" of the Chickasaw, traveled through Choctaw territory carrying a message from the Creek, Shawnee, Cherokee, Abenaki, and other smaller groups from the regions north and south of the Ohio and from throughout the Southeast. Taski Etoka's message was stark. American aggression was well-known to all of them: the Americans "had taken lands from the Cheroquis" in the Cumberland and Holston Valleys and would soon try to take more. Uniting "their interests under the protection of the Spaniards" would offer the Indigenous peoples their best protection against the relentless Americans.[4]

By 1785, Americans had invaded much of trans-Appalachia. Thousands squatted north of the Ohio on lands claimed by the United States, while more than three thousand white families had settled between the Holston and French Broad Rivers, within the territory of the Overhill Towns district of the Cherokee.[5] Thousands more had invaded the lands of the Creek Confederacy along the border of Georgia, provoking frequent violence. By 1786, war had broken out across trans-Appalachia. North of the Ohio, members of the Northern Confederacy attacked European American settlements at Vincennes and regularly crossed the Ohio River to threaten settlers in Kentucky, who retaliated in kind.[6] Creek soldiers attempted to repulse American settlement by Georgians along the Oconee River, while in the Cumberland district combined parties of Cherokee, Creek, and Shawnee engaged white settlers in a near-genocidal conflict over land. Spanish officials in Louisiana, as well as in East and West Florida, often supported these Indigenous efforts with arms and ammunition.[7]

Spanish officials supported a pan-tribal alliance because they feared the consequences of American expansion for Spanish control over Louisiana. In 1785, the Georgia legislature created Bourbon County, an administrative district that was to stretch westward to the Mississippi and that encompassed the northern part of what the Spanish regarded as the Natchez district and included much of the land of the Creek, Choctaw, and Chickasaw. Georgia's legislature followed up by selling speculators millions of acres in the region surrounding the Yazoo River. Georgia was soon forced by the Continental Congress to repudiate its sales, but the creation of the county alarmed Spanish officials, as did Georgia's decision to dispatch commissioners to Spanish Natchez where they spread rumors of an imminent invasion by Kentucky militia. In 1791, to counter American claims to Spanish territory, Spanish officials began construction of a fort at the mouth of the Yazoo River at the site of present-day Vicksburg. Called Walnut Hills by the English and christened Nogales by the Spanish, the new fort bolstered Spanish control over both the land of the lower Mississippi Valley and the Mississippi River. The 1792 conference in New Orleans was convened not only to urge the creation of a formal alliance but also so that the Spanish could try to overcome Choctaw and Chickasaw objections to the presence of the Spanish fort on their lands.[8]

Between 1784 and 1795, as a new American government took shape in Philadelphia, the political alignments of trans-Appalachia shifted. Even as Americans consolidated their union, the Southern Confederacy proposed by Taski Etoka and supported by the Spanish governor never materialized, in large part due to conflicts within the Chickasaw nation over the tribe's relationship to the United States. As some Chickasaw sought peace with the United States, other Indigenous nations, like the Creek, doubled down in their hostility toward the United States and the Chickasaw, who the Creek saw as betraying Indigenous interests.[9] Spanish officials relied on their relationships with the Indigenous peoples of the region to secure the territory they claimed but walked a delicate path between encouraging Indigenous resistance to European American settlement and keeping all-out war from creeping into the lower Mississippi Valley.

As the abortive creation of Bourbon County and the contested construction of the Spanish fort at Nogales show, conflict over control of the Mississippi was a key factor in the ongoing imperial rivalry for control of the continental interior. Spain's 1784 decision to close the Mississippi was part of this larger contest for control of the Southeast and of trans-Appalachia more broadly. For Spanish officials like Carondelet, and his predecessor, Governor Esteban Miró, the river's closure represented both a threat and an opportunity. As Anglo-American settlers poured into trans-Appalachia, access to the Mississippi became increasingly important to those who had made the move. As masters of New Orleans, the Spanish had a powerful bargaining tool in their dealings with western settlers. Spanish officials came to believe that many Americans, like Andrew Jackson, might be willing to sever their attachments to the United States in order to gain access to the port. At the same time, Spanish officials risked antagonizing the growing American communities in the West, which soon outnumbered the miniscule Spanish military in the region.

Conflict surrounding Spain's decision to close the Mississippi River played out in multiple arenas. In New York, a divided Congress had to determine how the fractured polity should respond; in Philadelphia, the framers of the Constitution kept the issue on their minds as they drafted a new future for the thirteen states. In western Pennsylvania, Kentucky, the Northwest Territories, New Orleans, Natchez, and in the Chickasaw communities of Chokkilissa' and Chokka' Falaa', state, tribal, and individual actors adopted a variety of schemes and stratagems for obtaining control over the Mississippi and with it control over the Ohio and Mississippi Valleys. In the 1780s and 1790s, no power could unilaterally assert its interests in trans-Appalachia. All navigated within a complicated world governed by violence, trade, and diplomacy made more complicated by the emergence of a new, more powerful American government in the East.

4

An Imperial Problem

By 1784, the thirteen new states, as well as the union created by the Articles of Confederation, were experiencing an economic contraction. Congress, as well as most Americans and many Europeans, believed the land of trans-Appalachia represented the best path for redeeming the nation's credit and recovering commerce. "If it is managed well the sale of the lands will pay a considerable part of our national debt," one Massachusetts representative opined to Samuel Adams in spring 1785, while revolutionary theorist Tom Paine reassured Americans anxious about the independent states' financial future that "no nation under heaven hath such an advantage as" western land would prove to be to the American republic.[1] According to Paine, the West was to be "the fund by which the debt of America would in the course of years be redeemed."[2] Early explorations of those lands offered support for these views. "The general opinion of the goodness of the soil in this western country . . . has been increasing with every new investigation of it," the representatives of New Hampshire enthused to their governor. Hugh Williamson of North Carolina was certain sales would be brisk, as "the Climate on the West side of the Appellachian Mountains is more stable & more hea[l]thy than on the East Side."[3] Congress hoped that selling western lands would not only put specie into the Confederation's coffers but could also help sink the debt "by absorbing a great number of the public securities" that the Continental Congress had floated during the war.[4] Many agreed with William Johnson of Connecticut, who glumly commented to a colleague that "the Western Territory" was the nation's "only actual resource."[5] In contrast, some delegates, primarily those from New England, hoped for the revival of maritime trade. At the end of the Revolution, New England's maritime classes struggled with the loss of markets. England now used the same

Navigation Laws the former colonists had protested to exclude American merchants from both British mainland and colonial ports. Spain had also closed its markets to its former co-belligerents. Only France admitted American shipping to its European ports, but France refused to allow Americans to trade with its colonies. Many delegates to Congress believed that exporting American goods to foreign markets and gaining access to more ports as commercial carriers would be a more certain pathway to restoring public credit. Delegates from New England and the mid-Atlantic states believed that compared to rebuilding the Confederation's finances by selling western lands, reestablishing trade would be both more lucrative and much faster.[6]

The two financial visions came to a head in December 1784, when Congress was jolted by the news that Spain had closed the Mississippi River. Spain's decision precipitated an imperial struggle within the states, as it threatened the viability of both territorial expansion and commercial restoration; as a result, the closure of the river tested the feasibility of union. Between December 1784 and August 1786, the question of how to respond to the closure of the Mississippi dominated Congress.[7] Congress was initially united in its opposition to Spain's actions. In June 1785, James Monroe declared that he had "never seen a body of men collected in which there was less party for there is not the shadow of it here."[8] By August 1786, however, Congress was bitterly divided. New England, New York, and Pennsylvania shared maritime interests, which led them to coalesce into one faction, known as the "northern," or more often "eastern," states. Although the eastern delegates, like their southern counterparts, would have preferred to have seen the river open, especially as an avenue for engaging in trade with the Caribbean, their interest in finding new markets and reestablishing old commercial ties led them to prioritize developing a trading relationship with Spain over insisting on river access. Virginia, North Carolina, South Carolina, and Georgia had economies dependent on the export of agricultural goods and formed the "southern" interest; each of these states also had extensive claims to western lands and constituents who had invested heavily in those regions.[9] These distinctive interests led to bitter divisions between the commercial states, intent on opening trade with Spanish markets, and the states engaged in westward expansion, which demanded the immediate reopening of the river. These fissures developed along sectional lines that mirrored the states' economic interests.

The bitterness and vitriol that dominated congressional debates over the Mississippi destabilized the newly formed American states and underscored the weakness of the Articles of Confederation and the necessity of political transformation. The battle over negotiations with Spain forced the states to negotiate with one another.[10] While there was no singular cause behind the creation of the Constitution, conflicts within the states over taxation and monetary policies, intra-state conflict over the balance of power among the states, divisions over western expansion, and concerns about the new states' position on the international stage all offer powerful explanations for why leaders in every state decided that a reevaluation of the Articles of Confederation was necessary. The treaty with Spain over the Mississippi River was bound up in each of these questions.[11] First at the Annapolis Convention in 1786—held just as the Spanish treaty negotiations were coming to a head—and again at the Constitutional Convention, the conflict over the Mississippi and schisms it revealed helped to shape the U.S. Constitution.[12]

In the 1780s, as political leaders tried to muddle their way through the myriad conflicts the new states faced, they confronted the question of what the new entity they created should be. That it would be republican was a given, but beyond that, they struggled with the degree to which their new polity would be a union or a federation, content to rule at home or determined to project its authority at a distance. In other words, they struggled with the question of empire. Well before the Revolution, North American colonists had developed a continental vision for the British empire that cast the West as fertile ground for incorporation into the British sphere. After the Revolution, Americans transferred their expectations for expansion across the continent into their new governments. The development of the *Continental* Army, the *Continental* Congress, and the demonym "American" all point to the prominence of this expansive geographical view. Imagining the thirteen colonies as embodying an entire continent offered revolutionaries a powerful tool. "A sense that the army reflected the continent and that nature favored" the cause of American independence helped to bolster American confidence as they prepared to fight the far more powerful British.[13] Victory over the British seemed to validate these continental pretensions. Although western expansion presented immediate difficulties that the Continental Congress was incapable of overcoming, by the 1780s large swathes of Americans were nonetheless convinced that settlement would inevitably spread westward. Paine's link between western land and repaying the union's debts tied the success of the American experiment to western expansion, making the newly independent confederation imperial from its inception.

At the core of nascent ideas of American empire was trade.[14] As members of Congress debated how to construct their renewed league of nations, they struggled to create a system in which the periphery would be equal to the center, bound together by a system of reciprocal advantages and mutual obligations. In their view, the problem with the British system was that the connections were unequal; colonies, the "provincial periphery," were made to serve a dominant metropolitan core. As they worked to fashion a new government, they envisioned commerce as a pathway for uniting the Confederation's disparate parts. Inland trade, facilitated by the numerous watercourses that penetrated the continental interior—especially the Mississippi—could provide the means for independent freeholders to secure western lands while tying westerners to the East. Free trade—the ability to carry any good to any port—would allow the United States to seek out commodities and trade opportunities that would provide the greatest return and thus the greatest prosperity to both the government and its constituents.[15] While inland trade might tie the empire together, free trade would bind it. Treaty negotiations with Spain threatened both potential pathways to unity. The Mississippi Question brought to the fore the complicated relationships between trade and expansion that threatened the possibility of union.

The Winter of 1785

Both easterners and southerners recognized the importance of the Mississippi to giving value to western lands. Spanish control of the Mississippi—even before Spain closed the river to American trade—constituted a threat to the new nation's security by endangering the economic viability of western expansion as a means of restoring the United States' finances. Thomas Hutchins, the first geographer of the United States, predicted that the day was not far distant when "the trade, wealth and power of America will at some future period, depend and perhaps center upon the Mississippi." In the future, "the safety and commercial prosperity" of the states would "depend upon the share of the navigation of the Mississippi which shall be allowed to them" by Spain.[16] Mississippi trade would give value to Congress's land, provide western settlers with the cash they needed to pay taxes and purchase more land, and structure the orderly, agrarian frontier Congress hoped to create.

Spanish control of the Mississippi linked the issues of territorial expansion and international trade. As members of Congress awaited the arrival of a Spanish official authorized to negotiate with them, they faced increasingly dire economic conditions at home. The same depression that displaced farmers across the thirteen states was brutal for the merchants and urban dwellers who made their living in maritime trade. "A flourishing and successful commerce has not yet been numbered among the blessings that peace and independence have restored to the state," New York's Chamber of Commerce complained in spring 1785, and across the maritime states of New York, Massachusetts, and Pennsylvania the same lament could be heard. The war had devastated the economy of New England and the mid-Atlantic.[17] The ships, shipyards, and sailors of New York, Boston, and Philadelphia lacked employment. Pent-up consumer demand throughout the former colonies revived the import trade in British manufactured goods after the war, but Britain barred American shipping from entering both English and Caribbean ports and prohibited the importation of American fish and whale oil, two of New England's most important commodities.[18] A trade imbalance quickly developed, as the former colonists imported British goods in excess of the value of the raw materials they exported to England. American merchants were forced to remit scarce specie to balance the trade. American trade faced other woes as well. France, Congress's staunchest European ally, had restricted American access to its Caribbean ports, and ongoing conflict with the Barbary States of North Africa effectively barred Americans from venturing into the Mediterranean.[19] "Such universal complaints of dull times, want of money, and stagnation of trade, as prevail at present, can hardly be remembered at any period heretofore," a New York newspaper bemoaned.[20] A Portsmouth, New Hampshire, newspaper summarized the situation: "Ruin! Ruin! Ruin!—Yes Inevitable Ruin!" faced the state.[21] In the words of the merchants of Boston, the "state of our trade and navigation" was "alarming."[22]

The depression of 1785 made reviving external trade critically important.[23] New England's representatives were particularly interested in seeing the codfish trade reestablished. For a century prior to the Revolution, fishermen operating off Cape Cod and merchants from New England's coastal enclaves had depended on the export of fish. Trade with Spain was particularly important, in part due to the scale of the Spanish import market but also because of the role Spain played in a triangular trade among the United States, southern Europe, and England. Before the war, New Englanders had relied on three main markets. They exported the least desirable fish to the Caribbean as part of the provisioning trade, where it was used as a protein source for enslaved laborers producing sugar.[24] Mid-grade fish was exported to the islands off the coast of Portugal, Spain, and Africa, where it was exchanged for wine that was then either shipped to England or found its way back to American markets. The highest grade of fish, and the most important branch of the trade, went to southern Europe, especially to Spain. The prerevolutionary colonies had imported little from Spain beyond salt and wine, forcing Spanish merchants to remit the balance of the trade in the form of either bills of exchange or specie, which had injected much needed hard currency to both the English and North American economies.[25] New England delegates and merchants alike hoped that the postwar period would bring the reinstatement of the trade on the same footing as before the war, only without the mercantilist intervention of England, which had at numerous times placed restrictions on the trade. Realistically, the new states could not hope to unilaterally balance their trade with Britain: nothing grown or produced in the states and in demand in England equaled the value of the goods Americans imported. But balancing the trade, or at least lessening the deficit, might be possible if the trade in codfish, flour, and rice with Spain could be reinstated on its prewar footing. Both eastern and southern members of the political elite recognized the potential of Spanish trade and therefore the importance of the upcoming negotiations between Congress and the Spanish plenipotentiary. In January 1785, the young Virginia delegate James Monroe predicted that "with a little policy & good management we might not only enjoy our right to the Navigation in peace, but open an extensive, useful & very beneficial commerce with the subjects of the King of Spain ... which ... will be more lucrative to America than the trade of any power in Europe."[26]

In the weeks following the closure of the Mississippi, Congress was united in its opposition to Spain's decision and optimistic that an agreement could be reached that would both open the river and establish a trading relationship with Spain. They also hoped to settle the outstanding disagreements over the boundaries of the American confederation and the Spanish empire. As they awaited the arrival of Don Diego de Gardoqui, the Spanish official charged with negotiating with Congress, delegates pressed forward with plans for the sale of the lands claimed by Congress lying north of the Ohio River. Since 1777, conflicts over western lands had created controversy between those states with large claims west of the Appalachians and those without. In 1784, Virginia and New York had ceded the last of their claims to Congress, creating the congressional domain that would become the Northwest Territory.[27] By 1785, disposing of western lands was a priority for Congress, and thus the delegates spent the spring drafting a land ordinance designed to facilitate the orderly sale of the public domain.

The resulting document demonstrates that, although delegates feared the consequences of a closed Mississippi for western land prices, many members of Congress believed the river would soon be reopened. Hugh Williamson of North Carolina anticipated that Spain's actions would have no effect on the price of western lands. Writing to a former colleague, Williamson scoffed that while "some people fear that our Western Country may be affected by some claims which the court of Spain are said to have made to the exclusive navigation of the Mississippi," he doubted Spain would keep the river closed. He could not "believe that the Court of Spain was disposed to irritate or provoke a Nation who in a few Years must be sufficiently numerous to eat up the Dons in a month.... The Spanish will certainly be so prudent as suffer us to cultivate our Lands."[28] Although the delegates expected Gardoqui—who would arrive in New York six weeks after the ordinance was passed—to assert Spanish control over the Mississippi publicly, they seem to have imagined he would quickly yield on the issue, and that Spain's decision to close the river would be only a minor inconvenience in the broader plan of funding the government through the sale of western lands.

Selling western land and reestablishing trade with Spain represented diverging avenues for overcoming the new states' financial difficulties. Before Gardoqui's arrival, neither eastern delegates nor their southern counterparts viewed the two goals as mutually exclusive. Rather, they were complementary. Opening western lands and expanding agricultural production would provide more goods eastern merchants could use in Atlantic world trade. Increasing the amount of specie in circulation would benefit everyone. Williamson believed the issues of Mississippi access and Spanish trade would soon be resolved. Invoking Spain's former role as a major source of specie for North American merchants, he predicted that in the future, Spain "will furnish us occasionally with a few Dlrs & we shall fairly give them in Exchange a few Brls of Flouer."[29] Whether delegates regarded Atlantic trade or western land as the source of the new states' future prosperity, all could agree on the importance of concluding a treaty with Spain that would settle boundaries, establish trade, and determine the status of the Mississippi.

Negotiations Begin

IN JUNE 1785, Don Diego de Gardoqui, the Spanish minister to the United States, arrived in New York City. Negotiations between Secretary of Foreign Affairs John Jay and Gardoqui commenced soon after. During the Revolution, Gardoqui, the son of a Bilbao merchant and an official in the Spanish Ministry of Finance, had acted as Spain's agent by secretly funneling cash to the Americans; as the American minister to the court of Spain, Jay had acted in partnership with him. Now, the two men found themselves in opposition.

Congress had instructed Jay to negotiate a treaty that forwarded American interests on three key issues. The first was trade: Jay was to request that Spain open both its mainland and colonial markets to American merchants. The second was territory: Jay was to assert an expansive view of American holdings in the Southeast, claiming all lands north of the 31st parallel for the United States. The final issue was the Mississippi. Jay was to insist on an American right to navigate the Mississippi from its headwaters to the Gulf of Mexico. Gardoqui's instructions conflicted with Jay's on every count. Spanish policy barred its colonies from trading with anyone except for Spain itself; American access to Spain's Iberian ports would depend on the United States' agreeing to Spain's claims to territory and to the status of the Mississippi. Based on Gálvez's successes during the war, Spain claimed a northern border far to the north of the 31st parallel: a line running from the junction of the Mississippi and Tennessee River (near modern-day Paducah, Kentucky), and then eastward to the headwaters of the St. Marys River (near modern-day Atlanta, Georgia), and southward from the St. Marys to the Gulf of Mexico.[30] Finally, Spain held that because it possessed both banks of the river along the lower Mississippi, it had the right to control access to the river within its boundaries. On this, Gardoqui's instructions were firm: under no circumstances could Gardoqui permit American claims to the navigation of the Mississippi to be included in the treaty. Gardoqui's resistance to even considering reopening the Mississippi arose from Spanish concerns over the rapid growth of American settlement in the West. Gardoqui, as well as officials in Spain, feared that the avaricious and restless westerners would make poor neighbors and would soon embroil Spain in another North American war.[31] Moreover, they resented the threat to Spanish sovereignty posed by the United States' claims to what was, to their minds, a Spanish right.

Gardoqui's intransigence immediately divided Congress between those who believed that opening the river, thereby facilitating western expansion, was most important for establishing American prosperity, and those who saw reestablishing Spanish trade as critical to Congress's, and their constituents', financial stability. Concerned about the value of western lands and the interests of western settlers, southern delegates clamored for Mississippi navigation. The only way for the United States to use western lands to repay its debts was if western settlers had access to the Mississippi, as "to those in the least acquainted with that country, it is known that the value of their lands must altogether depend upon the right to navigate the Mississippi." If Congress were to "relinquish [that right it would] . . . check, perhaps destroy, the spirit of emigration, and prevent the accomplishment of the object proposed by the sale [of western lands]," the payment of the domestic debt.[32] Southern representatives predicted that if western settlers were denied access to the river, they might soon take matters into their own hands.

In contrast, eastern delegates wanted Spanish ports opened. Soon after the war, American ships had returned to Spanish ports like Bilbao and Cadiz, but without a treaty American shipping was vulnerable. Particularly concerning were Spanish prohibitions on the exportation of specie, the key draw for American merchants operating in southern European ports. As colonial subjects of Great Britain, New England merchants had been protected by British treaties that created significant exceptions to Spanish bullionist policies. Without such protections, accepting pay in Spanish specie was risky. American merchants operating in Spanish ports risked both arrest and confiscation of their property.[33] Easterners correctly believed that if Congress conceded its claims on the issues of boundaries and navigation, Spain might relent to fully reopening its ports. Despite what eastern delegates saw as this obvious benefit to ceding distant land the United States could neither protect nor hope to settle within the span of their lifetimes, southern delegates held firm to the necessity of opening the Mississippi and insisted on an expansive view of American boundaries. Under the Articles of Confederation, a supermajority of nine states was needed to ratify a treaty. With Congress divided between seven committed eastern states (New York, Massachusetts, Pennsylvania, Connecticut, Rhode Island, New Hampshire, and New Jersey) and five committed southern ones (Virginia, North Carolina, South Carolina, Georgia, and Maryland), it seemed there was no chance of any Spanish treaty being acceptable to more than a bare majority.[34]

For his part, Gardoqui was eager to get a treaty signed that could help secure Spain's territorial borders, slow western settlement, and prevent western settlers from attempting to take the Mississippi by force, and he saw his best chance in the eastern delegates who might be persuaded to give up American claims to the Mississippi in exchange for Spanish trade concessions. By November 1785, Gardoqui was employed in persuading eastern members of Congress "of the advantages that this country would receive if they would relinquish the pretension of trading on the Mississippi."[35] Flattery and bribery were his principal tools. In his first year in New York, Gardoqui plied Jay and the eastern delegates with 577 pesos' worth of "wine, chocolate, oranges, fruit [and] tobacco," small but impressive gifts intended to ingratiate himself and his national interests with American politicians. He also delivered a Spanish stallion, a gift from Carlos III, to John Jay, and a much-prized donkey to George Washington.[36] Gardoqui found it "easy to convince [the eastern delegates], [that] if it were not for the two issues of limits and the Mississippi," the Spanish empire would gladly help them meet their financial needs by expanding trade. Gardoqui was thrilled when John Hancock of Massachusetts was elected to serve as the president of Congress, as he was "from the country where I have the largest party."[37] Throughout 1785 and 1786, Gardoqui urged eastern delegates to prevail upon their southern colleagues to approve a treaty to open trade between the two nations.

After six months of fruitless negotiations, Jay's insistence on an American right to navigation of the Mississippi began to flag. In late November 1785, Gardoqui invited a carefully cultivated eastern delegate to join a secret negotiation session. Gardoqui used the opportunity to urge the combined eastern and Spanish agenda on Jay. Informing Jay "that negotiations [could] not continue without" the Americans' acknowledging the Mississippi as a Spanish river, Gardoqui convinced Jay to yield the American claim to the river. Jay, perhaps reluctantly, acknowledged that Spanish sovereignty over the Mississippi was not a subject for negotiation but rather a precondition for any subsequent negotiations on boundary limits or trade.[38] The two continued to negotiate in secret, even though they knew that any treaty that did not reopen the Mississippi could not obtain the nine votes necessary for ratification.

As eastern representatives became willing to trade Mississippi navigation for protection of their trade to Spanish ports, the gulf between them and their southern colleagues grew. "The seven Eastern states have common commercial interests [and] are under similar embarrassments,"

Rufus King of Massachusetts reminded Caleb Davis, the speaker of the Massachusetts House and himself a prominent merchant. King and others began to debate whether the eastern states should make a common cause by establishing an alliance within the broader American Confederation that might be able to conclude its own trading treaties. Article 6 of the Articles of Confederation stated that "no two or more States shall enter into any treaty, confederation or alliance whatever between them, without the consent of the United States in Congress assembled," but as the seven eastern states constituted a majority in Congress, consent would be easily obtained for a subsection of the Confederation to act unilaterally. By presenting a united front, the eastern states could force the "Southern States [to] relinquish their partial, and unfederal, policy" of insisting on a right to Mississippi navigation. With a guaranteed majority, a united eastern interest would be able to impose its will on the rest of the nation. Creating a separate "alliance" of eastern states might serve to "not only remedy all their Difficulties" but also "raise them to a degree of power and Opulence which would surprize and astonish." The moment that the eastern states joined together, King believed, "the southern states will sensibly feel their weakness, and accede to such measures as may be adopted by the majority of the Confederacy [the seven northern states]."[39]

In winter 1786, there was gathering interest in New England in severing completely the bonds that tied them to the South. "The United States, as they are called, seem to be little more than a name.... Different interests have pointed them, and are now pointing them, to different courses; hence instead of their giving mutual security by pursuing the same point, they really endanger each other by counter movements," General Benjamin Lincoln, who had just been replaced as secretary of war by Henry Knox, observed from his Massachusetts home. He saw no other recourse than "by a division," believing that in clinging to their mindless commitment to the union, the people were "deceiving themselves" and that no good could come of it.[40] Massachusetts delegate Theodore Sedgwick believed the union to be a "meer chimera," "even the appearance" of which "cannot in the way we now are long be preserved.... It well becomes the eastern and middle States, who are in interest one ... to consider what advantages result to them from their connection with the Southern States." For his part, Sedgwick was sure there were few. "It becomes us seriously," he urged a correspondent, "to contemplate a substitute; for if we do not controul events we shall be miserably controuled by them."[41] Easterners like Sedgwick believed that the threat of secession might accomplish what the ongoing debates between Gardoqui and Jay could not—the completion of a commercial treaty that could help alleviate New England's financial stagnation. Massachusetts delegate Nathan Dane suggested that southerners would "be alarmed even at the suggestion of a confederacy of the States north of the Potomac . . . and give up their opposition [to a treaty] to avoid such a measure."[42] Whether or not eastern talk of separation constituted actual planning for secession, it revealed the degree to which both northerners and southerners were becoming dissatisfied with union.

In August 1786, Congress ordered Jay to present the details of his negotiations with Gardoqui. Jay laid out what he saw as the benefits of the proposed treaty: Both nations agreed to most-favored-nation status; although Spain would admit American exports into continental Spanish ports on the same footing as domestic manufactures, American goods remained excluded from Spain's colonial ports. Spain promised to purchase—if prices were reasonable—American hardwood to serve as masts on Spanish ships and to pay for it in specie. Spain agreed to serve as a mediator between the United States and other powers, promising to intercede on the Americans' behalf with Britain to effect the withdrawal of British troops from the forts on the western frontier and to represent the Americans against the Barbary powers in North Africa.[43] The states and Spain agreed to protect one another's territorial integrity against any attacks—a stipulation that both curtailed possibilities for the United States to expand westward and obligated them to protect Spanish interests in North America, the Caribbean, and South America. Jay's written account to Congress of his year of negotiations included not only the agreement that he and Gardoqui had tentatively reached but also Jay's overall assessment of the treaty: "These articles need no comment. It is easy to perceive that we gain much," Jay reassured Congress, "and sacrifice or give up nothing."[44]

Nothing, that was, but the use of the Mississippi for a period of twenty-five to thirty years. "Many fruitless arguments passed between us," Jay informed Congress, but Gardoqui refused to yield on the issue of Mississippi navigation. Continuing to insist on it would be tantamount to opening hostilities with Spain—a battle that, as Jay saw it, the states had no hope of winning. The "Bourbon Compact" bound the royal family of France to support Spain in the event of a war between Spain and the United States, which would leave Congress without its most important ally. The states had no choice but to concede their claim to the river. A war over the Mississippi would leave the states poor, isolated, and under siege by the Catholic powers of Europe. Jay did not advocate a total surrender, but as he attempted to persuade southern delegates, "as the navigation is not *at present* important, nor will probably become much so in less than twenty-five or thirty years, a forbearance to use it while we do not *want it*, is no great sacrifice."[45]

The reaction among the delegates was instantaneous. Easterners, of course, argued in favor of the proposed treaty. Rufus King pointed to "the distressed state of the Eastern States." The treaty could resolve many of their financial problems, as Spain represented the "best market" for mid-Atlantic flour and New England fish, and the "fishery depended on a market."[46] Arthur St. Clair of Pennsylvania and Sedgwick of Massachusetts scoffed at the notion that the proposed treaty would hurt their southern brethren. These United States were, after all, a union, and the "benefits reaped [by] one member will redound to the advantage of the whole Union." To St. Clair—the future governor of the Northwest Territory—one of the most positive features of the treaty was its ability to "check the settlement of the Western country," an "event devoutly to be wished." The states had no business sending their scarce inhabitants westward to incite violence with Native Americans and embroil the United States in European conflicts, while a sudden flood of western lands on the market would lower land prices in the eastern states. Once people migrated westward, they became "lost both to the states from which they removed and to the Union."[47] The proposed treaty would allow the United States to avoid these calamities.

For men like St. Clair and King, the states' future wealth lay not in westward expansion but in revitalizing and developing the economy east of the Appalachians. Southerners disagreed. The proposed treaty, Charles Pinckney of South Carolina argued, "was wholly at the Expence of the [southern] States" and offered easterners precious little.[48] Southerners like Pinckney saw the future prosperity, stability, and prominence of the union as tied to western land. "The occlusion of the river," William Grayson of Virginia informed Congress, "would destroy the hopes of the principal men in the [southern] States" by driving down western land prices.[49] Virginia already had three counties west of the Appalachians and tens of thousands of western residents whose economic prospects and future ability to pay taxes would be devastated by the closure of the river. North Carolina was not far behind. The closure of the river would undermine the South's economy.

While the interests of each region were clear, the *nation*'s interests were less so. All agreed that the long-term closure of the Mississippi would diminish the value of the great "common fund" of the West. Yet the representatives of the different sections disagreed on what the consequences would be. Southerners regarded it as a disaster. Grayson believed that the treaty "would render the western country of no value & thereby deprive the U.S. of the fund on which they depended to discharge the domestic debt," while Pinckney reminded Congress that it had spent the spring of 1785 negotiating a land ordinance for the sale of the West that the new treaty would render moot.[50] In contrast, St. Clair dismissed these fears. To him, "the Redemption of the Debt by the Sale of those Lands" had always seemed to be "a Chimera." "If the public Credit has no better foundation [than the sale of western lands] it rests upon the baseless Fabric of a Vision," St. Clair argued. Moreover, attempts to settle western lands were likely to *increase* the public debt by incurring high costs for surveying the land and paying an army to protect settlers. "In [his] View," St. Clair informed Congress, "the Advantages [of the treaty] can Scarce be estimated for they go much farther than the mere commercial profit[,] they embrace the political Interests of the Nation and her future consequence with respect to other Nations."[51] In St. Clair's view, the interests of the nation were synonymous with the interests of easterners.

No matter what decision Congress made, it would betray part of the union. "Never has Congress had a more combative controversy," Gardoqui informed his superiors in his account of Congress's reaction to Jay's proposal.[52] The debates grew increasingly bitter. To King of Massachusetts, refusing to ratify the treaty would be "sacrificing the interest & happiness of a Million to promote the views of speculating land jobbers," while to Grayson of Virginia, ratifying would be akin to "disaffecting the S[outhern] States when they saw their dearest interests sacrificed & given up to obtain a trivial commercial advantage for their eastern brethren." The treaty would deprive one side or the other of "the only advantages which they could expect from the Union." "The States whose interests are now neglected," King was sure, would have no interest in remaining a part of the United States.[53] The Jay-Gardoqui Treaty had the power, in the words of St. Clair, to "Convulse the Union."[54]

Disunion, which that winter had been whispered quietly in New England coffeehouses, was now openly debated. Even as these debates were raging in Congress, Gardoqui organized a "secret meeting" with several of the eastern delegates to discuss the possibility of a treaty between the eastern states and Spain, in contravention of the Articles of Confederation.[55] James Monroe caught wind of it, writing to Thomas Jefferson in Paris that eastern delegates were holding "in this {city committees} for {dismembering the confederacy} & throwing {the states eastward the Hudson into} one {government}." He sent the same news to James Madison, adding that the idea of a separation "is talk'd of in Mass. familiarly & is suppos'd to have originated there."[56] Monroe seems to have been correct. New England merchants, already trading with Spain on a tenuous legal footing, were eager to conclude a separate treaty if one could be obtained. On August 11, 1785, the same day Gardoqui held his secret meeting with the eastern delegates, Nathan Dane, who was in Massachusetts on private business, reported to King that "prudent and discreet men concur with us . . . concerning the Spanish negotiation." King was unsurprised, as it would have been "strange to [him] if a contrary Opinion was entertained by any sensible man North of the Potomack."[57]

The Jay-Gardoqui Treaty never got the nine votes necessary for ratification; while the eastern states were able to enact a change in Jay's instructions, allowing him to negotiate without insisting on Mississippi access, southern intransigence on the issue revived the question repeatedly through the next several months. Despite the treaty's failure, the loss of trust between the two halves of the union persisted. Balanced between the interests of the eastern and southern states were westerners. In 1786, it was easy for many in Congress to dismiss western settlers. St. Clair doubted the ability of westerners to form a part of the union, labeling them "indifferent citizens" characterized by a "turbulence and ferocity of Disposition." Westerners were "a distinct People" with "little connection" to the society east of the Appalachians. In contrast, southerners regarded westerners as "brethren," but forfeiting the river, the southern delegates warned, would transform westerners into enemies. The most dangerous prospect of the Jay-Gardoqui Treaty, according to Pinckney, was that it would sever the connection between the Atlantic and western portions of the nation. He warned eastern delegates that if they agreed to the proposed treaty, they would "immediately destroy all connection between [eastern citizens] and the inhabitants of the western country." Worse still, westerners would not remain neutral, "for, after you have rendered [the West] thus dependant on Spain, by using the first opportunity in your power to sacrifice their interests to those of the Atlantic States, can they be blamed for . . . throwing themselves into her arms for that protection and support which you have denied them—for the enjoyment of that right which you have placed it out of your power to grant." Pinckney believed that this was perhaps the goal of the Spanish negotiating strategy all along, allowing Spain to "separat[e] the interests of the inhabitants of the western country entirely from us, and mak[e] [the West] subservient to her own purposes."[58] While Pinckney feared this eventuality, others disregarded it. To Henry Lee of Virginia, who had been one of the greatest recipients of Gardoqui's largess and one of Gardoqui's few southern adherents, it was clear that a separation between East and West was "a matter very likely to happen at any rate." And good riddance. "For if [westerners] have no regard for the general Good, and are not under the general Controul the sooner exterminated the better."[59]

News of the outbreak of Shays' Rebellion, which occurred as Congress was debating the Jay-Gardoqui Treaty, soon distracted eastern leaders from the possibility of a separate confederacy, though they continued to meet with Gardoqui privately to discuss advancing the eastern states' goal of a new trade treaty. By fall 1786, it was not only eastern delegates who were meeting with the Spanish envoy: westerners were as well. On August 27, as it became increasingly clear that the eastern states would yield Mississippi navigation to Spain, James White, a delegate from North Carolina who had speculated heavily in western land, met with Gardoqui to discuss westerners' response to the proposed treaty. These folk were, in White's words, "strong, accustomed to work, and venturesome, and I am persuaded that, as soon as they learn of the Cession, they will consider themselves abandoned by the Confederation and will act independently."[60] It would not be long before Gardoqui was convinced that without access to the Mississippi, "however strong the Government of the United States may become, I do not believe that it will ever be sufficiently powerful to bring into subjection the people dwelling beyond the Mountains."[61]

The Spanish Negotiations and the Imperial Settlement

Although congressional delegates were bound to secrecy on matters related to the Spanish treaty, by August 12, 1786, James Madison was already well-informed of the proceedings occurring in New York. For Madison, the division over the treaty was a major barrier to obtaining one of his dearest-held ambitions: the revision of the Articles of Confederation and the enhancement of federal authority. Even though Congress had not ratified the Jay-Gardoqui Treaty, the fact that many of the states were willing to do so threatened to "be *fatal*" to Madison's goal of expanding federal authority. For three years, he had been working to convince the Virginia legislature of "the *equal attention of Congress* to the *rights and interests of every part of the republic*," North, South, East, and West. One of his most powerful arguments had been his claim that greater central authority was necessary if the United States were to reopen the Mississippi.[62] Congress's willingness to cede American claims to the Mississippi had severely undercut Madison's argument among Virginians—even as it highlighted the necessity of revising the Articles of Confederation.

First at Annapolis in September 1786, and then in Philadelphia in spring and summer 1787, delegates from the various states met to consider changes to the Articles of Confederation. The Mississippi Question, which had exploded in Congress's lap in 1784, became a driving force behind negotiations to reshape the national government. Both the divisions the Jay-Gardoqui Treaty negotiations incited and the issue of obtaining Mississippi trade were referred to multiple times at the Constitutional Convention and became a central issue in the Virginia ratification debates. Obtaining Mississippi trade remained a key concern for southern delegates, who worked to craft a document that would prevent the central government from ceding it again by maintaining a role for the states within foreign policy. When examined carefully, the final form of the Constitution reveals just how deeply the Mississippi Question had permeated national politics.[63]

By the end of summer 1787, the divisiveness over the Mississippi River that had threatened the union had largely been resolved, and the central government at least was committed to the project of establishing an American right to Mississippi River trade. This was not a transformation of hearts and minds, with easterners and southerners coming to see eye to eye with one another's outlooks and developing a shared vision of a national future. Instead, it was the result of a series of calculated compromises. Although Congress was meeting in New York, and the convention had convened in Philadelphia, it seems that despite each body's vow of secrecy both groups were engaged in a delicate joint chess match. None of the issues of national importance—slavery, western expansion, commerce, and the Mississippi Question—was or could be addressed in isolation, and both bodies were invested in resolving these questions for the present and the future. First in July and then in September, the American political elite produced two documents central to American governance, each of which became foundational to the joint projects of American nationhood and American empire. In July, the members of Congress issued the Northwest Ordinance, setting important precedents for westward expansion. In September, the delegates to the Philadelphia Convention issued the Constitution. Although neither document explicitly evokes the Mississippi Question, the question of Mississippi trade was bound up with both.

On July 10, 1787, Benjamin Hawkins reported to the North Carolina governor that Mississippi navigation, "which is very interesting to the Western citizens of the southern States, as it regards their peace and welfare, has at length, from a variety of circumstances unnecessary as well perhaps as improper to relate, been put in a better situation than heretofore."[64] Hawkins's statement needs to be accounted for: as recently as the previous May, the same regional divisions that had prevailed in 1786 continued to divide congressional delegates. What then were the "circumstances" effecting Mississippi navigation that had suddenly improved?

Circumstantial evidence points to an explanation for the compromises that were made during the summer of 1787. While delegates in Philadelphia were debating the Virginia and New Jersey plans on the apportionment of representation in the nation's new government, their brethren in New York were enacting a bargain that was as essential to the success of both the Connecticut compromise and the eventual Constitution. Three days after Hawkins's cryptic message to Richard Caswell, Hawkins, along with the southern-dominated Congress, agreed to enact the Northwest Ordinance. In return for adopting the pro-eastern terms of the ordinance, southern delegates received a valuable quid pro quo: an American insistence on the right to navigate the Mississippi.[65] Although the drafters of the Constitution *could* have included language that would have both established the process of establishing new states and explicitly asserted a right to Mississippi trade, such language within the body of the Constitution would have rendered the document unratifiable. An unwritten—but explicit—agreement between northern and southern delegates helps explain how the convention resolved such issues.

In June 1787, Charles Thomson, secretary of Congress, wrote to the congressional representatives of Pennsylvania and North Carolina urging them to return to Congress. Rather than support a delegation in both New York and Philadelphia, several states had decided to economize by deputizing some, or all, of their congressional delegation to serve in the convention, leaving behind a skeletal Congress unable to transact business. A congressional quorum required seven states in attendance, but only five states—Massachusetts, New York, New Jersey, Virginia, and South Carolina—were present.[66] While Thomson had summoned North Carolina and Pennsylvania, it was North Carolina and Georgia that heeded his call. On July 1, William Blount and Benjamin Hawkins of North Carolina, along with William Few and William Pierce of Georgia, boarded a stagecoach and departed from Philadelphia bound for New York and the Continental Congress. Blount, in apprising Governor Caswell of his change of locale, explained that he "conceived it more for the benefit and honor of the [North Carolina] . . . to represent the State in Congress than to Continue in the Convention."[67] To Blount, returning to Congress represented an opportunity to reshape national policy toward the Mississippi. There were few, if any, members of Congress more invested in trans-Appalachia and in the opening of the Mississippi than Blount. He was a speculator first and a politician second. Called "the dirt king" by the Creek, he invested hugely in western property, acquiring land through any means available, purchasing acreage (legally and illegally) and bribing state commissioners to help him acquire his paper empire.[68] Although he claimed he came to New York to represent North Carolina's interests, he was certainly acting in his own best interests as well.

The arrival of the delegates from North Carolina and Georgia created Congress's first southern majority, providing southerners with their first opportunity to assert an American right to the Mississippi since the river's closure in 1784. Nathan Dane of Massachusetts wrote to his colleagues at the convention urging them to return to New York, where he was certain southerners were about "to renew the subject of the S[panish] treaty" while the "Eastern States" were not present in Congress.[69] Southerners were quick to stoke his suspicions: on July 4, the first day on which there had been a quorum since May 11, southerners presented the report of a southern-dominated committee that had been appointed to consider revisions to Jay's instructions regarding the Spanish treaty. The committee declared that any attempt to cede the Mississippi—or even to forbear its use—"would be obviously disagreeable to a large majority of the Citizens of the United States," and therefore the United States had an "indispensable obligation to preserve the right of the United States to their territorial boundaries"—the 31st parallel—"and the free Navigation of the Mississippi."[70] Yet, despite Dane's fears, the southern delegates did not move for a vote on the issue. Instead, Congress—under the leadership of temporary president William Grayson of Virginia—drafted the Northwest Ordinance.

The terms of the Northwest Ordinance are well-known: the ordinance prohibited slavery north of the Ohio, provided for the sale of western land, and established a governing structure for the West.[71] There is some evidence of sectional compromise in the document. While slavery was prohibited in the Northwest Territory, a fugitive slave clause recognized the legitimacy of slavery elsewhere. The ordinance reduced the number of states that could be created from the region from ten (as proposed in the Land Ordinance of 1784) to no more than five, a provision that would help keep sectional balance in Congress in the future. Still, it favored easterners and their interests, especially by recognizing northern opposition to the expansion of slavery.[72] Easterners would also become the first purchasers of western lands: on July 6, two days after the return of the southern delegates, Reverend Manasseh Cutler, a leader of the Ohio Company, a consortium of New England veterans and investors, approached Congress about purchasing a million acres of western lands in exchange for depreciated government securities.[73] Certainly, the Ohio Company's proposal weighed in the document's drafting.

That a southern-dominated Congress would pass an ordinance so clearly in the North's favor is surprising; yet, when placed side by side with events unfolding in Philadelphia, it becomes less so. On July 13, the same day that Congress passed the Northwest Ordinance, Gouverneur Morris of Pennsylvania warned the Philadelphia Convention that "if the Southn. States get the power into their hands, and be joined as they will be with the interior Country they will inevitably bring on a war with Spain for the Mississippi." "This language," Morris reminded his colleagues, "is already held."[74] Morris's reference to the Mississippi as a *casus belli* for the South hints at previous discussions within the convention for which we have no record. Piecing together the role that the Mississippi played in the convention is challenging, in part because the delegates sought to avoid contentious issues during the debates, using, as occurred with negotiations over the Northwest Ordinance, both compromises and side deals to arrive at a document that stood a chance of ratification. Nevertheless, the Mississippi Question played a role in debates over representation, the admission of new states, and the role of Congress—and therefore the role of states—in foreign policy.

Representation was a significant issue during the convention, and the issue of Mississippi played a surprising if perhaps coincidental role in its resolution. On July 1, Hawkins, Blount, Pierce, and Few left Philadelphia; on July 2, the convention debated the issue of representation in the upper and lower houses of the new government. While the large states wanted proportional representation in both houses, the smaller states argued for the need for equal representation in at least one house—the so-called Connecticut Compromise. With Few and Pierce absent, Georgia had just two remaining delegates. William Houston voted with the large states against the proposed compromise, while Abraham Baldwin—a native of Connecticut and a recent immigrant to Georgia—voted with the small states. The stalemate was a victory for the small states, whose insistence on equal representation had threatened the viability of the convention's project. Had Few and Pierce remained in Philadelphia, rather than in New York, they likely would have voted with the large states.

The Mississippi Question played a more direct role in the delegates' debates over the status of new states within the union, an issue that had consequences for representation in both the Senate and the House. The growth of North Carolina and Georgia in the 1780s, as well as the explosive growth of Kentucky, led many Americans to believe that the national balance of power would soon be shifted south.[75] Unless some mechanism for acknowledging population change was included in the Constitution, northerners might be reluctant to yield power as western and southern states grew. "If," George Mason of Virginia contended, "the Western States are to be admitted into the Union as they arise, they must . . . be treated as equals, and be subjected to no degrading discriminations." Mason may have endorsed western equality because he suspected westerners would share southern interests, a view that others found less convincing.[76] Gouverneur Morris of Pennsylvania disagreed with Mason; in his view, "The Busy haunts of men[,] not the remote wilderness, was the proper School of political Talents." He predicted—likely based on the recent experience of the Jay-Gardoqui debates—that "if the Western people get the power into their hands they will ruin the Atlantic interests."[77] Morris likely spoke for large numbers of eastern merchants, retailers, shippers, and sailors who had favored privileging trade over territorial expansion.

A central issue in the debate was the question of how, and whether, new states would be able to contribute financially to the union. Mason believed that the Mississippi River would be a pathway for westerners to one day be even "more wealthy than their Atlantic brethren." Mason believed that while "Spain might for a time deprive [westerners] of the natural outlet for their productions, yet she will, because she must, finally yield to their demands."[78] Madison agreed that western prosperity was imminent. According to him, "Imports and exports" would be the source of "future contributions" to the nation, and the West would be a fruitful source of both—provided the Mississippi was open.[79] Like Mason, Madison felt American trade on the Mississippi was inevitable and needed to be accounted for in the final document. Madison and Mason both contended that once Mississippi navigation was obtained, westerners would be fully able to participate in the union, contributing to it financially and giving it their loyalty. Hovering within this contention, though, was its natural converse: if Spain refused to open the Mississippi, westerners would remain poor and indifferent citizens, if they remained citizens at all. Western equality would hinge upon the opening of Mississippi River trade.

The role of the Mississippi Question in the Constitutional Convention is most evident in the debates over treaties. Although treaty-making was a prerogative of the president, many of the delegates feared that entrusting such powers in a single individual would be dangerous. Most delegates agreed that the Senate was the most logical branch for advising the president, but they differed over what fraction of senators would be needed to ratify any proposals. Southern delegates insisted that a two-thirds majority was necessary in order to protect southern interests. Otherwise, a situation like the 1786 vote over the Jay-Gardoqui Treaty—an attempt, as they saw it, to "sell the whole Country by means of Treaties"—might occur again. In contrast, James Wilson of Pennsylvania protested that insisting on a vote of two-thirds of the senators "puts it in the power of a minority to controul the will of a majority." Southern calls for requiring a super-majority to enact a treaty found support in a surprising corner: New England. Echoing Mason's sentiment, Elbridge Gerry of Massachusetts "enlarged on the danger of putting the essential rights of the Union in the hands of so small a number as a [simple] majority of the Senate," who might, he predicted, represent "perhaps, not one fifth of the people."[80] The provision was adopted.

Throughout the convention, southern delegates were committed to building institutional safeguards for their interests within the body of the Constitution itself. Although the Mississippi was not mentioned in the debates, the two-thirds requirement was intended as a protection for southern interests in the Mississippi. In 1788, during the Virginia ratification debates, North Carolina's Hugh Williamson wrote to Madison offering him support in overcoming the objections of those who insisted that the new Constitution threatened the project of obtaining Mississippi trade by reminding him that the two-thirds majority clause "was inserted [in the Constitution] for the express purpose of preventing a majority of the Senate . . . from giving up the Mississippi." Williamson's letter offers insight into the debate that the records of the conventions themselves do not. He reminded Madison that in insisting on the measure, the delegates had insisted that "the Navigation of the Mississippi . . . was not to be risqued in the Hands of a meer Majority."[81] Although there is no mention of this in any of the surviving notes of the delegates, the lessons of the 1786 negotiations over the Mississippi were well learned. Now, all that remained of the work of replacing the Articles of Confederation was to sell their production to the nation. In Virginia and throughout the South, the Mississippi Question would be at the core of the battle over ratification.

Ratification

IN NOVEMBER 1787, a convention held at Pittsburgh offered the Constitution a lukewarm endorsement. "Our prosperity," the convention reported, "depends on our speedy adoption of some mode of government more efficient than that which we now possess. . . . Of all people it becomes us of the western country more especially to desire an object of this kind."[82] Westerners had many reasons to want the powers of the central government fortified. Unlike residents of the Atlantic seaboard, westerners were dependent on the federal government. A stronger, well-funded Congress could support a larger army to protect western settlers and assert western interests on the international stage. Yet while many westerners believed a change was needed, they were not sure that the proposed Constitution would meet their needs.

Throughout the Kentucky, Pennsylvania, and western North Carolina countryside, opposition to the Constitution was widespread.[83] According to a letter circulated by the Fayette County, Kentucky, court, adopting the Constitution would strike at "the happiness & greatness of the Western Country." As the weaker partner, the West would suffer if the union were strengthened. By giving power to regulate commerce to Congress, the Constitution would "loose the Navigation of the Mississippi; population will cease, and Our lands become of little value." Inevitably, westerners protested, the West would lose by the adoption of the Constitution: it was too distant to matter, and its interests too opposed to those of eastern states.[84]

With public opinion in eastern Virginia split, Kentucky delegates had an important role to play at the Virginia ratifying convention in May 1788.

Anti-Federalists, led by Patrick Henry, targeted these delegates by focusing their speeches around Congress's failure to reopen the river. "Let us hear how the great and important right of navigating that river has been attended to," the fiery orator reminded his audience, "and whether I am mistaken in my opinion, that federal measures will lose it to us forever." To his view, despite the safeguards southern delegates had built into the Constitution, Mississippi navigation remained in jeopardy. The two-thirds of the votes needed to ratify a treaty might easily be obtained in a poorly attended Senate. Henry dolefully predicted that if the Constitution passed, the cession of the Mississippi would soon follow, rendering "the situation of our western citizens dreadful."[85]

Madison attempted to reassure the convention that the Mississippi was safe under the auspices of the new government; unfortunately, his vow of secrecy left him with little ammunition. "There are some circumstances within my knowledge which I am not at liberty to communicate," Madison told the convention. "Were I at liberty, I could develop some circumstances [that]would convince this house that this project will never be revived in Congress, and that, therefore no danger is to be apprehended."[86] Madison's response adds force to the claim that Madison had struck a bargain to protect American claims to the Mississippi, but it was a less-than-successful argument. Of Kentucky's fourteen representatives to the convention, ten voted against ratification.[87] While the convention ultimately voted eighty-nine to seventy-nine to ratify, the passage of the Constitution did little to mollify western dissent. Western delegates and settlers remained unconvinced that the new union would be any more successful than the old in securing Mississippi River trade.

Exploring the role of the Mississippi Question in the drafting and ratification of the Constitution adds a new dimension to a familiar story. Congress's tumultuous debates over the Mississippi in summer 1786 acted as a spur to the nation's political class to rethink the United States' governing document. In both overt and subtle ways, the controversy of the Jay-Gardoqui Treaty and the southern reaction to it helped to shape the ultimate structure, and even the adoption, of the new Constitution. The safeguards for Mississippi trade built into the Constitution— the requirement that two-thirds of the Senate needed to approve a treaty, as well as the insistence on the equality of new states admitted to the union—ultimately had less of an effect on federal policy toward the Mississippi River than did the compromise over the Northwest Ordinance. Madison's assurances at the Virginia ratification debates proved true: in the fall of 1788, Congress abandoned any plans to cede its claims to the Mississippi River. In what one historian has termed "a stunning fit of political amnesia," Congress denied that it had ever attempted to relinquish its right to Mississippi trade; reports otherwise were "not founded in fact."[88] Instead, Congress passed two resolutions. The first broke the injunction to secrecy on matters related to Mississippi navigation. The second stated the new policy of the United States toward the river: "The free navigation of the Mississippi is a clear and essential right of the United States," a claim that was, in the words of the North Carolina delegates, "not only supported by the express stipulations of treaties but by the great law of nature." In a secret resolution, Congress ended Jay's negotiations with Gardoqui, transferring all authority to treat with Spain to the new government created by the Constitution. Each of the measures passed without issue. The most bitter, contentious debate of the Confederation period, which had occupied Congress for two and a half years, disappeared in an afternoon.[89]

The justifications offered by the eastern delegates for their new stance were unconvincing to many southerners who were unaware of the bargain. The eastern delegates now claimed that "the subject [of Mississippi navigation] is ... much better understood.... The late Increase of Settlers in the western Country has been so rapid beyond all their ideas of profitability that they are now fully agreed ... that Nature and the fitness of things must have their due Operation," including giving westerners access to the river.[90] The compromise had paid off: in exchange for the Northwest Ordinance, easterners agreed to support southern claims to the river. When the new government took power, its official stance would be to assert an inviolable American right to navigating the Mississippi.

5

Trading without the River

In May 1787, Colonel Josiah Harmar, who would soon command a disastrous campaign against Native forces in the Ohio Country, reported to his superiors about a recent journey he had taken through Kentucky. In Kentucky, Harmar noted, "the free navigation of the Mississippi is the general subject of discourse." "As the prosperity of the Western world depends entirely upon this outlet," Kentuckians "look upon [the closure of the river] as the greatest of grievances." By 1786, the population of Kentucky stood at nearly forty thousand European American and enslaved Black residents; soon, Harmar predicted, they would "become so strong . . . as to force" the river to be open.[1] Some Kentuckians were already turning to violence: a group of Kentuckians had seized the cargo of a Spanish boat valued at £2,000, "a retaliation," Harmar reported, for the closure of the river.[2] A year later, Harmar—now a brigadier general—would report to Secretary of War Henry Knox that rumors were circulating that westerners were planning to invade Spanish territory. Harmar was unsure "whether the Kentucky, Cumberland people, and those below, [would] have the audacity to attempt to seize upon Natchez," and speculated that only an "insignificant banditti" were actually willing to attack their southern neighbors. Nevertheless, Harmar dispatched officers to sound out the inhabitants of Kentucky and the Cumberland about their plans toward the Spanish.[3]

Harmar's presence in the West demonstrates the growing role of the federal government in the region in the years following the signing of the Constitution. By 1787, American outposts in trans-Appalachia included not only Virginia's Kentucky and North Carolina's Washington and Cumberland districts but also nascent white settlements north of the Ohio. As the federal government reconstituted itself under the

Constitution, it sought to construct a "federalist frontier," characterized by orderly, compact settlement under the control and authority of federally endorsed elites. As Harmar's letter to Knox reveals, federal officials in the West were aware of the tide swell of western anger over the Mississippi. Not only plans for extralegal violence but also popular and clandestine movements for separation from their parent states, and from the union entirely, were widespread across the West. Integrating the region into the union was far more complicated than just dispatching federal governors, judges, and surveyors, or conscripting powerful local elites into positions within the federal government. Nor would it consist solely of selling western land. To transform the West into a full partner within the union, the federal government had to solve the problem of the West's lack of trade.[4]

In the decades following the enactment of the Constitution, westward settlement did not follow the trajectory of a metropole extending its reach ever further outward. Instead, the relationship between center and periphery was shaped by the West. Westerners deployed federal power in their own interests, in the process constructing federal law, expanding federal authority, and developing federal policy.[5] As Bethel Saler has pointed out in her work on frontier Wisconsin, "More often [than not], congressional policymakers and government officials reacted" to settlers' demands, "rather than initiating actions or new policies on their own."[6] Westerners—both Indigenous and European American—often shaped federal policy on the frontier, where federal actors lacked the authority or power to impose their will.

Mississippi River trade was an arena in which the interests of westerners aligned with those of the federal government. Trade was a principal component of the federalist view of western development. As Andrew R. L. Cayton described in his account of frontier Ohio, reformist-minded founders envisioned an American empire "guided by a superintending national authority" and "expanding through space and time simultaneously." These early American visionaries imagined the reality of the contested Ohio Valley transforming into "an urban, commercial West fully integrated into the Atlantic world."[7] In the mid-1780s, this view was widely held, especially among those organizing the new, large-scale settlements north of the Ohio. According to New Jersey congressional delegate John Cleves Symmes, who would soon invest heavily in what would be known as the Miami Purchase, while in the future the West would have "many Towns and even cities of the first distinction," for the moment the region's many "navigable Lakes and rivers [were] well adapted for commerce" and could function as centers of trade.[8]

Trade was important not only because it could make the West prosperous but also because it would bind the East and West together. Western expansion depended on the federal government's ability to overcome western settlers' willingness to separate themselves from central authority, a process that often involved federal policy evolving to align with western interests. During the Constitutional Convention, James Madison traded eastern recognition of American claims to the Mississippi for the passage of the Northwest Ordinance; by fall 1787, his compromise had borne fruit. Westerners no longer needed to convince Congress that they possessed a right to trade on the Mississippi. Yet congressional recognition of the claim was hardly the same as actually gaining access to the river, and westerners fumed over what they saw as the slow progress of the federal government in attempting to reopen the river. While the Spanish empire was often described as in decline, it was by no means decrepit, and it was more than willing to use its position to assert its control over the Mississippi. With the federal government relatively powerless to aid them in convincing Spain to open the river, individual westerners began acting independently to forge trade connections that would serve their own interests. Simultaneously, westerners began to use the federal government's failure to obtain for them their acknowledged "right" to Mississippi trade as a tool for asserting western interests against the federal government.

From 1787 to 1794, western actors sought to shape federal policy in ways that would promote the development of western trade. Westerners pursued two separate avenues in their efforts to obtain trade. In winter 1787, erstwhile western army officer and merchant James Wilkinson bribed his way south to New Orleans and offered to negotiate a separation between Kentucky and the United States in exchange for an exclusive right to navigate the Mississippi. In contrast, merchant Abijah Hunt, operating out of the newly settled town of Cincinnati, used the U.S. Army to overcome the problem of the closed Mississippi, an approach that helped to strengthen the bonds between East and West. While both methods helped to increase western trade, incomplete access to the Mississippi remained a central point of contention between easterners and westerners, keeping the question of western separatism alive. In the 1790s, the newly created Democratic-Republican societies of Kentucky, the Southwest Territory, and western Pennsylvania used their anger over the closure of the Mississippi as their central argument in criticizing the Federalist regime.

A River Closed

By 1786, western settlers faced an unusual problem: oversupply. Over the previous decade, settlers had brought millions of acres of western lands under cultivation. Western land produced more than three times the yields of eastern lands; farms in the fertile bluegrass region could produce between fifty and sixty bushels of corn an acre, amounts far in excess of the needs of a single family.[9] By 1787, an observer on the frontier reported that "consumption is not now ½ of the annual produce."[10] The effect of the oversupply was to drive down prices; one commentator noted that "flour and pork are now selling here at twelve shillings the hundred; beef in proportion; any quantities of Indian corn can be had at nine pence per bushel"—about fourteen cents.[11] Although this valuation was an exaggeration—the 1786 account book of Edmund Lynne, a Lexington merchant, valued a bushel of corn around sixty cents—in the rich agricultural lands of Kentucky limited demand kept the price of subsistence goods low.[12] With the river closed, new arrivals constituted the only consistent market, and as one Kentucky resident complained, even though "the emigration to this country is so very rapid that the internal market is very great . . . the quantities of produce [Kentucky farmers] now have on hand are immense."[13]

As Spanish officials had hoped, the 1784 closure of the Mississippi dampened the economy of the trans-Appalachia. The land market, which had caused such excitement from 1775 until 1784, cooled. "Land," Kentucky speculator William Christian informed a correspondent in March 1786, "universally falls throughout the District." Christian tied the decline in land prices directly to the closure of the Mississippi. With the river closed, prices for land had fallen by a third. Even land in the most settled portions of the district had lost value, falling from over seventy-five pounds per hundred acres to fifty. Like Christian, many speculators had purchased land at high prices; with the decline in market demand, those investments were at risk. Christian expected prices to continue to fall. He predicted that with the river closed, the pace of emigration would slow and many who already lived in Kentucky would soon depart, driving land prices down further. Christian's son-in-law, Alexander Bullitt, employed thirty enslaved people growing corn and tobacco on his plantation near Christian's home, but with no ability to market what his farm produced, Bullitt was growing discouraged. Bullitt and his wife—Christian's daughter—planned to "go to Georgia unless the river opens soon." Bullitt had "no notion of Staying [in Kentucky] without Exportation."[14] With

Kentucky's scant markets saturated with agricultural goods, settlers had no way to profit from their lands or to settle the substantial debts many had accrued in purchasing land in the first place.

In June 1786, Thomas Amis, a Tennessee trader and iron merchant, shipped a cargo of goods down to the mouth of the Mississippi despite the river's closure. At Natchez, the Spanish commandant confiscated his cargo of "142 Dutch ovens, 53 Pots and kettles, 34 Skillets ... [and] 50 Barrels of flour" "for the use of the crown of Spain." Amis received "no satisfaction for [the] said goods" and was forced to return to Tennessee overland, rather than traveling to Philadelphia by sea as planned.[15] Others suffered the same misfortune: according to one infuriated Kentuckian, during summer 1786 "large quantities of flour, tobacco, meal, &c. [were] ... confiscated" by the Spanish at Natchez.[16] Some hopeful traders lost more than merely money. Natchez merchant John Girault described American flatboats detained by the Spanish that were held for "upwards of fifty days till some died thro' mere want."[17] Although smuggling almost certainly occurred, the Spanish embargo effectively cut off European American settlers of Kentucky, Tennessee, and western Pennsylvania from access to the Atlantic.[18] "Men of large property"—presumably figures like Amis, who had lost the benefits of over a year's worth of labor, but also men like Bullitt, who found themselves with surplus produce on hand and no way of selling it—were "already ruined by their policy."[19]

Westerners responded to the seizures with anger. In fall 1786, a contingent of Kentucky militia under the command of George Rogers Clark seized merchandise belonging to three Spanish merchants near the village of Vincennes in what is now Indiana. In Kentucky and in North Carolina's western districts, public sentiment endorsed Clark's actions as fundamentally patriotic and perhaps the first salvo in a war for Mississippi trade that some had come to regard as inevitable. "We have taken all the Goods belonging to the Spanish Merchants at post Vincennes and the Illinois," a widely circulated pamphlet written by Georgia official Thomas Green crowed, "and are determined they shall not trade up the river provided they will not let us trade down it." In a letter that circulated along with his pamphlet, Green implicated Clark in a plan to invade Spanish Natchez. According to Green, Clark, "together with many other Gentlemen of merit ... engages to raise Troops sufficient and go with me to the Natchez to take possession and settle the lands."[20] Clark would spend years denying that he had any such intentions; nonetheless, Clark's seizure of Spanish goods at Vincennes reveals the growing tension in the West over the closure of the Mississippi. Clark's seizure and Green's pamphlet gave legitimacy to eastern fears of a rupture between East and West.

Going It Alone

JAMES WILKINSON was one of Kentucky's most vocal proponents of a separation. Born in 1757 in Maryland, Wilkinson trained to be a doctor before his education was interrupted by the outbreak of the Revolution. His natural charm and near-unparalleled abilities at self-promotion saw him rise through the ranks of the Continental Army, becoming brevetted as a brigadier general at the age of twenty, while his tendency toward shady dealings led him to be discharged twice during the war. In 1783, he came to Kentucky with his wife, Ann Biddle, daughter of the prominent Philadelphia family of merchants and future bankers, to open a store in Lexington. Once arrived, Wilkinson had, as one historian described it, "a finger in almost every Kentucky pie, including shipping, wholesale purchasing, retailing, a monopoly on salt, lead, and silver mining, banking, manufacturing, ferrying, and ... land speculation."[21] By the mid-1780s, Wilkinson had failed in almost all these endeavors, yet he spent lavishly entertaining Kentucky's elite.[22]

In 1786, Wilkinson was elected to serve as a local delegate at a convention debating a separation between Kentucky and Virginia. Wilkinson's election campaign hinged on marshaling western anger over the Mississippi. Even before Congress had begun debating the results of Jay's negotiations with Gardoqui, Wilkinson had come to view the Continental Congress in general as "hostile to this Western World," a view that the subsequent debates confirmed. "By not asserting the right of the union to the navigation of the Mississippi," Congress had "betray[ed] the trust reposed in them." Westerners therefore needed "to seek for Security to their Interests, by every means within their reach."[23]

In March 1787, Wilkinson set out on the Ohio River in a flatboat loaded with "flour, butter, bacon and tobacco," bound for New Orleans. Hoping to avoid having his cargo confiscated, Wilkinson eased his journey southward by sharing with Spanish officials news of political developments in Kentucky, including Clark's actions in Vincennes, and capitalizing on Spanish officials' fears of a possible invasion.[24] Wilkinson may have also bribed Spanish officials: one historian contends that Wilkinson gave the commandant of St. Louis two Virginia-bred horses.[25] This certainly sounds like Wilkinson. In 1791, he would instruct his agent to give "small gifts" to each of the Spanish officials he encountered on the way down the Mississippi.[26] Whatever Wilkinson exchanged for safe passage proved effective: when Wilkinson and his cargo landed in New Orleans in June, it was the first time in three years that American produce had (legally) arrived along the Mississippi River.

Wilkinson's arrival was welcomed by Louisiana governor Esteban Miró, who had been confirmed as the governor of Louisiana following Bernardo de Gálvez's departure. As the Anglo-American population of Kentucky and the Tennessee Valley exploded in the years following the Revolution, Miró had become increasingly concerned about the safety of the colony. From 1785 to 1787, Miró peppered his correspondence with reports of the threat to Spanish interests posed by American expansion.[27] By 1787, alarmed by both Thomas Green's pamphlet detailing Clark's supposed plan to descend on New Orleans and by Wilkinson's warnings that the Kentucky militia was planning a campaign, Miró was convinced that an attack was imminent. Miró believed that the Americans could "easily form an army of one hundred thousand men" (a dramatic overestimation: the census of 1790 would place the entire population of Kentucky and Tennessee, including noncombatants, at just over 100,000) to attack New Orleans. "Who can tell if this day they may be in Tennessee . . . constructing flat-boats . . . in order to come down after the snow melts," Miró wondered to his superiors. He was certain the westerners had plenty of provisions to supply an invading army, as the Tennesseans "had no place to sell" their goods since the Spanish had closed the Mississippi to American trade.[28]

Miró needed an ally in the American settlements, someone who could send advance word of any invasion plans and keep Spanish officials apprised of events occurring in the American settlements. With his military background and connections to the Kentucky elite, Wilkinson would serve admirably. Wilkinson spent the summer of 1787 in New Orleans, building relationships with Governor Miró and with Martin Navarro, the Spanish intendant—the officer charged with collecting the taxes and overseeing the treasury. Wilkinson took advantage of this entrée into New Orleans society to sell his cargo to good advantage, but the real profit in his trip had little to do with the sale of flour or tobacco. While in New Orleans, Wilkinson agreed to become Spain's agent in Kentucky in exchange for a healthy fee.

Although he feared the vulnerabilities of Louisiana, Miró had also come to imagine the Mississippi as a tool that could be used to pry

Anglo-American settlers away from the United States and attach them to the Spanish empire. Miró viewed Wilkinson as a means for obtaining that separation. In a memorial to imperial officials, Miró and Wilkinson considered it an "an absolute Fact that [the western] Settlements will continue subordinate and look up for protection to that power which secures them this most precious privilege [of Mississippi navigation]." As master of the river, Spain had an opportunity to detach the West from the union. Wilkinson proposed that "Don Diego de Gardoqui should without hesitation peremptorily and absolutely refuse to Congress the Navigation of the Mississippi," an act that would reveal the weakness of the Confederation and reinforce in the minds of westerners the growing sense that the Continental Congress was willing, if not eager, to sacrifice western interests.[29] Spanish officials could then swoop in and negotiate directly with westerners to reopen the Mississippi, bypassing Congress and thereby securing westerners' loyalty for Spain.

The Spanish would have to tread a careful line, as foreclosing the river could backfire, driving westerners to fulfil Miró's predictions of an invasion. To avoid this eventuality, Wilkinson suggested a self-serving proposition: Spain should allow limited trading privileges to "men of real influence." By allowing some controlled trade, Spain would "attach the leading characters in that Country to the interest of Spain ... cheer the People with the hope of a free and friendly intercourse, and prevent every act of outrage and hostility." If done correctly, Wilkinson predicted that "the transition from the renouncement of the federal Government of America to a Negociation with the Court of Spain would be natural and immediate."[30] As his first step toward implementing Wilkinson's scheme, Miró granted Wilkinson the exclusive privilege of trading Kentucky produce through New Orleans. In exchange, in August 1787 Wilkinson swore his loyalty and allegiance to the Spanish crown. Undoubtedly, Wilkinson left New Orleans well satisfied with the bargain he had struck. By December 19, Wilkinson had placed an order for two boats, each fifty feet long, that he planned to send to New Orleans the following spring.[31]

Wilkinson returned to Kentucky in the spring of 1788 in the full flush of victory, riding in the first coach to venture westward across the Appalachians.[32] Soon after his return, he began probing Kentucky politicians for their feelings on effecting what was often known as a "violent separation"—a complete rupture not only with Virginia but also with the union—and a subsequent alliance with Spain.[33] Wilkinson began by making his negotiations with Miró known to three of his associates: Isaac Dunn, his business partner in the Mississippi trade; prominent planter

Alexander Scott Bullitt; and lawyer Harry Innes. All three men approved the plan.[34] News that on July 3, in one of its final acts, the Continental Congress had refused Kentucky statehood led many to look favorably on Wilkinson's plan. Several of the leading men of Kentucky, including Thomas Marshall, George Muter, Caleb Wallace, Benjamin McDowell, and John Fowler, professed themselves willing to separate from the United States and eager for an alliance with Spain. The alliance, after all, would offer their best chance of obtaining what Congress seemed so unable to deliver: Mississippi trade.[35]

Despite Wilkinson's machinations, at the meeting of the Seventh Convention, held at Danville in November 1788, it quickly became clear that Wilkinson had overestimated the willingness of Kentuckians to separate from the union entirely. The assembled body of Kentuckians divided between those who supported a "condoned" separation from Virginia and American statehood and those who preferred a "violent" separation and political independence. The convention decided to petition Congress, appealing for statehood and admission to the union. The petition, drafted by Wilkinson, focused less on statehood and more on the status of the river. Calling for their eastern brethren to "attend to the wrong done to men and citizens," the petition urged easterners "to trace the Mississippi from the ocean" to Kentucky. Wilkinson, using a rhetorical style he often employed, implored Congress to consider whether "the God of wisdom and nature" could have intended to cut Kentuckians off from the river, a right, he asserted, Kentuckians had come to view as "natural." "Can," he exhorted, "the presumptuous madness of man imagine a policy inconsistent with the immense designs of the Deity." "Americans," he asserted, including both Kentuckians and all right-thinking easterners within the term, "cannot." Employing a metaphor for the body politic, Kentuckians reminded Congress that they were "a member" of the union. "Do not," they warned, "cut us off from your body" by failing to assert western claims to the river.[36]

In 1788, the economic and political situation of Kentucky changed once more when Spain decided, as a result of the machinations of Wilkinson and other westerners, to reopen the Mississippi to limited American trade. That spring, the first boatloads of western produce traveled downriver for sale in New Orleans.[37] Having the river open helped ease the financial problems of the trans-Appalachian West; the price of one hundred pounds of Kentucky tobacco, for instance, increased from $2.50 with the river closed to $9.00 a year later.[38] Nonetheless, Spain continued to restrict American trade on the river, levying heavy taxes on all American goods brought into Louisiana. In 1789, James Brown, brother to John, reported sarcastically to an eastern correspondent, "The Spanish have given us the mighty privilege of carying our produce down the Mississippi provided we pay fifteen per cent duty—are they not very kind?" Any goods brought downriver were then taxed again when they were exported onto oceangoing ships. Only Wilkinson and a select few other western leaders were exempt from the tax.[39] Spanish officials still periodically seized American cargoes, forcing their owners to accept bills of dubious value drawn on the Louisiana treasury.[40] The Mississippi Question remained a key point of division between westerners and the federal government. Without consistent access to trade, westerners continued to flirt with the possibility of separating from the union. Wilkinson had offered them a possible path they could pursue.

Ultimately, separatist schemes lost favor in Kentucky as western elites were enlisted into positions of power within the new state and national administrations taking shape. For his part, although James Wilkinson remained in contact with the Spanish through the next three decades, the departure of Governor Miró in 1791 and the opening of Mississippi trade more broadly diminished Wilkinson's utility to the Spanish empire. His political machinations, which were extensive, could fill a book, but his machinations over reopening the Mississippi trade and conspiring with Spanish authorities alone had serious repercussions for future western settlement.

Going It Together

ABIJAH HUNT offered westerners a different path forward. Few men played a larger role in establishing western trade and linking western commerce to eastern political and economic networks than Hunt. Although he played a key role in supplying the American army in Ohio, and at the time of his death was "the most extensive planter in the Mississippi Territory," Hunt is nevertheless relatively unknown.[41] But his position on the western frontier shows how integrally commerce was connected to the successful construction of federal authority in the West.

In 1790, Hunt arrived in the recently settled village of Cincinnati to join his brother Jesse in operating a store; soon, they were joined by another brother, Jeremiah, who joined the trading firm. Initially, they found a ready market in new arrivals streaming into the region, but their timing was poor. In response to increasing encroachment by thousands of white settler-colonists, Shawnee, Cherokee, and Mingo war parties intensified attacks on European American settlements. Undeclared war between the regions' Indigenous inhabitants, organized into a loose confederation, and the newly arrived settlers not only slowed the pace of arrivals but threatened to completely depopulate the region.[42]

The Hunt brothers decided to capitalize on the presence of the West's largest consumer: the U.S. Army. The ratification of the Constitution had led to a new deployment of American troops to the frontier, most of whom were stationed in Cincinnati at the nearby Fort Washington. Throughout the 1790s, the U.S. government, frustrated by repeated losses at the hands of the northern Indian confederacy, pumped an ever-increasing amount of money into the West, eventually tripling the U.S. Army's funding.[43] Much to the disgust of settlers in the recently created Southwest Territory, the federal government chose to concentrate its military efforts north of the Ohio, a choice that heightened the importance of Cincinnati.[44] Initially, American military efforts in Ohio were as much of a failure as they had been under the Articles of Confederation. In 1790, Shawnee and Miami troops defeated General Josiah Harmar, along with 200 regular soldiers and 1,200 Kentucky militia, along the Wabash River.[45] In 1791, a campaign led by Northwest Territory governor Arthur St. Clair met a similar fate. In a major military victory, a combined force of Miami, Shawnee, Delaware (Lenape), Iroquois, Ottawa, Ojibwe, Wyandot, and Potawatomi forces decimated St. Clair's army; of roughly 1,400 soldiers engaged, 918 were killed or wounded in the battle.[46] For Abijah Hunt, the success of the army mattered less than its presence. Beginning soon after his arrival, Hunt became a sutler—a civilian merchant who traveled with the army, supplying the troops' nearly insatiable desire for food, dry goods, and liquor.[47]

In 1794, the army and Hunt's fortunes changed when three thousand American troops under the command of General Anthony Wayne won a decisive victory at the Battle of Fallen Timbers. The event marked a turning point in the ongoing war for the Northwest. The subsequent Treaty of Greenville redrew the boundaries between Indigenous and white territory, pushing the latter far to the north of the Ohio. Immigration, which had stalled but not stopped during the previous five years of war, resumed. Recognizing that the situation between the region's Indigenous peoples and settlers was still volatile, in 1795 Wayne made the decision to order nearly all civilian merchants to leave the region west of the Miami

River. Hunt was one of only five merchants allowed to remain in the region, guaranteeing him a large share of the army's trade.

Hunt was not initially aware of Wayne's order. That spring, he had traveled to New Jersey to visit his family and to replenish his stock for his Cincinnati store. While in New Jersey, on April 29, 1795, Abijah met with his twenty-two-year-old cousin John Wesley Hunt to discuss establishing a retail store in Lexington, in the heart of Kentucky's fertile bluegrass region. Abijah proposed a simple partnership: he and John would each contribute £1,000 to the new venture. Abijah would do the buying while John would "place [him]self behind the counter . . . where I know," Abijah assured his young cousin, "you will shine."[48] Despite his youth, John Hunt had strong connections to eastern networks that made him an attractive trading partner. John's father was Trenton, New Jersey's leading merchant; John's older brothers, Wilson and Pearson Hunt, had already gone into business for themselves as retailers in Philadelphia.[49] A few days after the two men signed a contract creating their new partnership, Abijah embarked on a buying spree in Philadelphia. He purchased a wide array of items, including fabric, hats, and a large supply of dry goods, including coffee, as well as spices like pepper, allspice, brimstone, cloves, and cinnamon. He purchased knives, forks, inkstands, and brandy, along with a thousand flints—an essential component of frontier weaponry—and keg upon keg of bullets. Books, medicine, and even feathers rounded out his purchases.[50]

Abijah's largest purchase was from John's brother Wilson, from whose shop Abijah purchased over a thousand pounds of goods.[51] Abijah imagined that John's Philadelphia connections would be a key asset of their new Kentucky venture. John's brothers in Philadelphia would supply John and Abijah with imported and finished goods; because they were family, Abijah may have envisioned Wilson and Pearson taking both more care with the new firm's orders and perhaps extending them more generous credit than was typical (and, indeed, John and Abijah did take advantage of Wilson and Pearson by not repaying their debts to them as quickly as they did to other firms). Philadelphia-based Wilson and Pearson could aid their brother and cousins by acting as eastern agents for the western Hunt enterprises by sending remittances, forwarding invoices, and assembling future cargoes for transport west. John and Abijah's first advertisement, which ran in the *Kentucky Gazette* in July 1795, illustrated the importance of the interconnectedness of the Hunt family traders. John and Abijah promised their customers the lowest prices in the area, which, they asserted, they were able to offer thanks to "the terms ... laid in at in Philadelphia."⁵²

In Lexington, John and Abijah joined a bustling community of merchants. When the Hunts opened their doors, there were as many as twenty mercantile establishments vying for the trade of Lexington. Despite the lack of market access caused by the closed Mississippi, Kentucky's settlers had become increasingly enmeshed in an Atlantic world of consumer goods.⁵³ From their post in the Kentucky bluegrass, John and Abijah Hunt were the westernmost outpost of networks of credit and exchange that stretched across the Atlantic. East Coast merchants, like Wilson and Pearson Hunt, imported manufactured goods; as retailers, they then extended credit to their western counterparts like John and Abijah, who hoped to repay their debts through sales of the merchandise.⁵⁴ The lack of cash among the settlers of Kentucky and Ohio meant that retailers like John and Abijah sold most of their goods either on credit or in exchange for "country produce." Without access to the Mississippi, merchants like the Hunts found themselves with an overabundance of local products on their hands.

Fortunately, Abijah Hunt found an outlet for the produce he and John had accumulated. In winter 1796, General Wayne grew frustrated with "the Extortions, Abuses & Excesses daily committed by the Swarm of Petty Traders & Smugglers who [creeped] into" the army's encampments. On February 27, 1796, Wayne ordered his officers to select one individual who would serve as the army's "Grand Sutler"—a post frequently used by the British Army—who would be responsible for providing the troops with "a Competent supply of wholesome groceries & Provision," as well as a "suitable Assortment of Dry Goods." The grand sutler would be responsible for licensing other merchants to act as "petty sutlers." One man would now be able to control the trade of the entire western army. Abijah Hunt was appointed to the post—thanks in large part to his personal friendships with Caleb Swan, the army paymaster, and with James Wilkinson, who in 1791, having become less useful to the Spanish, had rejoined the American army.⁵⁵

Abijah's appointment as grand sutler meant that the Cincinnati branch of the Hunt family enterprises found itself in "want [of] much larger Supplies of Country Produce" than had previously been the case.⁵⁶ Abijah had found a ready market for all the flour, bacon, and whiskey John could acquire through trade at their Lexington store. John and Abijah's Kentucky-based firm would sell the country produce it accumulated to

Abijah, Jeremiah, and Jesse's store in Cincinnati. Abijah would then broker the sale of that food to himself in his capacity as grand sutler. He would then sell it all to the army.

On the eighteenth-century trans-Appalachian frontier, trade with the army offered something that was not available from almost any other outlets: cash. Trade with the army provided an alternative to the limited export market available to western farmers. The army required a nearly endless supply of horses, oats, flour, beef, and whiskey, driving up prices in Kentucky. The army's demand for butter, for instance, meant it retailed for three times more near Cincinnati than it did elsewhere in Kentucky. Henry Toulmin, a French traveler who visited Kentucky in 1793, reported that while "cash used to be very scarce in Kentucky," of late it had become "more plentiful, on account of the army."[57]

Despite the infusion of cash the army brought, it was only rarely that the federal government shipped specie—gold and silver—to the Ohio Valley frontier. Instead, much of the money flowing into the West from the federal government came in the form of notes drawn on the Department of War.[58] Caleb Swan, the army's paymaster and Abijah Hunt's close friend, brought the government's bills west, where he advertised in the pages of the *Centinel of the North Western Territory*, Cincinnati's first newspaper, that he had available bills of exchange "at ten days sight, [drawn] on the secretary of War in Philadelphia."[59] Swan used the notes to pay local merchants for supplies for the troops. John Bartle, an early Cincinnati merchant, recalled that he would then take these drafts and "[cash] them in Lexington at a premium of two and a half percent. Whence they would be remitted to Phil[adelphia] to purchase goods for the new settlements of Kentucky."[60]

Swan also used the drafts to gather money locally to pay the army. For the most part, bills drawn on the secretary of war were not issued directly to the troops. Army privates typically earned three dollars a month; negotiating a bill of exchange for such a small amount was not feasible, nor would it have been possible to have issued the thousands of such notes it would have required to pay the entire army. Instead, Swan turned to merchants like the Hunts. In June 1796, for instance, a bill drawn on Secretary of War James McHenry was issued to the firm of Jeremiah and Abijah Hunt "for the sum of Three Thousand Dollars on account of the pay &c. Of the Army for two months."[61] Jeremiah and Abijah, along with other merchants, bought the army's bills in exchange for local currency—specie, bills of exchange, and occasionally banknotes—which was then distributed to the troops. Unsurprisingly, much of that money would later find its way back into the Hunts' pockets: on payday, troops went on spending sprees, settling their debts acquired since their previous payday and exchanging their wages for coffee, sugar, bacon, brandy, and of course whiskey, which sutler Abijah Hunt delivered to their encampments.[62] Because the army's bills were a form of currency that could be used to settle western merchants' debts with their eastern counterparts, the bills held tremendous value on the cash-scarce Ohio frontier. As grand sutler, Abijah secured for himself and his brothers and cousins a steady stream of currency they could remit to their creditors back east. By moving the government's money back and forth across the Appalachians, the Hunt family solved the crucial problem of how a distant government could pay and feed an army in the field. However, the model that Abijah Hunt adapted was untenable in the long term. With the Indigenous peoples north of the Ohio largely defeated by 1796, the army's role in the West shifted, and the Hunt family needed to find a new outlet for their trade.

While Wilkinson exercised his special trading privileges and the Hunt family used the army to get around the problem of the closed Mississippi, most westerners sought a different path forward. The desire to obtain Mississippi trade came to define westerners' relationship with the central government and with the Federalist Party. Western anger and frustration that Congress—which included many individuals who were now Federalist officials—had agreed to cede American claims to the river shaped western politics. Westerners became committed opponents of the Federalists. By 1792, opposition to Federalist policies was growing nationally. Democratic-Republican societies formed across the United States. Given the widespread dislike of the Federalist Party in the West, it is not surprising that by 1793, three Democratic-Republican societies had formed in Kentucky to widespread approbation. In western Pennsylvania, four more societies took shape in 1794.[63] These seven groups offered a distinctively western critique of the Federalist government. Whereas elsewhere, opposition to the Washington administration's policies toward the French Revolution drove political protest, in the West the closure of the Mississippi and the failure of the federal government to provide westerners with a trade outlet dominated the political discourse emerging from these societies.[64]

Congress's inability to open Mississippi River trade was a catalyst for the unrest that rocked Western Pennsylvania in 1794. Although the series of small skirmishes that erupted around Pittsburgh that summer are usually referred to as the "Whiskey Rebellion," westerners' anger went far beyond complaints about an unpopular tax on alcohol; across the West, Democratic-Republican societies used protests against the tax to give voice to westerners' anger over the Mississippi Question. In general, westerners did not object to the tax itself; rhetorically at least, western Democratic-Republican societies acknowledged the right of the government to place a tax on alcohol production, no matter how much they might dislike it. Nevertheless, they objected to the government's requirement that the taxes, "as if designed with peculiar inequality and hardship," were "made payable in specie only."[65] Westerners were struck by the seeming heartlessness of a policy that demanded their scarce resources of gold and silver while simultaneously withholding access to that specie by failing to open the Mississippi. By demanding cash but failing to provide markets, the federal government was, it seemed, purposely alienating its western citizens. "Money is to be taken from us by an odious and oppressive Excise," one of Kentucky's Democratic-Republican societies lamented, "but the means of procuring it, by the exercise of our just right [Mississippi Navigation], is denied."[66]

Accusing Congress of failing to assert their right to trade down the Mississippi "in a manner consistent with the justice they owe this part of the Union," the societies used the memory of the Jay-Gardoqui Treaty negotiations as a symbol of all the problems that westerners faced at the hands of an arbitrary eastern government. Pennsylvanians reminded Congress that during the 1786 negotiations, eastern delegates had argued that ceding western claims to the river would result in advantages to the nation writ large.[67] Westerners believed they had not yet experienced those benefits. By 1794, the Democratic-Republicans confidently asserted that "the inhabitants of the Western Country had a right to expect" the federal government to take "effectual measures to obtain from the King of Spain an acknowledgement of their undoubted right to the free navigation of the River Mississippi."[68] If the government was not prepared to enact policies that benefited both portions of the nation equally, the citizens west of the Alleghenies would be forced to take drastic action. Threatening to repeat the former colonies' actions during the Revolution, the society members warned Congress that "attachment[s] to governments" "cease to be natural, when they cease to be mutual."[69] The threat of disunion, which had played such a large role in the crafting of the Constitution, offered western citizens a tool to assert their will against the federal government.

When members of one of Pennsylvania's Democratic-Republican Societies met in Pittsburgh in April 1794, just two months before the Whiskey Rebellion came to a head, they remonstrated not about the tax on whiskey but about their anger at the river's continued closure. Collectively, they described their conception of what they were increasingly coming to see as a comprehensive right to the navigation of the Mississippi: "When we talk of this right, we mean not only that of descending the stream, without toll, duty, or restriction; but the use of every port free upon its banks as a natural appendage of the river; and if those who inhabit these ports will not give the free entrance of them to the tenants in common of the right, it is an injury."[70] A week later, a separate meeting accused Congress of failing to assert westerners' right to trade down the Mississippi "in a manner consistent with the justice they owe this part of the Union." Recalling the "proposition made in Congress some years ago of bartering [the Mississippi] away for a time, in consideration of some advantages in trade to the sea coast settlements," western Pennsylvanians reminded Congress that at the time "it was asserted that a greater interest would result to the United States in general" in exchange for westerners' sacrifice of the Mississippi. "But," they queried, zeroing in on their primary complaint in 1786, which remained problematic in 1794, "who gave [Congress] a power to sacrifice a part for the whole?"[71]

As western anger over the closure of the Mississippi grew, the right to trade transformed from a natural right, which could not be taken away, to a positive right, one that the federal government had a sacred duty to protect. By failing to act, Congress had betrayed its westernmost citizens. True, there as had yet been "no positive surrender of the right; but there has been what may be called a negative surrender; to wit, an acquiescence in our privation of it." It was not enough for the government to agree with westerners' claims to a natural right to navigation; it was the government's duty to provide them with that right. Thus, the Democratic Republicans argued that "the inhabitants of the Western Country had a right to expect" the federal government to take "effectual measures to obtain from the King of Spain an acknowledgement of their undoubted right to the free navigation of the River Mississippi."[72] Worse yet, by enacting trade and taxation policies that sacrificed the interests of the western part of the nation in favor of the eastern seaboard, the government confirmed once again westerners' suspicions that they were not fully incorporated into the union. If the government was not prepared to enact policies that benefited both portions of the nation equally, westerners were prepared to take drastic action. A Pennsylvania group calling itself the "citizens west of the Allegheny Mountains" warned Congress that while they "yield[ed] not in patriotism to any of their fellow-citizens: but patriotism, like every other thing, has its bounds," and the twinned burdens of specie-only taxation and the closed Mississippi pushed against the boundaries of what westerners were willing to tolerate.[73] The powerful ideology that had motivated the Revolution, the idea that the contract between the governed and the government could be broken in the event the government failed to meet its obligations to the people, now motivated westerners to protect themselves against the nation's new government.

In May 1794, frustrated over both foreign policy that denied them access to the Mississippi and domestic policy that demanded scarce specie, the residents of Lexington, Kentucky, gathered to voice their contempt of Washington's administration. Much of their opposition centered on John Jay, who had been dispatched to England to negotiate a new treaty. In the West, opposition to Jay extended beyond fears of Anglophilia. Jay's appointment "brought . . . strongly to the recollection of the people" of Kentucky "his former iniquitous attempt to barter away their most valuable right." In Lexington, the townspeople "could not refrain from openly testifying their abhorrence of this man, whose appointment . . . they consider[ed] tragically ominous." To express their anger, the Kentuckians constructed an effigy of Jay, hung a copy of "[John] Adams' defence of the American Constitutions" around its neck, and symbolically executed their nemesis with a specially built guillotine before setting the figure ablaze.[74] Western Pennsylvanians and Kentuckians protested Federalist policy about the Mississippi far more than they protested a specific tax on whiskey. When the Democratic-Republicans emerged as a viable alternative to Federalist rule, westerners were more than ready to embrace the alternative.

By 1794, if not even earlier, western farmers were placing Atlantic trade at the apex of their understanding of political economy. Trade was neither incidental nor secondary but so profoundly central to the desires and aspirations of western settlers that the lack of markets changed their understanding of the role of government in society and their understanding of their own relationship to the federal government. For James Wilkinson and for many other westerners, loyalty to the United States—or to any empire—was instrumental, a tool that could be engaged to obtain privileges and opportunities that contributed directly to one's own gain.

While westerners' threats to withdraw from the union—and federal officials' fears of that eventuality—cannot be dismissed, westerners deployed those threats as instrumentally as they employed their loyalty.

Abijah Hunt also used the federal government to acquire the economic advantages he sought. But his actions served to strengthen the power of the federal government in the West and thereby helped diminish the potency of western threats of separation. With the army deployed against Indigenous peoples, and its cash shoring up Kentucky's economy, withdrawal from the union became increasingly less likely, even as the population of the West surged and western anger smoldered. For all of the Democratic-Republican societies' bellicose threats, the fact remains that they limited their opposition to Federalist policies to political rhetoric, as opposed to armed conflict.

For their part, eastern Federalists were quick to dismiss westerners' claims of government neglect. Federalists responded to the petitions of the Kentucky and Pennsylvania Democratic-Republican societies with derision. The *Gazette of the United States* reported mockingly that a right to trade along the Mississippi "is held by the Church of Kentucky, to be *jure divino*." Mississippi trade was "a right they claim, and which they passionately and clamorously call upon the United States to vindicate for them, with a threat that if refused they will take redress into their own hands." Such a claim—and such a threat—could not stand. "If the Kentuckians" followed through on their threat to attack Spanish holdings directly to open the river, they would find themselves "disowned by the general government . . . left alone to the Consequences of their own presumption and iniquity."[75] The editor of New York's Federalist mouthpiece the *American Minerva* cast suspicion on western threats to secede if the Mississippi were not opened. "Do these people," the Federalist editors queried, "suppose that *passion* and *fury* will frighten three or four millions of *steady independent people*, who *reason* before they *act?*" Drawing a clear distinction between rash and impetuous westerners and a stolid and respectable East, eastern Federalists dismissed the very premise underlying western claims to the Mississippi.[76] Opening the river "was an affair belonging to men or rather to kings"—in other words, it would not be Kentucky settlers but eastern political elites who could best reopen the river. That being the case, the Kentuckians might as well "go whistle" for their supposed "right."[77]

Westerners' access to the Mississippi would ultimately be decided by treaty. But the members of both the western Democratic-Republican societies and their Federalist rivals in the East overlooked a key factor in determining the nature of Mississippi trade. While Spain might claim ownership of the Mississippi, its claim to dominance in the region was no less contested than the American one. The Spanish controlled New Orleans, but they could not control the waters of the Mississippi. For the United States, obtaining Mississippi access would ultimately require negotiating not only with Spain but with the region's Indigenous peoples as well.

6

Chickasaw Country

In October 1787, Carlos de Grand Pré, the Spanish commandant of Natchez, reported on the arrival of a flatboat from Fort Pitt. As was customary with arriving Americans, Grand Pré examined the men in detail about their journey down the river and their purpose in visiting Natchez. The Pennsylvanians carried some very interesting news: at Fort Pitt, a U.S. Army officer had ordered them to take aboard "the two great Chickasaw and Choctaw chiefs who had just arrived in a coach from Philadelphia at the expense of the General Congress." "They say," Grand Pré informed Miró, "that these two chiefs were invited by the Congress to go to Philadelphia where a treaty was made with them, forming an alliance against the Talapoosa [Creek] Indians." Congress had given each of the chiefs "a badge and a medal on which their names are stamped," promising them aid in fighting against the Creek. In return, "the two chiefs are to have their people armed immediately" to join nine hundred Virginians who would march with them against the Creek.[1]

The Americans could not recall the names of the Chickasaw and Choctaw chiefs they had presumably carried downriver for several weeks. Four delegates, representing the Choctaw, Chickasaw, and Cherokee nations were in Philadelphia during the summer of 1787; the two chiefs referenced in Grand Pré's letter were Choctaw chief Taboca and Chickasaw war captain Muckleshamingo.[2] When the two men arrived in Philadelphia in July 1787, they encountered the members of the Constitutional Convention, who persuaded them not to go onto New York where the sparsely attended Congress had just signed the Northwest Ordinance, providing a model for the sale of Indian country.[3] Savvy politicians, Taboca and Muckleshamingo must have recognized the role that western lands played in Congress's ongoing negotiations. Grand Pré certainly did.

"It is the intention and purpose of the Congress," the commandant informed Miró, "after having reduced or destroyed the Talapoosas [Creek], to put on public sale all the lands on the [eastern] bank of the Ohio from Fort Pitt to its confluence with the Mississippi. The profit from it," Grand Pré continued, "is to serve as payment in part for the continental debt."[4]

The meeting of Spanish officials, Americans from the Ohio Valley settlements, and Chickasaw and Choctaw leaders on the docks of Natchez was not unusual in the lower Mississippi Valley in the second half of the 1780s. Stepping onto the Ohio and Mississippi Rivers compressed distances between faraway places and disparate peoples, moving goods and people as well as information. By 1787, Spanish officials collected and reported on the information passing through the region, and news like that provided by the American traders was quickly passed along. After the Revolution, both the United States and Spain sought to expand their influence in the Southeast by establishing new trade and diplomatic relationships. For their part, the Chickasaw had established peaceful relationships with both the American and the Spanish empires. However, the Chickasaw disagreed over which party could best provide the trade goods that formed the heart of these exchanges. Since at least 1780, the Chickasaw had been divided into two factions. One faction, led by Ugulayacabé (Wolf's Friend), preferred a closer alliance with the Spanish as a European partner; in June 1784, at a Spanish-Chickasaw conference in Mobile, Chickasaw leaders agreed to allow only Spanish traders in Chickasaw country in exchange for Spanish help in keeping prices fair and encouraging peace among the region's Indigenous people.[5]

Despite agreeing to this treaty, Piominko led a substantial minority of Chickasaw who preferred the Americans to the Spanish. In 1786, at Hopewell Plantation in South Carolina, Piominko and a delegation of other Chickasaw leaders negotiated a treaty with the United States that confirmed to them all of the land that the Chickasaw had claimed as of 1782. The Chickasaw also made a major concession to the Americans: they agreed to the creation of an American trading post, to be built along Ocochappo Creek (now Bear Creek) near what is now the Mississippi-Alabama border, close to the ancient trading road that would eventually become known as the Natchez Trace.[6] To make it clear that the Chickasaw intended to allow Americans to use the land but by no means to cede it to the Americans, Piominko carefully sketched the location of the proposed fort onto a map that the American commissioners provided. While the Americans would benefit from such a trading post, so would the Chickasaw, who would have far easier access to imported goods if the Americans were operating from within Chickasaw territory. While the distinction between pro-Spanish and pro-American mattered tremendously in terms of the diplomatic tactics of the Chickasaw, internally, in their dealings with one another, there was little difference between the two groups. There was widespread tolerance among the Chickasaw for Piominko and his actions, as the broader Chickasaw agenda was to obtain as many concessions as possible from both the Spanish and the Americans in order to build Chickasaw strength.[7]

In the southeastern borderlands, the United States had no greater supporter than Piominko. In the latter half of the 1780s, Piominko would fight alongside Cumberland settlers against the Cherokee and Creek; in the 1790s, he would lead a band of Chickasaw soldiers north to join the U.S. Army in Ohio in its battle against the Northern Confederacy and travel to Richmond to remind Americans of their obligation to support the Chickasaw. Throughout, he would fiercely defend Chickasaw interests, both by securing his people's territory and by promoting trade with the United States. Establishing trade while maintaining independence was key to the Chickasaw's diplomacy in the decade following the Revolution. Balanced between the Spanish and American empires, by the mid-1790s the Chickasaw found their position growing increasingly precarious.

A World at War

THE BOY who would become known as Piominko was born in the Chickasaw village of Chokkilissa' (Old Town) around 1750.[8] He never knew his father, who died in a skirmish with Shawnee who were attempting to settle on Chickasaw land along the Cumberland River near the site of Nashville before he was born. Among the matrilineal Chickasaw, the death of a father did not connotate a loss of identity. Yet Piominko's matrilineal forebears were only loosely connected to the Chickasaw. Piominko's mother was Chakchiuma, a group that was closely affiliated culturally and linguistically with the Choctaw and Chickasaw. In 1730, a series of attacks by both Choctaw and Chickasaw forces had all but decimated the Chakchiuma; the survivors had scattered to join the two larger groups, intermarrying with each. Although no longer a distinct people, occasionally Chakchiuma individuals acted as emissaries between the warring Choctaw and Chickasaw due to their kinship connections with both groups.⁹ Piominko's mother had scattered familial connections across the Southeast. For his part, the young Piominko spent much of his youth and adolescence living among the Cherokee, near his uncle Cherokee chief Little Turkey. With the Cherokee, he learned the skills needed by a man of his age and position. He returned to the Chickasaw in the mid-1770s, near the outbreak of the Second Cherokee-British War, already a man and skilled fighter. He rose quickly through the ranks of Chickasaw warriors, eventually acquiring the title of Piominko, or Mountain Leader, a mark of his military skill.¹⁰

The title "Piominko" was a high honor. The Piominko who would become a staunch ally of the American interest was not the first to carry the name. In the decades prior to the American Revolution, the legendary Chickasaw leader Paya Mattaha (Oppoia Mattaha) was also known as "Piomingo." It was largely through Paya Mattaha's efforts that the Chickasaw finally made peace with their traditional enemies, the Choctaw and the Quapaw, as well as the Cherokee and Creek, and who helped the Chickasaw maintain a careful neutrality throughout the Revolution.¹¹ The death of Paya Mattaha in 1784 threatened that neutrality, as did the withdrawal of the British from the region. The Chickasaw were then left to contend with the Spanish and the Americans, both of whom were assuming new roles in the region.

Neither the Spanish nor the British—or their American successors—fully understood the structure of Chickasaw leadership. Unlike other southeastern Indian groups, which were often divided internally, the Chickasaw's small numbers and decades of warfare had allowed them to centralize authority within the tribe. The Chickasaw were led by the civil chief, or Minko. The Minko "ruled"—or, more accurately, led—for life. When a Minko died or could no longer serve, his successor was chosen from among his sisters' sons. The position was thus both hereditary—limited to the members of the Minko clan—but also merit-based. As the civil chief, the Minko was responsible for managing the Chickasaw's relations peacefully, conducting foreign diplomacy and keeping the peace internally. The Minko was assisted by the Tisho Minko, who was responsible for leading the national council, which was composed of the chiefs and prominent warriors of the various Chickasaw towns. The council acted as a deliberative body, negotiating and arguing before presenting their decisions to the Minko, who could then choose to enforce or veto the council's decisions. The Minko had to tread carefully if he chose to veto the council's actions, for each town chief was democratically chosen by the residents of the various towns and contradicting the council's wishes could easily upset the people more broadly.

The Minko and council were joined by another branch of government: the war chief. This position was chosen from among the members of the red moiety and was responsible for planning the Chickasaw's military strategies. The war chief was selected by the warriors for his military prowess; hence, any Chickasaw man from a red town stood a chance of being chosen. This was Piominko's path. By 1783, he was widely recognized as one of the most important leaders of the Chickasaw and the chief of Chokka' Falaa', a "red" town known to white people as Long Town. By 1786, he had apparently been elected the war chief of the Chickasaw nation.[12]

A Changing Economy

THE AMERICAN REVOLUTION accelerated significant changes already underway within the Chickasaw economy. In 1758–59, peace with the Choctaw, brokered by the Chakchiuma, allowed the Chickasaw to leave the shelter of Chokkilissa' and begin dispersing, reoccupying abandoned village sites and moving onto land that had lain fallow for decades. By the 1780s, Chickasaw lived in both sprawling towns and on scattered homesteads.[13] New settlement patterns were driven by new economic endeavors. By 1790, nearly every aspect of the Chickasaw economy looked different than it had just thirty years earlier. The Chickasaw were still producing traditional crops of corn, beans, and squash but also an increasing number of European cultivars. That year, when U.S. Army major John Doughty traveled through Chickasaw country, he reported that Chickasaw farmers produced ample "provisions [of] Hogs, Poultry, Eggs, Beans, Corn & the finest Potatoes I ever saw," and "appear[ed] to be verging fast towards the State of farmers."[14]

While Doughty's comment encapsulates white American's dismissive attitudes toward Indigenous husbandry, it also points to a real shift taking place in Chickasaw cultural practices. Although a majority of Chickasaw men engaged in annual hunts that allowed them to acquire meat for their families and hides for trading with European American merchants and would continue to do so through the first decades of the nineteenth century, the Chickasaw were embracing animal husbandry and diversifying their approach to agriculture. As early as the 1760s, as the advent of peace allowed the Chickasaw to move away from Chokkilissa', Chickasaw farmers used their more dispersed settlement pattern to raise animals to supplement their diet, beginning a transition to animal cultivation that would become widespread by 1810. While most white people on the frontier allowed their hogs and cows to roam at will, the Chickasaw penned their livestock, which required more intensive husbandry but kept pigs and cows from competing for some of the wild food stocks on which the Chickasaw continued to rely.[15]

Doughty may have been impressed by the Chickasaw's farming but the Chickasaw themselves were worried. "Never before," Piominko informed the American officer, were the Chickasaw "in such Distress for Want of Powder, Lead, Blanketts, Strouds, &C." The overhunting of white-tailed deer in the region, coupled with the failure of both American and Spanish officials to provide the Chickasaw with convenient trading opportunities, had severely limited the Chickasaw's ability to obtain the consumer goods, especially gunpowder, that they relied on. Piominko attributed this poverty directly to the United States' failure to provide them with the trading post agreed to in his negotiations with the Americans. "At Hopewell in 1786," Piominko bitterly reminded Doughty, Americans had promised "that Traders should be sent amongst them to supply them with Powder & Lead to hunt, & with Goods to cloth their Women & Children, but as yet they had received nothing but promises." Piominko felt betrayed by Congress's failure to provide the Chickasaw with adequate trade.[16]

The failure of the Americans to live up to the terms of the Treaty of Hopewell was hardly a new complaint. In 1787, Chickasaw Minko Chinubbee, known as the Chickasaw "king," had attempted to present the same protest to Congress.[17] That same year, in a letter to American Indian agent Joseph Martin, Piominko complained of the American delay in building a trading post on Chickasaw land. At Hopewell, the Chickasaw had agreed to allow the Americans to build a trading post on their lands. Since that time, though, the Americans had failed to provide the Chickasaw with either a trader or trade goods. "This makes us very uneasy," Piominko warned the American officer; it seemed that the United States intended "to jockey us out of our lands," not establish a trading relationship. Piominko remarked that while the Americans were failing to construct a trading post, the Spanish continued to trade with the Chickasaw and intimated that the Chickasaw might soon become even more favorable to the Spanish than they already were. After all, Piominko noted, "[we] must have trade from someplace.... Necessity will oblige us to look to new friends if we cannot get friends otherwise." The Americans were not the only ones to receive this message. In 1786, a Spanish official in Mobile reported to Governor Miro that Taski Etoka, Chinubbee's predecessor as Minko, had been complaining about the high prices of Spanish goods and the low values given for Chickasaw furs. American traders, Taski Etoka informed the Spanish official, had already entered Chickasaw territory, offering "all the goods he might want" in exchange for a treaty with the Chickasaw. Economic considerations were a key factor in Chickasaw diplomacy.[18]

By 1790, the Chickasaw were hoping to avoid dependence on either the Americans or the Spanish. Meanwhile, in the absence of trade, Doughty informed his superiors, "I am led to believe that the Chickasaws & Choctaws are really in a very distressed situation."[19] In particular, they faced increased hostility from their neighbors the Creek, who wanted the Chickasaw to join with them in forming a confederation to fend against American incursions into southern Indian Territory. Unlike the Creek, however, who were pressured by American settlers on the western frontier of Georgia, the Chickasaw were buffered from direct encroachment by Americans by their advantageous position along the Mississippi. Many among the Chickasaw, but especially Piominko, believed they had more to gain than to fear from the Americans, especially if American traders could offer abundant and cheap goods in exchange for Chickasaw deerskins. For the Chickasaw, obtaining frequent trade with either American or Spanish officials was important not only because of their desire for consumer goods but because they, like most southeastern Indians, had become dependent on European guns and gunpowder for warfare. This was hardly a new transition for the Chickasaw: throughout much of the seventeenth century, ending with the Yamasee War in 1715, the Chickasaw had dominated a regional trade in enslaved Indians because of their greater access to European guns through their alliance with the British. Many groups of southeastern Indians, particularly the Choctaw, had fallen victim to the much less numerous Chickasaw over several decades of raiding. After the Yamasee War, the trade in enslaved Indians declined but the necessity of being at least as well-armed as their neighbors had already become apparent to the Chickasaw.[20] By the 1790s, having access to guns and gunpowder was a necessary precondition to maintaining control over Chickasaw territory. Without the arms and ammunition that only trade could provide, the Chickasaw were vulnerable to both Indigenous and European American threats.

There were two causes of the Americans' failure to open trade with the Chickasaw. One cause was ongoing conflicts between the Chickasaw and the Kickapoo north of the Ohio and the Creek and Cherokee south of the Tennessee River, which made it dangerous for American traders to visit Chickasaw territory. A second arose from the same problem that had created issues for European American settlers in Kentucky: Americans' lack of access to the Mississippi. While the Chickasaw could direct the flow of traffic along the river, the Spaniards could keep Americans from navigating the lower part of the river, especially the approach to New Orleans. "As long as the Spaniards continue their present System of Monopoly & their Embarrassment in trade," Doughty informed Secretary of War Henry Knox, it would be impossible for an individual trader to establish a prosperous firm near the Chickasaw. Instead, Doughty advocated for the creation of a military-style trading post on the east side of the Ohio, below the mouth of the Tennessee, that could serve as depot for trade with the Indigenous peoples living on the cluster of rivers that ran together in the region. Without such a fort, "there is no Trader that will support [the trade] in competition with Spaniards." While Doughty believed that "the American Merchant of Capital will be able to undersell the Spaniards," as goods purchased in Philadelphia and shipped across the Appalachians and down the Ohio were still cheaper than purchasing goods brought upriver from New Orleans, the Spaniards would have a clear advantage on the return journey laden with the primary element of Indigenous-American trade—pelts. Spanish merchants could bring large cargoes of fur to New Orleans, where they could be shipped out to the Atlantic world. But with the river closed, American merchants would need to bring their "remittances up the Mississippi & Ohio and then to Baltimore or Philadelphia," a lengthy journey that would "destroy all Prospect of Profit to the trader."[21] A trading fort, subsidized by the federal government, could help to offset these disadvantages by allowing traders to operate closer to American settlements in Cumberland and Kentucky. The prospect of the enormous profits to be made by an individual who could capitalize on the location to serve communities north, south, east, and west of the Ohio River would make the trade both more secure and more lucrative for the trader.

For both the Americans and the Chickasaw, the creation of greater trade connections would serve their respective interests. While Doughty acknowledged that he was "far from proposing [that] the Profits of [the] Trade" from a centralized trading post were "any great national Object to my Country," his proposal nevertheless "deserve[d] their Attention as a political Engine giving [the United States] a concomitant Influence [as the Spanish] over the Savages who, if brought against us, can only be subdued at the Expence of much Blood & Treasure." For Piominko, establishing a trading post would create the ability to continue to play the Americans off against the Spanish while also giving the Chickasaw a strategic advantage in their ongoing contests with the Kickapoo, Creek, and Cherokee. For his part, Doughty recognized that the Chickasaw could be used as an ally against both Spanish and Indigenous threats in the Mississippi Valley. Enroute to the Chickasaw, Doughty and his men were attacked by a Cherokee patrol on the Tennessee River. The United States would benefit from receiving Chickasaw support against the threat posed by the Cherokee to American interests in the Tennessee Valley.[22]

By the mid-1790s, the Chickasaw relationship with the United States had grown increasingly strong as a result of relationships nurtured by Piominko. In 1791, in response to a request from the War Department, Piominko led a group of forty or fifty warriors to join U.S. forces under Arthur St. Clair in fighting against the Northern Confederacy in the Ohio Country, an act intended to demonstrate the friendship of the Chickasaw to the Americans in hopes of future military aid in their own contests against the Creek and Cherokee. Immediately dispatched to act as scouts, the Chickasaw troops, including Piominko and two other prominent leaders, William and George Colbert, were not present at the battle that became known as St. Clair's defeat, an unmitigated disaster for the American army. In recognition of their service, Piominko and the Colberts each received a handsome military uniform and a large silver medal.[23]

By 1793, the Chickasaw were facing their own disaster, as crop failures and an escalation of conflict with the Cherokee and Creek threatened the Chickasaw with starvation. Piominko appealed for relief to General James Robertson, the founder of Nashville who in 1792 was appointed by territorial governor William Blount as the first U.S. Chickasaw agent. In addition to food, Piominko requested the Americans send him ammunition, guns, powder, flint, lead, and heavy arms that could be used to guard recently fortified Chickasaw settlements. In a letter from Piominko that Robertson forwarded on to President Washington, Piominko reminded the Americans that it was "on [their] account that the [Chickasaw were] struck, for the last talk sent to us by the Creeks, when we told them we were perfect friends with the United States and would listen to no talk of war against them their [the Creek] answer was, the Virginians [Americans] were liars ... that the Chickasaws were fools not to join all other Indians to cut off the Virginians, and that the Chickasaws would know their error before long, as they, the Creeks, and Northwards, would fall on them."[24] Robertson emphasized this point in the letter he sent to accompany Piominko's request for aid, reminding the president that the Chickasaw and their Choctaw neighbors were the United States' only Indian allies. If the "Chickasaw and Choctaws have been persuaded to have joined" the emerging Southern Confederacy being spearheaded by Alexander McGillivray of the Creek, "all the Indians between the Mississippi and the Apalachian mountain, would have been at war with the United States."[25]

The Chickasaw Bluffs

After the Revolution, the Chickasaw continued to use control of the Chickasaw Bluffs to negotiate improved access to trade goods as the Americans and Spanish jockeyed with one another to convince the Chickasaw to allow them access to the site. As early as 1782, Governor Miró proposed building a fort at the bluffs to "protect the navigation" on the Mississippi.[26] In 1786, an exploratory party of Americans from the Cumberland district examined the bluffs, but the threat of violence kept them from remaining permanently. In late 1792, Miró's replacement as the governor of Louisiana, Francisco Luis Héctor, Baron de Carondelet, tried to persuade the Chickasaw to allow Spain to place a fort on the bluffs in exchange for constructing a trading post there as well.[27] In part, Carondelet was acting in response to the delivery at the Chickasaw Bluffs of food and ammunition to Piominko from the U.S. government. To Carondelet, the Chickasaw receiving presents from the United States at the bluffs was a precursor to the construction of an American trading house at the site. To offset this eventuality, the Spanish deployed an enlarged fleet of river galleys along the Mississippi but also increased their efforts to persuade the Chickasaw to allow them to construct a trading post and fort in their territory. For their part, the Chickasaw had no intention of allowing the Americans or the Spanish to build a post at the bluffs. They instructed the Spanish to construct a post along the Yazoo River, some thirty leagues to the south. As for the possibility of an American settlement at the bluffs, Ugulayacabé promised the Spanish that he would either "die or drive the Americans from Chickasaw Bluffs."[28]

In the early 1790s, both the Chickasaw and the Spanish feared an American invasion of the lower Mississippi Valley, and particularly of the bluffs. In early 1795, the state of Georgia approved the Yazoo Act, placing more than 40 million acres of land between the Appalachians and the Mississippi up for sale, and dispatched four commissioners to Spanish territory to inform European American settlers that they now fell under a new jurisdiction. While the Yazoo Act completely ignored the claims of the region's current residents, both Indigenous and European American, it demonstrated the growing self-confidence of Americans interested in speculating in the lands of the lower Mississippi Valley, adding new strength to Spanish fears of a possible settlement at the site and greater urgency to Spanish appeals to the Chickasaw to let them create a fort on the bluffs. The Spanish were also concerned by what seemed to be growing friendship between Piominko's faction of the Chickasaw and the U.S. government. In 1794, Piominko had led a delegation of nearly twenty chiefs to Philadelphia to meet with President Washington. In that meeting, Piominko secured a commitment from the U.S. government to preserve the boundaries of Chickasaw territory and to keep Americans from purchasing Chickasaw land, effectively canceling the Yazoo Act.[29] In 1795, a branch of the Chickasaw led by William Colbert proposed the construction of a joint Chickasaw-American fort along the Tennessee River to protect both the Chickasaw and the Cumberland settlers to the north from possible attacks by the Cherokee and Creek.[30]

For the Chickasaw, the situation was complicated by the resumption of war with the Creek and violent incidents with the Cherokee, which threatened to become war. To fight either group, the Chickasaw would need guns and ammunition that they could receive only from Spanish or American sources. While Piominko and the Colberts gambled on a relationship with the United States as the best chance for protecting Chickasaw interests, Ugulayacabé continued to see the Spanish as the nation's best ally. In both cases, however, the Chickasaw were becoming ever more worried about the dual problems of violence and land encroachment.

On May 30, 1795, after years of intensive negotiations, the Chickasaw finally agreed to the proposed Spanish fort on the Chickasaw Bluffs. Don Manuel Gayoso de Lemos, the governor of Natchez, took possession of the bluffs for Spain, promising Ugulayacabé that Spain was not claiming the land for itself; rather, it proposed to build a fort on the site that would be "for [the Chickasaw's] benefit as well as that of the Spanish nation." He promised Ugulayacabé that the fort would be well-armed and fortified, in order to protect against a concerted American attack. On June 20, Ugulayacabé returned to the site with a delegation of fellow

Chickasaw chiefs to solidify the exchange. As Piominko had insisted to American officials nearly a decade earlier, the event was commemorated by drawing a map that detailed the cession. While Piominko, who objected to allowing a Spanish post at the site, informed Gayoso that "it is the voice of the whole Chickasaw Nation in general that you should leave the Chickasaw Bluffs as you found it, and return home to your own land immediately," a few members of his faction did attend the talks, which seemed, despite Piominko's arguments, to have widespread support among the Chickasaw. While the Spanish worked to hastily construct a fort, the assembled Chickasaw headmen inquired once more when a trading post would be built near their lands.[31]

News from Spain

IN SEPTEMBER 1795, American diplomats in Madrid brokered an agreement between the United States and Spain. Although Thomas Pinckney, the U.S. minister to England, ultimately led the final negotiations for the treaty, William Short, a protégé of Thomas Jefferson and the brother of a prominent Kentucky merchant and land speculator, spent more than two years negotiating with Spanish secretary of state Manuel Godoy y Álvarez de Faria to determine the boundary between the two empires in North America and to settle the issue of American claims to Mississippi trade. On his arrival in Spain in February 1793, Short had carried with him instructions issued by then-Secretary of State Thomas Jefferson that revealed the extent to which three years of western assertions of their right to Mississippi trade had been effective in influencing federal policy. Jefferson instructed Short to assert the United States' right to Mississippi trade as not only stemming from previous treaties but also on the basis of "The Law of Nature and of Nations." Citing natural rights theorists Hugo Grotius, Samuel von Pufendorf, and Emmerich Vattel, Jefferson echoed the political philosophy emerging from Kentucky, claiming that "if we appeal to [the Law of Nature and Nations], as we feel it written in the heart of man, what sentiment is written in deeper characters, than that the Ocean is free to all men, & the Rivers to all their inhabitants?" None, according to Jefferson. The rights of the inhabitants upriver to the "innocent passage" through the river where it passed through Spanish lands were based "on the ... natural relations [of] the soil & water." According to Jefferson, the right to Mississippi navigation was "as real as any other right however well defined." "Were it to be refused," "shackled by regulations not necessary for the peace or safety of its inhabitants," or "render[ed] . . . impracticable to us" by obstructionist actions on the part of Spain, the United States would have every right to "demand redress." Jefferson had come to agree with the westerners, asserting that "Spain does not *grant* us the navigation of the river. We have an inherent right to it."[32]

For two years, Short and his sickly co-negotiator, William Carmichael, had little luck in convincing Spain of the legitimacy of American claims to the Mississippi, despite the numerous arguments justifying those claims Jefferson had sent along to Short. Shifting European fortunes finally created an opening for the Americans to move the negotiations forward. In 1794, the army of revolutionary France had invaded northern Spain, and by 1795 the Spanish crown was eager to make peace with France. Yet the Spanish government knew that coming to terms with France would mean abandoning their 1793 alliance with Britain, which would inevitably lead Britain to declare war on Spain. When news arrived in Spain that the United States and England had concluded what would become known as Jay's Treaty, Spanish officials were eager to head off a possible military alliance between the United States and England. Suddenly, Godoy adopted a far more conciliatory attitude with the United States, and the decade of negotiations between the United States and Spain over the Mississippi and the American Southwest finally drew to a close.[33]

The Treaty of San Lorenzo, more commonly called "Pinckney's Treaty," surpassed Jefferson's and western settlers' wildest dreams: it opened the Mississippi to American trade, although the question of whether Spain acknowledged that the United States had a right to that trade remained unanswered. The treaty also ended the boundary dispute between the United States and the Spanish empire. Reversing the instructions the court had given to Gardoqui a decade earlier, the court of Spain agreed that the borders between the two empires would fall at the 31st parallel, the line the United States had agitated for since 1783, and which fell far to the south of the border Spain claimed by right of conquest. Pinckney's Treaty was, on paper at least, all that those Americans who had gambled on western lands could possibly have hoped for. The day news of the treaty arrived in Lexington, the "general joy of all ranks and descriptions of citizens, was never so conspicuous as on the . . . occasion; of which, the firing of artillery, tolling of bells, bonfires &c. &c. were evident testimonies!"[34]

On that Fourth of July 1796, the settlers of Kentucky, the United States' westernmost citizens, raised their glasses in sixteen toasts in honor of the sixteen states of the union—of which Kentucky was one. They drank not only to "The Patriots of 1776" but also to "The Spanish Treaty." They looked forward to a bright future, in which "agriculture and her handmaiden commerce" would assure "equal liberty through the world."[35] Access to trade and the pursuit of "liberty"—at least for white people—had become synonymous.

Word of the treaty garnered a very different reception in Chickasaw country. The Chickasaw response was universal outrage. A Spanish official reported that when the news arrived in the Chickasaw villages, they did "a thousand crazy things in the nation." The Spanish flag was torn down and stomped into the earth.[36] Ugulayacabé, accompanied by a hundred of his followers, visited the site of the recently constructed fort in December 1796. "We have seen the treaty; it has been read to us in our nation," Ugulayacabé informed the Spanish commandant on the bluffs where once, centuries earlier, his ancestors had rowed out to the middle of the Mississippi to destroy Hernando de Soto's forces. "We see," he accused, "that our [Spanish] Father not only abandons us like small animals to the claws of tigers and the jaws and wolves but encourages these same wolves to devour us." The Americans, he reminded the Spanish, were daily penetrating further into Chickasaw lands, competing with them for pelts and putting pressure on them to cede territory. "Do you believe, brother, that we do not see this? We have hearts to feel, eyes to see, ears to hear." The Americans have "the cunning of a rattlesnake that caresses the squirrel in order to devour it ... and no doubt in time will take this land as theirs and [all of] ours as well."[37]

The new territorial boundaries of the United States now encompassed all the lands of the Chickasaw, which Piominko had so carefully marked on his map in 1786. Although Spanish officials in the Mississippi Valley promised to support the Chickasaw and their interests, they were nearly as outraged as the Chickasaw at the terms of the treaty, which undid more than a decade of diplomatic maneuvering in the region. Madrid had consulted neither its representatives along the Mississippi nor its Indigenous allies as it once more redrew lines on parchment that would have real consequences for peoples thousands of miles away. The geopolitical calculus of inter-imperial negotiations that had guided Chickasaw actions for nearly two decades was at an end.

In 1796, Piominko traveled to Philadelphia accompanied by a delegation that consisted of not only fellow Chickasaw leaders, including George Colbert, but also representatives of the Choctaw, Cherokee, and Creek. Such a journey would have been nearly unthinkable only eighteen months prior. In April 1795, Creek soldiers had attacked Chokka' Falaa', Piominko's village, where they found the Chickasaw reinforced by a hundred Anglo-American volunteers from the Cumberland district and by a four-pound cannon given to the Chickasaw by the Americans in 1793. A second Creek attack in September was even more consequential, as Chickasaw troops under George Colbert had again driven off the Creek. Exhausted by the ongoing warfare, both sides agreed to a truce, ending the war along the Chickasaw's eastern border and drawing a decade of war and near-warfare to a close.[38]

In Philadelphia, while on a state-arranged visit to the Peale Museum, the delegation encountered another diplomatic party: leaders of the Northern Confederacy, including members of the Shawnee, Miami, Ojibwa, and Pottawatomi, who were also in the city meeting with President George Washington and Secretary of War James McHenry. A decade prior, envoys from the Northern Confederacy had journeyed south to convince the southwestern Indians to join them in fighting the Americans; they had found a receptive audience among all but the Chickasaw. Now, the Northern Confederacy itself had been defeated, badly beaten at the Battle of Fallen Timbers in 1794.

The visit to the museum turned into an impromptu summit, as many of the leaders of the largest tribes met together in council for perhaps the first time ever. For Washington and McHenry, the chance encounter offered an opportunity to meet with nearly all the Indigenous groups with whom the United States had either military, economic, or diplomatic relations all at once, far from the Indians' centers of power and their supporters. Amid a backdrop of the museum's portraits and natural history artifacts, many of which came from country claimed and frequented by the gathered Indigenous groups and their ancestors, the unusual, and perhaps unprecedented, diplomatic event unfolded.[39] Near the end of the meeting, which focused on reducing hostility among the western tribes, Piominko rose to address those assembled around him. "The Red People have all finished their Talks," and they now agreed that "if any of their Blood is spilt, to enquire into the reason before they strike—by that means peace will be preserved."[40]

Only three months prior to the meeting at Peale's Museum, on August 3, 1796, the U.S. Congress had proclaimed the fully ratified Pinckney's Treaty to be in operation, profoundly shifting the balance of power in southern trans-Appalachia but also in the West more broadly. The southern Indians meeting with Washington, Knox, and their northern

MAP 2. In 1795, Spain and the United States signed the Treaty of San Lorenzo (Pinckney's Treaty). Spain recognized American claims to all territory north of the 31st parallel, a region that included both Natchez and the Chickasaw homeland. The treaty also reopened the Mississippi River to American trade.

counterparts confronted a transformed political landscape. In the North, the Northern Confederacy's loss at Fallen Timbers in August 1794 and the passage of the Treaty of Greenville, which ceded Indian lands in the Ohio Valley to the United States, marked the beginning of a world transformed, a process accelerated by the terms of Jay's Treaty, in which Britain finally withdrew from its western posts. Southern Indians too confronted a new world. As a condition of Pinckney's Treaty, Spain agreed to withdraw as an imperial force in much of southern trans-Appalachia, a condition that weakened the Indians politically and militarily in their dealings with the U.S. government. Pinckney's Treaty also violated several diplomatic agreements between the Spanish and the Chickasaw, Creek, Talapuche, Alibamon, Choctaw, and Cherokee, ceding lands to the United States that Spain had promised to protect. All the lands that in 1786 Piominko had so carefully traced on his map were now claimed by the United States and confirmed by Spain. Piominko was aware of all of this as he spoke to the assembled crowd at Peale's Museum. As the leader of the only group that had fought alongside American warriors and supported American interests in trans-Appalachia, Piominko recognized these changes and their likely consequences. Already, "the Country [was] over-run" by white people. In order for peace to last, they would need to be constrained in their actions against the other peoples in the region. Piominko closed the conference with a prediction. The Americans "will be apt, by their encroachments to do mischief," Piominko told his assembled audience. "This is all I have to say."[41]

PART III

Western Trade, Atlantic World, 1796–1803

―•―

B Y FALL 1795, the Washington administration had successfully resolved several longstanding issues with tremendous significance for trans-Appalachia. Although the Treaty of Paris of 1783 had transferred all the British posts south of the Great Lakes to the United States, the transfer did not occur until over a decade later, which allowed the British to monopolize the fur trade of the Great Lakes and to funnel clandestine support to members of the Northern Confederacy. In 1794, John Jay negotiated a treaty with England that, while widely unpopular, promised to finally transfer the posts to the United States. Jay's Treaty was a contributing factor in the Washington administration's accomplishing its second objective: ending the violence that had engulfed the region north of the Ohio River for the previous twenty years. Once Jay's Treaty was in place, the British withdrew their support from the regions Indigenous combatants. On August 20, 1794, Jay's diplomacy bore fruit when General Anthony Wayne defeated the Northern Confederacy at the Battle of Fallen Timbers. In August 1795, Wayne presided over treaty negotiations in which the region's Indigenous inhabitants agreed to cede what is now southern and central Ohio to the United States.[1]

Peace unleashed a tide of new settlement. New Jersey congressman-turned-land speculator John Cleves Symmes reported to a friend that "all Kentucky and the back parts of Virginia and Pennsylvania are running mad with expectations of the land office opening in this country—hundreds are running into the wilderness . . . locating and making elections of land."[2] Thousands of European Americans flooded westward to Ohio, while thousands more who had been relegated to tenancy in Kentucky abandoned their farms to seek independent proprietorships in Ohio.[3] To meet the demands of the incoming settlers and hoping to avoid the persistent issues of squatters' taking residence on federal land, in 1796 the government established two new land offices, one in Pittsburgh and one in Cincinnati, which joined a preexisting office located in Marietta, along the Ohio River. Yet without market access, the new arrivals lacked the means to pay for western land. The treaty with Spain, completed in October 1795, offered a path forward. The federal government, land speculators, and western settlers could finally hope to transform western land into cash. After the treaty's enactment in spring 1796, land speculator John Graham of Richmond, Virginia, reported to his business partner that he expected "the Spanish Treaty must have a good effect [on land prices] as it will greatly encourage emigration from the Eastern States." Graham's enthusiasm was well warranted: between 1795 and 1796, the value of Graham's lands north of the Ohio increased dramatically, rising from one dollar per acre to four.[4] Just as in Kentucky, land values in the Northwest Territory were tied to access to the Mississippi River.

Like frontier Kentucky, the economy of the Ohio Country was based on land, but the land market north of the Ohio looked radically different from its southern counterpart. In the Northwest Territory, the market for land was dominated by a small group of large land companies and a cadre of surveyor-speculators who held smaller, but nevertheless impressive, tracts across the region. Beginning in 1787, the federal government sold millions of acres of land in the Northwest Territory at a steep discount to private organizations. The first of these land-speculating organizations was the Ohio Company of Associates, a group of New England veterans who formed a joint colonization-speculation land venture. Several members of the conglomerate were also part of the far more secretive Scioto Land Company, which would fail spectacularly a few years later. The third large land company, the Miami Company, was spearheaded by former congressional delegate John Cleves Symmes and made up primarily of investors from the mid-Atlantic region, many of whom were from Symmes's home state of New Jersey.[5] Paying for the land using depreciated government currency and generous credit, the proprietors of the Ohio, Scioto, and Miami Companies claimed millions of acres of the Northwest Territory, at the rate of about ten cents per acre. All of this land was subject to the federal survey, which broke up the western landscape into neat, easily locatable parcels. The one region where this did not hold true was in the Virginia Military District (VMD). Lying between Symmes's purchase and the Ohio Company's lands, the VMD was a region of more than 4 million acres that the federal government set aside to allow Virginia to fulfill the promises it had made to those who had enlisted during the Revolution. In the VMD, the land market closely resembled Kentucky's. The region was excluded from the orderly survey that parceled out land elsewhere in the Northwest Territory; within the VMD, surveyors used the metes and bounds system that had caused so much confusion south of the Ohio. Moreover, absentee speculators were able to attain large amounts of land in the district by purchasing land warrants issued to veterans who lived on the Atlantic side of the Appalachians. Thus, like many other regions of the West, the VMD was subject to a double speculation, first in Virginia land warrants and then through the hope that land values in the region would rise as settlement grew.[6]

By 1795, a new market in Ohio lands was emerging that differed in substantial ways from previous distribution systems. From the beginning of white settlement in the region, land companies and the federal government centralized the distribution of land in the Northwest Territory. In Ohio, land speculators had to compete with the federal government to attract purchasers for their lands. To compete, speculators had to be willing to retail land in small quantities to individual purchasers, something the federal government was not yet willing to do in the 1790s. Speculators also needed to extend credit to purchasers, a practice the government initially resisted. Because land speculators had to compete with federal land sales, they tended to offer greater flexibility than landowners elsewhere, and land purchasers operated from a position of greater power.[7] Speculators' relatively generous policies, coupled with federal surveying practices that offered greater security of land titles, tended to make Ohio an attractive place for settlers seeking land. For their part, eastern investors took note of the sudden popularity of Ohio Country lands. Large numbers of new speculators, content to hold western lands for a few years until the increase in settlement raised their value, purchased their first lands in the Northwest Territory between 1795 and 1796.

In 1796, the speculators received a boost from the passage of a new land law. The Land Act of 1796 responded to frontier settlers' protests at the government's longstanding policy of selling land only in the six-mile square divisions known as townships, which, at two dollars an acre, were far too expensive for almost any private purchaser. The new law authorized the sale of land in more reasonable 640-acre parcels but set the price for western lands at a minimum of two dollars per acre. For the first time, though, the federal government extended credit to the public. Land claimants were required to provide a 5 percent downpayment at the moment of purchase; they then had a year to repay the remaining 95 percent of the purchase price. Initially, land speculators had good reason to hope that the new law would help them compete favorably with federal land sales. As most land companies had used discounted government paper to purchase their lands for pennies on the dollar, they could afford to offer lands at a price much lower than two dollars an acre, and many offered much more extensive credit.[8]

The speculative frenzy in Ohio lands came to a halt in February 1797, when the Bank of England suspended specie payments, an act with tremendous consequences for the economy of the United States, including the Northwest Territory. The bank's actions triggered a curtailment of credit and the onset of the "Panic of 1797," which ushered in a substantial downturn in the American economy. Speculators who only a year earlier had been eager to purchase Ohio lands now became eager to sell them, sometimes in parcels as small as fifty acres. Desperate to obtain payment immediately, some speculators turned to leasing as a means of generating income from their holdings. Increasingly, credit played a significant role in the sale of lands. Settlers purchasing lands from speculators typically paid from one-quarter to one-half the asking price as a down payment, with the remaining balance due over the course of several years. Frontier speculator Nathaniel Massie, who owned more than 65,000 acres in the VMD, typically required payment within twelve to twenty-four months.[9]

Because of the cash scarcity in frontier Ohio, speculators were often willing to accept payment in agricultural commodities. Symmes advertised that "clean wheat and rye may be delivered ... in payment of any debt due him on bond, note, or contract," at the rate of five shillings to a bushel, while in 1800 Robert McClure offered "for sale eighty-three acres of excellent first rate Land" in exchange for "good merchantable flour."[10] Animals, both dead and alive, were also used as a medium for acquiring lands. In 1801, Thomas McDonald offered to sell his land on Water Street in Cincinnati in exchange for "one third in cash down, and the balance in six months, payable either in young horses or cattle."[11] For his part, Symmes was willing to accept "cows under seven years old," as well as "young cattle" as settlement for any debt, including for land, while Massie coordinated for an associate to accept pork in exchange for land in 1801.[12] Small tracts, noncash payments, and the use of credit benefited potential purchasers over speculators. Meanwhile, men like Massie, McClure, and Symmes acquired large quantities of goods that needed to be sold in order to be translated into cash.

Speculators were willing to accept noncash payments for several reasons. The need to repay their own debts was paramount. Many of Ohio's largest land speculators held tens or even hundreds of thousands of acres of land in the region, much of it purchased on credit and with payments having already fallen due.[13] Their need for cash increased in 1798 when the territorial government enacted a land tax. The law required every landowner to bring a detailed list of all the lands they claimed within the territory to county commissioners, who would then divide the land into three classes—first rate, second rate, or third rate. Each class of land was taxed at a different rate: eighty-five, sixty, and twenty-five cents per a hundred acres respectively. If landowners failed to pay the tax, county sheriffs were authorized to hold a public auction to sell as much of the land as was necessary to pay the required tax.[14] For cash-poor farmers, who could not afford the $1,280 required to purchase federal land in the 640-acre townships dictated by the Land Act of 1796, the new territorial tax presented an opportunity to purchase far smaller lots of land for far less cash. For instance, in January 1800, the newspaper the *Western Spy* listed lands owned by seventeen individuals to be sold for unpaid taxes for as low as five dollars.[15] In the VMD, nonresident speculators felt the new tax law keenly: in 1802, 1,900 separate parcels of land with delinquent taxes were advertised for sale.[16] Given speculators' needs for immediate cash, by 1800 potential land purchasers in the Ohio Country faced a buyer's market, with multiple options for obtaining land.

The enactment of the Land Act of 1800 changed the market for land in the Northwest Territory once more. The act was driven by westerners' demands for changes to federal land policy. It reduced the amount of land settlers were required to purchase to 320 acres but kept the purchase price at $2 an acre. The law's major innovation, though, was the extension of far more generous credit.[17] Purchasers were required to pay an initial deposit of one-twentieth the value of the land on entry, with a second payment of the balance of one-fourth of the purchase price due within forty days. Then, the purchaser owed an additional fourth of the purchase price after two, three, and four years.[1] However, if at the end of five years they had failed to pay the total amount, they forfeited both the land and the cash they had paid to date. The government's offering of credit gave would-be purchasers the ability to obtain land for a small amount of cash upfront and then use the land to generate the money they required to pay off the balance. The act led to a renewed boom of land sales in the Ohio Country. In May 1801, the newly opened land office in Chillicothe sold over 99,000 acres of land, more than twice the total amount of land the entirety of the federal government had sold between 1787 and 1798.[18] With the federal government now offering generous terms, speculators scrambled to compete. To do so, they sold already cleared land and smaller parcels of unimproved land, or offered even more generous credit terms. They also continued accepting payment in produce.

Speculators' drive for cash, coupled with the Land Act of 1800, directly connected the purchase of Ohio lands with Mississippi River trade. Because settlers needed cash to pay the federal government, they had no choice but to focus on market relations from the moment they left the land office.[19] Local markets were difficult to come by. By 1800, the army was scattered, and although new arrivals streamed into the Ohio Valley, they did not bring sufficient cash to allow earlier purchasers to redeem their lands. Exporting marketable commodities, especially flour, whiskey, and pork, became the primary mechanism that would allow Ohio settlers to secure their lands.[20] Because speculators had been forced to accept produce in payment for lands, many of them accumulated large stores of commodities they needed to deliver to market in order to repay their own creditors and avoid defaulting on their taxes.[21] Land speculators had no choice but to partner with the region's merchants. Profiting from land required participating in trade.

In 1797, just as Pinckney's Treaty was being put into action, events on the international stage created new markets for Ohio Valley produce. In August 1796, Spain and France signed the Second Treaty of San Idelfonso, establishing an alliance between the two nations and jointly declaring war on Britain. The ongoing warfare in Europe spilled over to the Americas as European powers fought for supremacy on both land and sea. The mass mobilization of troops in Europe disrupted European food production, while the ongoing warfare disrupted trade. For the Spanish colonies in the Caribbean, a poor harvest in 1797 and repeated bouts of destructive hurricanes created near-starvation conditions. Hoping to avoid widespread famine, Spain opened its colonial ports to neutral shipping. With most of Europe at war, the United States emerged as the principal neutral carrier, carrying European manufactures to American ports and then reexporting them, along with foodstuffs, to ports across the Caribbean and Central and South America.[22] Smuggling, which had already been rampant, became legitimate trade and grew rapidly. For the farmers of the Ohio Valley, the European war created new opportunities. By 1801, ninety thousand barrels of American flour arrived in New Orleans and was exported to the Caribbean and to European ports.[23]

From 1797 to 1802, Pinckney's Treaty shaped western trade. In February 1802, Nathaniel Massie prepared to ship pork he had received in payment for land to New Orleans. His cargo of "ninety three barrels of pork and four of hog lard" was to be carried to Natchez, or if it could not be sold to advantage there, onto New Orleans. Massie hoped that Mississippi trade would help him finally achieve a profit from the 65,000 acres of Ohio land he claimed. He told his agent to sell each barrel of pork for no less than ten dollars at Natchez or twelve dollars in New Orleans. If the sale was successful, it would provide Massie with some much-needed cash to pay his taxes on Ohio land, facilitating the rapid expansion of the United States across trans-Appalachia.[24]

The passage of Pinckney's Treaty created new trade opportunities for the residents of the Ohio and Mississippi Valleys. In the Ohio Country, in Natchez, and in New Orleans, the trading patterns developed in the late 1790s would usher in profound consequences for people throughout the Atlantic world. As Massie's pork traveled downriver, it was joined by Pennsylvania flour and Kentucky whiskey. The addition of cotton, which had recently been adopted by planters in Tennessee and Natchez, further elevated the importance of this trade. Meanwhile, merchants at Natchez and in New Orleans received the river's cargo and arranged for its sale and passage to distant shores, while merchants in New York, Philadelphia, Havana, and Liverpool tracked the prices of commodities along the Mississippi. Meanwhile, the cash generated by Mississippi trade became increasingly important to both westerners and coastal merchants, and, perhaps more surprisingly, to the Chickasaw, who remained an important component of Mississippi River trade. As western produce poured into New Orleans, a growing number of Americans came to question the feasibility of relying on Spanish cooperation in conducting trade of such magnitude. In 1802, when Spain once more closed the Mississippi to American trade, the consequences of that decision, as well as the anger it generated, reverberated nationwide.

7

Cotton and the Americanization of Natchez

———•◆•———

In April 1797, Andrew Ellicott, the American official dispatched to Natchez to survey the new boundary between the United States and Spain, wrote to his superiors expressing his fears over the ongoing delay in transferring the region north of the 31st parallel to the United States. "I am now convinced," Ellicott informed Secretary of State Timothy Pickering, "that every impediment, that can be devised, & all the art, and duplicity that can be exercised, will be made use of by the officers of the Crown of Spain, to prevent the late treaty, being carried into effect." Six months had already passed since the date designated by the treaty for the handover of the territory. Ellicott had first become suspicious of the behavior of Spanish officials he met as he descended the Mississippi earlier that winter. The commandant of New Madrid had urged Ellicott, who was proceeding southward with all possible haste, to remain as his guest at the post for several weeks, while the commandant of the Spanish fort at the Chickasaw Bluffs, which was supposed to be turned over to the United States by the terms of the treaty, denied any knowledge of the treaty's existence.[1] Once Ellicott arrived at Natchez, he received excuse after excuse for why the new boundary could not be surveyed. His suspicions, already heightened, became a certainty: Spain had no intention of turning over Natchez.

Don Manuel Gayoso de Lemos, a career diplomat appointed governor of the Natchez district in 1787, led the Spanish fight to retain Natchez as well as the other western posts ceded to the United States by the terms of Pinckney's Treaty. By 1796, the town included two interdependent communities. On top of the bluff stood the Spanish fort, surrounded by the sprawling landholdings of Natchez planters. A single, narrow road snaked down the face of the cliff to the community at the base of the hill. "Natchez-under-the-Hill," as the collection of shops, stores, warehouses, and taverns between the base of the bluff and the shores of the Mississippi was known, would later become one of the most notorious cesspools of vice in the trans-Appalachian West, but it was also one of the major emporiums of western trade.[2] Unlike most of the European American communities in Louisiana, Natchez had few French families. Most residents were former British subjects who had settled in the region before the Revolution, Loyalists who had fled to British territory during the war, or former residents of the thirteen states who had chosen to take advantage of Spain's generous immigration policies. By 1796, the introduction of cotton cultivation was transforming the community of Natchez. The transfer of the region to the United States accelerated the pace of change.

The Americanization of Natchez involved much more than flying the stars and stripes over the former Spanish fort. Natchez became ever more integrated into Mississippi River trade. Its docks served two markets. First, merchants at this southernmost point of American trade facilitated the cross-border transportation of Ohio Valley produce. Natchez merchants disrupted but then organized the flow of produce from the Ohio Valley, facilitating the complicated process of importing goods to New Orleans and then exporting them throughout the Atlantic world. The second market was found in Natchez proper as cotton production became the region's premier crop.

Revolutionary Changes

BETWEEN 1784 and 1795, Spanish officials attracted American settlers by offering generous land grants to those who were willing to swear their allegiance to the crown of Spain. They confirmed British land grants to their current holders and eliminated an importation tax on enslaved Africans. Unusually within the Spanish empire, the Spanish government decided to allow Protestants to practice (privately) within their territory. By 1786, the population of Natchez was around two thousand people—of whom about nine hundred were enslaved. After James Wilkinson's visit in 1787, the town grew even more rapidly as Spanish officials adopted Wilkinson's proposals for attracting new emigrants. Americans arriving in the district who swore their allegiance to Spain received full political and civil rights, as well as the ability to import their own belongings, including goods intended for sale or export, creating a loophole that allowed some westerners like Andrew Jackson to subvert the Spanish ban on trade along the Mississippi.[3]

Generous Spanish land grants and the prospect of fortunes to be made in tobacco held out a potent lure to Anglo-American families contemplating western migration. In contrast to the policy of preemption prevalent in Kentucky and the Cumberland, would-be landowners in Natchez had neither surveyor nor entrance fees to pay to obtain legal title to a tract of land. The Spanish government did place certain conditions on obtaining title: in addition to swearing allegiance to the crown, Spanish policy dictated the owner had only a limited time to settle or the land reverted to the government. Moreover, the title remained in the crown's hands for three years after the grant was made. During that time, the settler could use the land but he or she could not sell it. The intention of this policy was to avoid the land speculation that had proved so common throughout the British colonies and in the American West.[4]

Because the Spanish offered land based on the size of an arriving household, Natchez attracted a disproportionate number of elite settlers who arrived with numerous enslaved people. Forcibly transporting enslaved people into the district offered white settlers three advantages. Because larger households received more land, transporting enslaved people multiplied the wealth of enslavers. Increased access to labor allowed enslavers to rapidly clear and plant the land with both subsistence and staple crops. Finally, enslavers used the bodies of enslaved people to transfer wealth from the eastern states to Spanish Natchez. Would-be colonists arriving from the new United States were allowed to import enslaved people free of charge, and enslaved people were always in demand in the slave-dependent staple crop economy of Natchez. An enslaved person purchased in Virginia or South Carolina could be sold for a profit in Natchez, or the person could be used to make the fertile topsoil of the lower Mississippi profitable.

Despite its small population, Natchez had outsized importance within the Mississippi Valley. Louisiana had never been a profitable colony, not to the French in their five decades of control of the region, nor to the Spanish who followed them. But following the American Revolution, Spanish authorities envisioned an expansive and flourishing region encompassing Natchez and West Florida. In 1789, they acknowledged the importance of Natchez by appointing Gayoso to serve as the district's governor. He was an excellent choice to govern an English-speaking community within a Spanish-speaking entity. Educated at Westminster College, he was fluent in English and rapidly accepted by the elite within the Natchez community, connections Gayoso cemented when he married the daughter of a leading Anglo-American planter following the death of his first wife.[5]

Mississippi Valley residents took advantage of the fluid understanding of loyalty prevalent in Natchez. In 1789, after swearing his loyalty to the Spanish king, Andrew Jackson obtained land in the region and began a profitable business importing goods and enslaved people into the district. He also took advantage of the fact that Natchez lay outside American legal jurisdiction. In 1790, Jackson and his future wife, Rachel Donelson Robards, fled from the Cumberland district, attempting to escape from Rachel's husband, Lewis Robards, who had threatened to force her to return to live with him in Kentucky. As a legal resident of Natchez and a vassal of the king, Jackson placed Rachel outside of the jurisdiction of any American court, making it impossible for Robards to commence civil proceedings against her or compel her to return to her marital home. A year later, Andrew and Rachel began living together in Natchez as man and wife, and would later claim to have married in Natchez in 1791, despite the fact that Rachel was still legally married to Robards.[6] Although the details of their courtship and illicit relationship would prove to be among the most contentious issues in Jackson's later political career, his actions in 1790 were similar to those of many Americans who took advantage of the proximity of Spanish jurisdiction to avoid prosecution for a variety of crimes in the United States. In 1794, another fugitive from justice, David Bradford, arrived in Natchez fleeing western Pennsylvania, where he had been among the leaders of the Whiskey Rebellion. Although Spanish officials were reluctant to allow someone who had so prominently defied governmental authority to remain in the district, they did not extradite the Whiskey rebels back to the United States.[7]

Although Natchez's residents hailed from across the United States, most of the new settlers, like the Whiskey rebels and the Jacksons, came from western regions with easy access to the Mississippi. From February to July 1790, fifty-seven boats carrying new emigrants arrived in Natchez; fourteen came from Pennsylvania, two from Cumberland, and thirty-eight from Kentucky.[8] Although the Spanish hoped that the new settlers could form a barrier to western American settlement, the effect of Spain's generous land-granting policy tied the two regions ever closer together.

One factor driving emigration to Natchez was Spanish policy toward tobacco. Since Spain's takeover of Natchez in 1783, the Spanish government had annually purchased 2 million pounds of Louisiana tobacco at inflated prices in an effort to secure the loyalty of British and French residents. Under the subsidy system, the Spanish government purchased tobacco from planters and paid them in cash or in bills drawn on the royal treasury; in turn, the planters paid that cash to local merchants, who advanced them goods during the year. In 1790, the Spanish government cut costs and slashed the amount of its subsidy to forty thousand pounds, setting off a seven-year-long depression in Natchez. Planters found themselves without the cash they needed to pay off the debts they had accrued during the boom years. To stave off unrest, Spanish officials issued two three-year stays on debt execution. Although the region's planters attempted to adopt indigo to replace tobacco, pests and the ecological degradation caused by indigo processing made it less lucrative than the planters had hoped.[9]

The planters needed a replacement for tobacco, and they found it in cotton. Here was a crop that would "reward industry and enterprise," William Dunbar, an early settler of Natchez and a prominent member of the American scientific community, reminisced. When "the Cotton Plant was introduced" in Natchez, "the golden dreams of the most sanguine seemed likely to be realized."[10] Natchez planters' transition to cotton coincided with Eli Whitney's 1793 popularization of the cotton gin. In 1794, Natchez produced 36,251 pounds of cotton; within a year, the town produced 154,195 pounds.[11] By 1796, a public cotton gin operated within the town.[12] In June of that year, Governor Gayoso could report that "every individual in this Government [Natchez] is just now attending their crops of Cotton that promises very advantageously."[13] Natchez planters embraced the new crop wholeheartedly.

It was also in June that Gayoso received word of Pinckney's Treaty. A Kentucky barge landed at Natchez carrying the unbelievable news that Spain had ceded the town to the United States. Gayoso hurried to reassure the people that "such rumors" of an American cession "should not be given any credit until received from our Court," but it was not long before the arrival of additional boats carrying newspapers with the printed text of the treaty confirmed that Spanish Natchez was to become American.[14] The news threw Gayoso and the countryside into uncertainty. Residents wondered what their status would be if they chose to remain in the district; they worried that while the treaty specified Spanish troops and residents alike had six months to evacuate the territory, taking "with them all the goods and effects which they possess," the treaty failed to mention what would happen to their land—the basis of the local economy and its primary source of wealth.[15] Questions about how the region would be administered also caused consternation. Would Natchez become a federal territory, like the region north of the Ohio River, or would it fall under the aegis of an existing state such as Georgia, which had attempted to claim the area surrounding Natchez for more than a decade?

While the townspeople wondered, Gayoso fumed. Pinckney's Treaty overturned a decade of Spanish diplomacy in the Southwest and left the Spanish colonies open to imminent attack. In 1793, after years of negotiations, Gayoso had signed a treaty of "amity, alliance, and trade" with the Chickasaw, Choctaw, Cherokee, Creek, Tallapoosa, and Alabama, promising that Spain would never cede the Natchez district; in return, Spain's Indian allies promised peace. If Spain were to "now deliver [its forts] to the destroyers of the red men [the Americans] we shall manifest ourselves as [the Indians'] most inexorable enemies" and expose all of Spanish Louisiana to attack.[16]

Gayoso was also angry at what he saw as the Spanish government's lack of patience. For eight years, Gayoso had been in contact with several members of the Kentucky and Tennessee elite, crafting plans to separate the West from the rest of the union.[17] He viewed the Whiskey Rebellion and recent agitation against the federal government in Kentucky, Tennessee, and Pennsylvania as likely to trigger a massive change in the political situation of the western United States. "The discord which now reigns in the American States could bring about the separation of many of them, which particularly alters the political status of that country, and subsequently the causes upon which our Court based itself in order to complete the treaty," Gayoso informed his superiors, urging them to delay implementation of the treaty.[18] He believed that if Spain could just be patient, there would be no need to transfer the territory north of the 31st parallel to the United States because westerners would take it upon themselves to transfer a much larger region to Spanish sovereignty.

Invoking the doctrine of "obedezco pero no cumplo"—"I obey but I do not comply"—Gayoso refused to evacuate Natchez as ordered by the treaty. "The treaty gives place for interpretations and questions to our Court," he informed his superiors. Each question "requires seven months for a decision," an optimistically short timeframe for sending and receiving news from Europe, given the distance between Louisiana and Spain and the time attending any diplomatic negotiation. In the meantime, Gayoso would refuse to transfer the territory until he received a response from Madrid. Thus, he felt, "without exposing Spain to any ill results or hostilities of any consequence," he could "differ with the said delivery for a period of two or three years." Gayoso was convinced that "the indispensable delays, which ordinarily occur in the execution of treaties of this nature, will give ample time for the paternal intercession of His Majesty in favor of [the residents of Natchez]."[19]

It was not long before the Spanish government, both in Louisiana and Spain, came to agree with Gayoso. As the terms of Jay's Treaty became better known, Spain began to regret the generosity of its concessions to the United States. Manuel Godoy, Spain's chief negotiator, dubbed the "Principe de la Paz" for his role in ending Spain's war with revolutionary France, now wished to renegotiate the terms of the American treaty of friendship and commerce to better align with Spain's interests. Moreover, even as it ceded the Natchez district to the United States, Spain was simultaneously attempting to sell Louisiana to France. In February 1797, Gayoso received orders from Louisiana governor Carondelet not to evacuate the Spanish posts at Natchez and upriver. Spain's new official policy was to delay the execution of the treaty.[20]

The first American to recognize Spain's refusal to implement the treaty was Andrew Ellicott, the American official appointed to survey the boundary between the United States and Spain. A meticulous mathematician, the Quaker Ellicott was no diplomat; he was known for being intransigent and pigheaded.[21] In the years before being dispatched to mark the 31st parallel and the boundary between the United States and Spain, Ellicott had surveyed the border between New York and Pennsylvania and had completed the survey of the Mason-Dixon Line after Charles Mason and Jeremiah Dixon were forced to abandon the project due to violence on the frontier. More recently, Ellicott had carved the diamond that would become Washington, DC, from Maryland and Virginia.[22] With no diplomatic experience, Ellicott would prove an interesting choice for navigating the complicated relationship emerging between Spain and the United States along the new southwestern border.

In 1797, the United States and Spain engaged in a bloodless conflict for sovereignty over the Natchez district against the backdrop of the planting season. Ellicott arrived in the district only to find the Spanish firmly entrenched. Neither Spain nor the United States wanted to make the first move to instigate an armed conflict. Ellicott lacked the personnel to force Spain to concede the territory or to unilaterally begin surveying the boundary; it is doubtful that his superiors in Philadelphia would have supported him had he taken violent action. Gayoso too lacked the strength to evict arriving American forces. Although both countries jockeyed for position against one another, it was the planters and merchants of Natchez who would decide the region's fate.

Reacting to the tension, the townspeople grew increasingly factionalized. According to Ellicott, Natchez's residents fell into three groups. The largest group, comprising "seven eights of the Inhabitants," were "either Americans, or those warmly attached to the interest of the U.S." "*Secondly*," there were "Old British subjects," who, though not Americans, were "decidedly in favor of [the government] of the U.S." when contrasted with that of Spain. Finally, Ellicott granted, there were "about eight persons . . . who [were] attached to the Spanish Interest."[23] If violence broke out, Ellicott believed the populace would support the United States. Gayoso—at least in his official correspondence—disagreed: the population was content with Spanish governance and in fact preferred it to American rule. Gayoso described the people of Natchez as "His Majesty's subjects," who had "[run] away from a stormy government" (that of the young United States) "in order to join the just and always reliable one of Spain."[24] The truth was probably somewhere in the middle: for most of the white residents of Natchez, whichever government could secure their land titles, get their crops to market, and ensure the prosperity of the community was the one they would support.

Religion brought the unrest at Natchez to a head. On June 9, a Mr. Hannon, described by one Spanish officer as an "Anabaptist sectary," was arrested and placed by Gayoso in the "calaboose" for allegedly preaching to a large crowd at the American encampment, violating Spanish prohibitions on the public practice of Protestantism.[25] According to Spanish accounts, as Hannon was dragged to jail by a Spanish soldier, he attempted to escape to the American encampment. A mounted Spanish officer captured him, but Hannon continued to plead with the American troops for aid, crying, "Help me citizens of the United States."[26]

Hannon's arrest was the flashpoint that brought the conflict between Spain and the United States into the open. A series of depositions taken by the Spanish government make it clear that Hannon's sins extended beyond religious transgressions. Hannon had spent the evening of June 8 carrying a petition against Spanish rule from door to door, eventually fighting with a loyal Spanish subject who took offense. According to Hannon's own testimony, he had been "so drunk on June 9 that he did not recall what had happened."[27] Other accounts claimed that Hannon had quarreled with some local Catholics then precipitously gone before Gayoso and demanded immediate action against his attackers.[28] What actually transpired matters less than the symbolic importance of Hannon's arrest to the citizens of Natchez. On one hand, by preaching publicly Hannon had violated Spanish law. On the other, he had done so while preaching within the boundaries of the American camp, under the American flag, on territory that had been ceded by treaty.

Hannon's arrest proved the tipping point in the political stalemate at Natchez—the moment when, in the words of Spanish officer, "the sedition of the inhabitants of this district began in favor of the" Americans.[29] Within a day, the population armed itself and took to the streets. The revolt had neither leaders nor a clear goal. Some Natchez residents "were for immediately attacking the [Spanish] fort," thereby expelling the Spanish from the region; others proposed seizing the Spanish gunboats that patrolled the Mississippi and "making themselves masters of the river," as the Loyalists had done in 1783.[30] Residents laid siege to the Spanish officers and soldiers, who took refuge in the fort. Gayoso attempted to deploy the local militia, but only 18 men, out of a population of 853 eligible soldiers, responded to his call.[31] These eighteen, combined with forty-one soldiers and a drummer boy, embodied Spanish power within the district. Ellicott, along with a small contingent of American soldiers, did their best to stay out of the conflict, attempting to frame the event as a revolt of the people of Natchez against the Spanish rather than as a conflict between the United States and Spain. They knew they could ill-afford to be blamed if violence broke out.

Despite being outnumbered by the townspeople, Gayoso refused to surrender; on June 14, five days after Hannon's arrest, he issued a proclamation pardoning the population and assuring them that there would be no negative repercussions if they would disperse and lay down their arms. Privately, he also accused Ellicott of responsibility for the populace's actions. Although he couched his accusations in the language of diplomacy (and in the language of honor, personal as well as national), Gayoso warned Ellicott that if Ellicott were involved in encouraging the rebellion, he would "make [Ellicott] answerable for the fatal Consequence that may ensue."[32]

Except for the Spanish fort and the American encampment, by mid-June all of Natchez was in the hands of the townspeople. Bands of armed men patrolled the roads, controlling access to the fort. Gayoso meanwhile put his men to work strengthening the structure; he posted double guards around the perimeter and redeployed the cannons, aiming them away from the river and toward the mainland, and even going so far as to spike the fort walls with gunpowder.³³ Nevertheless, there was only one armed encounter during the standoff: a skirmish that took place near a watchtower that, like most of the Spanish armaments in the region, had fallen into disuse. A gang of armed residents fired on a Spanish patrol, but no one was injured.³⁴

Although Hannon's arrest was the impetus for the Natchez Rebellion, it was not the cause. Several other factors were at play. Throughout spring 1797, rumors flew through the town, some in favor of the Spanish government, some in favor of the American. To justify their refusal to enact the terms of the treaty and hand over Spain's forts along the Mississippi, Spanish officers claimed they feared a possible British invasion along the Mississippi. Rumors that the United States had declared war on France as a result of French depredations on American shipping and the affronts of the XYZ Affair also inspired Spanish resistance.³⁵

Many residents saw different motives in the Spanish officials' refusal to surrender the forts. Throughout the spring rumors circulated that the Spanish were refortifying in preparation for invading Natchez. Ominous rumors that the Spanish planned to engage Indigenous allies to attack Natchez further alarmed the populace. Longstanding supposition, borne out by historical evidence, that Spanish officials had supplied arms and ammunition to the Cherokee and Creek to attack American settlers in Tennessee gave added weight to talk of an impending invasion by a force of Spanish and Indian soldiers.³⁶ Natchez residents' fear grew when a party of Choctaw returning from the western side of the Mississippi arrived in the village on June 20.³⁷

The most alarming rumor circulating was that the Spanish planned to march north from New Orleans with an army "to be principally composed of negroes & free Molattoes" that would "put to the Sword all the American troops at this place, & hang such of the Inhabitants as appeared decidedly in favour of the U.S." Because most Natchez landowners were enslavers, the fear of an incipient slave rebellion engendered by Spanish actions, or even the rumors of the proposed invasion, spurred the white residents to resist Spanish rule.³⁸

The passage of Pinckney's Treaty and the advent of cotton culture had acted as a catalyst for the rapid growth of the enslaved population of Natchez. African slavery had long been a part of everyday life in the town. In 1768, when British settlers first founded the community on the ruins of the former French settlement, they immediately introduced enslaved African labor. In 1785, the population of Natchez consisted of 1,121 white residents and 438 enslaved men, women, and children; by 1795, the population of Natchez had grown to 3,548 white and 1,800 enslaved people.[39] Within the next year, the number of enslaved people in the district rose to 2,110, 40 percent of the total population.[40] Although 814 children constituted the largest category of the enslaved in Natchez, by 1795 there were also 804 enslaved adult men in the village. In contrast, there were only 162 enslaved adult women.[41]

The presence of so many young, enslaved men without families alarmed many white inhabitants, particularly amid rumors of an invading army composed of people of African descent. Fears of slave revolt were near constant in Natchez. In 1795, an abortive rebellion of the enslaved population of Pointe Coupée, about eighty miles south of Natchez, sparked panic among the town's white residents. Although the plan was quickly detected, fear lingered and spread, in part because several enslaved people from the Natchez area were implicated.[42] The planters of Natchez were also alarmed by the recent slave rebellion in St. Domingue. In 1791, the enslaved population of the French-controlled half of Hispaniola rose up against their enslavers, in the process shaking slave regimes across the Atlantic world. By 1797, many white refugees of the conflict had fled to Louisiana, forcing enslaved laborers to emigrate with them. Committed to white supremacy, the Anglo-American residents of Natchez feared the consequences of Spain's more relaxed attitude toward race.

The crisis over the transfer of Natchez began in early April, just as the cotton season got underway. Like every crop, cotton has its own rhythm, and cotton plantations developed their own distinctive labor regime. Preparation for cotton planting began early in the spring by readying the field for cultivation. Enslaved women and children would be sent to the field to beat down the previous year's crop before the men plowed the field; planting began in early April and might extend into mid-May. The growing cotton then needed to be hoed to keep it clear of weeds, thinned to promote growth, and plowed once more to mound soil around the plants' roots (a process referred to as "dirting" or "molding") before being hoed and thinned a second time, work that extended from mid-June until mid-July.[43] One of the advantages of cotton cultivation, from the perspective of planters, was that it interfered only minimally with the rhythms of corn cultivation, which allowed cotton plantations to help feed themselves and their livestock. Corn could even be left ripe in the field until after the cotton harvest, allowing planters to produce both crops simultaneously.

Nothing, not even harvesting the food that would see the population through the winter, was allowed to interfere with the cotton harvest. Cotton picking began in September, when the first bolls opened, and often continued into January. Enslaved men, women, and children worked from before dawn until dark to bring in the crop, picking more than a hundred pounds of cotton a day at the height of cotton season. The cotton was then brought to the gin house, where enslaved people too young or too old to work in the fields removed debris as the crop lay drying in the sun. Then the ginning began in earnest, either in a gin constructed on a planter's property or at a public gin, where the gin owner typically kept some portion of the cotton for himself in exchange for cleaning the crop.[44] In the 1790s, the cleaned cotton was stuffed into large bags, weighing between 250 and 350 pounds each. The bags were made of hempen canvas and sewed together with rope. Once the cotton was cleaned and bagged, it was ready to be exported to market.

By June 1797, when Hannon was arrested, the crops were well-established, and white residents were able to devote more of their time to politics. During a June 20 meeting at Belk's Tavern, the population of Natchez declared their neutrality from Spain and the United States, and elected a seven-member committee to administer the town and carry on negotiations among the townspeople, the American officials, and the Spanish crown.[45] On June 24, faced with summoning troops from New Orleans—and, in doing so, fulfilling the population's fears—Gayoso officially acknowledged the neutrality of the citizens of Natchez. It would be a year before Natchez would finally be incorporated into the United States, on April 7, 1798.[46]

Western Merchants and the Americanization of Natchez

In 1798, just as the Spanish were beginning to evacuate the region, Abijah Hunt arrived in Natchez. The Treaty of Greenville and Jay's Treaty had diminished the importance of the army north of the Ohio, and Congress reduced the army from 5,120 to 3,359 men while simultaneously deploying them over a larger area.[47] Newly acquired outposts at Michilimackinac, Detroit, and Niagara suddenly formed the northernmost edge of the United States' defenses. Cincinnati no longer functioned as the central waystation in trade between the settlers of Kentucky and a captive military market in Ohio. Moreover, in 1798, the U.S. Army reorganized how it supplied its troops, dividing trans-Appalachia into six districts, which merchants bid on to supply.[48] Soldiers, of course, had no choice in where they were transferred. When the army was subdivided, many of the soldiers and officers indebted to the Hunts departed for the Natchez district.

With his primary source of income marching off, Abijah proposed to his brother Jesse Hunt that they send "a quantity of goods" downriver, "for the purpose of trading with the army."[49] Although Jesse opposed the move, Abijah decided to open a new branch of the store, this time in Natchez. The timing seemed fortuitous: John Hunt had grown frustrated with sharing his profits with a partner who was seldom present, and he and Abijah were preparing to amicably part when news of the troops' transfer arrived. As Abijah made his way down the Ohio, he continued to operate a mobile store from his flatboat, retailing whiskey, brandy, linen, thread, bacon, and tea to the settlers and soldiers he encountered traveling south. Once arrived at Natchez, Hunt established a store where he sold, in the words of one historian of early Mississippi, "white hats and ladies' 'delicate shoes.'"[50] Just as he had in Cincinnati, Abijah also dealt heavily in western produce.

Merchants like the Hunts were central to the trade of trans-Appalachia both before and after Pinckney's Treaty, but especially once Natchez became a part of the United States. In addition to retailing goods and acting as linkages in a chain binding the West to consumers and producers throughout the Atlantic world, they also acted as brokers, gathering local produce and shipping it downriver to be sold. Although western farmers were eager for the opening of international markets, few were interested in becoming merchants themselves. Many farmers chose to sell their produce locally to firms like the Kentucky or Ohio Hunts, or to Deaderick and Foster, who advertised in western journals like the newly begun Nashville *Tennessee Gazette* that they were willing to accept "Cotton, Hemp, Tobacco, and Flour" in exchange for "a large and generous assortment of Merchandize." Alternatively, farmers could consign goods to men like Nashville's John Caffery, who in autumn of 1800 offered to freight produce to New Orleans and act on his customers' behalf in selling their goods in New Orleans in exchange for "five per cent on the [sale]."[51] While some farmers built their own boats and carried their produce of flour, salt pork, hemp, lard, bacon, tobacco, and whiskey downriver on their own, merchants rapidly came to dominate river trade. In return for agricultural products, merchants offered western patrons store goods, store credit, or notes, usually payable in four or five months. Western merchants were key nodes in getting the produce of trans-Appalachia to markets.[52]

By leveraging his family's connections, Abijah was able to assemble large cargos that he could then import into New Orleans on his own account for the benefit of the entire family. In February 1800, Abijah wrote to his cousin John Hunt in Kentucky, requesting that John ship as much flour as he could acquire downriver as rapidly as possible. "Flour," Abijah informed John, "will meet with a ready Sail [sale] in this quarter as a number of American Gentlemen are waiting in N. Orleans for the arrival of the Boats." Abijah asked his cousin to purchase "1500 Barrels of Supr. fine flour at 6 Dolls. & under on 5 or 6 months credit," an easy task for John, stationed as he was among the farmers of the bluegrass. Abijah had no doubt that the flour would sell for "7 to 8 Dolls. pr. Barrel in Orleans," as, he believed, Americans "have permission to ship that article [flour] to England as it is in great demand there."[53] Abijah was well-informed. In 1800, Britain had suspended its corn laws, which traditionally barred the importation of flour, to help feed the populace during the ongoing wars with Napoleonic France. American merchants involved in the newly opened trade of the trans-Appalachian West stood to make a handsome profit by selling western produce to the hungry markets of wartime Europe.

Abijah Hunt also dealt with many smaller Kentucky and Tennessee traders who regularly sold him the contents of their flatboats. Nine months after urging his cousin to send as much flour as he could, Abijah purchased the cargo of Lexington merchant Samuel Postlethwaite, who ran a store and later a tavern in Kentucky. Postlethwaite had departed from Kentucky on September 13 on a boat he had grandly, and perhaps aptly, named the *Adventure*, and set sail for Natchez carrying a cargo that consisted of cordage, flour, bacon, linen, and blankets, assembled from the exchanges that occurred in his store in Lexington. When Postlethwaite arrived in Natchez on November 3, he quickly sold his cargo to multiple Natchez merchants, including Abijah Hunt.[54] Postlethwaite left Natchez with notes payable on March 1, 1801; his traveling companions, who had also sold a cargo at Natchez, left with a note on local merchants David Ferguson and Milling Wooley for $7,000—$2,800 was due that spring, the rest due in twelve months.[55] Within the year, Postlethwaite had also relocated to Natchez, hoping to take advantage of the opportunities the town provided.

While Abijah Hunt helped integrate Natchez into Ohio Valley trade, he also played a role in Natchez's newest economic endeavor: cotton. Even though the town of Natchez was in a political uproar throughout

1797, the planters of Natchez allowed nothing to interfere with the sowing of their cotton crops. By November, two Philadelphia merchants scouting out possibilities for profit observed that the "region for 50 miles around is inhabited by cotton planters . . . whose cultivation is the only thing the inhabitants of this whole area are involved in."[56] There was a "moral certainty of profiting advantageously," they believed, by establishing oneself as a merchant brokering the sale of Natchez cotton in exchange for goods imported from across the Atlantic. Abijah Hunt agreed. He became a cotton merchant in 1800 when he opened a public gin near his store in the community of Pine Ridge, charging his customers a percentage of their crop in exchange for use of the gin.[57] Hunt had a small advantage over his competitors as his customers were more likely to consign their crops to him, rather than pay to have the cleaned cotton carted off to the facilities of a different merchant.

There was money to be made in cotton, and the competition to find suppliers was fierce. Operating a gin, like Hunt did, was one avenue merchants could use to ensure they had large quantities of cotton available to ship downriver when the river's waters rose in the spring and American ships began arriving in New Orleans.[58] Many Natchez and New Orleans merchants employed agents to attempt to purchase the cotton crop while it was still being harvested. In 1801, one such agent, Shepherd Brown, reported to his New Orleans employers that "not less than 20 persons" were already in Natchez, attempting to purchase cotton, traveling from plantation to plantation in hopes of securing a large amount of the commodity. The resulting competition had driven up prices in Natchez, above the price New Orleans merchants expected they would be able to sell the cotton.[59] While dozens of planters grew cotton, the exportation of cotton from Natchez to New Orleans was dominated by a few large partnerships, many of whom partnered with Natchez merchants like Hunt.

Planters' profits depended on access to three things: land, labor, and markets. In 1799, the average cost of unimproved land south of Natchez was approximately fifty cents per acre, while improved land sold for two to ten dollars; a single cotton crop might clear one's entire debt for purchasing a farm.[60] In contrast to the cheapness of land, labor was extremely expensive in Natchez; the spectacular growth of the cotton market led to an increase in the price of enslaved laborers in the region. In 1798, the enslaved people of Natchez produced well over a million pounds of cotton annually, an increase of more than 2,600 percent in four years.[61] By 1799, transplanted Virginia farmer John Steele promised his brother that an enslaved man would sell for between $1,000 and $1,200 in Natchez, an amount, he predicted, the enslaved man's labor would likely pay for within the course of a single year.[62] That year, Natchez cotton sold for twenty cents a pound at New Orleans. On his plantation near Natchez, surveyor and scientist William Dunbar's enslaved workforce produced 20,000 pounds of cleaned cotton, netting around $4,000.[63]

Seeing an opportunity for profit, Abijah Hunt turned to selling a new commodity: enslaved people. It was not long after the popularization of the cotton gin that the domestic slave trade began to take shape, fueled by enslavers' demand for more captive laborers to grow cotton. In February 1800, Abijah wrote to John in Lexington. "Negroes are in demand & will Sell well." While flour and tobacco were currently "dull," whiskey and enslaved men and women would, Abijah assured John, "command money."[64]

When John and Abijah first ventured into bringing enslaved people from Kentucky to Mississippi, the trade was still in its infancy and lacked both the infrastructure and the accepted practices that would become commonplace in the 1820s, when the phrase "sold down the river" would encapsulate the experiences of hundreds of thousands of enslaved people.[65] Nevertheless, the brutal logic that underscored the domestic slave trade already operated. When Abijah first wrote to John asking him to gather a cargo of enslaved people, enslaved men of prime working age were trading for an average of $303 in Kentucky; in Natchez, in contrast, enslaved men sold for an average of $500.[66] Moreover, enslaved people, unusually for the Natchez marketplace, could be sold almost immediately for cash, a factor that was frequently at the front of Abijah's mind. In Ohio, Abijah had carefully structured his relationship with the army to supply the cash that kept his family's businesses running; in Natchez he found an even more lucrative avenue to financial liquidity in selling captive bodies.

The 1798 transfer of the region surrounding Natchez to the United States began the decades-long forced migration of enslaved peoples from the Upper South to the lower Mississippi Valley. As early as 1800, the pattern of migration was visible in the first census of the Mississippi Territory, which recorded that the enslaved population had nearly doubled, from 1,800 in 1795 to 3,489 at the turn of the century. The fortunes of Natchez would be built on the untold misery of thousands.[67]

As westerners had hoped, Pinckney's Treaty transformed the trade of the Mississippi Valley. But the change was not what they predicted. While western farmers could, as they had long demanded, now transport the flour, bacon, and whiskey of the Ohio Valley to the port of New Orleans, the transfer of Natchez had already changed the calculus of Mississippi River trade. Merchants like Hunt now funneled cotton to New Orleans, where ships bound for the eastern seaboard and Europe waited to bring the produce of the continental interior into the Atlantic world. Given the high demand for cotton in Europe, all involved in the trade expected high profits, and Natchez gained a reputation as a place where fortunes could be made.

In order for those fortunes to be realized, Natchez cotton had to be able to reach Atlantic markets. While the people of Natchez had forced the Spanish to acknowledge one article of Pinckney's Treaty through the threat of violence, continuing Spanish control of the Mississippi presented barriers to selling Natchez cotton. Natchez planters thus joined Ohio Valley settlers in a rallying call for federal intervention in trade relations along the Mississippi. As networks of merchants—like the Hunt family—reconfigured their trading strategies to include Natchez cotton, Mississippi River trade became more important to the nation at large. The U.S. territorial gains from the treaty, including the Natchez district, and the advent of cotton production in the region helped to elevate Mississippi trade as a national issue.

8

American Trade in a Spanish Port

ONCE THE river was opened, the agricultural produce of trans-Appalachia poured down the Mississippi. Along the Monongahela, Kanawha, Kentucky, Muskingum, Miami, Tennessee, and Cumberland Rivers, western farmers and merchants embarked with flour, salted meat, whiskey, cordage, and hemp for sale in New Orleans. French merchant François Michaux, who traveled through the West first in 1796 and again in 1802, reported that of the "85,570 barrels of flour" that floated past the new city of Louisville in the first six months of 1802, "more than two thirds of this quantity may be considered as coming from the state of Kentucky, and the rest from Ohio and the settlements situated on the rivers Monongahela and Alleghany [in Pennsylvania]."[1] Further downriver, produce from Nashville and the new state of Tennessee (admitted in 1796) joined the flow.

Above all other crops was cotton. In the mid- and late 1790s, farmers from the Gulf of Mexico north to the Ohio experimented with growing the staple. In 1796, Tennessee surveyor Daniel Smith speculated that cotton "must be a constant source of wealth to the planter. . . . It must be in constant demand in foreign markets."[2] Smith's prediction rapidly came true, as farmers and merchants in the Cumberland region around Nashville turned to cotton as a key commercial crop. In 1800, the Nashville partnership Hennen and Dixon accepted "Hemp, Pork, Flour, in barrels, cotton, bees-wax, and from 20 to 30 good Beef-Cattle" to settle its debts; by 1802, the merchants planned to accept only "Cash, or Cotton." By 1803, in a telling inversion of the traditional preference for cash, merchant Joseph Martin requested that "all those who cannot pay him their accounts in cotton . . . come forward and pay in cash." He planned to "purchase cotton therewith." These advertisements marked profound changes to the region from only a few years prior, when Michaux had speculated that "not one in ten of [the western inhabitants] are in possession of a single dollar."[3]

The opening of Mississippi River trade hinged on the right of deposit guaranteed by Pinckney's Treaty. Permission to "deposit" goods gave Americans the ability to transship merchandise imported into the colony—whether flour, tobacco, and cotton arriving from upriver, or fabric, house paint, and nails arriving from the East Coast—without paying Spanish import or export taxes. The right of deposit allowed the heavily laden flatboats that originated in Kentucky, Tennessee, or Natchez to unload their cargo in New Orleans, where the goods could be stored until their importer found a buyer who would then load them onto ships bound for ports throughout the Atlantic world. The right of deposit also allowed American merchants to bring in American finished goods destined for western settlements; on arriving in New Orleans, those goods would be transferred onto smaller, lighter boats capable of navigating against the currents and eddies of the Mississippi.

Beginning with the opening of the right of deposit in April 1798, every arriving American merchant or farmer was required to unload their cargo in the presence of a Spanish customs officer responsible for recording "everything that [was] deposited" in the port of New Orleans. Although Spanish officers could not inspect the goods themselves, they were charged with recording "the number of bales, sacks, boxes, and any other kind of packing, as well as marks, numbers, and any other identification marks" that made up each shipment.[4] The result of these efforts is a wonderfully rich account of the region's trade. Widespread smuggling means the record is by no means perfect, but the documentation that exists is remarkably complete. For each entry in the deposit, Spanish officials recorded the name of the importer; the origins of the imported goods; the number of barrels, sacks, bales, or casks; the date of importation; and when the item was removed from the deposit, either through eventual sale to an American merchant who exported the goods out of the city or by paying taxes so the goods could be sold within Louisiana. For most of the items brought to the deposit, the Spanish also recorded the name of the ship and the captain who carried away the goods, as well as their ultimate destination.

Records from the deposit reveal the astonishingly rapid growth of American trade in New Orleans. From 1798 (when only 56 entries were made) until 1802 (425 entries), New Orleans became an increasingly important port for Atlantic trade. Ships bound for Havana, Campeche,

Nassau, St. Croix, St. Thomas, Liverpool, Amsterdam, Bremen, New York, Philadelphia, and Charleston put in regularly at New Orleans. With Pinckney's Treaty in place and the deposit opened, American merchants found ample stores of western produce awaiting arriving vessels. Finally, western flour, tobacco, salt pork and beef, hemp, furs, hides, indigo, and increasingly cotton, could be exported throughout the Atlantic world.[5]

In New Orleans, the expanding continental and commercial interests of the United States converged and fused.[6] With the opening of the Mississippi River, New Orleans became the nexus in an Atlantic trade in western produce that brought Kentucky flour and Natchez cotton to consumers throughout the Atlantic world, and money—in the form of bills, notes, and specie—to Americans along the eastern seaboard and the Ohio and Mississippi Valleys.[7] This early trade increased exponentially each decade until the Civil War, becoming more sophisticated and tied to the development of U.S. financial and commercial networks.[8] Streams of produce, cotton, and humanity—much of it enslaved—flowed in and out of the city, shaping New Orleans and what would become known as the Deep South. This was a transformation that began in 1798 with the opening of the deposit and the enactment of Pinckney's Treaty.

On July 4, 1802, the *Rebecca* sailed into Liverpool harbor laden with Kentucky flour and Natchez cotton it had carried from the New Orleans deposit. Typical of the ships that moved among the eastern seaboard, New Orleans, and Europe, what makes the *Rebecca* distinctive are its unusually robust records, which make it possible to reconstruct the ship's journeys and through them the development of Mississippi River trade under the terms of Pinckney's Treaty. The story of the *Rebecca* represented a triumph of American diplomacy conducted by the Washington, Adams, and Jefferson administrations. Settlers of the Ohio Valley and merchants of the eastern seaboard had long envisioned a day when an American ship, sailing from a Spanish port and carrying American goods, could arrive in Britain, fulfilling the visions of Atlantic world trade that had fueled decades of speculative ventures. Only seven years earlier, during the signing of Pinckney's Treaty, few western settlers or eastern merchants could have foreseen the form this trade would take. To be sure, flour would form an important part of the *Rebecca*'s cargo. As Thomas Paine predicted in *Common Sense*, foodstuffs produced by the United States would "always have a market while eating is the custom of Europe."[9] But while flour remained central, it was cotton that promised to reshape American commerce.

Pinckney's Treaty created a legal fiction, allowing American trade to be conducted from a Spanish port. Ostensibly, the treaty "opened" the river and permitted western produce to flow into the Atlantic. In practice, this legal fiction threatened American trade through New Orleans and challenged Spanish imperial dominion, even as it tied Kentucky flour prices to European politics. The men who enabled New Orleans trade to grow under the operation of Pinckney's Treaty were constructing new networks and laying the groundwork for trading infrastructure that would be central to the expansion of the American empire throughout the continental interior and form the foundation of the international cotton trade, thereby transforming life for millions of enslaved people and the economies their work sustained. Gaining access to New Orleans seemed to vindicate westerners' claims that custody of the river was foreordained by both geography and providence. Although these claims would eventually butt up against the realities of imperial geopolitics, the opening of the river offered a glimpse of precisely the political economy that had driven settlement in the Ohio Valley. But not even the most sanguine early speculators had imagined the consequences of the explosion in cotton production.

By the mid-nineteenth century, cotton would become the lynchpin of an interdependent global economy that shaped modern capitalism. The links between the plantation regime of the Deep South and the capitalist regime of the factory have intrigued scholars since Louisiana senator John Henry Hammond declared cotton to be "king" in 1858. But for years before this regime was in place, the world of shopkeepers, river boatmen, importers, merchants, sailors, brokers, and manufacturers in and around New Orleans transformed goods into cash and credit throughout the Atlantic economy, as the remarkable records of the *Rebecca* show.

Trading in New Orleans under the terms of Pinckney's Treaty brought American merchants into direct conflict with Spanish imperial policy, even as colonial residents of New Orleans benefited enormously from the trade. Working together, Spanish officials and American merchants constructed mechanisms that allowed trade to continue, but they were constrained by distant authorities who asserted their control over the river, port, and New Orleans trade.[10] When war in Europe left the United States the only neutral shipper operating in the Caribbean, trade between New Orleans and England increased dramatically, escalating conflict with Spanish officials. American traders, merchants, sailors, river boatmen, and farmers shaped New Orleans trade largely without governmental interference, leaving the federal government little choice but to react to the shape it was taking.

Philadelphia's Flour in New Orleans

THE *REBECCA* was the property of William Taylor, a prominent Baltimore flour merchant. Well before the 1795 signing of Pinckney's Treaty, New Orleans had already become an important flour-trading destination. In the colonial era, New Orleans, and Louisiana more broadly, consistently struggled to produce enough food to feed itself. Under the French, and in the period between the Seven Years' War and the American Revolution, much of the deficit had been supplied by the mixed French and Indigenous communities in Upper Louisiana, places like Vincennes and Kaskaskia. When Spain closed the Mississippi in 1784, the Upper Louisiana flour trade was a casualty of the decision. The consequences of the closure for the city of New Orleans became clear in 1788, when more than 80 percent of the city was destroyed by a devastating fire. Along with the city's jail, military barracks, and arsenal, the fire destroyed the city's food warehouses. A second fire in 1794 had a similar effect, as did hurricanes that struck the city in the successive Augusts of 1793 and 1794, destroying the colony's unharvested crops.[11] Although Spanish policy officially barred American ships from arriving in port, following each disaster colonial officials issued calls of distress, promising merchants, most of whom were from Philadelphia, the ability to bring any cargo they wished to the port as long as any ship they sent carried flour.

Even when there were no active crises, New Orleans still imported the bulk of its flour from the mid-Atlantic, although few American ships entered New Orleans's harbor. Until 1795, both Spanish and American merchants were allowed to legally enter the French port of St. Domingue, and that port quickly emerged as a transshipment point for Pennsylvanian flour. As early as 1786, John Girault, a merchant in New Orleans, wrote to a correspondent that "it is totally impossible to introduce Flour here at present, and even if it was it would come to a very bad market much being brought from Philadelphia by way of the Cape of Port au Prince."[12] British trade goods often entered Louisiana via the same route, carried by American merchants to St. Domingue before being reexported to Spanish Louisiana.[13] Although technically illegal, colonial officials did little to intervene. Like their fellow Louisianans, they were also dependent on imported American flour for their daily bread. The 1791 revolt of the enslaved population of St. Domingue and the 1793 outbreak of war in Europe reshaped American trade with the Caribbean and elevated the importance of Spanish America, including New Orleans, as a destination for American exports. In 1790, the French West Indies accounted for "23 percent of the flour, 77 percent of the processed beef, 63 percent of the dried fish, 80 percent of the pickled fish, and 73 percent of the livestock exported from the United States." Likely some percentage of each of these purchases was actually transshipped to places like Louisiana or Havana.[14] Following the revolt, trade with St. Domingue declined for both American and Spanish traders, but trade between the United States and New Orleans increased.

Philadelphia and Baltimore merchants were drawn to Spanish colonial ports by the presence of specie. Throughout the eighteenth century, New Orleans always traded at a deficit, and Louisianan merchants had little choice but to export specie to balance their accounts with American merchants. In 1790, for example, about $400,000 in specie was transferred from Spanish Louisiana to American merchants via trade with St. Domingue.[15] Such transfers were always illegal. Spanish law prohibited the export of specie from the colony except for in return for slaves, and even then it was subject to a 3 percent duty. Despite this prohibition, Louisiana still presented perhaps the best chance for American merchants to obtain specie, as the reales, piastres, and pesos of Spanish America were the most desired currency in the United States.[16] Spanish officials were constantly complaining about the illegal export of specie. According to Don Diego de Gardoqui, the "shamelessness of the transgressors" who smuggled Spanish specie out of Louisiana "forced [him] to assail that evil of the exportation of specie, despite the fact that [he] was in a country [the United States] which thirsted for it."[17] With Spanish Louisiana unable to supply itself with basic foodstuffs, and Philadelphian merchants facing a severe cash shortage, it was little wonder that smuggling between the United States and the Spanish colonial outpost had become a "notorious [fact]."[18]

In 1797, the Spanish West Indies became an increasingly important destination for American flour after crop failures in the Caribbean spawned near-famine, forcing Spain to open its colonial markets.[19] For American merchants, the shift was doubly beneficial. Since the early 1790s, when war had initially engulfed Europe, Spanish officials had been reluctant to transport Mexican and Peruvian silver to the metropole, fearing (accurately) that it would prove an attractive target for belligerent privateers.

As a result, by the late 1790s Spain's specie stores came to be concentrated in its American ports, especially in New Spain and Cuba.[20] Some of that gold found its way to New Orleans as part of the colony's annual subsidy, but it did not take long before American merchants operating out of New Orleans wanted more direct access to these cash-rich markets. New Orleans became a frequent stop for American ships bound for Cuba. Nature facilitated this trade: soon after ships left the Mississippi and entered the Gulf of Mexico, the "Loop Current," an oceanic phenomenon, drew them to the southeast, close to the port of Havana, before pushing them eastward through the Florida straits. The powerful current then merged with the Gulf Stream, propelling ships up the eastern coast of the United States or eastward toward Europe.[21] New Orleans became a popular spot for American merchants to purchase cargoes of grain and salted meat that could be exported to Cuba. For instance, in 1801, Philadelphia merchants Reed and Forde predicted that their correspondents would find "liberal prices in New Orleans" for "Flour, Beef, Pork, hams, Butter & Lard" to ship to Havana.[22]

In the 1790s, American prosperity depended upon the United States' status as a neutral carrier. Anticipating the outbreak of a European war in 1790, Thomas Jefferson summarized American priorities in the upcoming conflict: "Our object is to feed and theirs to fight."[23] Once fighting broke out, American produce was shipped throughout the warring Atlantic. For the Spanish West Indies, the European war exacerbated periodic food shortages in the Caribbean that mid-Atlantic merchants like William Taylor, the owner of the *Rebecca*, moved to fill. When Spain opened its colonies to neutral shipping, flour merchants like Taylor were allowed to import not only foodstuffs but finished goods as well. Even as war disrupted trade, the *Rebecca* could be found moving among American, Spanish, and British imperial holdings. Ships like the *Rebecca* became the threads tying together an increasingly connected Atlantic world.

American Trade in a Spanish Port

THE FIRST sign that the *Rebecca* was approaching the mouth of the Mississippi was a sudden change in the water's color. About ten leagues off the coast, the green waters of the Gulf of Mexico became first whitish and then yellow; at the very mouth of the river, they turned into a churn "exactly like very dirty soapsuds," fresh enough to be scooped into cupped hands and drunk. For ships at sea, the main shipping channel of the Mississippi was barely discernable from the inlets and estuaries surrounding it, but sailors could be certain of their location when they spied a forty-foot wooden structure, constantly at risk of being swallowed by the sea, that marked the river's mouth.[24] Known as *La Balize* (the Beacon), the tower marked the river's channel and the entrance to Louisiana. The first stop for any ship bound for New Orleans, it was also the first sign to arriving American sailors that the Mississippi was a Spanish river. At the tower, the *Rebecca*'s captain, John McNeill, presented his papers to Spanish officials—declaring the ship's name, its provenance, and that it was owned by William Taylor of Baltimore. McNeill would have known what to expect: in the previous six months, the *Rebecca* had made two similar journeys to New Orleans. Each trip, as the ship lay at anchor, Spanish officials rowed out to the vessel to check the ship's manifest, matching items listed on parchment with the boxes, barrels, and bales that filled the ship's hold. McNeill and his crew would have stood by as a custom's official "locked and sealed" the ship's "cargo hatches" and placed a Spanish guard on board to prevent the ship from trading illegally before it reached New Orleans.[25] Arriving sailors, captains, and merchants could not have missed the signs that they were now in Spanish territory.

In addition to housing customs officials and a few soldiers, *La Balize* was homebase for twenty or so Spanish pilots. A shifting sandbar formed by the incessant churn of thousands of tons of silt that the Mississippi accumulated in its journey to the ocean obligated American ships to hire Spanish pilots, who navigated the treacherous mouth of the river. Captain McNeill may have gritted his teeth as he paid the twenty-dollar-per-day piloting fee.[26] American merchants and captains resented paying the Spanish pilots, whom they complained about constantly and suspected of sabotage. Despite the pilots' "expertise," American ships frequently went aground in the river and were condemned as shipwrecked, leaving the honesty of their Spanish pilots in doubt. American merchant Evan Jones attributed the "quantities of goods however which have been lost out of different vessels, only run ashore at first, at the mouth of the River, and afterwards wrecked" to either "ignorance or negligence." At best, he believed, the pilots were lazy; at worst, they were deliberately beaching American ships so their accomplices on land could rush in and salvage the ships' cargoes.[27] In truth, it was more likely the river itself that prevented the deep-drafted ocean vessels from successfully navigating the channel. The sandbar often lay at a depth of only twelve or thirteen feet; many-ton vessels typically displaced fourteen or fifteen feet of water. With enough

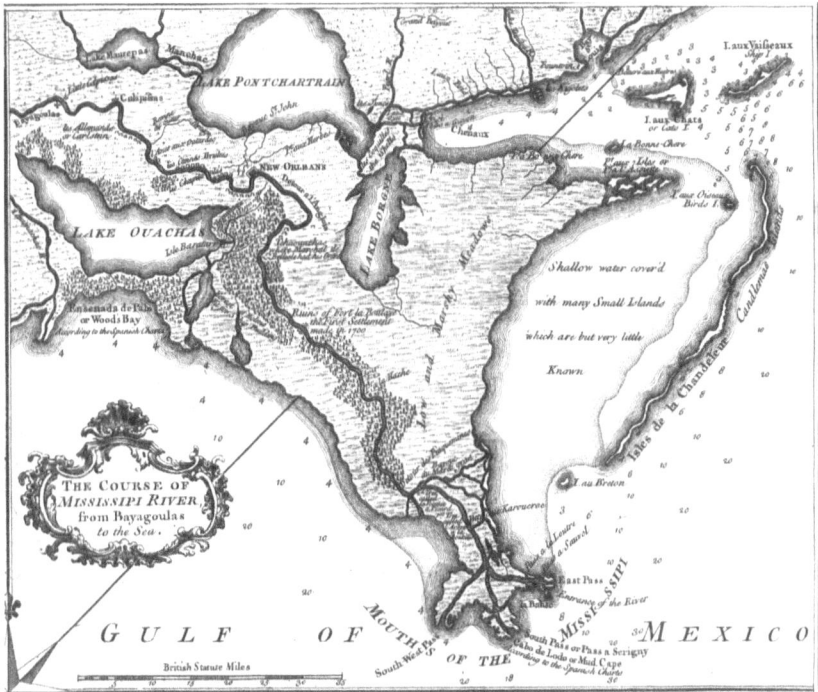

FIG. 4. Often blocked by mud and sand, the mouth of the Mississippi was guarded by the fort at *La Balize*. Ships bound for New Orleans still had several weeks to travel before arriving at the port. Thomas Jeffrys and Louis Brion de la Tour, *Plan of New Orleans the Capital of Louisiana; with the Disposition of Its Quarters and Canals as They Have Been Traced by Mr. de la Tour in the Year 1720*, London, 1759. (Library of Congress Geography and Map Division, Washington, DC)

momentum, a ship might plow through two to three feet of loose mud but not more; a slight miscalculation could cost substantial damage or time. Captains like John McNeill had no choice but to accept that from *La Balize* north, the Spanish would try to control every aspect of the river's trade. Although permitted to sound the Mississippi to determine its depth, it was illegal for American ships to record their findings, a regulation that saw at least one American captain imprisoned.[28] Spanish policy required Americans to depend on the dubious expertise of Spanish pilots to navigate the river's treacherous waters.

Once over the sandbar, the *Rebecca* would have trekked slowly northward, using sails and oars as it fought the constant southward flow of the river's current. Cumbersome oceangoing ships found themselves easily outpaced by smaller and more agile river vessels that took advantage of the river's eddies along the shoreline to make the journey north, carrying cargo and ferrying messages, alerting Spanish officials and New Orleans merchants to the imminent arrival of the *Rebecca*. For small craft, the journey could take a matter of days. For larger ships, the trip from coast to port could take six weeks or more if a ship were delayed by shallow water or unfavorable winds. Traveling through the watery swamps of the lower Mississippi, the *Rebecca* likely proceeded unimpeded until it arrived at Fort Plaquemine, where Spanish officials would again demand the ship's papers and question Captain McNeill about his cargo. If his answers passed muster, the ship would proceed upriver until finally coming to anchor off the port of New Orleans.

During shipping season, in the spring and again in the fall, the river in front of the city was alive with boats. Vessels like the *Rebecca*, large enough to cross the Atlantic, anchored offshore; an army of tenders, rowboats, and pirogues shuttled goods and people from ships to shore. Smaller ships engaged in the coasting trade might tie up along the levee—a mound of dirt that doubled as a seawall, marketplace, and promenade for those with leisure enough to stroll under the canopy of orange blossoms the city had planted along its top. An army of free and enslaved stevedores and longshoremen loaded and unloaded the arriving and departing ships. Hucksters, many of them members of the free African American community of New Orleans, walked along the levee, calling out their wares, some of which was purchased by the riverboat crews who kindled fires along the shore to cook their suppers. Dotted among the larger ships were flatboats. American sailors strolling the levee in their rough canvas pants were joined by the river boatmen, many of them young men from the western settlements who had never seen anything like the hustle and bustle of New Orleans. Regardless of where they hailed from, disdainful New Orleanians referred to these men as Kentuckians, a term they ascribed to the unwashed, unruly, and usually drunk boatmen who caroused in the city's seedier districts.[29]

Two men were likely on hand to greet the *Rebecca* on her arrival in New Orleans. First was New Orleans merchant John McDonogh, to whom the cargo of the *Rebecca* was consigned. Along with his business partner William O. Payne, McDonogh acted as William Taylor's New Orleans agent. Born in Baltimore in 1779 and indentured to Taylor in 1795, McDonogh quickly earned Taylor's trust and affection. Despite McDonogh's youth, Taylor dispatched him to New Orleans to act as his agent when McDonogh completed his apprenticeship in 1800. McDonogh traveled to New Orleans via London, where he persuaded William's brother, the merchant John Taylor, to invest in a cargo of finished goods that McDonogh could sell in New Orleans. Persuaded by McDonogh's promises of "great returns... faithfully" remitted in six months, as well as by his brother's evident trust in the young man, John Taylor agreed to invest heavily in New Orleans trade.[30] The terms were simple: Taylor's ships departed from Baltimore loaded with finished goods, which McDonogh was to sell in New Orleans or Natchez, for cash if possible; if not, then in exchange for country produce, which could then be remitted either to John Taylor in London or his brother William in Baltimore. William Taylor's ships, including the *Rebecca*, would carry the large shipments of goods McDonogh had assembled.[31]

The *Rebecca* was a small, fast ship, and William Taylor and John McDonogh kept her busy. In November 1801, the *Rebecca* arrived in New Orleans from Amsterdam. In early February 1802—loaded with sugar, indigo, vanilla, and 239 bales (approximately 65,000 pounds) of cotton—the *Rebecca* sailed for Baltimore.[32] Within a month, it was enroute back to New Orleans, loaded with "two thousand three hundred and sixty six bars Iron; Fifteen Thousand Bricks; Sixty Barrels, Containing Tar, Rozin, Turpentine and Varnish; one cask Spirits Turpentine; Ten Cases, containing liquor cases; white nankeens and Painters Brushes; Eighteen anchors; eight and half dozen Windsor Chairs & two Settees." A mixture of naval stores, building materials, and household goods, the cargo was well-suited to the New Orleans and Natchez markets.[33]

The other man on hand for the *Rebecca*'s arrival was an official from the New Orleans Intendancy, the Spanish office charged with levying and collecting Spanish customs duties. This office was also responsible for supervising the American deposit. Prior to 1798, no one building was designated as the deposit. Instead, custom officials walked along the waterfront, making a record of every item imported by American merchants or in American ships, including the type of merchandise, containers, and any markings visible from the exterior. Far from being ineffective agents of a declining power, Spanish officials in New Orleans deployed formidable tools to strengthen the empire's hold on the Mississippi. By controlling Americans' knowledge of the river, their access to its ports, and the movement of American goods, Spanish officials asserted the sovereignty of their empire and regulated the presence of foreigners within the city.

In the event of a dispute between McDonogh and the customs official, McDonogh could appeal to the acting American consul at New Orleans, an office occupied in the spring of 1801 by planter Evan Jones. Two men had held the position prior to Jones. In 1798, New Orleans merchant Daniel Clark Jr., a native of Ireland and formerly a resident of Philadelphia, was appointed acting consul by Andrew Ellicott; later that year, William Hulings, who had made a fortune in New Orleans commerce under Spanish rule, was nominated to serve as vice-consul by President John Adams. All three men failed to gain official recognition from Spanish imperial authorities because Spanish law prohibited foreign consuls from operating within its colonial possessions.[34] After the enactment of Pinckney's Treaty, however, this prohibition became untenable. Although Spanish officials did not grant U.S. consuls official recognition, they nevertheless collaborated with them to shape Louisiana trade.

Men like Captain McNeill, John McDonogh, William and John Taylor, the unnamed Spanish customs officials, and Clark, Hulings, and Jones all helped to construct the complicated fiction of Pinckney's Treaty: they were pursuing American trade in a Spanish port. The trade that emerged took shape in ways that none of the contracting parties could have imagined. In New Orleans, American merchants and Spanish officials collaborated in an uneasy dance that all hoped would serve their interests, striking a delicate balance among preserving Spanish sovereignty, meeting the needs of the colonial population, and expanding American trade.

Spanish officials and New Orleans merchants had long worked in concert to circumvent mercantilist imperial policies.[35] While the Spanish metropole sought to confine colonial trade within the Spanish empire, Spanish officials in New Orleans could hardly afford to do so. New Orleans depended on imports of American flour to keep the population fed.[36] Following a devastating fire in 1788 and the outbreak of war with France in 1793, Louisiana increasingly depended on American shipping for both food and consumer goods, despite imperial laws that formally circumscribed American access to the port.[37]

Prior to Pinckney's Treaty, Spanish officials decided on a case-by-case basis whether American ships could trade in New Orleans. American merchants in Philadelphia and other Atlantic ports depended on local correspondents to ease the way for their cargo, often using bribery or personal connections and skirting the line between legal and illegal trade to keep people fed. By contrast, Pinckney's Treaty required open negotiation about issues of access, control, and taxation—all of which continued to center local interests over imperial concerns.

Every merchant involved in American trade in New Orleans confronted a problem with the arrival of every ship: deciding whether to send the goods north to the 31st parallel and Natchez, or to pay Spanish import taxes and sell the cargo in New Orleans. The first scenario was preferred by those who created the right of deposit: American goods, remaining in American hands, ultimately sold to Americans. McDonogh occasionally chose this course for the *Rebecca*'s cargo, which necessitated applying to the Spanish government for a permit to remove his goods from the deposit before embarking upriver. Because everyone involved in each transaction was American, the Spanish could monitor the trade but not interfere. By contrast, an arriving American ship carrying goods for the Spanish subjects of Louisiana was no longer participating in the deposit; instead, it was involved in the importation of goods to Louisiana. Foreign goods imported from the Atlantic by American shippers were subject to a 21 percent tax, while any western goods imported into New Orleans and sold locally were subject to a 6 percent tax. Western goods subsequently exported to American territory accrued an additional 6 percent tax.[38]

The Spanish taxes represented a real barrier to the functioning of the deposit. Profiting from a voyage depended on a ship finding a market for its cargo when it arrived at its destination. The population of Natchez was far too small to absorb the quantity of American shipping now arriving in New Orleans, while the 21 percent importation tax drove prices to intolerable levels. To avoid the tax, American shippers turned to subterfuge. Arriving in New Orleans, the ship's captain gave "a confidential" or fake "title . . . to some [Spanish] Citizen," thereby ensuring the ship was entered into customs logs as a Spanish ship and could sell its cargo at the far less onerous rate of 6 percent that was owed by Spanish citizens importing foreign goods. The practice of claiming false ownership was an open secret: ships captains, local merchants, and Spanish officials all collaborated to introduce goods into New Orleans at the lowest tax rate possible. During his short-lived service as American consul, Daniel Clark described to Secretary of State Timothy Pickering how the resulting system worked: "Altho' the vessel is really American navigates at sea under that flag and is known to be such to every officer of the Colony"— such that even Spanish officers would issue the ship the "necessary vouchers and Certificates" required to prove American ownership—in order "to comply with the orders of the Court she must appear on the Custom House Books as a Spanish Vessel." According to Clark, this deception was a necessity, "as American vessels which do not get naturalized cannot afford to come here." Avoiding the higher tax required arriving in ballast, making the New Orleans–bound portion of the journey worthless. Only by claiming to be Spanish could American ships afford trade at New Orleans.[39]

Widespread subterfuge created problems for the deposit. "It results that there really is no American Shipping in Orleans to carry off the Produce deposited there in virtue of the Treaty," Daniel Clark informed Pickering in April 1798.[40] A month later, the partners Lanthois and Pitot informed John and Abijah Hunt that the tobacco they had shipped southward to be entered into the American deposit could not be sold. "We are sorry to tell you that there is not in this harbor a single vessel having entered into, without a Spanish permit, and for that reason [they are] forbidden to receive American properties. . . . It is to be feared," the Creole traders warned the western merchants, "that we shall not have the much wanted opportunities to bring soon away all the American produce in this place."[41] Spanish ships—whether truly Spanish or merely pretending—that carried American goods from the deposit needed to pay a 12 percent tax: 6 percent of the produce's value to import foreign goods into the colony; 6 percent more to export them. Frustration with this system was widespread. Merchants resented how the same barrel of flour, remaining in the same warehouse, could fluctuate between being imported—and therefore taxed—or being duty-free by virtue of having been "deposited" and remaining in American hands.

American merchants, residents of New Orleans, and Spanish officials all had a personal stake in solving the issues caused by divergent tax rates. War in Europe had spilled over into the Caribbean, where British warships and privateers preyed on Spanish shipping. Meanwhile, England had blockaded Spanish ports, locking in the Spanish merchant marine. As a result, New Orleans suffered under "a scarcity of overseas goods which are necessary for the subsistence and clothing of the inhabitants of the various classes," an issue of concern to residents and their colonial rulers.[42] With French shipping similarly depressed, Americans became—almost by default—the only source through which the colony could acquire imported goods.[43] New Orleans residents valued the increased goods brought by American shippers, which helped keep food costs low and provided desirable consumer goods to the city. Working closely with Don Manuel Gayoso de Lemos—recently elevated to the governorship of Louisiana—and Spanish intendant Juan Morales, Daniel Clark negotiated a solution letting Americans import goods at the same tax rate as Spanish merchants, which would allow them to both keep the cost of consumer imports low and participate in the American deposit. In June 1798, Morales and the Chamber of Commerce decreed a 6 percent tax on goods brought by any neutral ship. Although it opened the port to all neutral nations, as Morales reminded Clark, "since the Americans are the people who by virtue of their geographical location and their right to the free navigation of the Mississippi River are able to trade with this city," the decree would primarily apply to American shipping.[44]

In New Orleans, Spanish officials and American merchants negotiated mutually beneficial solutions to problems created by imperial policies. The New Orleans officials acted without the approval of their imperial superiors, the captain general in Cuba or the Council of the Indies in Spain. Morales attempted to persuade his superiors to approve the measure by appealing to their pocketbooks, arguing that a lowered tariff would cut down on smuggling and boost imports to the colony, thereby raising the crown's revenue. Even though the change in tariffs would certainly make "Spain's commerce with this province apt to fall off," little trade occurred between Spain and the colony in the first place. Aggressively enforcing Spanish mercantilist policies and keeping the excessively high tariff in place would only create additional problems within Louisiana.

Officials in Madrid disagreed with Morales. In April 1799, they demanded the 21 percent tax be reinstated. When news of the decree arrived in New Orleans, American trade briefly ground to a halt. American ships could still carry away deposited American produce without paying a duty, but ships that had already entered New Orleans harbor and not yet sold their goods were subject to the new rates. Evan Jones, who had recently replaced Clark as the acting U.S. vice-consul, wrote to Secretary of State Timothy Pickering that "several American vessels are now lying here, without having obtained permission to sell their cargoes."[45] The effects of the change might have been devastating had Morales not decided to ignore orders from the Spanish crown. Deeming trade shortages in New Orleans too acute, Morales returned New Orleans trade to its former footing, reinstating the 6 percent tax. But the brief suspension of trade impressed upon the growing number of American merchants in New Orleans that despite the opening of the Mississippi, trade in New Orleans was subject to the will of the Spanish crown.

Clark's and Jones's negotiations with Spanish officials also eased a growing political problem for the United States. The opening of the official Spanish deposit in New Orleans and the transfer of Natchez to American sovereignty occurred within a week of one another, but the 21 percent tax left unclear whether the citizens of Natchez would benefit from the trade of the deposit—as Abijah Hunt discovered when his tobacco arrived in New Orleans to find no American buyers. As Natchez planters began bringing their cotton to New Orleans for export, they were sure to "imbibe [a] disadvantageous impression" of their newfound American citizenship if American ships were unable to export their crops. Natchez residents might have accepted American hegemony, but if it could not find outlets for their trade, Clark warned federal officials, "they may be induced to consider the blessing of becoming American Citizens in a wrong light as at present they only perceive its immediate disadvantages."[46]

Despite the ongoing debates over duties, Payne and McDonogh knew that the first ships to arrive at their destinations with that year's crop would earn the highest returns, so they worked hard to ensure they had a cargo ready to load as soon as the *Rebecca* could be unloaded and reoutfitted for the outbound journey. McDonogh and Payne purchased merchandise from local farmers and merchants, including cotton and sugar, which they then shipped on behalf of their patron William Taylor. Sometimes they arranged to carry products belonging to others on freight. The cargo carried from the port of New Orleans on the *Rebecca* in spring 1802 consisted of 50 bales of cotton—property of Taylor—along with 1,330 barrels of flour belonging to Captain John Brown of Kentucky and his associates.[47] The cotton that McDonogh and Payne shipped aboard the *Rebecca* was a partial remittance for the nearly $200,000 worth of goods that Taylor had invested in New Orleans trade since 1800. The ship departed from New Orleans with a mix of goods from the American deposit and Spanish Louisiana.[48]

American—or Spanish—Trade

On May 21, 1802, the *Rebecca* departed New Orleans. Captains often received only loose instructions from the merchants who owned the vessels they sailed. Charged with selling a ship's cargo to good advantage and finding return cargo at reasonable prices, captains had tremendous leeway in how trade was conducted. Captain John McNeill had instructions to sail first for Havana and then on to Liverpool, but he had discretion over where to sell his cargo. The *Rebecca* sailed out of New Orleans in the company of the *Eliza*, bound for New York, and the *Polly*, bound for Baltimore, but was briefly detained on May 23 at the mouth of the river when the ship's draw proved too deep for the narrow passage. Despite the delay, the *Rebecca* was soon Cuba-bound. Finding the Havana market already flooded with American flour, much of it from New Orleans, McNeill quickly sailed for Liverpool, making the passage from New Orleans in just thirty-six days.[49]

McNeill was lucky. In the late 1790s, the Caribbean was a dangerous place for American shipping. War in Europe had spilled over into the Western Hemisphere, and Britain, France, and Spain were engaged in a fierce battle for control over the Caribbean, "whose seas," according to American secretary of state Timothy Pickering, "swarm[ed] with privateers and gun boats." With the onset of war, much of the British and French merchant marine accepted letters of marque from their respective crowns and turned privateer. American shipping was a favored target. Between June 1796 and June 1797, more than three hundred American ships were captured by French privateers; each ship taken was a blow to the owner and to the merchants whose cargo it carried.

By the time the American deposit in New Orleans opened in the spring of 1798, the French had placed an embargo on all American shipping, allowing privateers to step up their depredations.[50] In 1799, Captain William Lark, who sailed between Philadelphia and New Orleans for the merchant house of Reed and Forde, discovered just how dangerous the Caribbean had become. Between February 11 and 23, Lark's ship was captured three times, first by British and French privateers and then by the British Navy. Each time the ship was captured, it was searched "down to the keel" by privateers in search of "contraband goods." While the British were content to hold the ship for four days, French privateers seized every case of wine, destroyed the hogsheads of codfish—creating a putrid mess on the ship's deck—and "took all our Spare rigging & Stores" before allowing the ship to depart. Despite these losses, Lark's ship got off easily. The French privateers also had in their possession another American ship, the *Mercury*, sailing out of Charleston. Having taken a large part of its cargo, the privateers planned "to burn [the *Mercury*] and the remainder" of its wares, a fate guaranteed to terrify Captain Lark into submission. Despite his ship having been boarded on three separate occasions and robbed of its provisions and extra sails, Lark was lucky that his ship avoided the fate of the doomed *Mercury*, which French privateers turned into a flaming pyre in cruel commemoration of the hopes of American shipping.[51] Both ships got off easily in comparison to the *Fair American*, a Philadelphia ship captured off of St. Thomas. Six days after leaving the port, a ship calling itself the *Nancy*, and bearing a striking resemblance to the *Fair American*, sailed into St. Thomas. An investigation revealed the deception. In the ship's cabin, customs officials found a grisly arena of blood spatter and cutlass slashes that showed the fate of the crew of the *Fair American*.[52]

Privateering exposed the fractures in the legal fiction of New Orleans as an American port embedded in Spanish territory. A privateer's success depended on capturing ships whose cargo would be considered a valid prize—meaning that the ship, cargo, or crew could be proved the property or produce of a belligerent nation. New Orleans was a Spanish port; British privateers could therefore capture ships trading in the city. But American ships carrying goods to or from the American deposit in New Orleans were trading solely in American goods and were not subject to seizure by foreign powers. If such a ship traded with the Spanish residents of New Orleans, however, it became a neutral ship trading enemy produce, and from the British perspective it was then subject to seizure. Rare was the privateer who carefully distinguished between a ship using New Orleans as an American port of call and a ship entering the port to trade with Spanish residents. On the other hand, if the ship or any part of its cargo was destined for the English market, that made it fair game to French privateers. Because American ships trading in New Orleans carried cotton bound for England's textile industry, the port's trade was exceptionally vulnerable. Ships bound to and from New Orleans were constantly harassed, as it remained unclear whether New Orleans was an American or Spanish port.

Luckily, the *Rebecca* avoided capture. On July 4, 1802, the ship arrived in Liverpool. On arrival, Captain McNeill would have set out to find the establishment of consignment agent V. Pearse Ashfield, William Taylor's agent in the British cotton trade. Liverpool merchants like Ashfield often functioned as brokers, acting as go-betweens among merchants importing cotton and the spinning manufacturers who wished to purchase it. A broker's success depended on close relationships with importing merchants, developed primarily by extending credit. In 1803, when the New Orleans house of Shepherd Brown and Company established a connection with the Liverpool firm of Rathbone, Hughes, and Duncan—the largest importer of American cotton in Liverpool—the terms of their agreement included extending to the American merchants an "advance from 1/3 to 3/4th the probable proceeds."[53] This advance would be used by the Liverpool firm to pay the fees attendant to selling the cotton, with the balance directed as the cargo's owners dictated. In exchange for arranging the cargo's sale, brokers like Ashbrook received a customary commission of 2.5 percent; if the broker also helped organize a cargo for the ship's outward journey, the percentage typically rose to 5 of 6 percent, as well as interest levied on the value of the advance.[54]

Ashfield's next task was to remit the funds to Taylor. When Ashfield received the *Rebecca*'s cargo, he quickly sent an advance in the form of a bill drawn on himself to William's brother John, the London merchant. On August 25, Ashfield remitted the £1,300 he expected the *Rebecca*'s cotton to fetch to John Taylor on William Taylor's behalf, which John then used to repay a portion of his own debts within the port of London. Ashfield then went about finding a buyer for the cotton. He soon found there were no takers. New Orleans cotton arriving in Liverpool initially received a mixed reaction from the British textile industry. While in general "New Orleans cotton when good [was] a favorite description with the Manufacturers," as Rathbone, Hughes and Duncan informed Brown and McDonogh in 1803, "of some late years its reputation has been materially injured by the badness of the quality and its being [badly] packed."[55] William Taylor warned McDonogh that "New Orleans cotton is now in the lowest estimation" in the Liverpool market, occasioned by complaints that New Orleans shippers brought "many bags . . . of a very bad quality and many not cleaned at all."[56] It seems that cargo like the *Rebecca*'s occasioned such complaints: the fifty bales of cotton, much of it unwisely carried across the Atlantic on the ship's deck, arrived badly damaged. Moreover, the fortunes of New Orleans cotton in the British market rose and fell with demand for the product and with British manufacturers' perceptions of its quality. In 1798, New Orleans cotton sold for 21.5 pence in Liverpool, or 39 cents a pound.[57] The price was roughly the same in 1800, but by 1802 it had fallen precipitously to 15.5 pence—just under 29 cents a pound.[58]

The low price of cotton in the summer of 1802 was caused by events occurring far from Liverpool. Signed early that summer, the Treaty of Amiens ushered in the first—and, it would turn out, the only—year of peace Britain experienced in a decade, while "vast importations of cotton from all parts" received earlier that year had "reduced the prices [of cotton] very much." Ashfield found the *Rebecca*'s cargo particularly problematic. Despite being an American ship, its cotton could not be proved an American product. In 1802, England levied duties on all imported cotton. While American cotton paid 10 shillings and 6 pence per 100 pounds,

Louisiana cotton—deemed the produce of Spain—paid 14 shillings. Because John McDonogh had failed to obtain proof that the fifty bales of cotton aboard the *Rebecca* were American grown, his cotton was taxed at the higher rate. Eventually, Ashfield sold the *Rebecca's* cotton, but for only about two-thirds the usual price, or £713.1.1 (an amount that, after duties and commission, netted William Taylor £557.17).[59]

To recover the funds he had already advanced, Ashfield attempted to write bills drawn on John Taylor amounting to the difference between the advance and the selling price. But in October, John notified Ashfield that he could no longer honor any notes drawn on him.[60] Calling together his creditors, Taylor asked for more time to receive the remittances he was certain would soon arrive from his brother in Baltimore and their partners in New Orleans. His letters to McDonogh grew increasingly strident as his financial situation worsened. By the spring of 1803, he had suspended payments to his creditors. McDonogh's inability to assemble shipments that would balance John Taylor's accounts and the constant delays in bringing goods between New Orleans and London nearly bankrupted Taylor and left Ashfield holding the bag.[61]

Returning Home

In late July, the *Rebecca* sailed out of Liverpool laden with twenty-seven crates of earthenware, demands for William Taylor to pay the money owed Ashfield, and a request that William honor a bill of exchange for eight hundred pounds that Ashfield had issued to Captain Brown.[62] Just as he had for William Taylor's cotton, Ashfield had advanced Brown a substantial sum against the eventual sale of the flour brought aboard the *Rebecca*. But unlike the cotton, the flour earned more than the advance. On the ship's arrival in Baltimore, Taylor would honor the bill of exchange and issue Brown bills of his own that Brown could carry home to Kentucky.

As an East Coast merchant in the New Orleans cotton trade, William Taylor fulfilled various functions. First, he owned several of the ships he fitted out and dispatched to New Orleans and Liverpool. He shipped cargo intended for the New Orleans and Natchez marketplace, importing both the prosaic—"bricks, glue, oil, soap . . . salt, spades, frying pans, raisins, and crackers"—and the luxurious. In 1801, he dispatched "70 doz. men's white silk stockings, 18 gross white playing cards, 312 doz. kid gloves of assorted finishes, lengths, and colours," along with thousands of bottles of French wine from Bordeaux to Natchez.[63] For Taylor, Natchez and

New Orleans occupied just one node in an expansive network of Atlantic trade spanning the Caribbean and Europe. Other East Coast merchants who invested in New Orleans trade maintained relations that stretched across the globe. In 1796, the Philadelphia partners of Reed and Forde, who were heavily involved in the Mississippi flour trade, sent a cargo of wine to India.[64]

East Coast merchants were also responsible for insuring the ships they sent to sea. The prevalence of privateers in the Caribbean drove up the cost of insurance for ships and goods bound for New Orleans.[65] To reduce these high costs, some East Coast merchants armed their vessels to convince their underwriters that they could sail safely. Philadelphia merchant Daniel Coxe outfitted his ship the *Star* with twelve small cannons, enough, he believed, "to resist any small French privateer," but not enough to offset the concerns of the underwriters, who charged 15 percent for insurance in June 1798, a fivefold increase over pre-conflict rates.[66]

William Taylor financed his purchases of European goods largely through credit, often extended by his brother John in London. In return for goods that East Coast merchants shipped south to New Orleans or west to the Ohio Valley, they expected remittances from their Atlantic world agents, often in the form of cotton, indigo, or peltry but ideally in specie. Specie was the factor that lured American traders into the New Orleans market. "Remittances must be had or ruin must follow," William Taylor wrote John McDonogh in 1802, only days before the *Rebecca* sailed. "A few Thousand Dollars in Specie occasionally would be of more convenience than I can describe."[67] William's brother John, whose finances teetered on the precipice of ruin, was even more emphatic that remittances be made in specie. Protesting what he believed was McDonogh's delinquency, John Taylor threatened bodily harm should McDonogh fail to settle their accounts, promising to hunt McDonogh down if "I can find him upon the face of God's almighty Earth."[68] These letters might have inspired McDonogh to greater effort: between September and December 1802, McDonogh and Payne remitted at least $30,000 in specie to William Taylor.[69] Still, the amount paled in comparison to the $200,000 Taylor had invested in New Orleans trade.[70]

If the merchants themselves are to be believed, few actually profited from the New Orleans trade. William and John Taylor sent John McDonogh increasingly frantic notes, first urging and then demanding remittances for cash advanced. Daniel Coxe, brother to financier Tench Coxe, found himself severely in debt thanks to his investments in New Orleans trade. In 1803, he wrote to his New Orleans partner Daniel

Clark that he would never have sent another ship to New Orleans save "the positive assurances" he received from a New Orleans correspondent who promised that he would "receive special Remittances in time to face the Engagements contracted for the purchase of their cargoes, in [addition] to the Rem[ittances] Indispensably necessary to extricate me from my former engagements & to reestablish my credit" in Philadelphia. This was "a point of the highest consequence," Coxe informed Clark, as he had "a considerable sum of paper afloat."[71] Finding themselves similarly situated in the summer of 1803, Reed and Forde urged Daniel Ferguson, a Natchez shopkeeper, to send a remittance as soon as possible. Cotton, if he had any "on hand," should be shipped immediately, provided Ferguson could include an accompanying certificate of American growth. But, Reed and Forde concluded, "we shall however prefer to receive Bills on Philada. Baltimore or New York even at 4 months sight to a shipment of Cotton."[72]

Despite the hardships of particular investors and merchants, Mississippi River trade played a key role in circulating money—specie as well as commercial credit—throughout the trans-Appalachian West and the Atlantic world. Consider the bill of exchange that Pearse Ashfield issued to Captain John Brown in exchange for the Kentucky flour shipped aboard the *Rebecca*. Although some of the flour had turned sour, Ashfield was able to dispose of the 1,300 barrels of Ohio Valley flour for £2,348. After paying the required fees, including Ashfield's commission, Brown and his associates netted £933—approximately $4,191. The bill that Brown received, denominated in pounds and payable in Liverpool, was eminently useful to East Coast American merchants needing to settle their debts with British creditors. This was exactly how William Taylor used it. By purchasing Ashfield's bill from Brown, in exchange for a bill drawn on himself, Taylor canceled part of his own debt in Europe. Brown could then take the bills he received from Taylor and either sell or use them to settle his own debts in Kentucky. Brown would have found an eager buyer in a merchant like John Hunt, who had debts to resolve back east. A bill drawn on Baltimore would have been of far greater value to Hunt's brothers Wilson and Peale in Philadelphia than a bill drawn on Hunt from Lexington, Kentucky. Although Brown and his associates ultimately netted only about $3,650—or $2.75 per barrel of flour—for their troubles, the payment was remitted in the form of a highly flexible bill drawn on William Taylor of Baltimore, exactly the type of bill that was in short supply in trans-Appalachia.[73]

In the summer of 1802, facing a dull market, William Payne decided to sever his partnership with John McDonogh. Payne left for New York, and McDonogh established a new partnership with Shepherd Brown, yet another William Taylor protégée. Together, Brown and McDonogh established two new partnerships. The first, John McDonogh Jr. and Company, was oriented toward the Atlantic and operated as an import/export business, trading with Europe and the eastern seaboard. A second partnership, Shepherd Brown and Company, was oriented toward the river; it would bring American produce—especially flour and cotton—to New Orleans, using their own ships and selling to customers in and north of New Orleans. By the summer of 1803, McDonogh was building his own warehouses to handle the volume of merchandise passing through his hands.[74] McDonogh was determined to take advantage of his position in New Orleans, the central nexus between the continental interior and the Atlantic world.

Under Pinckney's Treaty, the West finally gained the trade outlets it had pursued for decades. By 1801, more than eighty American ships, the bulk of them from Baltimore, New York, and Philadelphia, sailed into the port of New Orleans every autumn.[75] Still, despite the rapid growth of western trade, constraints placed on New Orleans trade by Spanish officials revealed the fiction of the deposit itself: American goods entering the Spanish port became subject to Spanish control. Pinckney's Treaty liberalized trade but did not open it. American interests in New Orleans remained subject to Spanish rules.

The voyages of ships like the *Rebecca* tied Ohio Valley trade to the Atlantic world while increasing the value of western lands. Pinckney's Treaty set in motion Mississippi River trade, intertwining the economies of trans-Appalachia with the southern and eastern United States through a series of overlapping cycles of labor, commerce, and cash—cycles that would grow and evolve as cotton production, along with the forced migration of enslaved and Indigenous peoples, expanded after the Louisiana Purchase. The *Rebecca* followed one such cycle, as people and goods traveled from the Ohio Valley to Natchez, New Orleans, the Caribbean, Europe, and the Atlantic Coast. A second necessary cycle took shape as well: the movement of goods and people from the Ohio Valley to Natchez and New Orleans, and the flow of money and men northward. Both cycles faced crucial choke points over which the United States exerted no control. The first was New Orleans, which was under the control of Spain. The second was along the Natchez Trace, which traveled north through the Chickasaw homeland.

9

The Chickasaw Trace

In 1801, Thomas Jefferson's first postmaster, Joseph Habersham, who had served as postmaster general under both George Washington and John Adams, wrote to Secretary of War Henry Dearborn with a request. The nation needed a road, Habersham argued—one that would create an overland route connecting the lower Mississippi with settlements in the new state of Tennessee. The lack of such a road had long been lamented. In 1799, Secretary of State Timothy Pickering complained to interim Mississippi territorial governor Winthrop Sargent "that the passage of letters from the Natchez is as tedious as from Europe."[1] It took at least two months, often three, for mail to reach Philadelphia from Natchez. Business mail might travel through New Orleans and then on to eastern cities with relative ease, but government correspondence was trickier. As masters of New Orleans, Spanish officials could intercept any mail traveling through the city, making the construction of a road between Tennessee and Natchez a matter of national security. "The public is considerably interested in preserving a proper communication with that distant frontier which is exposed both to the Spaniards & Indians & is quite seperated from the intervening possessions of . . . the United States," Habersham informed Secretary Dearborn.[2] In the event of an attack, the government of Mississippi would be completely isolated. A road connecting them to Tennessee would buttress the region's security, while a post road would allow both information and people to flow between the lower Mississippi Valley and U.S. settlements to the north. Because the route would pass through both a federal territory and the lands of the Choctaw and Chickasaw, the responsibility for creating the road fell to the federal government.

As the volume of western trade grew, a road became an economic necessity. Since the opening of the deposit, "the whole of the produce raised in Kentucky & Tennassee for exportation" had been "conveyed by boats down the Mississippi and the boats with the produce are generally disposed of at New Orleans." Every year, the scale of western trade increased, as did the number of boats making the journey southward to New Orleans. And with the produce came thousands of "hands," young men employed to pilot the boats from the Ohio Valley to the Mississippi. "It being found very expensive & difficult to navigate . . . back against the rapid stream of that river," the men who navigated the boats to New Orleans usually needed to find other transportation home. Within a few years of the opening of the deposit in New Orleans, thousands of westerners began streaming northward through Choctaw and Chickasaw country.[3]

In the eighteenth century, the route that would become known as the Natchez Trace went by many names—the Chickasaw Trace, the Path to the Choctaw, the Natchez Road, the Road to Nashville (going north) or the Road to Natchez (going south). Some called it the "road through the wilderness," while an American map produced in 1795 referred to it as Mountain Leader's Trace, in homage to Piominko, who traversed it often. Historically, the route consisted of a series of paths connecting Chickasaw villages in the Black Prairie to the north with the villages of the Choctaw and Natchez to the south. For centuries, the route had been instrumental to both warfare and trade. Stretching more than five hundred miles north and east of Natchez, the route as it would eventually take shape connected the lower Mississippi with crossings along the Tennessee River in northwestern Alabama, before turning toward the Cumberland and the settlements surrounding Nashville.[4] By 1797, some white settlements could be found just north of Natchez and south of Nashville, but the majority of the trail stretched through lands belonging to the Choctaw and Chickasaw, where it ran through the heart of Chickasaw settlement.

Over the late eighteenth century, Chickasaw political and economic leadership had coalesced into the hands of the Colbert family. James Colbert's political actions during the Revolution have already been discussed, but his family's role in Chickasaw history far exceeded his several years of piracy. In 1740, the Scottish-born Colbert had settled among the Chickasaw. He married a Chickasaw woman from a prominent family in 1758 and settled with her in the village of Chokka' Falaa'; in 1760, he took another wife, a common practice among the polygynous Chickasaw. Colbert's second wife, Noe, was also from Chokka' Falaa', as was his third wife, Sopha, daughter of one of the town chiefs. By 1775, Noe, Sopha, and Colbert's first wife (name unknown) had together borne eight children,

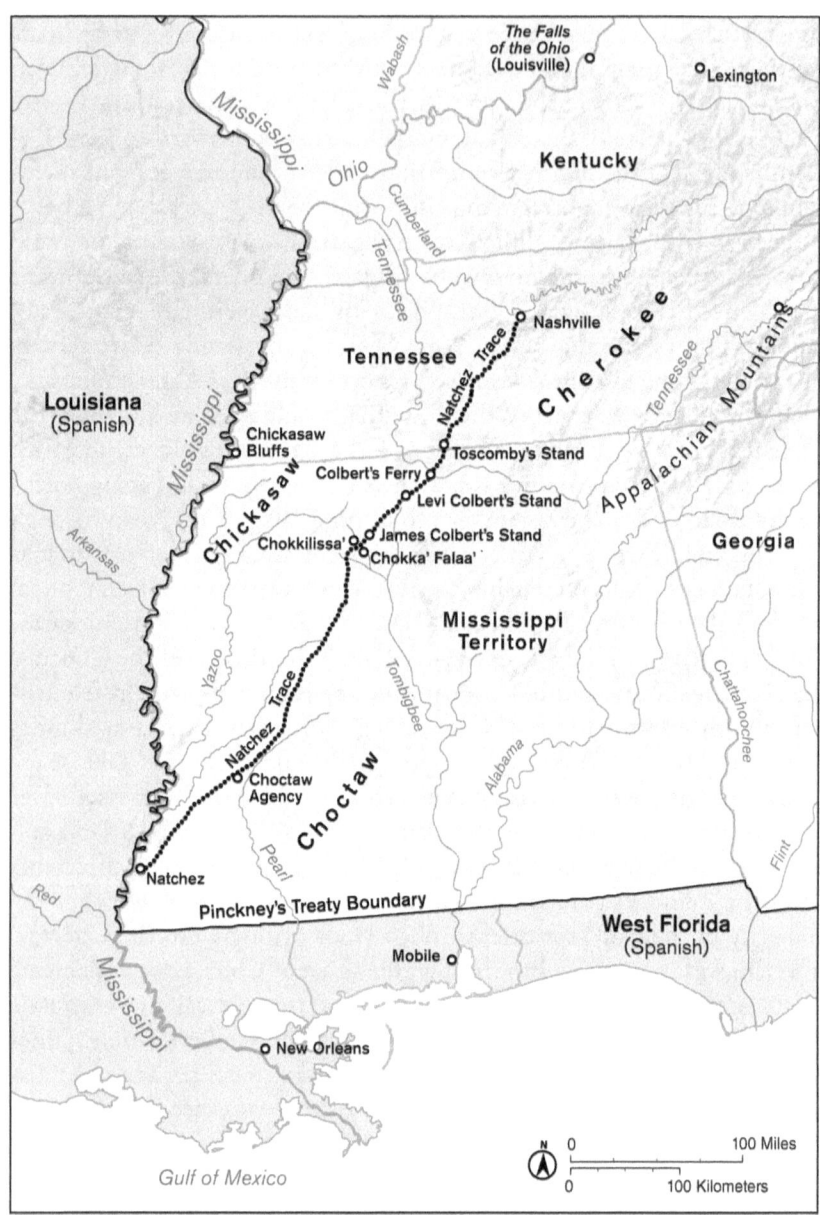

MAP 3. Thousands of European American boatmen trudged north along the Natchez Trace every summer. Increasingly, the Chickasaw moved away from their traditional communities around Chokkilissa' and Chokka' Falaa' to take advantage of new economic opportunities.

six boys and two girls: William (Achooshamaataha), Samuel, George (Toopo'li), Levi (Itti'iwaamba), James Pitman, Joseph, Sally, and Susan.[5] Over the next several decades, these children and their spouses would build on their intercultural heritage and their father's economic success in ways that would both secure their own financial well-being and have significant consequences for the Chickasaw more broadly.[6]

At the end of the eighteenth century, the Colberts became chief players in asserting Chickasaw control over what would become the Natchez Trace. Even before 1801, when the United States proposed construction of a post road along the Trace, the Colberts advanced Chickasaw interests by controlling traffic along the route. As the route grew in importance, it became a key avenue by which cash entered Chickasaw society. Much as Chickasaw control over the bluffs had provided a strategic advantage in negotiating with European powers, their control over the Natchez Trace became the means by which the Chickasaw defended their sovereignty against the United States. In the process, the Trace became a key means of accelerating economic changes underway in Chickasaw territory.

In the eighteenth century, roads constituted an important part of agricultural economies and a vital component of settler expansion. By the time Pinckney's Treaty began full operation in 1798, the federal government was already in the business of road-making. Post roads of the kind that Joseph Habersham wished to see established connected far-flung regions to central markets and distant authorities, and had the potential to link trans-Appalachia to the Atlantic seaboard.[7] Building a road to Natchez was an important step in securing the region's loyalty to the nation. With an economy largely oriented southward to New Orleans and the Atlantic, bonds tying Natchez to the rest of the nation were tenuous. A road stretching from Natchez to Nashville, and then on to settlements in Kentucky and Ohio, would bind westerners broadly to the nation's eastern half by facilitating the return of boatmen, and the cash they carried, to the Ohio Valley.

Although they might perform a similar function of linking distant markets, roads through Indian country were distinctive. To enter Indigenous territory, white people often needed a passport from state officials or from an Indian agent appointed by the federal government. Roads through Indian Territory were typically exempt from this requirement, creating zones of intense cross-cultural interactions.[8] Roads not only offered a means for Americans to pass through Indian Territory; they also brought Americans into the heart of Indigenous homelands. As a result, roads like the Natchez Trace became "arteries of settlement and expansion—facilitating, perhaps more than any other factor, the demographic explosion of the old Southwest." Established by treaty with southeastern Indians, roads through Indian country became discrete sites of contested sovereignty and tools of settler colonialism and imperial expansion.[9] Roads through Indian country created contiguity out of separation: by linking distant areas of white settlement, they united American markets while simultaneously penetrating Indigenous lands yet excluding Indigenous peoples.

The Chickasaw, especially the Colberts, had a distinctive relationship with the road that bisected their territory. They used their control over the Natchez Trace for their own purposes: to bargain with the U.S. government and build the Chickasaw economy.[10] By allowing Americans to cross Chickasaw territory safely, the Chickasaw slowed American efforts to obtain Chickasaw land. Simultaneously, the road drove the development of a service economy—headed by the Colberts—among the Chickasaw people. As money and men began flowing back to the Ohio Valley from New Orleans, Chickasaw control over the Natchez Trace became a key component of the diplomatic and political relationship between the Chickasaw and the U.S. government. As European American boatmen returning from New Orleans tromped through the Chickasaw homeland, the Colberts capitalized on Chickasaw control over this key linkage in the trade between trans-Appalachia and the Atlantic world.

Traveling the Trace

In 1801, the year Habersham urged Dearborn to employ the army to construct a road, nearly six hundred American vessels arrived at New Orleans from across trans-Appalachia.[11] Along with Ohio flour and Kentucky whiskey, some three thousand westerners flowed south annually in a seasonal inundation that helped shape public life in Natchez and New Orleans. Most western cargo was brought downstream in flatboats so ubiquitous they were often called "Kentucky boats," piloted by a captain who might own the boat's cargo along with a crew of four to five men. Cheaply constructed vessels—typically sixty feet long, fifteen feet wide, and four or five feet high—flatboats were essentially rafts with elevated sides, "great square boxes" that, rather than being sailed or rowed downriver, were "abandon[ed] . . . to the mercy of the stream." Boat hands were needed to paddle and pole to avoid obstacles and to navigate the often-shallow waters of the Ohio, but they could rely on the current for forward momentum and expect to be afloat for five or six weeks before arriving in New Orleans. The journey of merchant and astronomer Francis Baily was typical: he departed from Cincinnati on April 8, 1796, and arrived in Natchez on May 11; it took him another five days to reach New Orleans.[12] Like Baily's, most flatboats put in at Natchez for at least a few hours if not a few days. Along the city's docks, merchants like Abijah Hunt struck deals to purchase a flatboat's contents; other crews stopped only long enough to take in the town before traveling on to New Orleans.

Once in port, captains needed to sell their cargo before boatmen could expect their pay. It might take weeks to find buyers. Boatmen kept busy in the meantime retailing barrels of Ohio River water—far sweeter than the water available in New Orleans—and exploring the city's disreputable taverns.[13] Once the cargo was sold, boatmen received their wages of about thirty-five dollars each. It is easy to imagine that New Orleans, with its polyglot denizens and foreign government, would have been overwhelming to some and tantalizing to other boat hands, many of them Kentucky and Ohio farm boys.[14] Meanwhile, the residents of New Orleans denigrated all boatmen as "Kentuckians," regardless of origin, and often complained about their behavior while in port. "Gambling is very frequent, and our foolish Kentucky men spend and lose their money in this place most infamously," an anonymous visitor reported to a friend in 1801. "Large sums are frequently won & lost," another traveler noted, "especially [among] the Kentucky men—who are frequently stripped of all their profits ere' they return home."[15] Almost every observer commented on the boatmen's heavy drinking.

From New Orleans, Ohio Valley boatmen had several options for returning home. Those with means could book passage for Baltimore, Philadelphia, or New York aboard one of the many oceangoing vessels they found in port. Some westerners—usually large planters who had opted to control the sale of their crops directly—traveled on to the Caribbean or Liverpool to manage the sale of their produce, thereby avoiding paying commissions and generating business contacts abroad. Few boatmen could afford to travel as passengers; instead, they signed on as common sailors on oceangoing vessels, a practice that generated frequent complaints from U.S. consuls in New Orleans. In April 1801, Acting Consul Evan Jones reported to Secretary of State Pickering that American sea captains were attempting to take advantage of the annual arrival of backwoodsmen. "The great facility indeed, with which men are found, especially at this season, who come down in boats from the upper country," Jones reported, led oceangoing ship captains to "beat and abuse" their crews, hoping to force crew members to desert once they arrived in New Orleans. Financially, the crew's desertion would be a boon to the captain; crew members who sailed from eastern ports were paid a specific percentage of the voyage's profits, whereas backwoods settlers would "willingly work their passages to the Atlantic States."[16] Boatmen from western Pennsylvania were more likely to take this route, working their way north to Philadelphia before heading home overland along the well-traveled wagon road between the port and Pittsburgh.

Other westerners decided to return to the Ohio Valley by river, hiring on as part of a keelboat crew. Built long and skinny to slice through water, keelboats were more maneuverable than flatboats, taking advantage of eddies along the riverbank where the current was slower to move north. It was arduous work. When they could, keelboat crews rowed; when they could not, they poled. Each man stood near the gunwales with a long wooden pole, tipped with iron, held to his side. When the pilot gave the signal, they sank their poles into the water, braced it against their shoulders, and walked toward the stern, slowly inching the boat northward by essentially walking the distance they were traveling many times over, one sixty-foot length of the keelboat at a time. Sometimes, when the banks were clear, keelboat crews walked along the shore and pulled their boats northward; other times, they sent a few men ahead to tie a rope around a large tree, slowly wound the rope back up until they were parallel with the tree, and repeated the process. Keelboats were used mostly by fur traders, who carried large supplies of manufactured goods northward for trading with Indigenous peoples along the Mississippi, the Missouri, or one of their many smaller offshoots. Keelboat crews often comprised men from a mix of cultural backgrounds. No matter their nationality, this was difficult and dangerous work. It is hardly surprising that most Ohio Valley boatmen instead chose to walk home.[17]

Boatmen traveling back to the Ohio Valley overland returned first to Natchez, where they readied themselves for the 550-mile walk to Nashville and points beyond. Knowing that those who arrived in New Orleans first would sell their goods for the highest prices, they may not have paused in Natchez for long on their way south. But on the way north, they could take their time. For most boatmen, the attraction was not the town of Natchez, sitting high on a bluff overlooking the river; instead, their destination was the Natchez port, which had developed in the floodplain along the river's banks and was now home to a vibrant service economy that catered to the needs of Mississippi trade. Docks littered the waterfront, as did warehouses where consignment merchants could store goods. Natchez-under-the-Hill, as the port came to be called, quickly developed a reputation for sin and debauchery. James Hall, who visited Natchez in 1800, sardonically described the boatmen streaming into the city as not to his mind "the most regular livers." "Lodging either in their boats, or in and about the dram-shops" of Natchez-under-the-Hill, "thoughtless as sailors or soldiers, and as fond of whiskey," the Ohio Valley boatmen consumed "vast quantities of spirituous liquor." Gambling and prostitution were rampant.[18] By 1803, twenty-five licensed taverns served the little city.

Natchez—both Natchez-under-the-Hill and the more respectable town growing atop it—embodies the ways that Mississippi River trade was underpinned by slavery beyond the plantation. While almost all boatmen were white, the port of Natchez, like the port of New Orleans, depended on enslaved labor for the functioning of its trade. Black porters, longshoremen, carters, and draymen loaded and unloaded goods along the docks or stored them in the port's warehouses, and transported barrels of water from the river to the elegant dwellings atop the cliff. Although white, Native American, and free women of African descent worked as prostitutes, some of the sex workers who made Natchez-under-the-Hill notorious were enslaved. For these men and women, the annual arrival of the Kentucky boatmen brought a renewed season of exploitation.[19]

Few boatmen lingered long in Natchez on their return journey. Having arrived in New Orleans in April or May, they were typically on their way home by June or July, looking to avoid the worst of the summer's heat and the malaria and other diseases common to the lower Mississippi Valley. Often, Ohio Valley boatmen traveled north in groups, hoping for safety in numbers and company along a journey that would last for more than a month.

The Boatmen's Trace

IN THE 1790s, the Trace was not a road but "a skein of loosely braided tracks" that, like many western roads, "serpentine[d] through ... boundless forests," radiating outward from the Chickasaw homeland.[20] An ancient trading path connected the Chickasaw villages of the Black Prairie in the north with the villages of the Choctaw and Natchez to the south; a newer and increasingly well-trodden path connected the Chickasaw villages with the new European American settlement at Nashville. In many places, the way was more suggested than marked: the ground along the Trace was rough and broken, composed of a "sandy and gravelly soil," a path so narrow that "in many places [it was] hardly discernible" and travelers often lost their way.[21] Sitting atop the ridge that separates the Mississippi watershed from that of the Tombigbee River, the route travels through forests, barrens, and swamps. Finding potable water along its route was a constant concern, as was drowning in the path's numerous river crossings.[22] A journey along the Trace was best summarized by Philip Buckner, who recorded its highlights in an 1801 diary: "muskeetoos Gnats & water very bad."[23]

On July 4, 1797, the British merchant Francis Baily left Natchez along with twelve companions and thirty or forty horses laden with biscuit, flour, bacon, and dried beef to feed the party on its way north to Kentucky. The path was by no means deserted: early in their journey, Baily and his companions encountered a party of forty Indigenous warriors returning from a battle across the Mississippi, and at a crossroads connecting the Trace to the villages of the Choctaw they happened on two members of that nation who could point them further on their journey. Nature posed a far more formidable threat than people. Baily encountered alligators, storms, and a driving thirst relieved only by drinking the dew from grass after searching in vain for a water source.[24] In 1797, there were no inns or taverns along the way to accommodate travelers, and few places to acquire more supplies. Despite these difficulties, Baily's journey marked the beginning of a transformation in usage of the path that would accelerate over the next several decades. As American traffic on the Mississippi increased, the path through Choctaw and Chickasaw country became increasingly well-traveled and accessible.

Travel along the Trace was distinctive in two ways. First, while occasional travelers journeyed southward along the Trace, the annual influx of boat men overwhelmingly moved from south to north, shaping how the road came to be used. Second, it was widely known that travelers on the Natchez road carried "large sums of money."[25] This was certainly the case for Baily. On July 12, his party encountered a near disaster when, "by some unfortunate accident," one of the horses' saddles slipped, spooking the horse, who "was so frightened that he set off into the woods as fast as his legs could carry him.... The other horses seeing this, set off also; and in a moment we were left in a deplorable situation. Bereft of all our provisions and clothes, and deprived of every means of continuing our journey." Baily and his companions lamented the loss of their food stores but more alarming still was the loss of money. "Some of these horses," Baily recalled, "were laden wholly with dollars, the proceeds of the cargo some of our party had taken down the river." The fleeing horses carried with them the profits from years of labor.[26]

The merchants who facilitated Ohio Valley trade were responsible for much of the money that moved over the Trace.[27] Although journeys without incident went mostly unrecorded, the few reports of theft give a sense of the volume of money flowing along the Trace at the turn of the century. In 1799, an express rider working on behalf of Abijah Hunt was robbed of $20,000 on his journey to Cincinnati.[28] In 1802, a party of eleven men was robbed of $1,300 along the Trace; one traveler, luckier than his associates, fled at the first sign of thieves, "ran about two miles," and "concealed" saddlebags containing $2,300 in the woods.[29]

Baily and his companions—who eventually hunted down all of the escaped horses—became some of the first travelers to inject New Orleans specie into the economies of Kentucky, Tennessee, and Ohio. The opening of the New Orleans deposit in 1798 increased the number of men traveling along the Trace and the volume of cash they carried. In June 1801, the *Tennessee Gazette*, published in Nashville, reported, "From the best calculations we are able to make there has not less than 120,000 dollars crossed the Cumberland at this place from New Orleans and the Natchez, destined for Kentucky, and the back parts of Pennsylvania, and horseloads daily passing."[30] One early resident of Tennessee recalled that "most of the money in circulation in Tennessee, especially the mountainous portions," was carried to the district by flatboat men along the Trace.[31] That same year, reports from Kentucky echoed the *Tennessee Gazette*. The previous April, Kentucky judge Samuel Hopkins had informed a potential land seller that money was scarce in Kentucky; by the end of that summer, he reported a sea change in local circumstances. In September 1801, he wrote to his son that "70 horses & mules loaded with money from Orleans, Natchez &c have arrived in Kentucky & Tenassee this year tis Certain there is much more cash in Circulation of late."[32] The men walking north from Natchez frequently carried more money than they had ever seen in their lives.

Decades before Americans would settle along its boundaries, the Natchez Trace became a key artery of American expansion—not by promoting settlement but by enabling trade. The Trace tied together speculation in western lands with Atlantic world trade, binding trans-Appalachia into networks of exchange that stretched across the United States to the Caribbean and Europe. By 1802, the federal treasury could report that western residents had shipped 73,058 barrels of flour, 615 barrels of whiskey, and 67,692 pounds of bacon to Natchez; the proceeds, valued in excess of a million dollars, were carried along the Trace back to Kentucky, Tennessee, Ohio, and Pennsylvania.[33] The image of dusty, sunburned boat hands trudging hundreds of miles through the Mississippi Valley does not align with a view of Atlantic world trade as the province of merchants and seaports. When we examine the movement of goods, we expect to see ships—not hundreds of Opelousa ponies carrying cash through a Mississippi summer. Yet, with their money loaded onto horses, rolled into packs, or sewn up into shirts, returning boatmen became the final link in a chain of interactions allowing Ohio Valley settlers to transform western land into cash. By enabling this transformation, the Trace supported the value of investments made in Kentucky, Tennessee, and Ohio—by individuals and by the federal government.

The Trace helped to cement western loyalty to a national polity. The Adams administration recognized the importance of building a road connecting Natchez to the United States, but not until the presidency of Thomas Jefferson did efforts to improve the Trace begin in earnest. In 1801, Congress authorized a team of commissioners to negotiate with the Cherokee, Choctaw, and Chickasaw "to obtain their consent for opening a road which may facilitate the communication between Natches and the settlements on the Ohio," and "for the cession of some spots of ground, at convenient distances, whereon to erect houses for the accommodation of travellers." In Kentucky and Tennessee, where voting had heavily favored Jefferson, the federal initiative was regarded as a sign of the "friendly disposition of the executive towards" the union's western regions. The new road would not only provide "great aid" to western "commerce down the river"; it also signaled Jefferson's "disposition to advance, in every respect, this valuable and productive" territory.[34] In Nashville, the *Tennessee Gazette* hailed the proposal as demonstrating Jefferson's "mark[ed] . . . attachment to the interest of the most remote parts of the United States." Nothing "could tend more to the welfare of the Western country than" the construction of "a road from Nashville, to the Natchez . . . and the great advantages which we may expect from the American Union begin now to be manifested."[35] As an act of domestic policy, improving the Trace helped cement western loyalty not only to the nation but to the Democratic-Republican Party.

In fall 1801, commissioners General James Wilkinson, Indian Superintendent Benjamin Hawkins, and Andrew Pickens met with leaders of the three tribes. The Cherokee—who faced the greatest pressure from white settlement—refused to allow a road through their territory. Happily for the commissioners, the proposed route lay largely outside Cherokee territory. Facing a subsistence crisis caused by drought and the decline of their traditional game, the Choctaw agreed to cede more than 2.5 million acres in the southwest corner of their territory and gave the United States permission to construct a "wagon way" through their territory in exchange for a payment of $2,000.[36] Only the permission of the Chickasaw remained.

The Chickasaw Trace

When U.S. commissioners met with Chickasaw leaders at the Chickasaw Bluffs in October 1801, they met with representatives of a nation transformed. When Piominko—the old U.S. ally and savvy defender of Chickasaw interests—was born in the 1750s, nearly the entire Chickasaw nation lived huddled within the environs of Chokkilissa'. Perpetually at war with the Creek and Choctaw, the Chickasaw had abandoned earlier patterns of dispersed settlement in favor of defense. The advent of peace in the 1770s and 1780s allowed the Chickasaw gradually to spread outward and reoccupy traditional village sites. At the time of Piominko's death in 1798, most Chickasaw lived in traditional village sites. But by 1800, there were again noticeable shifts in settlement patterns. The process of dispersal begun in the 1780s had accelerated, as had changes in Chickasaw agricultural practices. Increasingly, instead of cultivating traditional food crops of corn, squash, and beans, the Chickasaw were turning to commercial farming. Many Chickasaw farmers had tried ranching, expanding their holdings to accommodate the needs of grazing animals. Others had begun to produce cotton, some of it used in domestic fabric production and some exported for sale elsewhere.[37]

These changes were significant. By 1801, Benjamin Hawkins, general superintendent of Indian affairs in the South, could report that the Chickasaw were "settling out from their old towns and fencing their farms. They have within two years fenced near 150 [farms], and all of the farmers have a stock of cattle or hogs."[38] By 1805, Philadelphia physician Rush Nutt reported that Chickasaw towns were nearly deserted. At Chokkilissa', "formerly the residence of the whole nation . . . not more than 8 or 10 families remain in the old fields. They have settled out & made tolerable farms with ... fences." At Piominko's Chokka' Falaa' the situation had changed even more. Although nearly five hundred people remained in the district, "all the Indians [had] removed out of long-town, & settled in different parts of the country." The advantages of the surrounding countryside in providing "range, water & timber" offered better opportunities for new pursuits, including cotton production and raising stock.[39]

The Chickasaw were reacting to a variety of stressors that wrought major changes in their economic practices. The rapidly shrinking white-tailed deer population and concomitant decline in deerskin trade was one factor. Another was Spain's increasing inability to act as a counterweight to American influences. A third was the "civilization policy" that characterized early U.S.-Indian affairs and which the Chickasaw used to their advantage. None of these differences led to wholesale cultural change, but together they prompted significant modifications to the organization of Chickasaw society.

The Chickasaw also reorganized themselves politically. In the eighteenth century, towns were the chief organizational component of Chickasaw governance. In 1800, the Chickasaw divided their territory into four regions, each with a council that included the headmen of every household in the district as well as the district's military leaders. The leaders of these local councils were authorized to speak on the district's behalf during national councils. While the district councils dealt with local matters—including the distribution of land, which was held in common—the national council negotiated with foreign leaders. Chickasaw practice was for the various councils to discuss upcoming meetings with foreign delegations well in advance, sharing the issues most likely to be discussed and developing consensus about a path forward. But the Chickasaw had also learned a lesson about U.S. diplomatic practices with Indigenous nations: the Americans were happy to treat with any leader who seemed likely to serve U.S. interests. They had only to recall their own experiences: although Ugulayacabé (leader of the Spanish faction) and Piominko had held relatively equal positions within Chickasaw society, the Americans were happy to engage Piominko to the exclusion of Ugulayacabé. To avoid this problem in the future, the Chickasaw turned to their traditional leadership position of the Tisho Mingo, the Minko's assistant. Henceforth, one Tisho Mingo would speak for the Chickasaw during negotiations, a position historian Ronald Eugene Craig likened to serving as the Chickasaw secretary of state.[40] Recognizing the importance of having a Tisho Mingo who was familiar with American motivations and understood English, the Chickasaw turned to George Colbert to serve as the reorganized government's first spokesperson.[41]

The 1801 meeting with the American commissioners marked Colbert's first opportunity to exercise his new role. The Chickasaw surprised the commissioners with how quickly they agreed for a road to be constructed through their lands. To deny access to the road would engender conflict with the federal government and the thousands of boatmen who journeyed through their territory each year.[42] Knowing this, the Chickasaw bartered the boatmen's safe passage through their territory to protect themselves from European American encroachment on their lands. The Chickasaw would permit the construction of a road and the passage of Americans along it, but they would make no further concessions. When the commissioners asked that two or three white families be allowed to build accommodations for travelers along the way, the Chickasaw refused. Although they agreed to further deliberations over how to establish stands along the road, the Chickasaw forbade "any of the whites [to] Settle on the road, or have any profit arising therefrom." Instead, the Chickasaw decided "that three Settlements be made by [their] own people" to see to the needs of travelers along the Trace. This refusal was directly tied to Chickasaw land distribution practices. Because land was held in common, only Chickasaw tribal members were eligible to hold property, and they refused to cede any of their lands. The Chickasaw drove this point home repeatedly. Chinubbee, the Chickasaw Minko, broke traditional protocols against the Minko speaking during diplomatic engagements to inform the commissioners that he was "very glad to hear" that their proposals did "not require the cession of land, or anything of the kind."[43] Speaking on behalf of the council and the broader Chickasaw people, Colbert explained that the Chickasaw intended that all "the advantages to be derived from" the road be reserved to them.[44]

While the resulting treaty strongly resonated with Chickasaw interests, there were aspects that particularly benefited the Colbert family. Colbert had brought the strategic importance of ferries to the attention of the national council in 1797, pre-reorganization, and was subsequently granted the privilege of operating a ferry along the Tennessee River, a privilege that was accompanied by permission to use a 350-acre parcel of land nearby.[45] In 1799, he and his brother Levi established a ferry at the Duck River to help travelers across. The opening of the Colberts' ferry proved so useful that it diverted the traditional route of the Trace nearly two and a half miles east. The ferry became a resting point and landmark along the Trace, giving the Colberts—and the Chickasaw more broadly—an opportunity to profit from the Americans passing through their territory. Establishing the ferry helped to drive Chickasaw dispersal. Many former residents of Chokka' Falaa' moved to the ferry site, drawn by their township affiliation with the Colberts and the certainty of new markets. By 1803, Chickasaw agent Samuel Mitchell reported that "the purpose" of such families moving was to "[furnish] travelers with corn and Meat."[46] Their relocation reinforced the profitability of the Colberts' business enterprises. The presence of the ferry and the possibility of obtaining much-needed supplies were both factors driving traffic along the Trace to the ferry. Despite the new location, Chickasaw cultural practices persisted even as the community adapted to new economic opportunities; most of the families who moved to the site shared traditional township affiliations with the Colberts.[47]

The Colberts not only built ferries to ease travelers' way along the Trace; they also constructed accommodations along the road. George Colbert operated a store and provided some basic accommodations on the south side of the Tennessee River; in 1801, a traveler on the Trace reported having purchased "7 quarts of whiskey at 1 Dol. Per quart and 4 dried fish at 6 pc apiece" at George Colbert's store.[48] Levi Colbert operated a store on the north side of the river, as well as a tavern and a store at Buzzard Roost, about eight miles south. The post of Tockshish, or McIntoshville—originally the home of British Indian agent John McIntosh—stood another fifty miles south and had a strong connection to the Colberts: John McIntosh was married to Sopha, James Logan Colbert's third wife. When McIntosh died, Sopha carried on running the inn by herself.[49] Further south still, Levi Kemp, who had a white father and Chickasaw mother, operated a stand near his home. The only other stopping point in Chickasaw territory was at the Chickasaw Agency, the home of the federal official charged with overseeing American relations with the nation.[50]

By 1801, not only were the Chickasaw raising ever-larger flocks of cattle, sheep, and hogs; they were also producing cotton. Eager to support this effort as part of its "civilization" policy, the federal government provided cotton cards, spinning wheels, and looms, along with American artisans to train Chickasaw in the use of these devices. In part, the effort was intended to force Chickasaw gender patterns to resemble American ones, as Chickasaw women joined their American contemporaries in the seemingly unending task of creating textiles. But its success was due to its alignment with Chickasaw interests: producing cotton, spinning thread, and weaving cloth allowed the Chickasaw to become less dependent on trading with U.S. merchants. In 1801, the federal government delivered material to the Choctaw to construct a cotton gin; when the Choctaw rejected it, George Colbert had it erected at what became known as Cotton Gin Port, a town on the eastern shore of the Tombigbee River. From there, it was easy to export Chickasaw cotton and deer hides to Spanish Mobile. Colbert's actions furthered the collective goal of greater Chickasaw independence while also accruing benefits to himself.[51]

As the number of travelers along the Trace increased, the Chickasaw positioned themselves to take advantage of the growing American presence. Even after they agreed to open the road, Chickasaw control over its resources—especially its ferry crossings, inns, and food supplies—allowed them to effectively control passage along the road. Their partnership in making the road more usable became a bargaining tool in their negotiations with U.S. government officials. When the United States approached the Chickasaw about selling some land north of the Tennessee River in 1805, their response was immediate: they would not sell. After all, at the treaty negotiations at the Chickasaw Bluffs in 1801, the American commissioners had promised to not "ask any further favors of us after we granted them the favor of a road through our nation."[52] By partnering with the United States to allow safe passage for Americans through their territory, the Chickasaw were able to resist ceding Chickasaw land.

Although the Chickasaw continued to assert their authority over the road, the federal government's determination to transform the Trace into a road arose from the desire to cement its authority in the Southwest. Even before the Chickasaw agreed to the road's creation, General James Wilkinson had already ordered four companies of soldiers to the northern end of the Trace to begin clearing the path; a second detachment of troops began widening the road from its southern terminus after the Choctaw agreed that it could pass through their territory. The work was tedious and difficult, clearing hundreds of miles of brush across a distance wide enough to allow for the passage of a wagon, building bridges where possible and felling logs to act as bridges where it was not. Construction was expensive and time-consuming; Wilkinson's troops never made it more than forty miles below Colbert's ferry, leaving much of the road untouched, and brush and trees were quick to reclaim what had been cleared.[53]

Nevertheless, it did not take long for the Natchez Trace to become the most important road in the Southwest. When U.S. mail began traveling up and down the Trace, it became a vital link connecting Natchez and the new Mississippi Territory to the rest of the United States: the U.S. government could now govern the region from a distance. It also allowed news to flow from south to north. When events occurred in Natchez, word arrived in Nashville ten days later and in Lexington soon after. The Trace provided a key link in a chain that allowed farmers in Kentucky, Tennessee, and the Ohio Territory to obtain the cash they needed to secure their lands and profit from the connections. Cash was never abundant in the West—or anywhere in the early republic, for that matter—but the opening of Mississippi trade, and of the Natchez Trace, eased the way for circulating currency to reach Nashville and move onward to Kentucky.

As a tool of union, the Trace quickly proved useful. In October 1802, when word arrived in Natchez that Spain had terminated the American right of deposit in New Orleans, riders were immediately dispatched along the Trace to bring the news to Nashville and Kentucky. Despite the U.S. government's attempts to improve the road, it took three weeks for the news to arrive in Nashville; it would be another eleven days before word reached Kentucky. It would not have taken long for the governors of Tennessee and Kentucky to summon their militias to march southward along the Trace. No longer dependent on the water levels of the Ohio and Tennessee Rivers, troops could now arrive in Natchez to protect American interests along the river faster than ever before. The only reason the Kentucky and Tennessee militias did *not* march south was the effort made by their governments to urge their populations to allow the federal government to attempt to reopen the river. But quick and violent action remained a possibility in ways it had not been previously. With a growing American population at Natchez and New Orleans, the Trace offered the United States a way to mobilize against foreign powers. It is no wonder that a few months earlier Wilkinson had asserted, "This Road being completed I shall consider our Southern extremity assured, the Indians in that quarter at our feet & the adjacent Province laid open to us."[54] As further word arrived that Spain had retroceded Louisiana and New Orleans to France, the Trace offered powerful reassurance to western residents of the United States that the federal government could assert its authority in the Mississippi Valley as it confronted the threat posed by France.

The Natchez Trace transformed the political economies of the communities it connected: in the lower Mississippi Valley, the Chickasaw homeland, middle Tennessee, Kentucky, and the Ohio Valley settlements beyond. Americans had spent years clamoring for Mississippi River trade yet had failed to realize the importance of this final link in the circuit tying trans-Appalachia to the Atlantic world. From 1798 until the widespread adoption of the steamboat in the 1810s, the Natchez Trace played a central role in transporting and generating cash for trans-Appalachia—cash that could be used to settle western debts with eastern merchants, pay taxes, and finance further land purchases. The Trace played an important part in justifying—*after the fact*—the decisions of thousands of European American families to gamble their futures in moving westward.

For the Chickasaw, the Trace also played a transformative role. Only recently have historians begun to genuinely integrate the experiences of Indigenous peoples into broader accounts of political economy, demonstrating how financial capitalism operated on Native peoples to hasten their dispossession.[55] As Emilie Connolly has shown in her account of the links among the federal government, state banks, and the dispossession of the Chickasaw, in the "unusual agreement" the Chickasaw negotiated with the federal government in 1832 and 1834, they would "receive as compensation for their land the entirety of the proceeds of its sale," placed into a trust by the federal government.[56] The experience of the Chickasaw in the 1830s tied directly back to the experience of the Chickasaw in the 1790s. As a result of their position along the Trace and savvy reinvestment of their profits, the Chickasaw were better capitalized and therefore better positioned than their southeastern neighbors to assert their interests. Yet, despite Chickasaw use of the Trace, the road nevertheless functioned as an agent of dispossession in its own right. By making western expansion profitable, the Trace contributed to the rapid growth of the cotton South, growth that would explode in the aftermath of the Louisiana Purchase.

Although the Chickasaw were essential actors in the opening of the Trace, enslaved men and women provided much of the labor that made travel along the trace possible. George Colbert enslaved roughly twenty people when he first began operating the ferry over the Tennessee River; in 1806, he would justify charging high rates to U.S. military personnel by explaining that three to five enslaved men operated his ferries, and the cost of purchasing and feeding them was especially high in Indian Territory.[57] For African Americans, the transformation of the Trace into an artery of western trade had longstanding consequences. While white boatmen traversed the path south to north, the smattering of settlers and missionaries heading south were often joined by coffles of enslaved people being forcibly relocated from Kentucky and Tennessee to the cotton fields of the lower Mississippi Valley. Tens of thousands of enslaved people, shackled two by two, shuffled southward along the road that had been opened by the federal government to serve western interests. As early as the 1790s, Natchez's infamous Forks of the Road slave market was constructed at the southern terminus of the Natchez Trace.[58]

10

Buying the Mississippi

———•◆•———

THE OPENING of the Mississippi brought prosperity to the trans-Appalachian West. In the late fall of 1802, James Garrard, Kentucky's second governor, proclaimed, "The earth still pours out for us lavishly products of every kind." "Our population, our agriculture, our mechanic arts, and our commerce by the Mississippi, are still in a progressive and improving state," but great things lay in store for the future. "Vessels built on our own rivers" would soon travel from the Ohio Valley, "transporting our commodities to the most distant quarters of the globe." Garrard had every reason to believe himself justified in holding "a flattering view of the resources and future greatness of our country." "Harmony," he concluded, "prevails among our citizens and confidence exists in the national government."[1]

Between January and October 1802, over 3 million pounds of Natchez cotton entered the New Orleans deposit; in May 1802 alone, 27,129 barrels of flour arrived in New Orleans from Kentucky, Tennessee, and the "American establishments" upriver—an amount that merchants could expect to sell for over £60,000 (or $274,000) in Liverpool.[2] Natchez was now "an extensive, opulent and privileged society," according to James Wilkinson.[3] For four years, westerners in Pennsylvania, Kentucky, Tennessee, and the Natchez district had access to Atlantic and European markets for their produce. "The extension of commerce here is now fully adequate to the agricultural interest," Kentucky judge Samuel Hopkins enthused in 1801, "a thing never known before in a Country of our age."[4] The opening of the Mississippi fulfilled western hopes, as produce from trans-Appalachia had entered the Atlantic world.

The trade through New Orleans was important not only to westerners. The day the *Rebecca* sailed out of New Orleans, bound for Havana and Liverpool, it left behind fourteen American vessels: the *Aurora* of New York was slated to sail to the Isle of Wight with a cargo of cotton; the *Thomas Wilson* of Philadelphia sailed for Liverpool with a cargo of flour and cotton, as did the *Commerce* of Norwich, Connecticut, and the *Patterson* of Providence, Rhode Island. The *Neptune* of Nantucket was preparing to set sail for the Scottish port of Greenock loaded with Natchez cotton, while the *Juliana* of New York and the *Betsy* out of Newburyport, Massachusetts, prepared to sail to New York and Boston, respectively, loaded with cotton. The *Fame*, the *Ceres*, and the *Maria Woods* each had cargoes of flour and destinations in the West Indies; the *York* and the *Carlotta* were Charleston-bound. The ever-growing swell of movement into the western regions laid the basis for rising exportation. In 1790, Kentucky's population stood at 73,677 and Tennessee's at roughly 35,000. By 1800, the population of Kentucky had more than doubled to 220,955, while the population of Tennessee had nearly tripled to 105,602.[5] Ohio, poised on the brink of statehood, now had 45,635 residents while the population of the Mississippi Territory, still only 7,600, was growing rapidly.[6] Two other ships moored in the Mississippi in the spring of 1802 hinted at this growth: the *Ohio*, sailing out of Philadelphia, was chartered to carry a cargo of flour to Liverpool, while the *Monongahela Farmer* was headed to New York loaded with cotton.[7]

But even as westerners extolled their achievements, their prosperity faced a significant new obstacle. By the Treaty of Ildefonso, King Charles IV of Spain ceded Louisiana to the French in exchange for Italian land to be given his son-in-law (and cousin) the Duke of Parma.[8] Ratified in 1800, the treaty's terms were kept secret until 1802, when peace in Europe finally ended nearly a decade of war. In late winter 1802, as European combatants waited to hear the terms of the Peace of Amiens (an uneasy truce between Britain and France), rumors of the Spanish retrocession of Louisiana were confirmed. Napoleonic France was to become the new neighbor of the United States.

The prospect of a French-owned Louisiana changed the calculus of North American geopolitics. "Louisiana is ceded to France, whose well-fleshed blood-hounds will be howling rownd the skirts of your naked plantations before you have time to collect the means of resistance," warned the *New York Herald*.[9] "Louisiana under the superintendence and protection of France, will form in a manner another new world," another New York paper reported.[10] Just as Spain once feared an expansive American republic arrayed along its borders, now the United States faced the specter of a creeping French power, under a Bonaparte with "no bounds to [his] ambition ... [and] no limit to his inordinate views."[11] Napoleon's armies had roared through Switzerland, conquered northern Italy, defeated the Holy Roman Empire, forced the Russian empire to withdraw from the war, and arrived at an uneasy peace with Britain, the world's greatest naval power. What chance would a small U.S. Army accustomed to fighting American Indians, and an active navy of only 195 men—officers and captains included—have against the French behemoth?[12] Newspapers up and down the coast compared the French in Louisiana to "a serpent at [our] feet, by which [we] will ultimately be devoured."[13]

These fears were not overblown. Americans and especially the Jefferson administration feared that the loss of U.S. trade through New Orleans would threaten the nation's continued unity. From 1786 until 1795, the U.S. government's inability to obtain New Orleans trade led repeatedly to western separatist movements, and President Jefferson and other prominent politicians feared that losing access to New Orleans would drive westerners to seek out a new government that could protect their economic interests. Jefferson placed retaining U.S. trade through New Orleans at the heart of his administration's response to the transfer of Louisiana. In April 1802, Jefferson sent a carefully worded letter to Robert Livingston, a prominent New Yorker and resident U.S. minister to France. The oft-cited letter, which evidence suggests Jefferson intended for French officials to read, invoked the threat of a possible American realignment with Britain in the event of a French takeover of New Orleans and offered a bleak—and likely overstated—assessment of the consequences of a French New Orleans for the United States. It also summarized Jefferson's thoughts on the importance of New Orleans. "There is on the globe one single spot," Jefferson informed Livingston and, presumably, French officials, "the possessor of which is our natural and habitual enemy. It is New Orleans, through which the produce of three-eighths of our territory must pass to market, and from its fertility will ere long yield more than half of our whole produce, and contain more than half of our inhabitants." The threat posed by retrocession was not the vague fear of a French colony along the banks of the Mississippi; it was an existential blow to union.[14] Charles Pinckney, stationed in Madrid as the U.S. minister to Spain, stated the administration's fears clearly: "Should the Western inhabitants ever have the Opinion or entertain the idea that it was to France they were to look for the permission to navigate & deposit & not to their own Government," the suspicion alone might "produce a

Separation." Jefferson's policy focused on retaining American trade through New Orleans in order to shore up the union between East and West.[15]

Expansion and commerce are often treated as separate goals of statecraft. In the trade of New Orleans, the two pursuits merged: the retrocession of Louisiana created a twofold crisis for the Jefferson administration.[16] Americans from across the political and geographic spectrum recognized that maintaining the nation's western possessions depended on providing westerners with commercial connections. A New York newspaper reported that the "disadvantages which will most probably result from" the cession for the nation's "western citizens ... are too obvious to require comment." Trade gave land worth, and if France controlled the Mississippi, "the produce of Kentucky, of the Natchez, and of all that immense portion of our territory which lies contiguous to the river, will be of little value to its owners."[17] To preserve western loyalty, Jefferson and his cabinet needed to safeguard western trade, without which the union would falter. Because continued western prosperity would depend on French goodwill, the administration needed to maintain a careful balance, ensuring "that nothing be said or done which will unnecessarily irritate our future neighbors, or check the liberality which they may be disposed to exercise in relation to the trade and navigation through the mouth of the Mississippi." Secretary of State James Madison urged Livingston to "patronize the interests of our Western fellow citizens, by cherishing in France every just and liberal disposition towards their commerce" through New Orleans.[18]

Jefferson and his cabinet had good reason to fear that the retrocession would cause another sectional crisis. That the crisis never materialized—that the West remained loyal to the union and allowed the federal government to resolve its concerns over Mississippi River trade—is testament to how attitudes had changed since 1786, and how western dedication to the Jeffersonian Republicans disposed them to await federal action. In part, this inclination was driven by changes to the nation's eastern half and attitudes there toward the West: connections between the two regions forged by increased trade inspired universal outrage at French control of the Mississippi, as easterners also lobbied for government action on the river. Indeed, Spain's decision to close the port of New Orleans, followed by news of the retrocession, drew calls for unity from across the nation, and precipitated the diplomatic negotiations that sealed the Louisiana Purchase and the fate of countless eastern merchants, western farmers, Native American proprietors, enslaved Africans, and European laborers who converted western cotton into marketable cloth.

The Closing of the Deposit

On October 16, 1802, acting on a secret order he received from Madrid, Juan Morales, the Spanish intendant of Louisiana, closed the American deposit and barred American shipping from New Orleans. With the advent of peace, Morales decreed, Spain was no longer required to admit the trade of neutral nations: "From this date the privilege which the Americans had of importing and depositing their merchandize and effects in this capital [New Orleans], shall be interdicted."[19] The news was shocking, threatening at one blow the trade networks created over the previous four years and catching even the Spanish governor of Louisiana by surprise. Hoping that the closure was a matter of local caprice rather than an act of imperial policy, the merchants of New Orleans, both American and Spanish, implored the intendant to reopen the right of deposit, claiming that by the Treaty of San Lorenzo, Spain had promised to allow Americans to deposit their goods at New Orleans. Were Spain to withdraw that permission, it was supposed to designate "another part of the banks of the Mississipi [as] an equivalent establishment." Arguing that the treaty stipulated only that the port remain open for three years, and that Spain could then close or continue the right of deposit at its discretion, Morales refused to change course. Americans would no longer be allowed to deposit their goods at New Orleans.[20]

In response, William Hulings, acting U.S. consul in New Orleans, dashed off a message to James Madison: "The difficulties and risks of property that will fall on the Citizens of the United States, if deprived of their deposit, are incalculable." American ships arriving in harbor from the eastern seaboard could not land their wares, while American flatboats arriving from upriver could no longer unload cargo in New Orleans. Cargo had to remain aboard the flatboat until being transferred onto an American ship—a method not only difficult but dangerous. Flatboats arriving from upriver were "so frail, and so subject to be sunk by storms, that they cannot be converted into floating Stores, to wait the arrival of Sea Vessels to carry away their Cargoes," Hulings warned.[21] Waiting the days or even weeks it could take to make a sale exposed both crew and cargo to constant danger. Once western farmers found a buyer and the produce was sold, the bulky hogsheads of tobacco, barrels of flour, or bags of cotton still needed transferring from flatboat to ship. A hogshead of tobacco generally weighed about five hundred pounds; after the widespread adoption of the cotton press, a bag of cotton could easily weigh over three hundred pounds. Transferring either from the deck of a flatboat to the deck

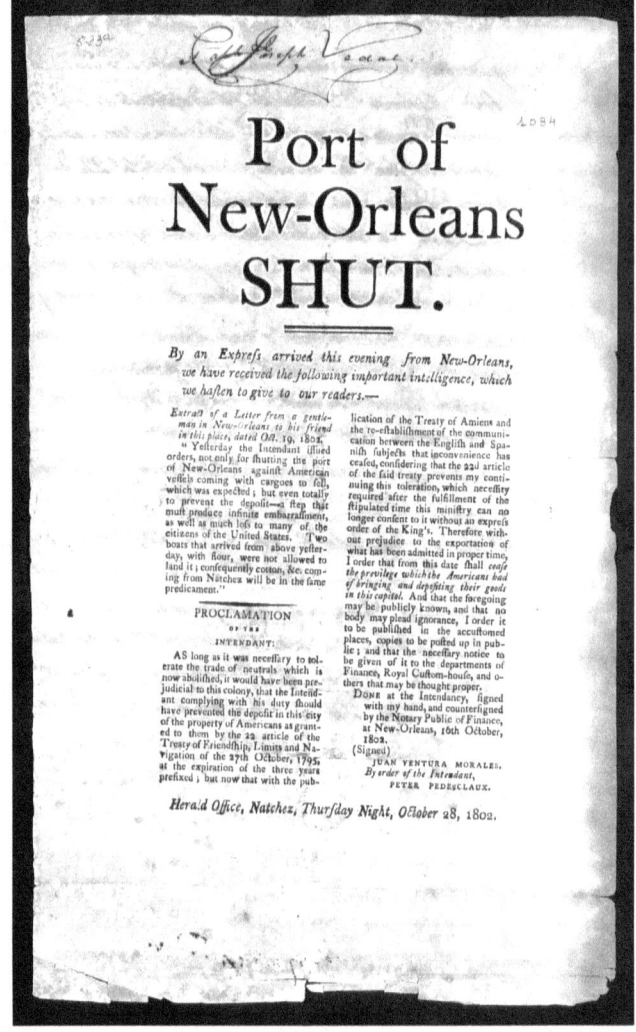

FIG. 5. This broadside, printed by Andrew Marschalk, editor of the *Mississippi Herald*, was rushed into production as soon as word of the closing of the deposit arrived in Natchez. It is highly possible that this broadside was how newspapers in the Ohio Valley and along the Atlantic heard of the port's closure. ("Port of New-Orleans SHUT," AGI, Cuba 95, 523a, fol. 1084, España, Ministerio de Educación, Cultura y Deporte, Archivo General de Indias. Courtesy of the Archivo General de Indias, Seville, Spain)

of sailing ship at anchor was exceptionally difficult work. An unfortunate gust of wind could dump a year's worth of produce into the muddy waters of the Mississippi.

In November 1802, such a disaster befell John Ellis and Gordon Forman, both of Natchez, who "had a boat in port [at New Orleans] with a quantity of Cotton which was not permitted to be landed." Because Morales had closed the deposit, the boat capsized "and nearly fifty bales fell into the river." The boat's crew was able to haul the cotton to shore, which the Spanish intendant deemed equivalent to importing it. Ellis and Forman had "much trouble to obtain permission to reimbark [the cotton], being obliged to petition the Intend. for that purpose."[22] Ellis and Forman were just two men among many—western farmers and eastern merchants alike—who faced ruin with the closing of the American deposit.

News of the closure rippled outward from New Orleans, traveling north along the Mississippi and the Natchez Trace and up the Atlantic Coast. By late November, word that the Spanish had closed New Orleans to American shipping arrived in Philadelphia; ten days later, the news reached Pittsburgh.[23] Meanwhile, an express rider dispatched from New Orleans arrived in Kentucky.[24] Within three months of Morales's decision, newspapers from Vermont to South Carolina carried news of the closing.[25] Accounts from New Orleans appeared in eastern papers, reporting that the intendant "positively [refused] to permit American vessels to land their cargo under any pretext." Moreover, "what is still more revolting and insufferable, a duty of 6 pr. cent is exacted on all the American produce which has arrived here since the proclamation." In other words, American ships arriving in New Orleans intending to trade with Americans were now required to pay import taxes on their goods, even if they were immediately exported from the colony. "From these circumstances," the correspondent warned Philadelphia readers, "you may figure to yourself the situation in which the inhabitants of the western country will be placed."[26] Many questioned *why* the intendant would close New Orleans—not only was the right protected by the terms of Pinckney's Treaty but it had also proved profitable to Louisiana over the four years it remained open—while others questioned whether the intendant had acted alone. The surprise and alarm expressed by both the new Spanish governor (Juan de Salecedo) and the Spanish minister to the United States (Carlos Fernandez Martínez de Yrujo) lent credence to the belief that Morales had acted independently. Whatever the conjectures as to motive, the outcry at its result was universal.

"The late act of the Spanish Government at New Orleans has excited considerable agitation at Natchez and its vicinity," reported Governor William C. C. Claiborne of the Mississippi Territory to President Jefferson. Claiborne's dispatch—sent overland as the river was now closed and no American ships were available to carry news to the East Coast—lamented present hardship and predicted future struggles: "It has inflicted a severe wound on the agricultural and commercial interests of this Territory, and will prove no less injurious to all the Western country."[27] Governor James Garrard of Kentucky concurred. Less than a month earlier, Garrard had waxed panegyric about Kentucky's prospects; by November, he warned the president that "the citizens of this state are very much agitated." The closing of the deposit spelled disaster for westerners. "This measure of the Spanish Government will, if not altered, at one blow, cut up the present and future prosperity of their best interests by the roots."[28] Even easterners recognized the danger. With the Mississippi shut, wrote a northern pamphleteer, "not a barrel of flour of our western states would reach the ocean. Our indigos and cottons would rot in the stores ... our sugar plantations on the banks [of the Mississippi], would be abandoned ... and what might be the effect on the *western states*, I forebear to conjecture, or I rather suppress what reflection forces me to suggest, as the consequence." "The very idea," he concluded, "communicates afflicting sensations" felt by all Americans.[29]

Cementing Western Loyalty

In 1802, national reaction to the closing of the Mississippi differed palpably from the reaction in 1784, when Spain first closed the river. This was no longer a "western" problem. News of the river's closing excited anger in Kentucky, but that anger was not directed at the federal government. Letters of concern and remonstrance flew east to members of Congress—with some westerners even calling for the creation of a military expedition to attack New Orleans—but they no longer threatened separation or the creation of a separate nation.[30] Westerners resolved to fight for their right to access the Mississippi trusted that the federal government shared their determination. Not only did westerners now insist that "harmony prevails among our citizens," they also described, throughout the West, a feeling that "confidence exists in the national government."[31] When the citizens of Frankfort, Kentucky, issued a remonstrance "To the President of the United States and the Senate and House," beseeching the government to restore the right of deposit, they did so in the language of national fidelity. Relying "with confidence on your wisdom and justice," the Kentuckians "pledge[d] [them]selves to support, at the expence of [their] lives and fortunes, such measures as the honor and Interest of the United States may require."[32] Tennesseans echoed their western neighbors, adding their own vote of confidence in the stability and utility of the union. The members of the Tennessee House of Representatives were adamant about their right to the navigation of the Mississippi, "holding it to be their duty ... to express their unalterable determination to maintain the boundaries and rights of navigation and commerce through the river Mississippi." Still, like their Kentucky brethren, they were committed to letting the federal government take the lead in reopening the river. The Tennesseans expressed "perfect confidence in the vigilance and wisdom of the executive," certain that the federal government would work to "[assert] the rights and [vindicate] the injuries of the United States."[33]

"From every quarter" of Kentucky, Tennessee, Ohio, and Mississippi, petitions "expressing the peculiar sensibility of the Western country" poured into Congress. The outpouring of western anger surprised no one, but the sentiment did not come solely from the West: calls to reopen the river arrived from across the United States. "There is," wrote Secretary of State James Madison, "but one sentiment throughout the Union with respect to the duty of maintaining our rights of navigation and boundary." In late December 1802, Madison informed Livingston that the closing of the Mississippi "has drawn forth the clearest indications, not only of the sensibility of the Western country with respect to the navigation of the Mississippi, but the sympathy of their Atlantic fellow-citizens on the subject."[34] George Clinton, governor of New York, mentioned the Mississippi in remarks to his state's legislature. Although the "late unwarrantable conduct of the Spanish intendant in New-Orleans" must excite "regret" among his listeners, Clinton was certain that Jefferson's administration would take the necessary steps to resolve the issue. "Should this not be the case and a more vigorous course become proper and necessary," then New York, which had "so eminently exerted itself in the establishment of American independence, will display equal firmness and patriotism in vindicating our national rights, from which ever quarter they may be assailed."[35] That Clinton—who in 1786 met regularly with Don Diego de Gardoqui and was more than willing to see the river closed—was now equally willing to endorse the possibility of violent action to reopen the river offers powerful evidence that national attitudes toward Mississippi

River trade, and the West broadly, had changed in the intervening decade and a half. New Yorkers were not alone in concluding that closing the deposit caused injury to the nation; according to one Philadelphia newspaper, it was "equivalent to a declaration of war against the United States."[36] Another reported that Jefferson was expected to act immediately, "as it is well understood, that every precautionary measure has been adopted by the Executive of the United States, to secure the peace, tranquility and prosperity of this remote, but important part of the Union."[37]

National outrage against the closing of the deposit likely helped mitigate western anger. Calls for violent action from across the union may even have dampened western enthusiasm for acting unilaterally. In 1787, Kentuckians set themselves in opposition to easterners and to the central government; by 1802, westerners were not so easily omitted from the U.S. imaginary. Easterners did not propose abandoning the West to Europeans, and any desire for western separatism was muted. It is possible that the timing of the closure in mid-October, and the fact that news of it did not reach Tennessee and Kentucky until the end of November, kept Kentuckians and Tennesseans from launching an offensive against New Orleans. But as 1802 came to a close, no armed action had occurred in either region.

The most important factor mitigating western violence in reaction to the closure of New Orleans was the trust westerners had come to feel in the Democratic-Republicans who held national office and enjoyed wide support across Kentucky, Tennessee, and the new state of Ohio, which was to be admitted to the union on March 1, 1803. Federalists in Kentucky were few and scattered. Various interests continued to vie with one another within the state, but the Democratic-Republicans so dominated local politics that support for Jefferson was nearly absolute. Describing the political situation in Tennessee, one historian of early America has noted that "antagonism to the eastern establishment, to the Federalists, and to Adams characterized the consensus of nearly the entire political world of the new state."[38]

In Kentucky, Tennessee, and Ohio, animosity toward the Federalists had several causes. Many leading Federalists had aligned themselves with the interests of eastern states during the 1784–87 crisis over the Mississippi. Animosity toward John Jay was particularly vitriolic, as proved when the residents of Kentucky burned him in effigy in 1794, but distrust and dislike of the entire Federalist Party was widespread. The legislature of Kentucky roundly rejected the Alien and Sedition Acts—passed by

Congress in 1798—demonstrating the strength of western adherence to the Democratic-Republicans. Tennessee residents had additional reasons for resisting the measures: the Washington and Adams administrations had failed to send troops to the southwestern frontier during its wars with the Cherokee, Chickamauga, and Creek.[39] In Tennessee's Hamilton district, "the most populous eastern region of the state," the grand jury passed a series of resolutions that declared the Alien and Sedition Acts "unconstitutional, oppressive, and derogatory to our general compact."[40] In the new state of Ohio, meanwhile, opposition to the Federalists was heightened by local anger at the party establishment that had controlled the territorial government and with it the distribution of land within the region. Although a strong Federalist contingent remained in the area surrounding the Ohio Company settlements, by 1802 "a coalition of [Ohioans]—urban traders, large landholders, and small farmers" joined together to wrest control from the Federalist governor, Arthur St. Clair.[41] The result was a staunchly anti-Federalist West.[42]

The Revolution of 1800 brought Thomas Jefferson to the presidency in a victory over John Adams and showed the decline of the Federalists nationally: they carried no state south of New Jersey or west of New Hampshire. The changes were particularly significant in the West. Thanks in part to the region's rapid growth, the Eighth Congress, convened in 1803, had thirty-five more seats than its predecessor. Whereas the Seventh Congress included 38 Federalists and 68 Democratic-Republicans—including two nonvoting western delegates—the Eighth Congress had 142 representatives of whom 103 were Democrats. The Seventh Congress saw the West represented by three delegates: two from Kentucky and one from Tennessee. In the Eighth, there were ten representatives from Kentucky, Tennessee, and Ohio, all of them Democratic-Republicans. In the Senate, the three western states were ably represented by six senators, one of whom—John Brown of Kentucky—was elected president pro-tempore of the Senate the day after Morales closed the deposit at New Orleans. Like the western delegates, the senators were all Democratic-Republicans and Jefferson supporters. In 1786, few western voices could be heard in the federal government and few delegates had ever traveled further west than Pittsburgh. Now, westerners were unquestionably a presence within Congress.[43]

The closure of the Mississippi and French control of New Orleans threatened once more to divide East from West. By now, the entire nation recognized that the Mississippi was the lever on which western loyalty to the union depended. Without it, the West would be sorely tempted, as it had been many times previously, to consider shifting loyalties. French control of the Mississippi could "have a powerful tendency to induce many of our valuable Western citizens to shake off their allegiance, and become *subjects* of the 'Great Nation'" of France, the editor of New York's *American Citizen* warned. "In such a case self interest . . . may subdue patriotism," and westerners would have little choice but to become part of an expansive French Louisiana.[44]

But by 1802, threats of western separation were less forceful and less likely. The editor of the *American Citizen* hinted at why: since New Orleans had been opened to American trade, "between three and four millions of dollars . . . in specie" had been brought from the port to the Atlantic states.[45] Four years of U.S. trade in New Orleans had reoriented American, Caribbean, and European markets. Eastern merchants like William Taylor of Baltimore or the Hunts of Philadelphia were now invested in western trade, especially in the movement of western cotton and flour to England. Wresting the West away from the United States would require the provision of enough shipping to allow western agriculturalists—especially those in the cotton-producing regions of the lower Mississippi and middle Tennessee—to transport their crops to European markets. As long as England remained the primary consumer of western cotton, perennially embattled France would be unable to fulfil the role played by eastern merchants that had developed under the terms of Pinckney's Treaty.

For Jefferson and his administration, fears of a separation between East and West lingered—perhaps with reason, as only a few years later Jefferson's vice president, Aaron Burr, would attempt to separate them once more. For disunion to take place, however, westerners would have needed to be confident that they could find a power capable of bringing their goods to international markets. Realistically, only England had the shipping capacity and demand for western produce to successfully challenge the region's allegiances. For the Jefferson administration, the possibility of British control over the southwest was the worst possible outcome amid the uncertainty caused by retrocession. Britain would be the "last of neighbors that would be agreeable to the United States"— far more threatening than either a weak Spain or a French colossus.[46]

Negotiating for the River

FOR HIS part, Jefferson recognized that his popularity in the West might help postpone a violent attack on Louisiana. But he needed to act quickly to keep westerners under federal control and to bolster connections between East and West. Moved not only by "the just sensibility of the portion of our fellow-citizens more immediately affected by the irregular proceeding at New Orleans" but also "by the regard due to rights and interests of the United States," Jefferson urged Congress "to lose not a moment in causing every step to be taken which the occasion claimed."[47] Madison was also convinced of the necessity for swift, decisive action to vindicate the U.S. government and allay the fears of western settlers. In 1786, Secretary of State John Jay had been willing to "forebear" American claims to the Mississippi; in 1802, Secretary of State Madison asserted an American right to trade along the river. "The Mississippi," Madison informed the U.S. representative in Spain, Charles Pinckney, was "everything" to westerners. "It is the Hudson, the Delaware, the Potomac, and all the navigable rivers of the Atlantic States, formed into one stream."[48] Pinckney hardly needed reminding of this fact. In 1786, he had been the most assiduous critic of Jay's proposal to cede Mississippi trade in exchange for a market in Atlantic cod; his cousin Thomas negotiated the treaty that bore Pinckney's name. Now Madison turned Jay's argument on its head. Western trade alone could more than justify any action the administration took to reopen the river. Considering the region's rapid growth, Madison predicted that the value of western crops would increase by 50 percent for the year 1802.

The surest way to secure the Mississippi would be to gain possession of the city of New Orleans. Even if "France considers Louisiana . . . as indispensable for her views," Jefferson told Livingston, "ceding to us the island of New Orleans and the Floridas" would allay western fears and give the United States imperial dominion over regions east of the Mississippi.[49] Possession of New Orleans and the colony of West Florida would give the United States access to the Mississippi as well as ownership of the Alabama River and the port of Mobile, which offered a second outlet for western produce. The extremely short portage between the bend of the Tennessee and the Tombigbee River, which eventually flows into the Gulf of Mexico, would reduce the time required for Tennessee cotton and flour to reach Atlantic markets.[50] Jefferson had good reason to hope that Napoleon might consider parting with the region. Both East and West Florida, though nominally under French sovereignty, had only a minimal European American presence. Both colonies were very much Indian country, home to the Choctaw, Chickasaw, Cherokee, Creek, Alabaman, and Seminole. Giving American farmers access to the Mississippi and Alabama Rivers, Jefferson wagered, would be more valuable to the United States than the colonies themselves would be to France. Jefferson proposed to Congress that a "minister extraordinary" be sent to negotiate, not only for the reopening of the Mississippi but also for "our object of purchasing New Orleans and the Floridas."[51]

According to Jefferson, "there could not be two opinions among the republicans as to the person" who should be sent. James Monroe's appointment as minister extraordinary would not only forward U.S. geopolitical goals; it would also serve to mitigate western anger over the closing of the Mississippi. In 1786, Monroe had warned Governor Patrick Henry of the movement afoot within Congress to cede Mississippi access. According to Jefferson, Monroe "possessed the unlimited confidence of the administration," and perhaps more importantly, of "the western people."[52] Monroe departed for Paris with instructions from Congress to negotiate "a cession of New Orleans and the Floridas to the United States; and consequently the establishment of the Mississippi as the boundary between the United States and Louisiana."[53]

When Monroe arrived in France, he carried two blank commissions appointing the bearer as the U.S. minister plenipotentiary to Britain. Congress had hedged its bets: if negotiations with France failed, then Monroe and Livingston—still U.S. minister to France—would need to depart for England to cement an alliance against the French. While the rapidly growing population of the American settlements in the trans-Appalachian West could easily supply enough soldiers to invade Louisiana, the British Navy could help prevent France from landing or supplying any troops it sent to the region. If France refused to sell New Orleans, the United States would immediately attempt to ally with Britain, which—it was widely assumed—would eagerly undertake any action to diminish their longtime continental enemies.[54]

The consequences of a failed treaty negotiation were not lost on Napoleon. Resumed warfare between France and Britain, which seemed likely to begin at any moment, weighed heavily on his mind. Moreover, the role he once envisioned for Louisiana—as a granary for the French Caribbean, particularly the island of St. Domingue—seemed less and less necessary as French military operations to reclaim the island proved increasingly disastrous. The twenty thousand troops Napoleon had deployed to "pacify" the rebelling former slaves were decimated by guerrilla warfare and yellow fever, the disease to which General Charles LeClerc, commander of French forces on St. Domingue and Napoleon's brother-in-law, succumbed in November 1802.[55] Without the valuable island to supply, France had little need for Louisiana.

On Easter Sunday, April 10, 1803, with the reclamation of St. Domingue looking increasingly like a lost cause, Napoleon called together Talleyrand, his foreign minister, and François Barbé-Marbois, director-general of the public treasury and one time intendant of St. Domingue and consular representative to the United States. Louisiana, in Napoleon's view, was already "entirely lost," and renewed war with Britain inevitable. France lacked the resources to protect a colony that Britain could easily seize by descending the Mississippi River from Canada. Distance and war made the situation urgent: "I have not a moment to lose," Napoleon informed his counselors, "in putting [Louisiana] out of [British] reach. I think of ceding it to the United States." While the Americans asked for "only one town in Louisiana," it appeared to Napoleon "that in the hands of this growing power, [the cession of Louisiana] will be more useful to the policy and even to the commerce of France, than if I should attempt to keep it."[56] "I renounce [Louisiana] with the greatest regret," Napoleon informed Barbé-Marbois, but "to attempt obstinately to retain it would be folly."[57] An American Louisiana was in the best interest of France.

Talleyrand opposed the cession of Louisiana, but Barbé-Marbois agreed with Napoleon's assessment and added another reason to divest France of the colony. Slavery, he argued, was entrenched in Louisiana and contrary to French law. The catastrophe in St. Domingue showed the dangers of both slavery and emancipation to civil society. "But," he offered, "there is another kind of slavery of which this colony has lost the habit: it is that of the exclusive system [of trade].... The reign of prohibitory laws is over, when a numerous population has decided to throw off the yoke." Over the previous four years, the population of Louisiana had become accustomed to trading with the world; it would be folly for France to reestablish mercantilist policies "in a country contiguous to one where commerce enjoys the greatest liberty." A motley collection of multiple ethnicities, Louisianans had been ruled by various governments and exhibited little loyalty to any one nation. They would pledge allegiance to "those princes whom they regard as the authors of their happiness." Such a population would never "permit [France] to enslave their commerce." The only way to make such a region into a colony would be by force of arms, at a moment when every soldier was needed for war with Britain. Barbé-Marbois agreed with Napoleon's cost-benefit analysis: in the final accounting, Louisiana was worth more to France in the hands of the United States than as a French colony.[58] The French ministers lost no time in implementing Napoleon's proposal. On April 11, Talleyrand approached Livingston with a startling suggestion: France would sell Louisiana.

When Monroe arrived on April 12, he and Livingston conferred. They had been authorized by Congress to negotiate the purchase of the city of New Orleans and the colonies of East and West Florida, or as much as France might be willing to sell. Now, France offered all of Louisiana—the territory lying along the western bank of the Mississippi River, along with its crown jewel, the city of New Orleans. Livingston and Monroe faced a conundrum. Negotiating to purchase Louisiana exceeded the authority granted to them by Congress, but France was unwilling to negotiate for the colony piecemeal. To acquire New Orleans, they would have to acquire the uncharted, unsurveyed, and unexplored continental interior as well. France's reversals in St. Domingue and imminent war with Britain had driven Napoleon to the negotiating table; there was no telling how long these circumstances would last, and no time to write to Congress for advice on how to proceed. Faced with a choice between acquiring Louisiana in its entirety and acquiring nothing, the American ministers began negotiating the purchase.[59]

It took three weeks to settle the terms of the Louisiana Purchase—three weeks to resolve a problem the nation had confronted for the previous two decades and to transfer millions of acres and tens of thousands of people to nominal U.S. sovereignty. The ultimate agreement left the western and northern boundaries of the purchase deliberately vague; only the eastern boundary—the Mississippi River—was defined. Barbé-Marbois proposed a purchase price of 100 million francs that the three men negotiated down to 60 million francs, or $11,250,000. The U.S. government also agreed to assume $3.75 million worth of American merchants' claims against the French government that had arisen due to French seizures of U.S. ships during the Quasi War. In a treaty of cession and two conventions, all signed on May 3, 1803, the United States assumed ownership of Louisiana.[60]

The deal was made possible by a British bank. The United States financed the Louisiana Purchase by issuing $15 million in bonds with an interest rate of 6 percent annually, not redeemable for fifteen years. They were to be sold by the Baring Brothers and Company of London and Hope and Company of Amsterdam, both prominent European banks with a long history of funding American interests. The terms of the agreement were such that a British bank provided cash to a foreign government—France—knowing that money would be used to fight the British crown and that the loan would make the United States Britain's greatest debtor. The fact that British authorities did not object to this arrangement reveals the extent to which they too wanted the question of Louisiana resolved, preferring the United States to Napoleonic France as a North American neighbor.[61]

In May, fearing western military action against New Orleans, the crown of Spain reopened the American deposit.[62] But what would have been happy news was rapidly overshadowed by word of Monroe and Livingston's amazing success in Paris, which arrived in Boston at the end of June. By July 3, word had reached Jefferson that the United States would now own all of Louisiana if the Senate ratified the treaty.[63] This put Jefferson, a strict constitutional constructionist, in a bind: nowhere in the Constitution was he given the power to purchase land. Throughout 1803, Jefferson contemplated adopting a constitutional amendment giving him the authority to do so, even drafting multiple versions of possible wording. Such an amendment was unlikely to be approved. Although it would probably make it through Congress, where Democratic-Republican representatives overwhelmingly predominated, it would struggle to be ratified by the state legislatures, five of which were controlled by the Federalists. Accordingly, when the Eighth Congress convened on October 17, Jefferson presented them with the treaty and conventions signed by Livingston, Monroe, and Napoleon. Although the Senate alone could vote to ratify the treaty, the House had an important role to play, approving the appropriation and determining payment methods for the necessary $15 million. Although seven Federalist senators opposed its passage, the Senate ratified the treaty on October 20.

The Louisiana Purchase faced mild opposition in the Federalist press and among Federalist politicians but was generally and overwhelmingly popular, particularly in the West. "Every face wears a smile, and every heart leaps with joy," Andrew Jackson wrote to Jefferson from his home near Nashville. "All the western Hemisphere rejoices in the Joyfull news of the Cession of Louisiana—an event which places the peace, happiness, and liberty of our country on a permanent basis."[64] When news that the

United States would take possession of New Orleans reached the nation's most distant outpost at Natchez, there were "universal demonstrations of joy." Governor William C. C. Claiborne ordered a "general illumination" of the town; residents held a parade and fired off "22 rounds" in celebration.[65] The *Scioto Gazette* of Ohio deemed the purchase an event that would "be considered as second only in importance to the establishment of national independence."[66] In Kentucky, seventeen toasts, one for each state of the union, were drunk in honor of the cession. The toasts congratulated Kentuckians on placing their trust in the president and congratulated Jefferson himself, "by whose wise measures we have acquired a new world." All over Kentucky, "difference of political opinion was forgotten, and perfect unanimity of sentiment prevailed."[67]

As Jackson intimated, to westerners the Louisiana Purchase constituted a second founding, a revised statement of what the United States was to be. The first founding had largely alienated westerners; the Louisiana Purchase served to draw them into the union, fashioning for them a position that lay not along the American periphery but at the heart of the newly created empire of liberty. The purchase finally secured westerners' right to Mississippi River trade, giving them "free and uninterrupted navigation of the Mississippi—The great incentive to industry," the mechanism by which hard work would receive "a certain prospect of obtaining its merited reward."[68] The purchase assured the West's prosperity; even as word of its achievement began circulating in the West, news arrived that the brigantine *Deane*, the first transoceanic vessel built along the waters of the Ohio, had arrived in Liverpool with a cargo of western cotton.[69] "Who now," westerners wondered, "would not live in such a land?"[70]

The Louisiana Purchase secured a curious double victory: both the commercial vision of a Federalist frontier, characterized by compact settlement and robust trade connections, and the expansive frontier of yeoman farmers envisioned by Thomas Jefferson. Long considered a part of the nation's inexorable expansion, the Louisiana Purchase established the United States as an empire. It more than doubled the size of the nation, opening up new fields of western investment that, like the earlier American wests, would clamor for access to national and international markets. These new calls would emerge in a very different context. Unlike American trade under Pinckney's Treaty, trade opened by the purchase was to be free of foreign interference. Western "agriculture may depend upon these steady markets which trade shall open to industry," finally turning western land into cash. American ownership of the Mississippi "open[ed] all the avenues of commerce from the most remote regions of the earth, to every part of North America," especially to the West.[71] Once cut off from the rest of the nation by the Appalachian Mountains, westerners were now bound to the East by the inexorable current of the Mississippi. They had truly become members of the union.

On December 20, William Claiborne and James Wilkinson formally accepted the transfer of Louisiana from France, raising the flag of the United States over the port of New Orleans. Two decades earlier, settlers in the trans-Appalachian West had clamored for the opening of the port as a means of getting produce from their nascent farms to market. Finally, the government had acted to secure it for them, obtaining in the process hundreds of millions of acres of new land that would itself become the province of boosters and speculators, a spectacular act of property creation with disastrous consequences for the land's Native American proprietors and for generations of enslaved Africans who would work land made profitable by the trade of the Mississippi River.

For the white Americans who celebrated the purchase, it was clear that the West had much to offer. Western land, with a market assured, seemed poised to rise in value. Already, a generation born and raised west of the Appalachians eyed the territory north of the Ohio and south of Tennessee as potential homes for themselves and their families. Western cotton, meanwhile, helped to balance the nation's trade deficit with England, giving eastern merchants greater access to British goods and British credit, while western flour, carried throughout the Atlantic world in ships belonging to eastern merchants, fed the enslaved men and women toiling on plantations in the Caribbean and the European laborers who converted western cotton into cloth. By acquiring the Mississippi, the United States gained the undisputed loyalty of its westernmost citizens. President Washington's prediction, made during his Farewell Address, that through commerce among the different regions the United States would develop an "indissoluble community of interest as one nation," had finally come to pass.[72]

Epilogue

By the time the venerable Joshua McQueen died in 1853 at the remarkable age of 106, the Ohio Valley had been transformed. In 1782, when McQueen had first ventured down the Mississippi carrying a cargo of flour, he had floated through Spanish, English, and Chickasaw territory. Now, the land on both sides of the Mississippi belonged to the United States. Little remained of three decades of Spanish rule over the region. Absent too were the Chickasaw, who had commanded the river in his youth. Multiple steamboat lines moved freight and passengers up and down the Mississippi and Ohio on a regular schedule, vying with one another in opulence, speed, and price. Joining these steamships was an annual armada of flatboats pouring out of newly settled territory far to the west of Kentucky. By the 1840s, more than four thousand flatboats, guided by twenty thousand boatmen, descended the Mississippi each year.[1] The produce of Kentucky and Ohio was joined by that of Indiana, Illinois, Missouri, Wisconsin, Minnesota, and Iowa, while together Arkansas, Alabama, Louisiana, Tennessee, and Mississippi produced nearly half of the United States' annual exports of cotton. New Orleans, at the mouth of the river, received it all.[2]

In the decades following the American founding, Mississippi River trade shaped the United States. The major developments of the antebellum era all depended on Mississippi River trade. Western expansion, the rise of King Cotton, the development of American industry, the spread of slavery, the policy of Indian removal, the flow of American commerce, the rise of American empire, and the fracturing of the American polity all resulted, in part, from the United States' 1803 acquisition of the Mississippi. Jefferson's empire of liberty was, in fact, an empire of commerce, as the expansion of American settlement led to the simultaneous demand for the expansion of markets. Throughout the first decades of the United

States' existence, American foreign policy was just as responsive to the demands of western settlers as it was to eastern merchants. The interests of the nation, East and West, united along the waters of the Mississippi. After the American Revolution, there were neither self-sufficient western farmers nor Indigenous peoples east of the Mississippi who were insulated from a web of expanding agricultural capitalism. Instead, American public policy, from its inception, revolved around connecting its growing population to Atlantic world markets.

Mississippi River trade offered a tool for empire-building that served as a necessary ancillary to the violence and settler-colonialism that characterized early American expansion.[3] The settlement of trans-Appalachia was alternately driven by interracial violence, cross-cultural cooperation, and intragroup conflicts over local authority, but underlying each of these issues were questions about the distribution of land and the ability to access ties to Atlantic world trade. For white settlers, the value of western lands rose and fell in proportion to their ability to achieve access to distant markets, access that, in the eighteenth century, meant controlling interior waterways. The transformation of the western landscape into property with a salable value laid the foundation for individual and national wealth. Mississippi River trade drove the gradual construction of the United States' contiguous empire.

The foundations for these changes were largely in place well before the first steamboat ventured down the Mississippi. In many ways, the plans of the earliest Kentucky boosters had in fact come to pass: Ohio Valley flour now fed enslaved people in the Caribbean and factory workers in England. River trade continued to give value to the lands of the continental interior. Had they witnessed the changes that occurred between 1803 and 1850, early settlers like McQueen, river merchants like the Hunts, and Atlantic merchants like John McDonogh and William Taylor would have been amazed at the scale of what had changed but likely not at the way it had changed.

By the time McQueen died, he and his second wife, a woman thirty-eight years his junior, had lived together on a small plot of land in Madison County, Kentucky, for more than forty years. He never grew wealthy but he did accumulate enough to leave a legacy for those of his thirteen children who outlived him.[4] In contrast, Abijah Hunt had died long before; in 1811, Hunt was killed in a duel with George Poindexter, Mississippi's first congressional representative. At his death, Abijah was extremely prosperous. Cotton was the business of Natchez, and Hunt was involved in every component of the trade. He acted as a commission agent for his clients and neighbors, exporting cotton to New Orleans. It was not long after the Louisiana Purchase before he dispatched his brother Jeremiah to represent the family's interests in England. At the five stores he owned in the Natchez district, he accepted cotton and cash in exchange for goods and operated public cotton gins where his poorer neighbors could process their crops in exchange for paying him a percentage of the cleaned cotton. He also grew cotton on his own plantations. Abijah was certainly successful: in 1808, he sold a plantation along the Bayou Pierre for $60,000. The purchase included not only land but also "the negroes on the said plantation amounting in number from sixty-one to sixty-five."[5]

In 1803, John Wesley Hunt abandoned retailing and turned his attention to producing and manufacturing hemp. At a factory in Lexington, Kentucky, Hunt used the labor of seventy-seven enslaved men, women, and children—many of them boys younger than sixteen—to wind and weave hemp products, especially cotton bagging, the thick, coarse cloth used to bind and protect bales of cotton for transport. He exported this cotton bagging to Natchez, where Abijah helped him sell it to cotton producers. Abijah advised, and John agreed, to accept cotton as payment. John sold the factory in 1813, becoming a merchant once more, this time using his connections in New Orleans and Philadelphia to connect eastern manufacturers with western markets and acting as a commission agent for western farmers. By the time of his death, John Wesley Hunt had become the first millionaire west of the Alleghenies.[6]

Kentucky bagging was often carried alongside enslaved Kentuckians being brought to the lower Mississippi Valley to be sold to cotton planters eager for enslaved laborers. Enslaved people arrived in Natchez in several ways: on flatboats floated down the Ohio and Mississippi Rivers, on steamboats that churned the three hundred miles up the Mississippi from New Orleans, or overland down the Natchez Trace to the Forks of the Road slave market, the second largest in the South. The rise of cotton was a direct cause of the movement of close to a million enslaved people through the domestic slave market. The infrastructure of Mississippi River trade was easily enlisted to transport commodified humans throughout the newest cotton-growing regions of the South.[7]

For the Chickasaw, the second decade of the 1800s also brought profound changes. As steamboats began operating along the Mississippi, the Natchez Trace declined in importance as a route for midwestern farmers to return home. In 1820, the United States completed construction of a military road, named for General Jackson, that connected New Orleans and Nashville. The new route shortened the journey by more than two hundred miles and bypassed the facilities the Chickasaw had constructed along the Trace. Instead, the new road passed through territory that the Chickasaw had ceded to the United States in the Treaty of the Chickasaw Council House in 1816, a treaty that was negotiated in the home of George Colbert.[8]

By 1830, determined to undermine tribal sovereignty, the state of Mississippi had abolished the Chickasaw government and extended state rule over Chickasaw and Choctaw territory. Chickasaw appeals to President Jackson failed; although many of the Chickasaw leaders knew Jackson, and several had fought alongside him against the Red Sticks in 1814, Jackson's reply to their appeals was dismissive. Only the states, he told them, had the right to make laws within their territories. Already, the Chickasaw faced near-constant intrusions onto their lands by aggressive settlers and squatters. If the Chickasaw remained in Mississippi, it would not be "possible you can live contented and happy," Jackson informed his former allies.[9] The era of Indian removal had begun.[10]

In 1836, the Chickasaw confronted a horde of white settlers and speculators intent on purchasing Chickasaw lands. At the time, Mississippi was in the midst of an economic bonanza as rapid immigration and easy credit funded land sales on a near-unprecedented scale. Since 1833, when twice as much land was sold in Mississippi as in any other state, it had been at the epicenter of a new southeastern land mania as more than seventy-five thousand white people moved onto recently ceded land. In 1835 alone, the federal government sold more than 3 million acres from the federal domain in Mississippi, much of it recently obtained from the Choctaw.[11] East Coast financiers, eager to fund the dispossession of Indigenous peoples, flooded the region with speculators and agents, many of whom colluded to keep the prices paid for Indigenous land low. Benjamin Reynolds, the U.S. agent to the Chickasaw, accepted payments and kickbacks from white purchasers in exchange for coercing Chickasaw landowners to sell at low prices. In return for their lands, the Chickasaw received an assortment of paper money drawn on dubious banks, which they were forced to accept, even as the Jackson administration's Specie Circular demanded that all payments for federal land had to be tendered in specie. Federal agents further dispossessed the Chickasaw by investing Chickasaw national funds in state bonds, forcing the Chickasaw to help finance their own displacement.[12] In the summer and autumn of

1837, four thousand Chickasaw departed from the eastern side of the Mississippi toward an uncertain future in the West. Ferried across the Mississippi from Memphis—once known as the Chickasaw Bluffs—they enacted the Chickasaw creation story in reverse.

By the time of Chickasaw expulsion in 1837, Memphis was an active river port busily engaged in Mississippi River trade. Founded in 1819 by Andrew Jackson and two colleagues, Memphis was named for the ancient Egyptian capital along the Nile River. Jackson may well have imagined that this new city might one day form the cradle of a great riverine empire of its own. Both before and after his presidency, Jackson would continue to be strongly associated with the lower Mississippi Valley. In 1814, he led an expedition of Kentucky, Tennessee, and Chickasaw militia against the British at New Orleans, striking a symbolic victory for the United States. He continued to maintain business interests in Natchez and New Orleans, partnering with John Coffee of Nashville to export cotton from the Cumberland. He invested heavily in land; much of his acquisition focused on sites like Memphis that had been strategically important to the people of the Southeast for centuries.[13] When Jackson won the election of 1828, there were nine more states than there had been forty years before, when he had stood on the banks of the Mississippi and sworn his allegiance to Spain. Jackson carried all of them. He was the first western president, the first president to have lived his adult life across the Appalachians, where an ever-larger number of Americans now made their homes. For Jackson, and for the United States, the Mississippi was no longer an edge but instead at the heart of an ever-expanding empire of commerce.

NOTES

Abbreviations

AGI, PC	Archivo General de Indias, Papeles procedentes de Cuba, Seville, Spain
DSG	Despatches of the Spanish Governors of Louisiana, 1766–92, transcriptions, Tulane University Special Collections, New Orleans
DUCO	Despatches from United States Consuls in New Orleans, 1798–1807, National Archives
FHS	Filson Historical Society, Louisville, Kentucky
GDUC	Gardoqui Dispatches, University of Chicago Library
HSP	Historical Society of Pennsylvania, Philadelphia
JCC	Ford et al., eds., *Journals of the Continental Congress*
JWHP	John Wesley Hunt Papers, Filson Historical Society
KHS	Kentucky Historical Society, Frankfort
LDC	Smith and Gephart, eds., *Letters of Delegates to Congress*
LRDS	Letters Received by the Department of State Relative to the Southern Boundary, Compiled 1796–1802, National Archives
MDAH	Mississippi Department of Archives and History, Jackson
NOPL	Special Collections, New Orleans Public Library
NTC	Natchez Trace Collection, University of Southern Mississippi
SPTL	U.S. Government, *State Papers and Correspondence Bearing upon the Purchase of the Territory of Louisiana*
UK	University of Kentucky Library, Lexington
WTP	William Taylor Papers, Library of Congress

Introduction

1. Juramento de Fidelidad, July 15, 1789, before Manuel Gayoso de Lemos and Josef Vidal, AGI, PC, legajo 2361. See also Remini, "Andrew Jackson Takes an Oath of Allegiance to Spain," 9; "Report of Americans Arriving at Natchez," July 5, 1788, AGI, PC, legajo 2361; and "Report of Americans Arriving at Natchez," December 31, 1788, AGI, PC, legajo 2361, in Kinnaird, *Spain in the Mississippi Valley*, 3, part 2:257–58, 264–65.
2. Din, "Immigration Policy of Governor Esteban Miró in Spanish Louisiana," 155–75.

3. Meacham, *American Lion*.
4. At the time of Jackson's vow, the lower Mississippi River Valley was both a borderland—a region contested among imperial powers—and a frontier— a meeting place among people of differing cultural backgrounds. Adelman and Aron, "From Borderlands to Borders," 815–16.
5. On the difficulty of traveling to Kentucky and the West in the 1780s, see Eslinger, *Running Mad for Kentucky*, 8–51.
6. For a broader picture of the United States' relationship with the Spanish empire in the Americas, see Lewis, *American Union and the Problem of Neighborhood*.
7. Ray, *Middle Tennessee*, 10–12; Friend, *Along the Maysville Road*, 133–34.
8. Friend, *Along the Maysville Road*, 133–34.
9. The "Mississippi Question" became a common term for the problem after the passage of Pinckney's Treaty in 1795; before that, the debates lacked a single designation. I expand the term backwards a decade to refer to the entirety of the conflict over the Mississippi. For this phrase, I am indebted to Arthur Preston Whitaker, who in the 1930s examined the role of the lower Mississippi River Valley within the broad arc of American politics, diplomacy, and trade. Throughout my work, I build on many of his insights, although ultimately my questions, narrative, and sources are different. Whitaker, *Mississippi Question*.
10. Gabriel Bolong, Deposition, October 17, 1795, Darlington Autograph Files, 1610–1914, DAR.1925.07, Darlington Collection, Special Collections, University of Pittsburgh.
11. Edelson, *New Map of Empire*, 17. On American empire more broadly, see Gilje, "Commerce and Conquest in Early American Foreign Relations"; Hartigan-O'Connor, *Ties That Buy*; and Breen, *Marketplace of Revolution*.
12. Onuf, *Statehood and Union*; Matson and Onuf, *Union of Interests*; Cayton, *Frontier Republic*; Gould, *Among the Powers of the Earth*. On the legal components of imperial expansion, see Ablavsky, *Federal Ground*. On the incorporation of western lands, see Van Atta, *Securing the West*, and Saler, *Settlers' Empire*.
13. Throughout, I use the terms "colonizers" and "settlers" to refer to people of European descent who were moving to new communities in trans-Appalachia. There is some disagreement among scholars over the accuracy of each term. Rob Harper argues that the terms "settlers" and "settlement" are associated with "peacemaking, compromise, and the benevolent ordering of the land," while in reality the process of western disposition was characterized by bloodshed and brutality. Harper, *Unsettling the West*, xii. Harper's point is well-stated, but my choice of the word "settler" is driven by a different logic. The people discussed here regarded themselves as settlers, in part due to the subordinate connotations of "colonist" they carried over from the Revolution. Lorenzo Veracini, a theorist of settler colonialism,

defines "settlers" as migrants who "are *founders* of political orders and carry their sovereignty with them." The individuals who migrated to the West were the creators of a new western political economy and hence seem to align with this definition. Veracini, *Settler Colonialism*, 3.

14. On "Facing East," see Richter, *Facing East from Indian Country*. In most accounts of the early United States, the West figures very little or not at all; in particular, the inhabitants of the trans-Appalachian West are usually absent from the story even if western lands are considered. Hendrickson, *Peace Pact*; Wood, *Creation of the American Republic*; Holton, *Unruly Americans and the Origins of the Constitution*. An exception to this is in discussions of the army. Edling, *Revolution in Favor of Government*. Gregory Ablavsky has written about the relationship between Indigenous peoples and the writing of the Constitution; see Ablavsky, "The Savage Constitution," 999. Another major exception is Merritt, Green, and Campbell, "Sectional Conflict and Secret Compromise."
15. Turner, "Significance of the Frontier in American History."
16. Whitaker, *Mississippi Question*; Whitaker, *Spanish-American Frontier*; Bemis, *Jay's Treaty*; Bemis, *Pinckney's Treaty*.
17. Limerick, *Legacy of Conquest*; Klein, "Reclaiming the 'F' Word."
18. Einhorn, *American Taxation, American Slavery*; Levy, *Freaks of Fortune*; Rockman, *Scraping By*; Matson, *Merchants and Empire*; Rosenthal, *Accounting for Slavery*.
19. Reda, *From Furs to Farms*.
20. Balogh, *Government Out of Sight*; Van Atta, *Securing the West*; Kastor, *Nation's Crucible*; Banks, *Chasing Empire across the Sea*; McMichael, *Atlantic Loyalties*; Cangany, *Frontier Seaport*; Hatter, *Citizens of Convenience*; Saler, *Settlers' Empire*; Harper, *Unsettling the West*; Sachs, *Home Rule*; Aron, *How the West Was Lost*; Buss, *Winning the West with Words*; Barr, *Boundaries between Us*; Hinderaker, *Elusive Empires*.
21. Aron, *How the West Was Lost*; Aron, "Pioneers and Profiteers"; White, *Middle Ground*; Usner, *Indians, Settlers, and Slaves*; Hyde, *Empires, Nations, and Families*; Richter, *Facing East from Indian Country*; Dupre, *Transforming the Cotton Frontier*; Morris, *Becoming Southern*. On the role of the federal government, see Saler, *Settlers' Empire*; Van Atta, *Securing the West*; Bergmann, *American National State and the Early West*; Griffin, *American Leviathan*; and Balogh, *Government Out of Sight*.
22. On western violence, see Saler, *Settlers' Empire*; Harper, *Unsettling the West*; Aron, *How the West Was Lost*; Eslinger, *Citizens of Zion*; Perkins, *Border Life*; Bergmann, *American National State and the Early West*; Griffin, *American Leviathan*; Nichols, *Red Gentlemen and White Savages*; Ray, *Middle Tennessee*; and Barksdale, *Lost State of Franklin*.
23. For an overview of Natchez in the antebellum period, see James, *Antebellum Natchez*. On the American Revolution in Natchez, see Haynes, *Natchez*

District and the American Revolution. On Spanish Natchez, see Weeks, *Paths to a Middle Ground*, and Holmes, *Gayoso*. On the rise of slavery in the region, see Libby, *Slavery and Frontier Mississippi*; Haynes, *Mississippi Territory and the Southwest Frontier*; and Hammond, *Slavery, Freedom, and Expansion in the Early American West*.

24. Baptist, *Half Has Never Been Told*; Beckert, *Empire of Cotton*; Dupre, *Transforming the Cotton Frontier*; Johnson, *Soul by Soul*; Johnson, *River of Dark Dreams*; Rockman, *Scraping By*; Karp, *This Vast Southern Empire*; Schoen, *Fragile Fabric of Union*; Berry, *Price for Their Pound of Flesh*. Three studies that do look at this early period are Rothman, *Slave Country*; Morris, *Becoming Southern*; and Hammond, *Slavery, Freedom, and Expansion in the Early American West*.

Part I

1. On John Dabney Shane, see Perkins, *Border Life*, 14–22.
2. John Dabney Shane (hereafter JDS), "Interview with Joshua McQueen," vol. 13, series CC, p. 127, Draper Manuscripts, Wisconsin Historical Society (hereafter DC, volume, series, page/item).
3. Tomás López, *Mapa de América, sujeto a las observaciones astronómicas, con todos los nuevos descubrimientos hasta ahora conocidos, 3 de mayo de 1794*, España, Ministerio de Defensa, Archivo General Militar de Madrid, Bibliothèque nationale de France, département Cartes et plans, GE C-7825; John Fielding, *A Map of the United States of America, as Settled by the Peace of 1783* (London, 1783), Library of Congress, Washington, DC, https://www.loc.gov/item/00552212/.
4. Dyson, *Early Chickasaw Homeland*, 7.
5. Atkinson, *Splendid Land, Splendid People*, 138.
6. Michael Blaakman has written on the "mania" for western land that permeated American society in the 1780s. Blaakman, *Speculation Nation*, 101–37; Aron, *How the West Was Lost*, 58–81.
7. Imlay, *Description of the Western Territory of North America*, 97, 108.
8. Sklansky, *Sovereign of the Market*; Mihm, "Follow the Money"; Mihm, *A Nation of Counterfeiters*.
9. JDS, "Interview with Joshua McQueen," DC 13CC127.
10. Ablavsky, *Federal Ground*; Harper, *Unsettling the West*; Saler, *Settlers' Empire*; Griffin, *American Leviathan*.
11. Lee, *Masters of the Middle Waters*, 3, 8; Usner, *Indians, Settlers, and Slaves*, 96–104.
12. Furstenberg, "Significance of the Trans-Appalachian Frontier in Atlantic History"; Hinderaker, *Elusive Empires*.

1. The Colonial River

1. "The Mississippi/Atchafalaya River Basin," U.S. Environmental Protection Agency, https://www.epa.gov/ms-htf/mississippiatchafalaya-river-basin-marb.
2. Even today, moving goods by barge is five times cheaper than relying on other modes of transportation. Joe Deaux and Diego Lasarte, "Mississippi Barge Snag Forces Goods onto Pricey Rail, Truck," Bloomberg.com, October 6, 2022, https://www.bloomberg.com/news/articles/2022-10-06/mississippi-river-drought-forces-goods-to-pricier-rail-trucks.
3. Morris, *Big Muddy*, 2.
4. Aron, *American Confluence*, 6; Pauketat, *Cahokia*, 9–10.
5. Barnett, *Natchez Indians*, 13–15. See also Ian W. Brown, "Plaquemine Culture in the Natchez Bluffs Region of Mississippi," in Rees and Livingood, *Plaquemine Archaeology*, 145–60.
6. "For over three hundred years," according to historian Dustin J. Mack, "Chickasaw storytellers have defined their ancestors' migration relative to the Mississippi River." Mack, "Chickasaws' Place-World," 9, 11 (quotations).
7. The two most important Chickasaw settlements were Chokkilissa' (Old Town) and Chokka' Falaa' (Long Town). Chokka' Falaa' has many spellings, the most frequent being Tchoukafala. Chokka' Falaa' is the site of the modern medical district of Tupelo. See Craig, "Colberts in Chickasaw History," 52–57, and Malinda Maynor Lowery, "Kinship and Capitalism in the Choctaw and Chickasaw Nations," in Garrison and O'Brien, *Native South*, 202. In choosing how to spell these names, I followed the usage adopted by the *Journal of Chickasaw History and Culture*. See Prewitt and Lieb, "A Tale of Two Cities."
8. Newhall, "The Chickasaw," 196.
9. On the characterization of the Chickasaw as "warlike," see Atkinson, *Splendid Land, Splendid People*, 26.
10. Atkin, *Indians of the Southern Colonial Frontier*, 67.
11. Mack, "Chickasaws' Place-World," 20.
12. Baron de Carondelet to Louis de Las Casas, New Orleans, May 22, 1793, quoted in Weeks, *Paths to a Middle Ground*, 128; Mack, "River of Continuity, Tributaries of Change," 180–89.
13. Mack, "River of Continuity, Tributaries of Change," 123.
14. Morris, *Big Muddy*, 1.
15. Barnett, *Natchez Indians*, 21–26.
16. Barnett, *Natchez Indians*, 30.
17. Kelton, *Epidemics and Enslavement*, 143–58.
18. Barnett, *Natchez Indians*, 38.
19. Ethridge, *From Chicaza to Chickasaw*, 237.

20. Barnett, *Natchez Indians*, 79; Milne, *Natchez Country*, 54; Ellis, *Great Power of Small Nations*, 47.
21. For more on the role of the Chickasaw as enslavers, see Snyder, *Slavery in Indian Country*, 46–79, and Kelton, *Epidemics and Enslavement*, 122–24, 137–43. On the persistence of the Chickasaw's relationship with the English, see Atkinson, *Splendid Land, Splendid People*, 20, and Weeks, *Paths to a Middle Ground*, 13.
22. Barnett, *Natchez Indians*, 45.
23. Barnett, *Natchez Indians*, 74, 75, 85; Milne, *Natchez Country*, 55; Usner, *Indians, Settlers, and Slaves*, 66.
24. Barnett, *Natchez Indians*, 83–84, 98.
25. Morris, *Big Muddy*, 78.
26. Morris, *Big Muddy*, 77.
27. Of the 291 transported to St. Domingue, only 160 survived the journey. Barnett, *Natchez Indians*, 105, 160, 118.
28. For a more detailed and nuanced discussion of the role of the Natchez War within the Indigenous world of the lower Mississippi Valley, see Ellis, "The Natchez War Revisited."
29. Libby, *Slavery and Frontier Mississippi*, 19.
30. Cowger and Caver, *Piominko*, 28.
31. Usner, *Indians, Settlers, and Slaves*, 28, 17–19.
32. Morris, *Big Muddy*, 70.
33. Vidal, *Caribbean New Orleans*, 49–51.
34. Usner, *Indians, Settlers, and Slaves*, 33–35; Vidal, *Caribbean New Orleans*, 55–58; Dawdy, *Building the Devil's Empire*, 14–15; Morris, *Big Muddy*, 74–75.
35. Vidal, *Caribbean New Orleans*, 58; Usner, *Indians, Settlers, and Slaves*, 41.
36. Morris, *Big Muddy*, 54–55, 61–63.
37. Aron, *American Confluence*, 31–32; Reda, *From Furs to Farms*, 14–16; Clark, *New Orleans*, 61–88; Usner, *Indians, Settlers, and Slaves*, 120–22.
38. Clark, *New Orleans*, 68–69.
39. Usner, *Indians, Settlers, and Slaves*, 80. Cécile Vidal discusses how in 1731 the colony suspended the African slave trade; subsequently, most of the enslaved people brought to the colony arrived from the Antilles. She also connects the end of slave importations to the slowing of economic and demographic growth. Vidal, *Caribbean New Orleans*, 18.
40. Usner, *Indians, Settlers, and Slaves*, 28, 97–98, 244–75, 100–103, 100 (quotation).
41. Clark, *New Orleans*, 58.
42. Usner, *Indians, Settlers, and Slaves*, 31.
43. For discussions of these outposts, see Usner, *Indians, Settlers, and Slaves*; Lee, *Masters of the Middle Waters*, 49–52, 73–74, 176–78; and Reda, *From Furs to Farms*, 14–41.
44. DuVal, *Independence Lost*, 16.

45. DuVal, *Independence Lost*, 9.
46. Weeks, *Paths to a Middle Ground*, 43; DuVal, *Independence Lost*, 229–38.
47. Atkinson, *Splendid Land, Splendid People*, 96.
48. Usner, *Indians, Settlers, and Slaves*, 121.
49. Libby, *Slavery and Frontier Mississippi*, 19; James, *Antebellum Natchez*, 19.
50. DuVal, *Independence Lost*, 91.

2. Kentucky Land, Cash, and the Mississippi

1. John May to Samuel Beall, January 20, 1781, Beall-Booth Family Papers, FHS.
2. George Washington to John Posey, June 24, 1767, in Abbott et al., *Papers of George Washington*, Colonial Series, 8:1–4.
3. Samuel Beall to John May, November 11, 1780, Beall-Booth Family Papers, FHS; Jillson, *Kentucky Land Grants*, 79–83.
4. Jillson, *Kentucky Land Grants*, 21, 36, 45.
5. Holton, *Forced Founders*, 30; Bouton, "A Road Closed," 861.
6. On the consequences of the Proclamation of 1763 for land speculation, see Holton, *Forced Founders*, 29–30, and Weaver, *Great Land Rush*, 193–94. The success of the proclamation in preventing speculation may be overstated; squatters ignored the line altogether, while several companies were organized to speculate in western lands during this time period. See Blaakman, *Speculation Nation*, 23–57.
7. Lachlan McIntosh to George Washington, March 12, 1779, in Chase et al., *Papers of George Washington*, Revolutionary War Series, 19:451–63.
8. Garrison, "A Memorandum of M. Austin's Journey," 525.
9. Aron, "Pioneers and Profiteers," 183–98.
10. Ablavsky, *Federal Ground*, 19–50; Aron, *How the West Was Lost*, 70–77.
11. Recently, historians' interest in land and its relationship to national and individual finances has surged. Michael Blaakman and John Van Atta have both examined how governmental policy and land speculation operated glove in hand in the construction of the American state; Blaakman has focused on the role that land came to play within the nation's evolving political and economic ideology. Frederika Teute and Stephen Aron have shown the rapid concentration of Kentucky land in the hands of elites, while Honor Sachs has demonstrated the consequences for the haves and the have-nots within Kentucky society. Aron, "Pioneers and Profiteers"; Watlington, "Discontent in Frontier Kentucky"; Watlington, *Partisan Spirit*; Abernethy, *Western Lands and the American Revolution*; Hammon, "Settlers, Land Jobbers, and Outlyers"; Van Atta, *Securing the West*; Blaakman, *Speculation Nation*; Teute, "Land, Liberty, and Labor in the Post-Revolutionary Era"; Sachs, *Home Rule*. Other historians have recognized the role of law and

violence in the earliest expansion of the United States. See Ablavsky, *Federal Ground*; Harper, *Unsettling the West*; Saler, *Settlers' Empire*; and Griffin, *American Leviathan*.

12. Onuf, *Statehood and Union*, xiii–xiv.
13. Imlay, *Description of the Western Territory of North America*, 97.
14. In 1824, Joseph Patterson published a pamphlet titled "An Interesting Narrative by Anne Jamison," which chronicles McMeans's experiences in Kentucky. There are three copies of the document that have been used by researchers. An original handwritten copy is held by the Newberry Library in Chicago in the Ayer Collection, manuscript no. 691. Other copies are held by the Draper Manuscripts of the Wisconsin Historical Society and the Filson Historical Society in Louisville, Kentucky. In writing this chapter, I relied on a typeset copy transcribed by Robert Aiken, one of McMeans's descendants, in 1904, held by the Western Reserve Historical Society and republished in 1964. Jamison, "An Interesting Narrative." I also relied on the work of Light Townsend Cummins, cited below.
15. Cummins, "'Her Weary Pilgrimage,'" 389–415.
16. For more on Lord Dunmore's War, see Harper, *Unsettling the West*, 44–66.
17. Friend, *Kentucke's Frontiers*,15.
18. JDS, "Interview with Joshua McQueen," DC 13CC121, 115.
19. Cresswell, *Journal of Nicholas Cresswell*, 76; Friend, *Kentucke's Frontiers*, 47.
20. Filson, *Discovery, Settlement, and Present State of Kentucke*, 24.
21. "Narrative of Levi Todd," DC 15CC158.
22. Bushnell, "The Virginia Frontier in History," 44.
23. Jamison, "An Interesting Narrative"; Cummins, "'Her Weary Pilgrimage,'" 395–96.
24. Cummins, "'Her Weary Pilgrimage,'" 396.
25. JDS, "Interview with Berg Stites," DC 13CC87.
26. Ellen Eslinger, "Introduction," in Eslinger, *Running Mad for Kentucky*, 12–28.
27. See "Certificate Book of the Virginia Land Commissioners"—that is, the Kentucky Secretary of State's "Doomsday Book," a record of the commissioners' hearings held in reaction to the land law of 1779. For Andrew McMeans's petition, see pages 433–34.
28. Locke, *Second Treatise on Government*, 21. On preemption, or the "right of first occupancy" (already a misnomer, as western lands were owned by Native nations), see Ablavsky, *Federal Ground*, 40; Tomlins, *Freedom Bound*, 133–90; and Aron, *How the West Was Lost*, 58, 70. On the connections between "wasted" land and Indigenous dispossession, see Banner, *How the Indians Lost Their Land*, 21–35.
29. Locke, *Second Treatise on Government*, 21.
30. Jefferson, *A Summary View of the Rights of British America*, 147; "Fifth Virginia Convention, Proceedings of Forty-Second Day of Session, Monday

June the 24 1776," in Van Schreeven, Scribner, and Tarter, *Revolutionary Virginia*, 7:593.
31. Garrison, "A Memorandum of M. Austin's Journey," 526.
32. For a summary of the land law of 1779 and its consequences, see Teute, "Land, Liberty, and Labor in the Post-Revolutionary Era," 3, 185–94.
33. Lachlan McIntosh to George Washington, March 12, 1779, in Chase et al., *Papers of George Washington*, Revolutionary War Series, 19:451–63.
34. JDS "Interview with Isaac Clinkenbeard," DC 11CC1.
35. Michael Blaakman has illustrated how these laws, although intended to favor the interests of smallholders, were used by speculators to exclude smallholders from the market in Kentucky lands. Blaakman, *Speculation Nation*, 138–74.
36. Hening, *Statutes at Large*, 9:359. In October 1777, the state legislature decreed that "an annual quitrent of two shillings ... shall be allowed the sum of two shillings and six pence current money." This rate of exchange remained constant for two years, and the land law imposed the same valuation, as the ten shillings were "to be discharged in current money, at the rate of thirty three and one third per centum exchange." This valuation of specie remained constant although the value of the Virginia pound continued to fluctuate.
37. Hening, *Statutes at Large*, 10:40.
38. Hening, *Statutes at Large*, 10:35–65, 160.
39. For more on these markets, see Blaakman, *Speculation Nation*, 138–74.
40. Adkinson, "Saddlebag Notes"; Harrison and Klotter, *New History of Kentucky*, 54; Watlington, *Partisan Spirit*, 12–14; Ablavsky, *Federal Ground*, 32.
41. Adkinson, "Saddlebag Notes."
42. John Lewis land grant, November 19, 1796, Lewis Family Papers, Hannah Holborn Gray Special Collections, University of Chicago Library; Patrick Henry land grant to William Duvall, John Hawes, and John May, June 1, 1786, FHS.
43. See "Certificate Book of the Virginia Land Commissioners."
44. Aron, *How the West Was Lost*, 72.
45. "Certificate Book of the Virginia Land Commissioners," 433–34.
46. Hening, *Statutes at Large*, 10:178.
47. John Floyd to William Preston, January 19, 1780, DC 17CC120; John Fleming to Anne Fleming, December 3, 1779, Fleming Papers, FHS; John May to Samuel Beall, March 15, 1780, Beall-Booth Family Papers, FHS.
48. John Floyd to William Preston, December 19, 1779, DC 17CC122; January 19, 1780, DC 17CC120.
49. Hening, *Statutes at Large*, 10:280.
50. John May to Samuel Beall, c. March 1780, Beall-Booth Family Papers, FHS.

51. Hammon, "Initial Land Acquisition in Kentucky."
52. Hening, *Statutes at Large*, 10:431, 432, 465.
53. Aron, *How the West Was Lost*, 79–80, 119.
54. The most thorough study of the role the Mississippi played in the development of the West can be found in Whitaker, *Mississippi Question*.
55. Untitled anonymous pamphlet, c. 1788–92, Bullitt Family Papers, FHS.
56. On the American Revolution in the Gulf South, see DuVal, *Independence Lost*; Haynes, *Natchez District and the American Revolution*; Quintero Saravia, *Bernardo de Gálvez*; and Atkinson, *Splendid Land, Splendid People*.

3. The River at War

1. Patrick Henry to Bernardo de Gálvez, October 20, 1777; January 14, 1778, in Kinnaird, *Spain in the Mississippi Valley*, 2, part 1:241, 248–49.
2. DuVal, *Independence Lost*, 41.
3. James, *Oliver Pollock*, 251, 230; Cummins, "'Her Weary Pilgrimage,'" 401–3, 413; Randall, "George Rogers Clark's Service of Supply"; Jamison, "An Interesting Narrative."
4. Cummins, "'Her Weary Pilgrimage,'" 401–3, 413; Randall, "George Rogers Clark's Service of Supply"; Jamison, "An Interesting Narrative."
5. Haynes, *Natchez District and the American Revolution*, 42, 47.
6. Haynes, *Natchez District and the American Revolution*, 45, 36–44.
7. DuVal, *Independence Lost*, 136.
8. Haynes, *Natchez District and the American Revolution*, 111–21.
9. DuVal, *Independence Lost*, 90–92, 94–99.
10. George Rogers Clark to Unknown, June 26, 1783, in Palmer et al., *Calendar of Virginia State Papers*, 3:501.
11. Alexander Cameron, quoted in Mack, "River of Continuity, Tributaries of Change," 198.
12. Cummins, "'Her Weary Pilgrimage,'" 401. On tenancy in Kentucky, see Sachs, *Home Rule*, 77–78.
13. Jamison, "An Interesting Narrative."
14. Cummins, "'Her Weary Pilgrimage,'" 402–3; Atkinson, *Splendid Land, Splendid People*, 108; Fraser, "Fort Jefferson," 16.
15. Gibson, *Chickasaws*, 13.
16. Jamison, "An Interesting Narrative."
17. Jamison, "An Interesting Narrative."
18. Haynes, *Natchez District and the American Revolution*, 82–86.
19. Din, "Arkansas Post in the American Revolution," 16; Haynes, *Natchez District and the American Revolution*, 142–46. See also Corbitt, "James Colbert and the Spanish Claims to the East Bank of the Mississippi," 458–60.

20. "Declaration of Labbadie," July 5, 1782, in Kinnaird, *Spain in the Mississippi Valley*, 2:32.
21. Mack, "River of Continuity, Tributaries of Change," 178–79, 199–203.
22. Haynes, *Natchez District and the American Revolution*, 150–51.
23. Affidavit of Robert Trimble, May 19, 1819; Pension Application File S. 36102 for service of Sergeant Joshua McQueen (Col. John Gibson, 13th Virginia Regiment, Revolutionary War), Case Files of Pension and Bounty-Land Warrant Applications Based on Revolutionary War Service, Pension and Bounty Land Warrant Application Files, National Archives, roll 1700, images 624–25. In a subsequent affidavit submitted in 1828, Joshua McQueen stated he might have enlisted in 1776. He also served as a private in Colonel Gibson's Virginia regiment.
24. JDS, "Interview with Joshua McQueen," DC 13CC116.
25. On the departure of the two convoys from Pittsburgh, see William Irvine to Robert Morris, April 29, 1782, in Butterfield, *Washington-Irvine Correspondence*, 202. On McQueen's role, see JDS, "Interview with Joshua McQueen," DC 13CC116. On Pollock's involvement, see James, *Oliver Pollock*, 230.
26. William Irvine to Robert Morris, April 29, 1782, in Butterfield, *Washington-Irvine Correspondence*, 202.
27. Haynes, *Natchez District and the American Revolution*, 89–90.
28. On the multicultural world of Spanish Louisiana, see DuVal, *Independence Lost*, 135–36, and Rodriguez, *Spanish New Orleans*, 58–60.
29. JDS "Interview with Joshua McQueen," DC 13CC126.
30. Cummins, "'Her Weary Pilgrimage,'" 401–3, 413; Randall, "George Rogers Clark's Service of Supply"; Jamison, "An Interesting Narrative."
31. Cummins, "'Her Weary Pilgrimage,'" 390.
32. Jamison, "An Interesting Narrative."
33. For a more detailed description of Spanish objections to the Anglo-American Treaty of Paris, see Bemis, *Pinckney's Treaty*, 47–70. The correspondence of Don Diego de Gardoqui goes into detail regarding Spanish indignation toward the British and American claims in the region; see, for instance, "Response to the Proceeding of Senor Vicente Manuel de Zespedes [Cespedes]," August 6, 1786, vol. 1, GDUC. The dispatches consist of the correspondence of high-level Spanish officials in both the New World and Spain.
34. Jenkinson, *Collection of All the Treaties of Peace*, 3:397.
35. Jenkinson, *Collection of All the Treaties of Peace*, 3:396.
36. Jenkinson, *Collection of All the Treaties of Peace*, 3:396.
37. José de Gálvez, Minister for the Department of the Indies, summarized Spain's official attitudes in a letter to the Continental Congress, Philadelphia, November 16, 1784, in *JCC*, 27:689. Arthur Preston Whitaker also

explained Spain's goals in closing the Mississippi. Whitaker, *Mississippi Question*, 7–9.
38. "Copia de carta escrita por Don Diego de Gardoqui, al Governador de Florida," June 30, 1786, vol. 1, box 22, folder 2, GDUC.
39. Spain had cultivated diplomatic ties with the Choctaw, Chickasaw, and Creek nations prior to the Revolution. The British trading house of Panton and Leslie continued to operate among the tribes of the Southeast with a Spanish license. For a detailed examination of Native American trade and diplomacy in the region, see Weeks, *Paths to a Middle Ground*.
40. "Notes on John Jay's Conference with Floridablanca," September 23, 1780, in Johnston, *Correspondence and Public Papers of John Jay*, 1:424–25.
41. Lewis, "Anglo-American Entrepreneurs in Havana," 115, 118–21. On the Philadelphia-Cuba flour trade, see also Johnson, "El Niño, Environmental Crisis, and the Emergence of Alternative Markets," and Hunter, "Wheat, War, and the American Economy during the Age of Revolution."
42. Don Diego de Gardoqui to Unknown, San Ildefonso, July 25, 1784, Diego de Gardoqui Papers, Tulane University Special Collections.
43. Quoted in Cummins, "'Her Weary Pilgrimage,'" 411.
44. Will of Joshua McQueen, May 7, 1846, in *Kentucky, U.S., Wills and Probate Records*, image 352. McQueen's grave stands in Old Bott Cemetery, Millville, Woodford County, Kentucky. The gravestone lists his birth and death dates as October 15, 1746, and April 17, 1853.
45. Gould, *Among the Powers of the Earth*, 11–12.
46. Sachs, *Home Rule*, 37–40; Aron, *How the West Was Lost*, 100; Harrison, *Kentucky's Road to Statehood*, 12.

Part II

1. Baron de Carondelet to Conde de Aranda, November 13, 1792, no. 22, AGI, PC, legajo 177, quoted in Weeks, *Paths to a Middle Ground*, 87; Atkinson, *Splendid Land, Splendid People*, 155.
2. Friend, *Kentucke's Frontiers*, 135.
3. DuVal, *Independence Lost*, 296.
4. Juan de la Villebeuvre to Baron de Carondelet, October 12, 1792, quoted in Weeks, *Paths to a Middle Ground*, 86.
5. Nichols, *Red Gentlemen and White Savages*, 48.
6. Griffin, *American Leviathan*, 190–211; Harper, *Unsettling the West*, 145–72.
7. DuVal, *Independence Lost*, 301. On violence in what would become Tennessee, see Barksdale, *Lost State of Franklin*, 91–117, and Ray, *Middle Tennessee*, 19–40.
8. Weeks, *Paths to a Middle Ground*, 48–50, 59–62, 84–87.
9. DuVal, *Independence Lost*, 307.

4. An Imperial Problem

1. Samuel Holton to Samuel Adams, April 11, 1785, in *LDC* 22:320.
2. Paine, *Common Sense*; Paine, *Public Good*, 6 (quotation).
3. New Hampshire Delegates to Meshech Weare, May 29, 1785; Hugh Williamson to Thomas Ruston, November 2, 1784, in *LDC*, 22:414, 9.
4. New Hampshire Delegates to Meshech Weare, May 29, 1785, in *LDC*, 22:414.
5. William Johnson to Roger Sherman, April 20, 1785, in *LDC*, 22:348; Onuf, *Statehood and Union*, 30.
6. Van Cleve, *We Have Not a Government*, 36–39; Gould, *Among the Powers of the Earth*, 119–21.
7. The debate over how to respond to the closure constituted, in the words of historian Samuel Flagg Bemis, "the most serious issue that agitated the Continental Congress during its five years of peacetime history." While Bemis likely overstated the case, the question of the Mississippi and the pursuit of a treaty with Spain were key points of division within Congress and the states at large. Bemis, *Pinckney's Treaty*, 85.
8. James Monroe to Thomas Jefferson, June 16, 1785, in Boyd et al., *Papers of Thomas Jefferson*, 8:217.
9. This view of sectional distinctions as the result of economic similarities among states differed from later conceptions of sectional identity based on shared social and political attitudes. Revolutionary-era Americans often ascribed nefarious motives to their sectional rivals; as divisions over slavery grew in the antebellum era, sectional differences became morally charged. Maryland typically identified with the southern bloc, while New Jersey and Delaware were in the eastern camp. McCoy, "James Madison and Visions of American Nationality in the Confederation Period," 237. See also Onuf, "Federalism, Republicanism, and the Origins of American Sectionalism," 22.
10. A growing body of work points to the international consequences of the U.S. Constitution. According to Leonard J. Sadosky, "In the process of negotiating with extranational polities, and often because of it, the individual American states reassessed how they related to one another." Sadosky, *Revolutionary Negotiations*, 4. For other works on the evolution of the Constitution as a tool for international relations, see Totten, "Security, Two Diplomacies, and the Formation of the U.S. Constitution," 79–80, 101–9; Gould, *Among the Powers of the Earth*, 130–35; and Cutterham, "The International Dimension of the Federal Constitution," 504–11.
11. Bouton, *Taming Democracy*, 61–104; Holton, *Unruly Americans and the Origins of the Constitution*; Feer, "Shays's Rebellion and the Constitution"; Szatmary, *Shays' Rebellion*; Hendrickson, *Peace Pact*, especially 211–20;

Matson and Onuf, *Union of Interests*; Gould, *Among the Powers of the Earth*, 130–35; Edling, *Revolution in Favor of Government*, parts 2 and 3.
12. Van Cleve, *We Have Not a Government*, 161–85; Merritt, Green, and Campbell, "Sectional Conflict and Secret Compromise."
13. Drake, *Nation's Nature*, 194.
14. Edelson, *New Map of Empire*, 17. According to Paul Gilje, "Anglo Americans believed that their empire was built upon commerce and not conquest." Gilje, "Commerce and Conquest in Early American Foreign Relations," 737.
15. Onuf, *Jefferson's Empire*, 68–69; Matson and Onuf, *Union of Interests*, 20–26.
16. Hutchins, *Historical Narrative and Topographical Description of Louisiana*, 27, 22–23.
17. *Loudon's New York Packet*, March 14, 1785; Kaminski, *George Clinton*, 96–106.
18. Matson and Onuf, *Union of Interests*, 44.
19. Tucker and Hendrickson, *Empire of Liberty*, 28.
20. *Independent Journal*, March 1, 1786.
21. *New-Hampshire Mercury and the General Advertiser*, March 15, 1785.
22. *Pennsylvania Journal*, May 11, 1785.
23. Rufus King to Elbridge Gerry, May 19, 1785, in *LDC*, 22:396.
24. On the provisioning trade, and difficulties with Great Britain and Spain in general, see Richard Henry Lee to Patrick Henry, December 18, 1784, in *LDC*, 22:75–76. On France's behavior toward American fisheries, see Elbridge Gerry to Thomas Jefferson, September 12, 1785, in *LDC*, 22:631–32.
25. Lydon, *Fish and Flour for Gold*, 3, 23, 88.
26. James Monroe to Patrick Henry, January 1, 1785, in *LDC*, 22:99.
27. Onuf, *Origins of the Federal Republic*, 76–80.
28. Hugh Williamson to Thomas Ruston, March 2, 1785, in *LDC*, 22:240–41.
29. Hugh Williamson to Thomas Ruston, March 2, 1785, in *LDC*, 22:240–41.
30. Bemis, *Pinckney's Treaty*, 64.
31. Diego de Gardoqui to Conde de Gálvez, Viceroy of Mexico, August 23, 1785, legajo 3891, 3:304, GDUC.
32. "Mr. Charles Pinckney's Speech, in Answer to Mr. Jay, Secretary for Foreign Affairs, on the Question of a Treaty with Spain, Delivered in Congress, August 16, 1786," in *JCC*, 31:943.
33. Lydon, *Fish and Flour for Gold*, 238.
34. Dickson, "James Monroe's Defense of Kentucky's Interests in the Confederation Congress." During the summer of 1785, Congress changed its instructions to Jay several times but continued to maintain that Jay could not accept any treaty that did not acknowledge American claims to the Mississippi.
35. Diego de Gardoqui to José Moñino y Redondo, Conde de Floridablanca, November 21, 1785, 4:34, box 22, folder 2, GDUC.

36. Diego de Gardoqui to Conde de Floridablanca, New York, June 19, 1786, 4:110, box 22, folder 2, GDUC; Bemis, *Pinckney's Treaty*, 73; Kukla, *Wilderness So Immense*, 74.
37. Diego de Gardoqui to Conde de Floridablanca, November 21, 1785, 4:34, box 22, folder 2, GDUC.
38. Diego de Gardoqui to Conde de Floridablanca, November 21, 1785, 4:34, box 22, folder 2, GDUC.
39. Rufus King to Caleb Davis, November 3, 1785, in *LDC*, 22:719.
40. Benjamin Lincoln to Rufus King, February 11, 1786, in King, *Life and Correspondence of Rufus King*, 1:157, 160.
41. Theodore Sedgwick to Caleb Strong, August 6, 1786, in *LDC*, 23:436.
42. Nathan Dane to Edward Pulling, January 8, 1786, in *LDC*, 23:85.
43. Diego de Gardoqui to Conde de Floridablanca, November 21, 1785, 4:44–57, box 22, folder 2, GDUC. Jay's August 3 address to Congress laid out the agreements that he and Gardoqui had reached as early as the previous February. Bemis, *Pinckney's Treaty*, 77–78. For Barbary pirates, see Bemis, *Pinckney's Treaty*, 77n23.
44. John Jay, Address to Congress, August 3, 1786, in U.S. Government, *Secret Journals of the Acts and Proceedings of Congress*, 4:51.
45. John Jay, Address to Congress, August 3, 1786, in U.S. Government, *Secret Journals of the Acts and Proceedings of Congress*, 4:53.
46. Charles Thomson, Notes of Debates, August 16, 1786, in *LDC*, 23:486.
47. Arthur St. Clair, Speech, August 18, 1786, in *LDC*, 23:492, 493; Charles Thomson, Notes of Debates, August 18, 1786, in *LDC*, 23:496–97.
48. Charles Pinckney, Speech, August 16, 1786, in *JCC*, 31:942.
49. Charles Thomson, Notes of Debates, August 16, 1786, in *LDC*, 23:485.
50. Charles Pinckney, Speech, August 16, 1786, in *JCC*, 31:493; Charles Thomson, Notes of Debates, August 16, 1786, in *LDC*, 23:485.
51. Arthur St. Clair, Speech, August 18, 1786, in *LDC*, 23:492.
52. Diego de Gardoqui to Conde de Floridablanca, August 20, 1786, 2:226, box 21, folder 5, GDUC.
53. Charles Thomson, Notes of Debates, August 16, 1786, in *LDC*, 23:486.
54. Arthur St. Clair, Notes of Debates, August 17, 1786, in *LDC*, 23:491.
55. Diego de Gardoqui to Conde de Floridablanca, August 6, 1786, 2:225, box 21, folder 5, GDUC.
56. James Monroe to Thomas Jefferson, August 19, 1786, in *LDC* 23:500 (materials marked {} were in cipher); Monroe to James Madison, August 12, 1786, in *LDC*, 4:464.
57. Rufus King to Nathan Dane, August 17, 1786, in *LDC*, 23:488; Lydon, *Fish and Flour for Gold*, 239–40.
58. "Pinckney's Speech," in *JCC*, 31:945.
59. Arthur St. Clair, Notes of Debates, August 18, 1786, in *LDC*, 23:490.

60. "Summary of a Conversation between James White and Gardoqui, August 26, 1786," in Corbitt and Corbitt, "Papers from the Spanish Archives Relating to Tennessee and the Old Southwest" (1944), 84.
61. Diego de Gardoqui to Conde de Floridablanca, October 28, 1786, in Corbitt and Corbitt, "Papers from the Spanish Archives Relating to Tennessee and the Old Southwest" (1944), 87.
62. James Madison to Thomas Jefferson, August 12, 1786, in Boyd et al., *Papers of Thomas Jefferson*, 10:229–36.
63. Frederick W. Marks III discussed how foreign affairs, including trade and defense, played a significant role in the writing of the Constitution. As Marks suggested, this understanding does not need to replace our understanding of the social forces driving constitutional reform but can help us to better understand the actions and motivations of the members of the Constitutional Convention. Throughout his book, Marks emphasized the importance of reinstating American trade to the British West Indies, but trade with Spain's colonial possessions might have been at least equally important. Marks, *Independence on Trial*, 52–95.
64. Benjamin Hawkins to Richard Caswell, July 10, 1787, in *LDC*, 24:351–52.
65. Van Cleve, *A Slaveholders' Union*, 158.
66. Charles Thomson to William Bingham, June 25, 1787, in *LDC*, 24:343. The letter to the North Carolina delegates is mentioned by Thomson in his note to Bingham but is no longer extant.
67. William Blount to Richard Caswell, July 10, 1787, in *LDC*, 24:350.
68. Ablavsky, *Federal Ground*, 8.
69. Nathan Dane to Rufus King, July 5, 1787, in *LDC*, 24:348.
70. July 4, 1787, *JCC*, 32:299–300.
71. For the most thorough account of the ordinance, see Onuf, *Statehood and Union*.
72. Van Cleve, *A Slaveholders' Union*, 154–55.
73. Cayton, *Frontier Republic*, 24–26.
74. Convention debates, July 13, 1787, in Farrand, *Records of the Federal Convention of 1787*, 1:604.
75. McCoy, "James Madison and Visions of American Nationality in the Confederation Period," 228.
76. George Mason, speaking in convention, July 11, 1787, in Farrand, *Records of the Federal Convention of 1787*, 1:586, 578.
77. Gouverneur Morris, speaking in convention, July 11, 1787, in Farrand, *Records of the Federal Convention of 1787*, 1:583.
78. George Mason, speaking in convention, July 11, 1787, Farrand, *Records of the Federal Convention of 1787*, 1:579.
79. James Madison, speaking in convention, July 11, 1787, Farrand, *Records of the Federal Convention of 1787*, 1:584–85.

80. George Mason, August 15, 1787; James Wilson, September 7, 1787; Elbridge Gerry, September 8, 1787, in Farrand, *Records of the Federal Convention of 1787*, 2:297, 540, 548.
81. Hugh Williamson to James Madison, June 2, 1788, in *LDC*, 25:136–37.
82. *Pittsburgh Gazette*, November 17, 1787.
83. On Kentucky's opposition, see subsequent paragraphs, as well as Watlington, *Partisan Spirit*, 147–56. On Pennsylvania's opposition, see Cornell, "Aristocracy Assailed."
84. "Circular Letter to the Fayette County Court, Danville, Ky.," February 29, 1788, in Kaminski et al., *Documentary History of the Ratification of the Constitution*, 8:435.
85. "The Virginia Convention," June 9, 1788, in Kaminski et al., *Documentary History of the Ratification of the Constitution*, 9:1051.
86. James Madison to the Convention, June 13, 1788, in Robertson, *Debates and Other Proceedings of the Convention of Virginia*, 248.
87. Talbert, "Kentuckians in the Virginia Convention of 1788," 187.
88. Van Cleve, *A Slaveholders' Union*, 161.
89. September 15, 1788, *JCC*, 34:531–35.
90. Hugh Williamson to Samuel Johnston, September 17, 1788, in *LDC*, 25:376–77.

5. Trading without the River

1. Watlington, *Partisan Spirit*, 70.
2. Colonel Josiah Harmar to Henry Knox, May 14, 1787, in Smith, *St. Clair Papers*, 2:19–22.
3. Colonel Josiah Harmar to Henry Knox, January 10, 1788, in Smith, *St. Clair Papers*, 2:38–40.
4. A widespread consensus has emerged among historians who study the West that the federal government, far from being absent in the region, was in fact at its strongest, most active, and most visible along the nation's peripheries. See for instance Balogh, *Government Out of Sight*, 151–218. At the same time, historians have taken seriously contemporary concerns that western settlers, far from being willing agents of American empire, were open to approaches by European powers and were prepared to separate themselves from the rest of the union entirely. In a recent account of the growth of federal authority in the West, Gregory Ablavsky has captured this reality, arguing that the West was at once "a space of robust, nearly unchallenged federal authority . . . [and] a borderland marked by flux, contestation, and uncertain sovereignty where the success of the United States in securing its tenuous hold" seemed unlikely. Ablavsky, *Federal Ground*, 15.

5. In his account of the Southwest Territory, Ablavsky contends that local western actors utilized federal law as a tool for asserting their interests within the territory, a process that strengthened the relationship between the East and the West while, somewhat ironically, expanding federal authority, not at the behest of the government but to fulfil the needs of western settlers. Other accounts of federal authority have focused on violence, land distribution, and slave policy in the process of state-building in the West, recognizing the active role of westerners in contesting and shaping federal actions. Harper, *Unsettling the West*; Griffin, *American Leviathan*; Nichols, *Red Gentlemen and White Savages*; Bergmann, "A 'Commercial View of This Unfortunate War'"; Bergmann, *American National State and the Early West*. Those who have examined the role of violence in the West typically draw a sharp distinction between the employment of the federal army north of the Ohio and the seemingly uncontrolled violence of the Southwest Territory. Cayton, "'Separate Interests' and the Nation-State." On land policy, see Van Atta, *Securing the West*; Hammond, *Slavery, Freedom, and Expansion in the Early American West*; and Hammond, "Slavery, Settlement, and Empire."
6. Saler, *Settlers' Empire*, 39.
7. Cayton, *Frontier Republic*, 21.
8. John Cleves Symmes to Joseph Ward, July 24, 1786, in LDC, 23:411.
9. Eslinger, "Farming on the Kentucky Frontier," 21; Friend, *Along the Maysville Road*, 115.
10. Harry Innes to John Brown, December 7, 1787, Harry Innes Papers, Library of Congress.
11. "A Copy of a Letter from a Gentleman at the Falls of Ohio, to His Friend in New England, Dated December 4th, 1786," in U.S. Government, *Secret Journals of the Acts and Proceedings of Congress*, 4:321.
12. Garcia, "A Great Deal of Money," 189.
13. "A Copy of a Letter from a Gentleman at the Falls of Ohio, to His Friend in New England, Dated December 4th, 1786," in U.S. Government, *Secret Journals of the Acts and Proceedings of Congress*, 4:321. In 1785, the price of pork in Philadelphia was typically twice that of Kentucky. U.S. Bureau of Labor Statistics, *History of Wages in the United States*, 21.
14. William Christian to Unknown, March 30, 1786, Bullitt Family Papers, FHS.
15. Deposition of Thomas Amis, November 15, 1786, in U.S. Government, *Secret Journals of the Acts and Proceedings of Congress*, 4:325–27.
16. "A Copy of a Letter from a Gentleman at the Falls of Ohio, to His Friend in New England, Dated December 4th, 1786," in U.S. Government, *Secret Journals of the Acts and Proceedings of Congress*, 4:321.
17. John Girault to William Clark, July 2, 1785, DC 1M114–15.

18. Whitaker, *Spanish-American Frontier*, 95.
19. "A Copy of a Letter from a Gentleman at the Falls of Ohio, to His Friend in New England, Dated December 4th, 1786," in U.S. Government, *Secret Journals of the Acts and Proceedings of Congress*, 4:320.
20. Thomas Green to Unknown, December 23, 1786, in U.S. Government, *Secret Journals of the Acts and Proceedings of Congress*, 4:321.
21. Watlington, *Partisan Spirit*, 89.
22. James Wilkinson to James Hutchinson, August 18, 1786, in "Letters of Gen. James Wilkinson," 63.
23. James Wilkinson to James Hutchinson, May 4, 1786, in "Letters of Gen. James Wilkinson."
24. Shepherd, "Wilkinson and the Beginnings of the Spanish Conspiracy," 494.
25. Andro Linklater asserts that Wilkinson gave Francisco Cruzat two Virginia-bred thoroughbreds, but he offers no source for this claim. Linklater, *Artist in Treason*, 82.
26. James Wilkinson to Hugh McIlvain, March 17, 1791, Harry Innes Papers.
27. Esteban Miró to Don Bernardo Troncoso, New Orleans, June 11, 1785, legajo 1387, no. 1, DSG. Miró was almost certainly referring to Kentucky when he mentioned Virginia; Esteban Miró to Don Josef de Espeleta, January 28, 1788, legajo 1394, DSG.
28. Esteban Miró to Don Joseph de Espeleta, February 20, 1788, legajo 1394, no. 48, DSG.
29. William R. Shepherd quotes much of Wilkinson's memorial verbatim; see Shepherd, "Wilkinson and the Beginnings of the Spanish Conspiracy," 499.
30. Shepherd, "Wilkinson and the Beginnings of the Spanish Conspiracy," 499.
31. Agreement between James Wilkinson and William Pope, December 19, 1787, Harry Innes Papers.
32. Watlington, *Partisan Spirit*, 145–46.
33. Wilkinson told few of his colleagues of his plans to turn the West into a Spanish colony. Watlington, *Partisan Spirit*, 143.
34. For a very detailed discussion of the complicated party politics of Kentucky and Wilkinson's role in Kentucky politics both before and after his journey to New Orleans, see Watlington, *Partisan Spirit*, 79–187.
35. Watlington, *Partisan Spirit*, 145.
36. Littell, *Political Transactions in and Concerning Kentucky*, appendix, 47–48.
37. Five boats belonging to James Wilkinson arrived in New Orleans on June 15, 1788. Potter, *Passports of Southeastern Pioneers*, 13, 15.
38. Pelzer, "Economic Factors in the Acquisition of Louisiana," 117.
39. James Brown to Captain John Preston, September 3, 1789, Joseph Adger Stewart Collection, FHS. This is corroborated by Daniel Clark Jr., "Extract

from a Paper on the Commerce of Louisiana, Supposed to Be Referred to in a Letter from Mr. Daniel Clark to the Secretary of State, of the 18th, April, 1798," in U.S. Government, *American State Papers: Miscellaneous*, 1:709. Spain continued to limit not only riverine but maritime trade as well, restricting it as much as possible to Spanish-owned trips.

40. See, for instance, Baily, *Journal of a Tour in the Unsettled Parts of North America*, 286–89.
41. The major exception to this are the works of Ramage: *John Wesley Hunt*, and "Hunts and Morgans." Some of the subsequent material also appears in Susan Gaunt Stearns, "The Sutler's Empire: Frontier Merchants and Imperial Authority, 1790–1811," in Blaakman, Krutz, and Arista, *Early Imperial Republic*, 45–62.
42. Nichols, *Red Gentlemen and White Savages*, 42.
43. Nichols, *Red Gentlemen and White Savages*, 164.
44. Cayton, "'Separate Interests' and the Nation-State," 66.
45. Nichols, *Red Gentlemen and White Savages*, 116.
46. Hurt, *Ohio Frontier*, 114–18.
47. Bergmann, *American National State and the Early West*, 134.
48. Abijah Hunt to John W. Hunt, April 30, 1795, JWHP, FHS.
49. Ramage, "Hunts and Morgans," 43.
50. "Invoice, Philadelphia, May 11, 1795," Whelan & Miller; "Philadelphia, May 18th, 1795," Taylor & Newbold, John Wesley (Morgan) Hunt Collection, FHS; Ramage, "Hunts and Morgans," 25.
51. Ramage, "Hunts and Morgans," 26.
52. *Kentucky Gazette*, July 25, 1795; Ramage, "Hunts and Morgans," 27.
53. Elizabeth Ann Perkins characterized Kentuckians' involvement in markets as following "a remarkably sophisticated, international pattern of consumption [which] laid a cultural base for American life." Perkins, "Consumer Frontier," 493, 499. Much of Perkins's article focuses on a sampling of the 541 transactions recorded in the Hunts' daybook. James A. Ramage's dissertation and book also focus on the operations of this store. Ramage, "Hunts and Morgans."
54. Ramage, "Hunts and Morgans," 24.
55. Jeremiah Hunt to John W. Hunt, March 11, 1796, Hunt Morgan Papers, UK; Burton, "General Wayne's Orderly Book"; Delo, *Peddlers and Post Traders*, 21; Ramage, *John Wesley Hunt*, 27.
56. Jeremiah Hunt to John W. Hunt, March 11, 1796, Hunt Morgan Papers, UK.
57. On the price of butter in Kentucky, see Toulmin, *Western Country*, 62; on the increase of cash in Kentucky, see Toulmin, *Western Country*, 126.
58. The role of the army in injecting specie and providing a market outlet for the West has been discussed by numerous authors, among them Bergmann,

American National State and the Early West, 132–36; Cayton, "'Separate Interests' and the Nation-State," 53; and Downes, "Trade in Frontier Ohio," 477.
59. *Centinel of the North Western Territory*, January 9, 1796; Bill of Exchange, June 26, 1796, Hunt Morgan Papers, UK. See also Downes, "Trade in Frontier Ohio," 478.
60. Mansfield, *Memoirs of the Life and Services of Daniel Drake*, quoted in Downes, "Trade in Frontier Ohio," 478.
61. Bill of Exchange, June 26, 1796, Hunt Morgan Papers, UK.
62. Bergmann, *American National State and the Early West*, 135, 134.
63. Link, *Democratic-Republican Societies*, 13–14. Link's account is still one of the most detailed works available that discusses all of the nations' Democratic-Republican societies. Other works on the Democratic-Republican societies include Philip S. Foner's anthology of documents relating to the societies, which includes a lengthy discussion of earlier scholarship. Foner, *Democratic-Republican Societies*, 1–53; Sioli, "The Democratic Republican Societies at the End of the Eighteenth Century," 289.
64. Although it is possible that portions of the records of these clubs have not survived, nearly every surviving document, with the exception of the first circulating letter issued by the Kentucky Democratic-Republican societies, deals with Mississippi navigation. Orihel, "'Mississippi Mad,'" 403–4.
65. *Kentucky Gazette*, September 29, 1787.
66. Democratic Society of Kentucky, "To the Inhabitants of the United States West of the Allegany and Apalachian Mountains," December 13, 1793, Harry Innes Papers.
67. "Response to an Address from the Democratic Society of Kentucky, April 26, 1794," in Foner, *Democratic-Republican Societies*, 131.
68. "Resolutions Adopted on the Free Navigation of the Mississippi," *Kentucky Gazette*, November 16, 1793.
69. "Remonstrance of the Citizens West of the Allegany Mountains," 1793, Harry Innes Papers.
70. *Independent Gazetteer*, May 10, 1794.
71. "Response to an Address from the Democratic Society of Kentucky, April 26, 1794," 131.
72. "Resolutions Adopted on the Free Navigation of the Mississippi," *Kentucky Gazette*, November 16, 1793.
73. "The Remonstrance of the Citizens West of the Allegany Mountains, to the President of the United States of America," n.d., Harry Innes Papers.
74. *Kentucky Gazette*, May 31, 1794.
75. *Gazette of the United States and Evening Advertiser*, March 10, 1794.
76. *American Minerva*, reprinted in the *Columbian Centinel*, January 25, 1794. Both journals were organs of the Federalist Parties of their respective cities.
77. *Gazette of the United States*, March 10, 1794.

6. Chickasaw Country

1. Carlos de Grand Pré to Esteban Miró, October 26, 1787, in Kinnaird, *Spain in the Mississippi Valley*, 3, part 2:236.
2. Charles A. Weeks claims that the unnamed Chickasaw chief who accompanied Taboca to Philadelphia was Piominko, while Mary Sarah Bilder offers strong evidence that it was Muckleshamingo. See Weeks, *Paths to a Middle Ground*, 57, and Bilder, "Without Doors," 1722.
3. O'Brien, *Choctaws in a Revolutionary Age*, 65.
4. Carlos de Grand Pré to Esteban Miró, October 26, 1787, in Kinnaird, *Spain in the Mississippi Valley*, 3, part 2:236. On the presence of Indigenous leaders in Philadelphia in the summer of 1787, see Bilder, "Without Doors," 1718–53. For the Chickasaw specifically, see Flaherty, "'People to Our Selves,'" 76–77.
5. Atkinson, *Splendid Land, Splendid People*, 124.
6. Atkinson, *Splendid Land, Splendid People*, 129–30.
7. James R. Atkinson has offered two explanations for Piominko's stance. The first is that Piominko resented the Spanish for inciting earlier attacks on the Chickasaw by the Kickapoo. A second explanation is that, having seen first the French and then the British displaced in the lower Mississippi Valley, Piominko may have recognized the growing influence of the United States as a potentially useful partner in trade and diplomacy in the region. Atkinson, *Splendid Land, Splendid People*, 137–38.
8. Chokkilissa' was situated just north of the present-day site of Tupelo, Mississippi. It has been spelled many different ways, including Chukalissa. By the eighteenth century, many European Americans referred to this community as "Big Town," which adds to naming confusion. Chokkilissa' was a white, or peace, town.
9. Cowger and Caver, *Piominko*, 8; Greg O'Brien, "Quieting the Ghosts: How the Choctaws and Chickasaws Stopped Fighting," in Garrison and O'Brien, *Native South*, 58–59.
10. Cowger and Caver, *Piominko*, 10–12.
11. DuVal, *Independence Lost*, 17.
12. Atkinson, *Splendid Land, Splendid People*, 126.
13. Washburn, "Directing Their Own Change," 97.
14. Storm, "Up the Tennessee in 1790," 131.
15. Washburn, "'Labor in the Field Is Much Changed,'" 96–97n75.
16. Storm, "Up the Tennessee in 1790," 124.
17. Flaherty, "'People to Our Selves,'" 77.
18. Piomingo to Joseph Martin, February 15, 1787, in Palmer, *Calendar of Virginia State Papers*, 4:241; Atkinson, *Splendid Land, Splendid People*, 133–34.

19. Storm, "Up the Tennessee in 1790," 124.
20. See Snyder, *Slavery in Indian Country*, especially chaps. 1 and 2.
21. Storm, "Up the Tennessee in 1790," 127–28.
22. Storm, "Up the Tennessee in 1790," 122, 128–29.
23. Atkinson, *Splendid Land, Splendid People*, 148–49, 152–54.
24. Atkinson, *Splendid Land, Splendid People*, 157; Chickasaw Chiefs to General James Robertson, February 13, 1793, in U.S. Government, *American State Papers: Indian Affairs*, 1:442–43.
25. "Extract from a Letter of Brigadier General [James] Robertson," March 12, 1793, in U.S. Government, *American State Papers: Indian Affairs*, 1:441.
26. Esteban Miró to Bernardo de Gálvez, June 5, 1782, in Houck, *Spanish Regime in Missouri*, 1:214–18.
27. Weeks, *Paths to a Middle Ground*, 131.
28. Manuel Gayoso to Baron de Carondelet, July 25, 1793, AGI, PC, 178, in Corbitt and Corbitt, eds. "Papers from the Spanish Archives Relating to Tennessee and the Old Southwest" (1962), 94–97.
29. Atkinson, *Splendid Land, Splendid People*, 164–65.
30. Cowger and Caver, *Piominko*, 108–9.
31. Weeks, *Paths to a Middle Ground*, 136–40.
32. "Report on Negotiation with Spain," March 18, 1792, in Ford, *Works of Thomas Jefferson*, 422, 425, 426–27, 434–35. For more on these negotiations, see Bemis, *Pinckney's Treaty*.
33. Bemis, *Pinckney's Treaty*, 227–29.
34. *Kentucky Gazette*, March 26, 1796.
35. "Lexington, July 9," *Kentucky Gazette*, July 9, 1796.
36. Deville Degoutin to Baron de Carondelet, San Fernando de las Barrancas, Aug. 22, 1796, AGI, PC, bundle 34, no. 16, quoted in Weeks, "Of Rattlesnakes, Wolves, and Tigers," 500.
37. Weeks, "Of Rattlesnakes, Wolves, and Tigers," 511–13.
38. Cowger and Caver, *Piominko*, 109–14.
39. Sellers, *Mr. Peale's Museum*, 69–70.
40. Cowger and Caver, *Piominko*, 114–18; "Speech to the Indians from the Secretary at War" (quotation).
41. Cowger and Caver, *Piominko*, 114–18; "Speech to the Indians from the Secretary at War" (quotation).

Part III

1. Lakomäki, "'Our Line,'" 601–3.
2. John Cleves Symmes to Jonathan Dayton, August 6, 1795, in Bond, *Correspondence of John Cleves Symmes*, 172, 174–75.
3. Hurt, *Ohio Frontier*, 189.

4. The quotation and statistic are both from Scheerer, "For Ten Years Past," 13.
5. For general overviews of the Ohio, Scioto, and Miami Companies, see Cutler, *Life, Journals, and Correspondence of Reverend Manasseh Cutler;* Jones, *The King of the Alley*, 119–23; Shannon, "The Ohio Company and the Meaning of Opportunity in the American West"; Cayton, *Frontier Republic*, 13–32; Rohrbough, *Trans-Appalachian Frontier*, 84–86; Maulden, *Federalist Frontier*, 27–34; and Goodwin, "Development of the Miami Country."
6. Scheerer, "For Ten Years Past," 7–13; Bean, "Marketing 'the Great American Commodity,'" 156–58.
7. Scheerer, "For Ten Years Past," 13–16. See also Hinderaker, *Elusive Empires*, 249.
8. Bean, "Marketing 'the Great American Commodity,'" 157.
9. Bean, "Marketing 'the Great American Commodity,'" 166; Scheerer, "For Ten Years Past," 17, 10.
10. *Western Spy, and Hamilton Gazette*, December 3, 1800.
11. *Scioto Gazette*, January 9, 1802; Hurt, *Ohio Frontier*, 172.
12. *Western Spy, and Hamilton Gazette*, November 5, 1799; Charles Wilkins to Nathaniel Massie, December 28, 1801, in Massie, *Nathaniel Massie, a Pioneer of Ohio*, 175–76.
13. Bean, "Marketing 'the Great American Commodity,'" 166.
14. The law was reenacted in December 1799, when the first meeting of the territorial legislature was held. Bogart, *Financial History of Ohio*, 11–13.
15. *Western Spy, and Hamilton Gazette*, January 7, 1800.
16. Bond, *Civilization of the Old Northwest*, 338.
17. Hinderaker, *Elusive Empires*, 249; Hurt, *Ohio Frontier*, 168.
18. Rao, "Thomas Worthington and the Great Transformation," 28. Between 1787 and 1798, the federal government sold only 43,573 acres of land and received $100,674 in return. U.S. Government, *American State Papers: Public Lands*, 1:73.
19. Hinderaker, *Elusive Empires*, 249.
20. Downes, "Trade in Frontier Ohio," 484–85.
21. For instance, on May 2, 1798, Samuel P. Duvall offered several tracts of land in exchange for the "next crop of tobcco [sic], wheat, flour, hemp or merchandise." *Kentucky Gazette*, May 2, 1798; Rao, "Thomas Worthington and the Great Transformation," 24–25.
22. Matson, "Accounting for War and Revolution," 193, 195–96; Salvucci, "Supply, Demand, and the Making of a Market," 40–44.
23. Clark, *New Orleans*, 214.
24. Nathaniel Massie to Thomas James, February 3, 1802, in Massie, *Nathaniel Massie, a Pioneer of Ohio*, 189–90.

7. Cotton and the Americanization of Natchez

1. Andrew Ellicott to Timothy Pickering, April 14, 1797, LRDS, vol. 1.
2. In 1808, a traveler to Natchez described Natchez-under-the-Hill as a "resort of dissipation." Henry Ker, quoted in James, *Antebellum Natchez*, 169.
3. The 1785 figures are from "Census of Louisiana in the Years 1785," DUCO. A full description of Spanish land distribution policy in Louisiana from the year 1799 can be found in "Regulations Regarding the Concessions of Ownerless Lands and Lots of the Province of Louisiana, Compiled for the Intendente the Commissioner in Charge of This Matter," Spanish Louisiana Collection, Williams Research Center, Historic New Orleans Collection. Although the policies outlined in this collection are in regard to Louisiana, they are extremely similar to the policies in place in Natchez. For more on early Natchez, see James, *Antebellum Natchez*, 3–30.
4. Holmes, *Gayoso*, 35.
5. Holmes, *Gayoso*, 4, 122–26.
6. Owsley, "The Marriages of Rachel Donelson," 482–88.
7. Baldwin, *Whiskey Rebels*, 265.
8. James, *Antebellum Natchez*, 41.
9. The system was similar to the cycles of indebtedness of tidewater tobacco planters; however, the presence of an annual payment in cash by the government gave settlers greater freedom as they knew the price their tobacco would earn in advance of sale. Breen, *Tobacco Culture*, 106–22. On tobacco production in Natchez, see Haynes, *Mississippi Territory and the Southwest Frontier*, 11–12, and James, *Antebellum Natchez*, 48–50.
10. "Notices of the Life and Character of W. D. Late of the Forest Near Natchez, 1810," William Dunbar Papers, Mississippi Department of Archives and History, Jackson.
11. On the 1794 number, see Haynes, *Mississippi Territory and the Southwest Frontier*, 13. For the 1795 number, see "Resumen General del Padron del Dist. De Natchez a finis del Ano de 1795," Daniel Clark, DUCO.
12. Holmes, *Gayoso*, 99–100.
13. Manuel Gayoso to Daniel Clark Jr., June 17, 1796, DUCO.
14. Manuel Gayoso to Baron de Carondelet, Natchez, June 2, 1796, DSG, 11:327.
15. "Treaty of Friendship, Limits, and Navigation between Spain and the United States."
16. Manuel Gayoso to Manuel Godoy, June 12, 1796, quoted by Baron de Carondelet to Don Louis de las Casas, June 18, 1796, DSG, 11:326. On the 1793 treaty, see James, *Antebellum Natchez*, 60, and Holmes, *Gayoso*, 151–54. For more on Spanish diplomacy in the Southwest, see Weeks, *Paths to a Middle Ground*, especially 126–41.

17. On Esteban Miró's and Gayoso's continued involvement in schemes for western separation, see James, *Antebellum Natchez*, 58–59, 62.
18. Manuel Gayoso to Baron de Carondelet, Natchez, June 7, 1796, DSG, 11:330.
19. Letter of Manuel Gayoso, quoted in Baron de Carondelet to Don Louis de Las Casas, June 18, 1796, DSG, 11:324–26.
20. James, *Antebellum Natchez*, 63–64.
21. D. Clayton James described Ellicott as "irascible." James, *Antebellum Natchez*, 65. On Ellicott more broadly, see Mathews, *Andrew Ellicott*.
22. Bush, *Surveying the Early Republic*, 9.
23. Andrew Ellicott to Timothy Pickering, April 14, 1797, LRDS, vol. 1.
24. Baron de Carondelet (quoting Manuel Gayoso) to Senor Don Luis de las Casas, June 18, 1796, DSG, 11:321.
25. In the various accounts gathered at the time, he was referred to by several names: Janan, Innan, or Hannaw.
26. "Diary Recorded by the Captain of the Fixed Regiment, Manuel de Lanzos," DSG, 11:398–412.
27. Holmes, *Gayoso*, 191.
28. Ellicott makes this claim, for instance. Ellicott, *Journal of Andrew Ellicott*, 97–100.
29. "Diary Recorded by the Captain of the Fixed Regiment, Manuel de Lanzos," DSG, 11:398–412.
30. Andrew Ellicott to Timothy Pickering, June 27, 1797, LRDS, vol. 1.
31. "Resumen General del Padron del Dist. De Natchez a finis del Ano de 1795," DUCO.
32. Manuel Gayoso to Andrew Ellicott, June 13, 1797, LRDS, vol. 1.
33. Holmes, *Gayoso*, 193; "Diary Recorded by the Captain of the Fixed Regiment, Manuel de Lanzos," DSG, 11:398–412.
34. Andrew Ellicott to Timothy Pickering, June 27, 1797, LRDS, vol. 1.
35. Andrew Ellicott to Timothy Pickering, June 6, 1797, LRDS, vol. 1.
36. See Caughey, *McGillivray of the Creeks*, 33–35.
37. Holmes, *Gayoso*, 194.
38. Andrew Ellicott to Timothy Pickering, June 27, 1797, LRDS, vol. 1.
39. James described the population growth of Natchez as "unprecedented for the region." James, *Antebellum Natchez*, 42. The 1785 figures are from "Census of Louisiana in the Years 1785"; the figure from 1795 is from "Resumen General del Padron del Dist. De Natchez a finis del Ano de 1795," both of which are included in DUCO. The 1795 census distinguishes by race but not by condition of servitude. The census enumerates 1,780 "negros" and "negras" and 114 "mulatas" and "mulatos." While there were a few free Black people in Natchez, the records indicate that it was not a large community. The figure given above of 1,800 enslaved people in Natchez is an

underestimate. The majority of those listed as "mulato" or "mulata" were young—77 of the individuals classified in this way fell into the youngest age classification.
40. James, *Antebellum Natchez*, 45.
41. There was no similar sex imbalance among those characterized as "mulatos"—in 1795, there were nineteen adult men classified as "mulatos" in Natchez and eighteen adult women. "Resumen General del Padron del Dist. De Natchez a finis del Ano de 1795," DUCO.
42. Libby, *Slavery and Frontier Mississippi*, 37.
43. Libby, *Slavery and Frontier Mississippi*, 42.
44. Libby, *Slavery and Frontier Mississippi*, 41–44.
45. Andrew Ellicott to Timothy Pickering, June 27, 1797, LRDS, vol. 1.
46. James, *Antebellum Natchez*, 71, 75.
47. Alexander Hamilton to James Gunn, December 22, 1798, in Syrett, *Papers of Alexander Hamilton*, 22:388–90; Prucha, *Sword of the Republic*, 54.
48. Bergmann, *American National State and the Early West*, 133. Ten additional districts were created on the Atlantic side of the Appalachians.
49. Deposition of Andrew Burd, Abijah Hunt Papers, Dolph Briscoe Center for American History, University of Texas, Austin. The date marked on this deposition is 1809, but this may refer to a different deposition. All the other depositions in this case were given in 1803; there is an added addendum in a different handwriting, and it seems likely only that section was gathered in 1809.
50. James, *Antebellum Natchez*, 157.
51. *Tennessee Gazette*, April 21, 1801; October 22, 1800.
52. Ambler, *History of Transportation in the Ohio Valley*, 94, 97. On the role of merchants in frontier trade, see Gruenwald, *River of Enterprise*, 43–61. Advertisements listing produce merchants were willing to accept in exchange for store goods abound in western newspapers. On the length of credit given, see Abijah Hunt to John Hunt, February 6, 1800, Hunt Morgan Papers, UK.
53. Abijah Hunt to John W. Hunt, February 6, 1800, Hunt Morgan Papers, UK.
54. Samuel Postlethwaite claimed his companions sold their goods to "Messrs. Fergman & Wooley." David Ferguson and Milling Wooley operated a firm together in Natchez and served as the western agents of the Philadelphia firm of Reed and Forde. See Reed and Forde to David Ferguson, March 13, 1802, Reed and Forde Papers, HSP, and Postlethwaite, "Journal of a Voyage from Louisville to Natchez," 328.
55. Postlethwaite, "Journal of a Voyage from Louisville to Natchez," 328.
56. Louis Tarascon, Journal, 1799, FHS.
57. Claiborne, *Mississippi as a Province, Territory, and State*, 143. Typically, public cotton ginners charged their patrons 10 percent for cleaning.

58. Box 1, folder 1, Abijah and David Hunt Papers, MDAH.
59. Shepherd Brown to John McDonogh, November 28, 1801, quoted in Atherton, "John McDonogh," 459.
60. This was the case of John Hutchins, whose first crop of cotton—cultivated, he would claim later, entirely by himself and one enslaved worker—cleared his entire debt for his property. Anderson, "The Narrative of John Hutchins," 22–23. The price of land is given by Holmes, "Cotton Gins in the Spanish Natchez District," 170.
61. The figure most often quoted for cotton produced in Natchez in 1798 is 1.2 million pounds; however, this number, in the words of its author, Daniel Clark Sr., rather "exceeds the truth." Using his estimate of 4,000 bales, and the average weight of his nephew's cotton bales of 1798, which was 270 pounds, we reach an estimated weight of 1,080,000 pounds of cotton. For that year, the amount of cotton recorded in New Orleans was approximately 606,900 pounds—however, this amount would omit cotton brought into the deposit the subsequent spring. Daniel Clark Sr. to William C. C. Claiborne, June 18, 1800, in Sargent, *Papers in Relation to the Official Conduct of Governor Sargent*, 26; "Libro de registro del depósito de las mercancías compra das por los Americanos en Nueva Orleans, años 1798–1802," legajo 631A, PC, AGI. The 1.2-million-pound figure has been widely quoted: Holmes, *Gayoso*, 100; James, *Antebellum Natchez*, 52; Hammond, *Slavery, Freedom, and Expansion in the Early American West*, 18.
62. Libby, *Slavery and Frontier Mississippi*, 38.
63. Rowland, *Life, Letters and Papers of William Dunbar*, 10; "Prices Current, Liverpool," March 22, 1800, Clifford Family Papers, HSP.
64. Abijah Hunt to John W. Hunt, February 28, 1800, JWHP, FHS.
65. Although it is impossible to be sure, it is likely the Hunts were among the first Americans to import large numbers of enslaved people to Natchez for sale. By the 1820s, the business of slave trading came to be dominated by firms that focused on transporting enslaved laborers to the expanding cotton frontier. Johnson, *Soul by Soul*, 47–57; Baptist, *Half Has Never Been Told*, 179–80.
66. Bogert, "Sold for My Account," 6.
67. The figure from 1795 is from "Resumen General del Padron del Dist. De Natchez a finis del Ano de 1795," DUCO; the figure for 1800 is the entirety of the enslaved population as counted on the 1800 census, when the majority of the population of Mississippi lived in Natchez. U.S. Census Office, *Return of the Whole Number of Persons within the Several Districts of the United States*, 3.

8. American Trade in a Spanish Port

1. Michaux, *Travels to the West of the Alleghany Mountains*, in Thwaites, *Early Western Travels*, 3:240.
2. Smith, *Short Description of the State of Tennessee*, 25.
3. Michaux, *Travels to the West of the Alleghany Mountains*, in Thwaites, *Early Western Travels*, 3:269.
4. Manuel Gayoso to Manuel Godoy, July 31, 1798, DSG, 11:476.
5. For previous works that have used the records of the deposit, see Clark, *New Orleans*, 202–74, and Whitaker, *Mississippi Question*, 85–97, 138–42.
6. Walter Johnson makes a similar point, referencing a later period, stressing the interconnections between "the cotton planters in Louisiana and cotton brokers in Liverpool, of the plantations of the Mississippi Valley and the textile mills of Manchester," but arguably what New Orleans tied together extended far more broadly to include the farmers of the Ohio Valley and merchants from the eastern seaboard. Moreover, the pattern for these connections was in place earlier than much of the history of the cotton trade implies: by 1798, the patterns that would dominate the cotton trade, "the largest single sector of the global economy in the first half of the nineteenth century," had taken shape. Johnson, *River of Dark Dreams*, 10.
7. Jessica M. Lepler's work on the flow of credit and information through the Atlantic economy demonstrates that by 1830, New Orleans had become central to both American and European finance. In the 1790s and early 1800s, these connections were by no means as extensive; their origins are explored here. Lepler, *Many Panics of 1837*, 23–41. On money, specie shortages, and bills of exchange in the early republic, see Sklansky, *Sovereign of the Market*, parts 1 and 2; Poovey, *Genres of the Credit Economy*, 35–55; Matson, *Merchants and Empire*, 69–71, appendix B; and Mihm, *A Nation of Counterfeiters*, 26–62.
8. Johnson, *River of Dark Dreams*; Baptist, *Half Has Never Been Told*; Beckert, *Empire of Cotton*; Schoen, *Fragile Fabric of Union*.
9. Paine, *Common Sense*, 63.
10. Historians of American ports, like Cathy D. Matson, have explored how commodities moved through networks of Atlantic world merchants, while others, like Brian Schoen and Sven Beckert, have focused specifically on the movement of cotton and its role in structuring Atlantic world trade. In contrast to New York, the focus of Matson's study, New Orleans trade was developed by American merchants but in a Spanish city, a factor that influenced how trade could operate. As the center of Mississippi River trade, New Orleans served a broader and more complex hinterland than New York. Both Schoen and Beckert focus on East Coast cotton production in Georgia and South Carolina and arrive in the Mississippi Valley after

the Louisiana Purchase. Matson, *Merchants and Empire*, 121–214; Schoen, *Fragile Fabric of Union*, 36–60; Beckert, *Empire of Cotton*, 136–99. Several other authors have focused on the movement of goods through the Atlantic economy and into the backcountry but not on the simultaneous movement of agricultural commodities into the Atlantic world. Martin, *Buying into the World of Goods*, 11–66; Gruenwald, *River of Enterprise*, 68–75. A few texts have focused on the Mississippi River trade in agricultural goods and animal hides but not on what happened to those goods once they were transported overseas. Usner, *Indians, Settlers, and Slaves*.

11. David Roth, "Louisiana Hurricane History," National Weather Service, 13, https://w2.weather.gov/media/lch/events/lahurricanehistory.pdf.
12. John Girault to William Clark, July 13, 1786, DM 1M137.
13. The contours of this trade are described by Clark, *New Orleans*, 326–35.
14. Coatsworth, "American Trade with European Colonies," 246.
15. Arena, "Philadelphia–Spanish New Orleans Trade, 1789–1803," 133; Whitaker, "The Commerce of Louisiana," 198.
16. Whitaker, "Reed and Forde," 244; Clark, *New Orleans*, 235; Arena, "Philadelphia–Spanish New Orleans Trade in the 1790s," 433.
17. "Opinion of Diego de Gardoqui on the Commerce of Louisiana," July 1790, in Whitaker, *Documents Relating to the Commercial Policy of Spain*, 119.
18. "Opinion of Diego de Gardoqui on the Commerce of Louisiana," 117.
19. Salvucci, "Anglo-American Merchants," 136.
20. Bouton, "Flour for Pesos," 505.
21. Maul, "The Annual Cycle of the Gulf Loop Current."
22. Reed and Forde to John O'Bannon, June 5, 1801, Reed and Forde Papers, HSP.
23. Thomas Jefferson to James Monroe, July 11, 1790, in Boyd et al., *Papers of Thomas Jefferson*, 17:25.
24. Much of what follows is drawn from an account by John Pintard, a prominent New Yorker who visited New Orleans in 1801. Pintard, "New Orleans, 1801."
25. Manuel Gayoso to Manuel Godoy, July 31, 1798, DSG, 11:480.
26. Clay and Army Department, *History of Navigation on the Lower Mississippi*, 22. A 1764 study of the mouth of the river shows how shallow it was. See "The Entrance of the River Mississippi at Fort Balise Taken in the King's Ship Nautilus in the Year 1764" (London: Sayer and Bennett, 1794). An account of that voyage appears in Rea, "A Naval Visitor in British West Florida," 147–50. On ships' risking sailing through the sandbar, see Sir John Lindsay to Governor George Johnstone, January 2, 1765, British West Florida Transcripts, 41–43, Alabama State Department of Archives and History.

27. Evan Jones to Timothy Pickering, New Orleans, May 15, 1801, DUCO. Jones made similar complaints in a letter written two weeks earlier. Evan Jones to Winthrop Sargent, governor of the Mississippi Territory, April 18, 1801, DUCO. Sargent was already on his way out by the time Jones wrote to him; Jones's likely intention in writing to Sargent was to convince him to carry news of the difficulties faced by Americans trading in New Orleans back to the Atlantic Coast.
28. Daniel Clark to James Madison, June 22, 1802, DUCO.
29. Vidal, *Caribbean New Orleans*, 359–60; Allen, *Western Rivermen*, 128–29.
30. John Taylor to John McDonogh, October 6, 1802, John McDonogh Papers, Tulane University Special Collections.
31. Atherton, "John McDonogh," 457.
32. Receipt, November 19, 1801; Bill of Lading, 5 January 1802, Payne and McDonogh Papers, NOPL.
33. Bill of Lading, February 17, 1802, John Minor Wisdom Collection, MDAH.
34. Simeonov, "'With What Right Are They Sending a Consul,'" 22–27.
35. Clark, *New Orleans*, 230–36. While some contemporaries and historians understood the prevalence of smuggling within the Spanish empire as a sign of its decline, Jesse Cromwell and Casey S. Schmitt, among others, have argued instead that smuggling *strengthened* the empire. Cromwell considers smuggling a "safety valve" that allowed Spanish regulations to stand by ensuring the colonial population had its needs met. Schmitt argues that the empire itself depended on extralegal trade: despite technically violating the law, Spanish colonial officials used what they obtained from illegal trade to support Spanish imperial interests. Smuggling was not the result of a weak imperial center or the inherent venality of Spanish officials in colonial backwaters; smuggling was a strategy that shored up imperial power and strengthened colonial loyalty. Schmitt, "Virtue in Corruption," 82, 85–94; Cromwell, *Smugglers' World*, 18. On the acceptance of smuggling as a strategy embraced by colonial officials, see Karras, "'Custom Has the Force of Law,'" 282–84, 287–90.
36. Clark, *New Orleans*, 233.
37. Woodward, "Spanish Commercial Policy in Louisiana, 1763–1803," 145.
38. Daniel Clark to Timothy Pickering, April 18, 1798, DUCO; Clark, *New Orleans*, 242–43.
39. Daniel Clark to Timothy Pickering, April 18, 1798, DUCO.
40. Daniel Clark to Timothy Pickering, April 18, 1798, DUCO.
41. Lanthois and Pitot to Abijah and John Hunt, May 27, 1798, Hunt Morgan Papers, UK.
42. Manuel Gayoso to Manuel Godoy, July 31, 1798, DSG, 11:483.
43. The War of the First Coalition and the early Napoleonic Wars left the United States as the only neutral carrier available to western European nations. See Hill, "Prologue to the Quasi-War," 1039–47.

44. "Juan Ventura Morales, Intendant *Ad Interim* of Louisiana and West Florida, to Daniel Clark, Jr., Acting Vice Consul of the United States, Relative to the Commerce of Neutral Nations in New Orleans," June 13, 1798, in Whitaker, *Documents Relating to the Commercial Policy of Spain*, 201.
45. Evan Jones to Timothy Pickering, October 7, 1799, DUCO. Also described in Clark, *New Orleans*, 243–44.
46. Daniel Clark to Timothy Pickering, April 18, 1798, DUCO.
47. This Captain John Brown appears to not have been a relative of John Brown the Kentucky senator.
48. "Libro de registro del depósito de las mercancías compra das por los Americanos en Nueva Orleans, años 1798–1802," legajo 631A, PC, AGI, gives the amount of cotton purchased by John McNeill from the American deposit in May 1802 as 920 pounds and 3 sacks—approximately 1,820 pounds.
49. *Daily Advertiser*, June 14, 1802; Bill of Lading, May 21, 1802, Payne and McDonogh Papers, NOPL.
50. Timothy Pickering, Report, June 22, 1797, in U.S. Government, *American State Papers: Foreign Relations*, 2:29; "Pho." Guillot to Reed and Forde, July 15, 1798, Reed and Forde Papers, HSP.
51. William Lark to Reed and Forde, February 24, 1799, Reed and Forde Papers, HSP.
52. Arena, "Philadelphia–Spanish New Orleans Trade, 1789–1803," 69–70.
53. Rathbone, Hughes, and Duncan to Shepherd Brown and Co., December 12, 1803, Shepherd Brown and Company Papers, NOPL. For more information on Rathbone, Hughes, and Duncan, see Krichtal, "Liverpool and the Raw Cotton Trade," 69.
54. Clark, *New Orleans*, 310; Hall, "Emergence of the Liverpool Raw Cotton Market," 70–72, 78–80; Hall, "Business Interests of Liverpool's Cotton Brokers," 341–45; Hyde, Parkinson, and Marriner, "Cotton Broker and the Rise of the Liverpool Cotton Market," 76–81; Krichtal, "Liverpool and the Raw Cotton Trade," 50.
55. Rathbone, Hughes and Duncan to Shepherd Brown and Co., December 12, 1803, Shepherd Brown and Company Papers, NOPL.
56. The first quote is from an unsigned letter certainly written by William Taylor to John McDonogh, August 16, 1802, John McDonogh Papers, Tulane University Special Collections; the second is from Pearse Ashfield to William Taylor, April 23, 1802, WTP.
57. Price is given in Liverpool Price Current, enclosed by Robert Gladstone to Daniel Coxe, May 18, 1798, Tench Coxe Papers, HSP. The exchange rate between the dollar and the pound in 1798 was $4.39 to £1, according to "Measures of Worth."
58. Pearse Ashfield to William Taylor, July 22, 1802, WTP.
59. Pearse Ashfield to William Taylor, August 25, 1802, WTP.

60. Pearse Ashfield to William Taylor, September 22, 1802, WTP.
61. Atherton, "John McDonogh," 470.
62. Pearse Ashfield to William Taylor, July 23, 1802, WTP.
63. Swearingen, "Luxury at Natchez in 1801," 189.
64. Thomas Morgan Jr. to Reed and Forde, November 6, 1796, Reed and Forde Papers, HSP.
65. Kingston, "Marine Insurance in Philadelphia during the Quasi-War with France," 171–81.
66. Daniel W. Coxe to Tench Coxe, May 20, 1798; unsigned, June 13, 1798; Daniel W. Coxe to Tench Coxe, June 30, 1798, Coxe Family Papers, HSP.
67. William Taylor to John McDonogh and William Payne, May 5, 1802, John McDonogh Papers, Tulane University Special Collections.
68. John Taylor to John McDonogh and William Payne, October 6, 1802, John McDonogh Papers, Tulane University Special Collections.
69. McDonogh and Payne remitted $30,000 "Spanish Mill'd" or "Mexican" dollars in several smaller shipments during the fall of 1802. "Bill of Lading for the *Eliza*, September 14, 1802"; "Bill of Lading for the *Cygnet*, September 26, 1802"; "Bill of Lading for the *George*, October 5, 1802"; "Bill of Lading for the *Eleanor*, December 3, 1802"; "Bill of Lading for the *Matilda*, December 4, 1802," all Payne and McDonogh Papers, NOPL.
70. William Taylor to McDonogh and Payne, April 30, 1802, John McDonogh Papers, Tulane University Special Collections.
71. Daniel W. Coxe to Daniel Clark, August 26, 1803, Daniel W. Coxe Papers, HSP.
72. Reed and Forde to Lyman Harding, Esq. (attorney for Daniel Ferguson), February 28, 1803, Reed and Forde Papers, HSP.
73. John Brown, Ethan Allen Brown, and Henry Abbett to William Taylor, September 25, 1802, WTP.
74. Atherton, "John McDonogh," 464–65, 469.
75. Clark, *New Orleans*, 228.

9. The Chickasaw Trace

1. Timothy Pickering to Winthrop Sargent, May 20, 1799, copy, box 3, folder 28, NTC. The usage of the phrase "the Natchez" was common in the eighteenth century.
2. Joseph Habersham to Henry Dearborn, March 12, 1801, copy, box 3, folder 28, NTC.
3. Allen, *Western Rivermen*, 57.
4. Clark and Guice, *Frontiers in Conflict*, 86.
5. Craig, "Colberts in Chickasaw History," 112–24.

6. Although their historical significance is incontestable, the loyalties and actions of this complex family are not so readily intelligible. In 1981, Arrell Morgan Gibson contended that "the most intriguing feature of the Chickasaw economy in the period before removal was its complete domination by a mixed-blood clique headed by the Colbert brothers." That designation—"mixed-blood"—suggests to other historians a western understanding of race at odds with the perspectives of late eighteenth-century Chickasaw, in whose matrilineal culture the clan and affiliations of mothers mattered far more than that of fathers. Gibson's division of the Chickasaw into mixed-blood and full-blood factions violated contemporary understandings of cultural membership. But there is no denying Gibson on another front—that the Colberts' financial and political interests expanded in lockstep, which Gibson took as evidence that their actions were largely self-serving. Gibson, *Chickasaws*, 149–50. More recently, Theda Perdue, Ronald Eugene Craig, James R. Atkinson, Natalie Inman, and Jeffrey Washburn have contended that the Colberts acted not only in their own but also in the Chickasaw's interest—that they were committed to maintaining Chickasaw land claims and cultural practices even as they profited from their position as cultural brokers. Craig, "Colberts in Chickasaw History," 28–33; Inman, *Brothers and Friends*, 93–101; Perdue, *Mixed Blood Indians*, 47; Atkinson, *Splendid Land, Splendid People*, 199; Washburn, "'Labor in the Field Is Much Changed,'" chaps. 4–6.
7. John, *Spreading the News*, 53.
8. Angela Pulley Hudson's focus is on Creek roads, but the same point was certainly true for the roads that passed through Chickasaw territory. Hudson, *Creek Paths and Federal Roads*, 6.
9. Ford, *Settler Sovereignty*, 68–69.
10. Washburn, "'Labor in the Field Is Much Changed,'" 109–11.
11. Whitaker, *Mississippi Question*, 139.
12. Baily, *Journal of a Tour in the Unsettled Parts of North America*, 231–98.
13. Pintard, "New Orleans, 1801," 222.
14. Allen, *Western Rivermen*, 89.
15. Whitaker, *Mississippi Question*, 44; Pintard, "New Orleans, 1801," 233.
16. Evan Jones to Timothy Pickering, April 15, 1800, DUCO.
17. Allen, *Western Rivermen*, 69–72.
18. Hall, "Brief History of the Mississippi Territory," 556; "Speech to the Grand Jury," May 19, 1800, *Natchez Impartial Observer*.
19. Many of the early nineteenth-century visitors to Natchez commented on the presence of sex workers in the port's taverns; prostitution also occurred aboard flatboats, likely by even more marginalized women. One account from 1808 described these women as "copper colored." Much extant work on race, slavery, and sex-work focuses on New Orleans, or on the

phenomenon of "Fancy Girls," enslaved women often sold specifically for sex-work. The women who worked aboard Natchez flatboats almost certainly did not fall into this category. For an early account of prostitution in Natchez, see Schultz, *Travels on an Inland Voyage*, 2:136. On enslaved sex workers and their archival absences, see Fuentes, *Dispossessed Lives*, 46–70.

20. Michaux, *Travels to the West of the Alleghany Mountains*, in Thwaites, *Early Western Travels*, 3:203.
21. Baily, *Journal of a Tour in the Unsettled Parts of North America*, 355–56.
22. Clark and Guice, *Frontiers in Conflict*, 86.
23. Buckner, "Diary of Captain Philip Buckner," 191.
24. Baily, *Journal of a Tour in the Unsettled Parts of North America*, 334–54.
25. *Charleston Daily Courier*, October 3, 1803.
26. Baily, *Journey of a Tour in the Unsettled Parts of North America*, 348.
27. Postlethwaite, "Journal of a Voyage from Louisville to Natchez," 327.
28. *North American*, April 26, 1799.
29. *Vermont Mercury*, June 21, 1802.
30. *Tennessee Gazette*, June 24, 1801.
31. Guild, *Old Times in Tennessee*, 324.
32. Samuel Hopkins to Samuel G. Hopkins, September 1, 1801, Samuel Hopkins Papers, KHS.
33. *United States Gazette*, April 20, 1802.
34. *National Intelligencer and Washington Advertiser*, August 26, 1801.
35. *Tennessee Gazette*, August 12, 1801.
36. "Treaty with the Choctaw, 1801," in Kappler, *Indian Affairs: Laws and Treaties*, 2:56–58; White, *Roots of Dependency*, 28. On the size of the cession, see "Chocktaw History," Mississippi Choctaw, https://www.choctaw.org/about-us/tribal-history/.
37. Atkinson, *Splendid Land, Splendid People*, 183–85.
38. Benjamin Hawkins to R. J. Meigs, October 26, 1801, Manuscript Records of the Bureau of Indian Affairs, National Archives.
39. Rush Nutt, quoted in Atkinson, *Splendid Land, Splendid People*, 185–86.
40. Craig, "Colberts in Chickasaw History," 217–19.
41. Smithey, "Transformation of Early Nineteenth Century Chickasaw Leadership Patterns," 33.
42. "Minutes of a Conference Held at the Chickasaw Bluffs, by General James Wilkinson, Benjamin Hawkins, and Andrew Pickens, Esquires, Commissioners of the United States, with the King, Chiefs, and Principal Men, of the Chickasaw Nation," October 24, 1801, in U.S. Government, *American State Papers: Indian Affairs*, 1:652.
43. Tisshamastubbe, "A Talk from the King Chiefs and Warriors of the Chickasaw Nation to the Secretary of War, Delivered by Tisshamastubbe,

Speaker for the Chickasaws," doc. 123, box 89, series 488, Mississippi Territory Administration Papers, MDAH.
44. "Minutes of a Conference Held at the Chickasaw Bluffs," October 24, 1801, in U.S. Government, *American State Papers: Indian Affairs*, 1:652; Atkinson, *Splendid Land, Splendid People*, 189–91.
45. Craig, "Colberts in Chickasaw History," 214–15, 223.
46. Samuel Mitchell to William C. C. Claiborne, January 23, 1803, box 2, file 17, NTC; Washburn, "'Labor in the Field Is Much Changed,'" 114.
47. My thanks to Jeffrey Washburn for illustrating this point.
48. Quoted in Phelps, "Stands and Accommodations," 46.
49. Craig, "Colberts in Chickasaw History," 213.
50. Craig, "Colberts in Chickasaw History," 265.
51. Atkinson, *Splendid Land, Splendid People*, 184, 191.
52. "Chennabe [Chinubbee], Major George Colbert, Okoye, and Charles Fox to General Robinson, January 25, 1805," *American Historical Magazine* 5, no. 1 (1900): 77–79.
53. Atkinson, *Splendid Land, Splendid People*, 191; Clark and Guice, *Frontiers in Conflict*, 86.
54. Manuscript Map of the Survey of the Route from Nashville, Tennessee, to Grindstone Ford, Mississippi, 1801–1803, map 17, Records of the Post Office Department, National Archives.
55. Saunt, "Financing Dispossession"; Connolly, "Panic, State Power, and Chickasaw Dispossession."
56. Connolly, "Panic, State Power, and Chickasaw Dispossession," 683.
57. Craig, "Colberts in Chickasaw History," 120, 216, 255.
58. The Forks of the Road market eventually became the headquarters of Franklin and Armfield, the largest domestic slave traders in the early republic era and the second largest slave market in the country. As early as 1790, auctions were held at the site. See James, *Antebellum Natchez*, 46. On the domestic slave trade and Franklin and Armfield, see Schermerhorn, *Business of Slavery*, 124–68.

10. Buying the Mississippi

1. *Columbian Courier*, December 3, 1802.
2. "Flour 45 s/ p barrel and very little at market." Pearse Ashfield to William Taylor, March 18, 1802, WTP.
3. James Wilkinson to Isaac Guion, May 20, 1797, reel 6, J. F. H. Claiborne Collection, MDAH.
4. Samuel Hopkins to "Mr. Alves," November 22, 1801, Samuel Hopkins Papers, KHS.
5. "Resident Population and Apportionment of the U.S. House of Representatives, Tennessee," U.S. Census Bureau, http://www.census.gov

/dmd/www/resapport/states/tennessee.pdf; "Resident Population and Apportionment of the U.S. House of Representatives, Kentucky," U.S. Census Bureau, http://www.census.gov/dmd/www/resapport/states/kentucky.pdf.
6. "Resident Population and Apportionment of the U.S. House of Representatives, Ohio," U.S. Census Bureau, http://www.census.gov/dmd/www/resapport/states/ohio.pdf; "Resident Population and Apportionment of the U.S. House of Representatives, Mississippi," U.S. Census Bureau, http://www.census.gov/dmd/www/resapport/states/mississippi.pdf.
7. These ships are also all listed in the records of the American deposit for May 1802. There is some ambiguity about a few of these names, as English names were often Hispanicized by the recorders. The *Carlota*, for instance, may have been the *Charlotte*. "Libro de registro del depósito de las mercancías compradas por los Americanos en Nueva Orleans, años 1798–1802," AGI, PC, 631A.
8. On the retrocession, see Whitaker, *Mississippi Question*, 176–86.
9. *New York Herald*, February 9, 1803—quoting a letter of a year earlier.
10. "Louisiana II," *American Citizen*, April [?], 1802.
11. "Louisiana," *American Citizen*, April 1, 1802.
12. In 1801, Congress reduced the U.S. Navy to 6 commissioned ships, 9 captains, 36 lieutenants, and 150 midshipmen. While the law passed under the Adams administration, the Jefferson administration was responsible for implementing it. Allen, *Our Naval War with France*, 255.
13. *Mercantile Advertiser*, June 9, 1802.
14. Lewis, *American Union and the Problem of Neighborhood*, 25–28; James E. Lewis, "A Tornado on the Horizon" in Kastor and Weil, *Empires of the Imagination*, 117–42.
15. Charles Pinckney to James Madison, August 24, 1802, in Brugger et al., *Papers of James Madison*, Secretary of State Series, 3:514; Lewis, "A Tornado on the Horizon," 122–25.
16. In 2017, Paul Gilje urged historians to "alter our understanding of the relative importance of commerce and expansion in early America" by arguing that many of the United States' earliest expansionist moments were byproducts, and not goals, of an American diplomacy focused around obtaining commercial benefits for the new nation. In Gilje's formulation, the Louisiana Purchase was an "accidental and incidental consequenc[e] of diplomatic activities aimed at protecting American commerce." Gilje, "Commerce and Conquest in Early American Foreign Relations," 736–37 (quotations).
17. *American Citizen*, June 16, 1802.
18. James Madison to Robert Livingston, September 28, 1801, in Brugger et al., *Papers of James Madison*, Secretary of State Series, 2:142–47.
19. "Extract from a Publication Made 16th October, 1802, by Juan Ventura Morales, Intendant of the Province of Louisiana, &c," in U.S. Department of State, *A Message from the President of the United States*, 8.

20. "Treaty of Friendship, Limits, and Navigation between Spain and the United States; October 27, 1795" (quotation); Whitaker, *Mississippi Question*, 192–99.
21. William Hulings to James Madison, October 18, 1802, DUCO.
22. William Hulings to James Madison, November 25, 1802, DUCO.
23. "New Orleans, October 20th, 1802," *Gazette of the United States*, November 23, 1802; "New-Orleans Shut," *Pittsburgh Gazette*, December 3, 1802.
24. "Highly Important," *Palladium*, November 29, 1802.
25. News reached New York City on November 22 and Philadelphia on November 23. News reached Pittsburgh on December 3, and the December 18 *Scioto Gazette* of Chillicothe, Ohio, reported the closing of the deposit. An article appeared in Charleston, South Carolina, in the *City Gazette and Daily Advertiser* on December 10, and word reached Middlebury, Vermont, on December 8. "New-York, November 23," *City Gazette and Daily Advertiser*, December 10, 1802; "We Are Informed by Captain Sinclair," *Middlebury Mercury*, December 8, 1802.
26. "Extract of a Letter from New-Orleans," *Philadelphia Gazette*, December 16, 1802.
27. "Governor Claiborne to the Secretary of State, Near Natchez, October 18, 1802," in *SPTL*, 55.
28. "The Governor of Kentucky to the President of the United States, Frankfort, KY, November 30, 1802," in *SPTL*, 55.
29. Camillus, *Mississippi Question Fairly Stated*, 18.
30. For resolutions sent eastward by Kentuckians, see *Palladium*, December 2, 1802.
31. *Columbian Courier*, December 3, 1802.
32. *Palladium*, December 2, 1802.
33. *Tennessee Gazette*, February 16, 1803.
34. "James Madison, Secretary of State, to Robert R. Livingston, Minister to France, December 23, 1802," in *SPTL*, 67.
35. *Kentucky Gazette*, March 1, 1803.
36. "Extract of a Letter from a House in New Orleans, to a Gentleman of this City," *Poulson's American Daily Advertiser*, November 27, 1802.
37. "Of New-Orleans," *Philadelphia Gazette*, November 24, 1802.
38. Bradburn, "A Clamor in the Public Mind," 581–82; Ray, *Middle Tennessee*, 41, 43.
39. Ray, *Middle Tennessee*, 25–26, 31–32.
40. Bradburn, "A Clamor in the Public Mind," 582.
41. Cayton, *Frontier Republic*, 76.
42. Whitaker, *Mississippi Question*, 224.
43. On January 27, 1803, Representative Thomas Davis of Kentucky rose before Congress to present the Kentucky legislature's petition regarding the closure of the deposit. *Kentucky Gazette*, February 22, 1803.

44. *American Citizen*, June 16, 1802.
45. *American Citizen*, June 16, 1802.
46. James Madison to Rufus King, July 24, 1801, in Brugger et al., *Papers of James Madison*, Secretary of State Series, 1:464–70. American fears of a British-controlled Southwest are discussed in Lewis, "A Tornado on the Horizon," 119.
47. "President's Message, December 22, 1802," in *SPTL*, 53.
48. "Mr. Madison, Secretary of State, to Charles Pinckney, Minister to Spain, November 27, 1802," in *SPTL*, 64.
49. Thomas Jefferson to Robert Livingston, April 18, 1802, in Boyd et al., *Papers of Thomas Jefferson*, 37:263–67.
50. Lewis, *American Union and the Problem of Neighborhood*, 31. The bend in the Tennessee River was at the core of numerous speculation schemes in the eighteenth century.
51. "President Jefferson to Mr. Monroe, January 13, 1803," in *SPTL*, 68.
52. "President Jefferson to Mr. Monroe, January 13, 1803," in *SPTL*, 68.
53. "James Madison, Secretary of State, to Robert R. Livingston, Minister to France, January 18, 1803," in *SPTL*, 70.
54. James Madison to Robert Livingston and James Monroe, April 18, 1803, in Brugger et al., *Papers of James Madison*, Secretary of State Series, 4:527–33. On a possible alliance between the United States and Britain, see DeConde, *This Affair of Louisiana*, 112–17.
55. On Louisiana as a "granary," see DeConde, *This Affair of Louisiana*, 97, and Gleijeses, "Napoleon, Jefferson, and the Louisiana Purchase," 238. On yellow fever's role in the disastrous campaign, see Gleijeses, "Napoleon, Jefferson, and the Louisiana Purchase," 246, and DeConde, *This Affair of Louisiana*, 149.
56. Barbé-Marbois, *History of Louisiana*, 264.
57. Napoleon to François Barbé-Marbois, April 10, 1803, quoted in Bush, *The Louisiana Purchase*, 59.
58. Barbé-Marbois, *History of Louisiana*, 268–69.
59. Lewis, *The Louisiana Purchase*, 56–59.
60. Lewis, *The Louisiana Purchase*, 56–59.
61. Rory T. Cornish, "Baring Brothers," in Rodriguez, *The Louisiana Purchase*, 25–26.
62. Whitaker, *Mississippi Question*, 231.
63. DeConde, *This Affair of Louisiana*, 178.
64. Andrew Jackson to Thomas Jefferson, August 7, 1803, in Smith et al., *Papers of Andrew Jackson*, 1:354.
65. *Hive*, September 20, 1803, claimed that news arrived on August 7; the *Western American*, September 13, 1803, claimed that the news arrived on August 5.

66. *Scioto Gazette*, October 1, 1803.
67. *Kentucky Gazette*, August 16, 1803.
68. *Scioto Gazette*, October 1, 1803.
69. *Western American*, October 13, 1803.
70. *Kentucky Gazette*, August 16, 1803.
71. *Scioto Gazette*, October 1, 1803.
72. George Washington, Farewell Address, September 19, 1796, in Twohig et al., *Papers of George Washington*, Presidential Series, 20:703–22.

Epilogue

1. Allen, *Western Rivermen*, 145.
2. U.S. Department of Commerce and Labor, *Cotton Production*, 20.
3. See Griffin, *American Leviathan*, 152–83, and Saler, *Settlers' Empire*, 13–82.
4. Will of Joshua McQueen, May 7, 1846, in *Kentucky, U.S., Wills and Probate Records*, image 352.
5. Libby, *Slavery and Frontier Mississippi*, 52. On Abijah Hunt, see Stearns, "The Sutler's Empire," 45–62.
6. Ramage, *John Wesley Hunt*, 61–70; Hopkins, *History of the Hemp Industry in Kentucky*, 117–21.
7. Baptist, *Half Has Never Been Told*, 25–54; Levy, *Freaks of Fortune*, 23–24; James, "The Role of the Natchez Trace in the Development of the Nation," 29; Rothman, *Ledger and the Chain*, 64–68.
8. Davis, *Way through the Wilderness*, 81–82; Doherty, "The Colbert-Walker Site," 62–64.
9. *Niles Register*, September 18, 1830.
10. Claudio Saunt suggests abandoning this term for the more specific and accurate "deportation." Saunt, *Unworthy Republic*, xii–xiii.
11. Rothman, *Flush Times and Fever Dreams*, 4.
12. Saunt, *Unworthy Republic*, 170.
13. In addition to founding Memphis, Jackson also speculated near Florence, Alabama, at the region known as Muscle Shoals. Chappell, "Some Patterns of Land Speculation in the Old Southwest," 469, 472–73.

BIBLIOGRAPHY

Newspapers

American Citizen (New York)
American Minerva (New York)
Centinel of the North Western Territory (Cincinnati)
Charleston [SC] Daily Courier
City Gazette and Daily Advertiser (Charleston, SC)
Columbian Centinel (Boston)
Columbian Courier (New Bedford, MA)
Daily Advertiser (New York)
Gazette of the United States and Evening Advertiser (Philadelphia)
Hive (Northampton, MA)
Independent Journal (New York)
Independent Gazetteer (Philadelphia)
Kentucky Gazette (Lexington)
Loudon's New York Packet
Mercantile Advertiser (New York)
Middlebury [VT] Mercury
Natchez [MS] Impartial Observer
National Intelligencer and Washington Advertiser
New-Hampshire Mercury and the General Advertiser (Portsmouth)
New York Herald
Niles Register (Baltimore)
North American (Philadelphia)
North American and United States Gazette (Philadelphia)
Palladium (Frankfort, KY)
Pennsylvania Journal (Philadelphia)
Philadelphia Gazette
Pittsburgh Gazette
Poulson's American Daily Advertiser (Philadelphia)
Scioto Gazette (Chillicothe, Ohio)
Tennessee Gazette (Nashville)
United States Gazette (Philadelphia)
Vermont Mercury (Rutland)
Western American (Bardstown, KY)
Western Spy, and Hamilton Gazette (Cincinnati)

Pamphlets, Broadsides, and Other Publications, Historical and Contemporary

Abbot, W. W., ed. *The Papers of George Washington*. Confederation Series. 6 vols. Charlottesville: University Press of Virginia, 1992–97.

Abbot, W. W., et al., eds. *The Papers of George Washington*. Colonial Series. 10 vols. Charlottesville: University Press of Virginia, 1983–95.

Anderson, John Q. "The Narrative of John Hutchins." *Journal of Mississippi History* 20, no. 1 (1958): 1–29.

Atkin, Edmond. *Indians of the Southern Colonial Frontier: The Edmond Atkin Report and Plan of 1755*. Edited by Wilbur R. Jacobs. Columbia: University of South Carolina Press, 1954.

Baily, Francis. *Journal of a Tour in the Unsettled Parts of North America in 1796 and 1797*. London: Baily Brothers, 1856.

Barbé-Marbois, François, Marquis de. *The History of Louisiana: Particularly of the Cession of that Colony to the United States of America; with an Introductory Essay on the Constitution and Government of the United States*. 2 vols. Philadelphia: Carey and Lea, 1830.

Bond, Beverley W., Jr., ed. *The Correspondence of John Cleves Symmes: Founder of the Miami Purchase*. New York: Macmillan, 1926.

Boyd, Julian, et al., eds. *The Papers of Thomas Jefferson*. 37 vols. to date. Princeton, NJ: Princeton University Press, 1950–.

Brugger, Robert J., et al., eds. *Papers of James Madison*. Secretary of State Series. 12 vols to date. Charlottesville: University of Virginia, 1986–.

Buckner, Philip. "Diary of Captain Philip Buckner." *William and Mary Quarterly*, 2nd series, 6, no. 3 (1926): 173–207.

Burton, C. M., ed. "General Wayne's Orderly Book." Michigan Pioneer and Historical Society *Historical Collections* 34 (1905): 341–733.

Bush, Robert D., ed. *Surveying the Early Republic: The Journal of Andrew Ellicott, US Boundary Commissioner in the Old Southwest, 1796–1800*. Baton Rouge: Louisiana State University Press, 2016.

Butterfield, C. W., ed. *Washington-Irvine Correspondence: The Official Letters*. Madison, WI: David Atwood, 1882.

Camillus. *The Mississippi Question Fairly Stated, and the Views and Arguments of Those Who Clamor for War, Examined, in Seven Letters*. Philadelphia: William Duane, 1803.

Carter, Clarence Edward, ed. *Territorial Papers of the United States*. 28 vols. Washington, DC: Government Printing Office, 1934–75.

"Certificate Book of the Virginia Land Commissioners, 1779–1780." https://www.sos.ky.gov/land/non-military/settlements_preemptions/Pages/Kentucky-Doomsday-Book.aspx#:~:text=Kentucky's%20%22Doomsday%20Book%22%20is%20a,under%20Virginia%20Land%20Law%20A.

Chase, Philander, et al., eds. *The Papers of George Washington. Revolutionary War Series*. 28 vols to date. Charlottesville: University of Virginia Press, 1985–.

Corbitt, D. C., and Roberta Corbitt, eds. "Papers from the Spanish Archives Relating to Tennessee and the Old Southwest, 1783–1800." *East Tennessee Historical Society's Publications* 16 (1944): 79–84.

———. "Papers from the Spanish Archives Relating to Tennessee and the Old Southwest." *East Tennessee Historical Society's Publications* 34 (1962): 86–105.

Cresswell, Nicholas. *The Journal of Nicholas Cresswell, 1774–1777*. New York: Dial Press, 1924.

Cutler, William P., ed. *Life, Journals, and Correspondence of Reverend Manasseh Cutler, LL.D.* Cincinnati: Robert Clarke, 1888.

"The Definitive Treaty of Peace, 1783." Avalon Project, Yale Law School, https://avalon.law.yale.edu/18th_century/paris.asp.

Ellicott, Andrew. *The Journal of Andrew Ellicott: Late Commissioner on Behalf of the United States during Part of the Year 1796, the Years 1797, 1798, 1799, and Part of the Year 1800: For Determining the Boundary between the United States and the Possessions of His Catholic Majesty in America, Containing Occasional Remarks on the Situation, Soil, Rivers, Natural Productions, and Diseases of the Different Countries on the Ohio, Mississippi, and Gulf of Mexico, with Six Maps*. Philadelphia: Budd and Bartram, 1803.

Farrand, Max, ed. *The Records of the Federal Convention of 1787*. 4 vols. New Haven, CT: Yale University Press, 1911–37.

Filson, John. *The Discovery, Settlement, and Present State of Kentucke*. 1784; reprint New York: Corinth, 1962.

Foner, Philip S., ed. *The Democratic-Republican Societies, 1790–1800: A Documentary Sourcebook of Constitutions, Declarations, Addresses, Resolutions, and Toasts*. Westport, CT: Greenwood Press, 1976.

Ford, Paul Leicester, ed. *The Works of Thomas Jefferson*. 7 vols. New York: G. P. Putnam's Sons, 1904.

Ford, Worthington Chauncey, et al., eds. *Journals of the Continental Congress*. 34 vols. Washington, DC: Government Printing Office, 1904–37.

Garrison, George P. "A Memorandum of M. Austin's Journey from the Lead Mines in the County of Wythe in the State of Virginia to the Lead Mines in the Province of Louisiana West of the Mississippi, 1796–1797." *American Historical Review* 5 (1900): 518–42.

Hall, James. "A Brief History of the Mississippi Territory, 1801." *Mississippi Historical Society Proceedings* 9 (1906): 539–73.

Hamilton, Stanislaus Murray, ed. *The Writings of James Monroe*. 7 vols. New York: G. P. Putnam's Sons, 1898–1903.

Hening, William Waller, comp. *The Statutes at Large: Being a Collection of All the Laws of Virginia, from the First Session of the Legislature, in the Year 1619*. Vols. 9–10. Richmond, VA: J. and G. Cochran, 1821–22.

Henry, William Wirt. *Patrick Henry: Life, Correspondence and Speeches*. 3 vols. New York: Charles Scribner's Sons, 1891.

Houck, Louis, ed. *Spanish Regime in Missouri*. 2 vols. Chicago: R. R. Donnelley and Sons, 1909.

Hutchins, Thomas. *An Historical Narrative and Topographical Description of Louisiana, and West Florida, Comprehending the River Mississippi with Its Principal Branches and Settlements*. Philadelphia: Thomas Hutchins, 1784.

Imlay, Gilbert. *A Description of the Western Territory of North America; Containing a Succinct Account of Its Climate, Natural History, Population, Agriculture, Manners and Customs . . . to Which Is Annexed a Delineation of the Laws and Government of the State of Kentucky . . . in a Series of Letters to a Friend in England*. Dublin: William Jones, 1793.

Jamison, Anne (McMeans). "An Interesting Narrative" (1824). Edited by Joseph Patterson. In "Annals of the Robert Aiken Family," 11–18. Western Reserve Historical Society, Cleveland.

Jefferson, Thomas. *A Summary View of the Rights of British America. Set Forth in Some Resolutions Intended for the Inspection of the Present Delegates of the People of Virginia, Now in Convention*. Philadelphia: Dunlap, 1774. Reprinted in Thomas Paine, *Common Sense*, edited by Edward Larkin, 133–51. Peterborough, ON: Broadview Press., 2004.

Jenkinson, Charles, ed. *A Collection of All the Treaties of Peace, Alliance, and Commerce, between Great-Britain and Other Powers*. 3 vols. London: J. Debret, 1785.

Johnston, Henry P., ed. *The Correspondence and Public Papers of John Jay*. 4 vols. New York: G. P. Putnam's Sons, 1890.

Kaminski, John P., et al., eds. *The Documentary History of the Ratification of the Constitution*. 37 vols. to date. Madison, WI: Wisconsin Historical Society, 1976–.

Kappler, Charles J., ed. *Indian Affairs: Laws and Treaties*. 7 vols. Washington, DC: Government Printing Office, 1904.

Kentucky, U.S., Wills and Probate Records, 1774–1989. Provo, UT: Ancestry.com Operations, 2015.

King, Charles, ed. *The Life and Correspondence of Rufus King*. 6 vols. New York: G. P. Putnam's Sons, 1894–1900.

Kinnaird, Lawrence, ed. *Spain in the Mississippi Valley, 1765–1794*. 3 parts. Annual Report of the American Historical Association for the Year 1945, vols. 2–4. Washington, DC: Government Printing Office, 1946–49.

"Letters of Gen. James Wilkinson Addressed to Dr. James Hutchinson, of Philadelphia." *Pennsylvania Magazine of History and Biography* 12, no. 1 (1888): 55–64.

Littell, William. *Political Transactions in and Concerning Kentucky: From the First Settlement Thereof Until It Became an Independent State, in June, 1792*. Frankfort, KY: William Hunter, 1806.

Locke, John. *Second Treatise on Government*. Indianapolis: Hackett, 1980.
Mansfield, Edward D. *Memoirs of the Life and Services of Daniel Drake, M.D.* Cincinnati: Applegate, 1855.
Marshall, Humphrey. *The History of Kentucky. Exhibiting an Account of the Modern Discovery; Settlement; Progressive Improvement; Civil and Military Transactions; and the Present State of the Country.* 2 vols. Frankfort, KY: George S. Robertson, 1824.
Massie, David Meade. *Nathaniel Massie, a Pioneer of Ohio: A Sketch of His life and Selections from His Correspondence.* Cincinnati: Robert Clarke, 1896.
Michaux, François André. *Travels to the West of the Alleghany Mountains: In the States of Ohio, Kentucky, and Tennessee, and Back to Charleston, by the Upper Carolinas; Comprising the Most Interesting Details on the Present State of Agriculture, and the Natural Produce of These Countries: Together with Particulars Relative to the Commerce That Exists between the Above-Mentioned States, and Those Situated East of the Mountains and Low Louisiana, Undertaken, in the Year 1802.* London: D. N. Shury, 1805.
Paine, Thomas. *Common Sense*. Edited by Edward Larkin. Peterborough, ON: Broadview Press., 2004.
———. *Public Good*. Philadelphia: John Dunlap, 1780.
Palmer, William, ed. *Calendar of Virginia State Papers and Other Manuscripts, 1652–1781, Preserved in the Capitol at Richmond.* 11 vols. 1875–93; reprint New York: Kraus, 1968.
Pintard, John. "New Orleans, 1801: An Account by John Pintard." Edited by David Lee Stirling. *Louisiana Historical Quarterly* 34, no. 3 (1951): 218–33.
Postlethwaite, Samuel. "Journal of a Voyage from Louisville to Natchez 1800 by Samuel Postlethwaite." *Bulletin of the Missouri Historical Society* 7 (1951): 312–29.
Potter, Dorothy Williams. *Passports of Southeastern Pioneers, 1770–1823: Indian, Spanish, and Other Land Passports for Tennessee, Kentucky, Georgia, Mississippi, Virginia, North and South Carolina.* Birmingham, AL: Banner Press, 2010.
Robertson, David, ed. *Debates and Other Proceedings of the Convention of Virginia.* Richmond, VA: Enquirer-Press, 1805.
Sargent, Winthrop. *Papers in Relation to the Official Conduct of Governor Sargent.* Boston: Thomas and Andrews, 1801.
Schultz, Christian. *Travels on an Inland Voyage through the States of New-York, Pennsylvania, Virginia, Ohio, Kentucky and Tennessee: and through the Territories of Indiana, Louisiana, Mississippi and New-Orleans; Performed in the Years 1807 and 1808; Including a Tour of Nearly Six Thousand Miles.* 2 vols. New York: Isaac Riley, 1810.
Smith, Daniel. *A Short Description of the State of Tennessee: Lately Called the Territory of the United States, South of the River Ohio.* Philadelphia: Lang and Ustick, 1796.

Smith, Paul H., and Ronald M. Gephart, eds. *Letters of Delegates to Congress, 1774–1789.* 25 vols. Washington, DC: Library of Congress, 1976–2000.

Smith, Sam B., et al., eds. *The Papers of Andrew Jackson.* 11 vols. to date. Knoxville: University of Tennessee Press, 1980–.

Smith, William Henry. *The St. Clair Papers: The Life and Public Services of Arthur St. Clair.* 2 vols. Cincinnati: Robert Clarke, 1882.

"Speech to the Indians from the Secretary at War, Urging Peace into the Future, and Replies, 2 December 1796." In "Papers of the War Department, 1784 to 1800," Center for History and New Media, http://wardepartmentpapers.org.

Storm, Colton, ed. "Up the Tennessee in 1790: The Report of Major John Doughty to the Secretary of War," *East Tennessee Historical Society's Publications* 17 (1945): 119–32.

Syrett, Harold C., ed. *The Papers of Alexander Hamilton.* 27 vols. New York: Columbia University Press, 1961–87.

Thwaites, Reuben Gold, ed. *Early Western Travels, 1748–1846,* 32 vols. Cleveland: A. H. Clark, 1904–7.

Toulmin, Harry. *The Western Country in 1793: Reports on Kentucky and Virginia.* Edited by Marion Tinling and Godfrey Davies. San Marino, CA: Huntington Library and Art Gallery, 1948.

"Treaty of Friendship, Limits, and Navigation between Spain and the United States; October 27, 1795." In Samuel Flagg Bemis, *Pinckney's Treaty: A Study of America's Advantage from Europe's Distress,* 391–411. Baltimore: Johns Hopkins Press, 1926. Also available at the Avalon Project, Yale Law School, http://avalon.law.yale.edu/18th_century/sp1795.asp.

Twohig, Dorothy, et al., eds. *The Papers of George Washington.* Presidential Series. 21 vols. Charlottesville: University Press of Virginia, 1987–2020.

U.S. Census Office. *Return of the Whole Number of Persons within the Several Districts of the United States: According to "An Act Providing for the Enumeration of the Inhabitants of the United States," Passed February the 28th, One Thousand Eight Hundred.* Washington, DC: William Duane and Son, 1802.

U.S. Department of State. *A Message from the President of the United States, Transmitting a Report from the Secretary of State, with the Information Requested in a Resolution of the House, of the 17th Instant, Relative to the Violation on the Part of Spain of the Twenty-Second Article of the Treaty of Friendship, Limits, and Navigation between the United States and the King of Spain.* Washington, DC: William Duane, 1802.

U.S. Government. *American State Papers, Documents, Legislative and Executive, of the Congress of the United States.* 38 vols. Washington, DC: Gales and Seaton, 1832–61.

———. *Annals of Congress; or, The Debates and Proceedings of the Congress of the United States; with an Appendix, Containing Important State Papers and Public Documents, and All the Laws of a Public Nature; with a Copious Index,*

Compiled from Authentic Materials by Joseph Gales, Senior. 42 vols. Washington, DC: Gales and Seaton, 1834.

———. *Secret Journals of the Acts and Proceedings of Congress, from the First Meeting Thereof to the Dissolution of the Confederation.* 4 vols. Boston: Thomas B. Wait, 1820–21.

———. *State Papers and Correspondence Bearing upon the Purchase of the Territory of Louisiana.* Washington, DC: Government Printing Office, 1903.

Van Schreeven, William J., Robert L. Scribner, and Brent Tarter, eds. *Revolutionary Virginia: The Road to Independence.* 7 vols. Charlottesville, VA: University Press of Virginia, 1973–83.

Vattel, Emmerich de. *The Law of Nations; or, The Principles of Natural Law Applied to the Conduct and the Affairs of Nations and Sovereigns.* 1758. Indianapolis, IN: Liberty Fund, 2008.

Whitaker, Arthur Preston, trans. and ed. *Documents Relating to the Commercial Policy of Spain in the Floridas with Incidental Reference to Louisiana.* Deland: Florida State Historical Society, 1931.

Manuscript Sources

Assembly Papers Correspondence, 1801–3, 1806, 1809–11, 1814–15, series 520, box 29404. Mississippi Department of Archives and History, Jackson.

Beall-Booth Family Papers. Filson Historical Society, Louisville, KY.

British West Florida Transcripts. Alabama State Department of Archives and History, Montgomery.

Brown, Colonel John, and Major General Preston Brown Papers. Manuscripts and Archives, Yale University Library, New Haven, CT.

Brown, John, Miscellany. Filson Historical Society, Louisville, KY.

Bullitt Family Papers. Filson Historical Society, Louisville, KY.

Butler, Richard, Diary. Butler Family Papers. Special Collections, Louisiana State University, Baton Rouge.

Campbell, Arthur, Papers. Filson Historical Society, Louisville, KY.

Claiborne, J. F. H., Collection. Mississippi Department of Archives and History, Jackson.

Clifford Family Papers. Historical Society of Pennsylvania, Philadelphia.

Coxe, Daniel W., Papers. Historical Society of Pennsylvania, Philadelphia.

Coxe Family Papers. Historical Society of Pennsylvania, Philadelphia.

Darlington Collection. Special Collections, University of Pittsburgh.

Democratic Society of Clark County Records. Kentucky Historical Society, Frankfort.

Despatches from United States Consuls in New Orleans, 1798–1807. General Records of the Department of State, Record Group 59, Microcopy No T225. National Archives, College Park, MD.

Draper Manuscripts. Wisconsin Historical Society, Madison.
Dunbar, William, Papers. Mississippi Department of Archives and History, Jackson.
Fleming, Edmonds, Papers. Filson Historical Society, Louisville, KY.
Gardoqui, Diego de, Dispatches, Durrett Collection. Hannah Holborn Gray Special Collections, University of Chicago Library.
Gardoqui, Diego de, Papers. Tulane University Special Collections, New Orleans.
Greenberry, Dorsey, Papers. Historic New Orleans Collection.
Hopkins, Samuel, Papers. Kentucky Historical Society, Frankfort.
Hunt, Abijah, Papers. Dolph Briscoe Center for American History, University of Texas, Austin.
Hunt, Abijah and David, Papers. Historic New Orleans Collection.
Hunt, Abijah and David, Papers. Mississippi Department of Archives and History, Jackson.
Hunt, John Wesley, Papers. Filson Historical Society, Louisville, KY.
Hunt, John Wesley, Papers. Kentucky Historical Society, Frankfort.
Hunt, John Wesley (Morgan), Collection. Filson Historical Society, Louisville, KY.
Hunt-Morgan Papers. Filson Historical Society, Louisville, KY.
Hunt Morgan Papers. Special Collections, University of Kentucky Library, Lexington.
Innes, Harry, Collection. Kentucky Historical Society, Frankfort.
Innes, Harry, Papers. Manuscript Division, Library of Congress, Washington, DC.
Letters Received by the Department of State Relative to the Southern Boundary, Compiled 1796–1802; Commission Established under Article III of the October 27, 1795, Treaty between the United States and Spain. U.S. Commission; Records of Boundary and Claims Commissions and Arbitrations, Record Group 76. National Archives, College Park, MD.
Lewis Family Papers. Hannah Holborn Gray Special Collections, University of Chicago Library.
Livingston, Edward, Papers. Special Collections, Princeton University, Princeton, NJ.
Manuscript Records of the Bureau of Indian Affairs, Record Group 75. National Archives, College Park, MD.
McDonogh, John, Papers. Tulane University Special Collections, New Orleans.
Minor Family Papers. Special Collections, Louisiana State University, New Orleans.
Mississippi Territory Administration Papers, 1769, 1788–1817. Mississippi Department of Archives and History, Jackson.
Natchez Trace Collection. University of Southern Mississippi, Hattiesburg.

Papeles Procedentes de Cuba, Legajo 2361, Legajo 631A, 549, 631, 89, 582A, 514, 519A. Archivo General de Indias, Seville, Spain.
Payne and McDonogh Papers. Special Collections, New Orleans Public Library.
Pension and Bounty Land Warrant Application Files, 1800–1960, Record Group 15. National Archives, College Park, MD.
Petitions, 1802–1804, series 524, box 168. Mississippi Department of Archives and History, Jackson.
Records of the Post Office Department, Record Group 28. National Archives, College Park, MD.
Reed and Forde Papers. Historical Society of Pennsylvania, Philadelphia.
Shepherd Brown and Company Papers. Special Collections, New Orleans Public Library.
Short, William and Peyton, Papers. College of William and Mary, Williamsburg, VA.
Spanish Governors of Louisiana Dispatches. Louisiana Research Collection, LaRC.B-317. Tulane University Special Collections, Tulane University, New Orleans.
Spanish Louisiana Collection. Historic New Orleans Collection.
Stewart, Joseph Adger, Collection. Filson Historical Society, Louisville, KY.
Tarascon, Louis, Journal, 1799. Filson Historical Society, Louisville, KY.
Taylor, William Papers. Manuscript Division, Library of Congress, Washington, DC.
Wilkinson, James, Papers. Manuscript Division, Library of Congress, Washington, DC.
Wilkinson-Stark Papers. Historic New Orleans Collection.
Wisdom, John Minor, Collection. Mississippi Department of Archives and History, Jackson.

Secondary Sources

Abernethy, Thomas Perkins. *Western Lands and the American Revolution.* New York: D. Appleton-Century, 1937.
Ablavsky, Gregory. *Federal Ground: Governing Property and Violence in the First U.S. Territories.* New York: Oxford University Press, 2021.
——— . "The Savage Constitution." *Duke Law Journal* 63 (2013–14): 999–1089.
Adelman, Jeremy, and Stephen Aron. "From Borderlands to Borders: Empires, Nation-States, and the Peoples in between in North American History." *American Historical Review* 104, no. 3 (1999): 814–41.
Adkinson, Kandie. "Saddlebag Notes: The Kentucky Land Grant System," *Circuit Rider* 13, no. 3 (1990): i–iv. https://www.sos.ky.gov/land/resources/articles/Documents/SaddlebagNotes.pdf.
Allen, Gardner Weld. *Our Naval War with France.* Boston: Houghton Mifflin, 1909.

Allen, Michael. *Western Rivermen, 1763–1861: Ohio and Mississippi Boatmen and the Myth of the Alligator Horse*. Baton Rouge: Louisiana State University Press, 1990.
Ambler, Charles Henry. *A History of Transportation in the Ohio Valley*. Glendale, CA: Arthur H. Clark, 1932.
Arena, C. Richard. "Philadelphia–Spanish New Orleans Trade in the 1790's." *Louisiana History* 2, no. 4 (1961): 429–45.
Aron, Stephen. *American Confluence: The Missouri Frontier from Borderland to Border State*. Bloomington: Indiana University Press, 2005.
———. *How the West Was Lost: The Transformation of Kentucky from Daniel Boone to Henry Clay*. Baltimore: Johns Hopkins University Press, 1996.
———. "Pioneers and Profiteers: Land Speculation and the Homestead Ethic in Frontier Kentucky." *Western Historical Quarterly* 23, no. 2 (1992): 179–98.
Atherton, Lewis E. "John McDonogh—New Orleans Mercantile Capitalist." *Journal of Southern History* 7, no. 4 (1941): 451–81.
Atkinson, James R. *Splendid Land, Splendid People: The Chickasaw Indians to Removal*. Tuscaloosa: University of Alabama Press, 2004.
Baldwin, Leland D. *Whiskey Rebels: The Story of a Frontier Uprising*. Pittsburgh: University of Pittsburgh Press, 2010.
Balogh, Brian. *A Government Out of Sight: The Mystery of National Authority in Nineteenth-Century America*. Cambridge, UK: Cambridge University Press, 2009.
Banks, Kenneth J. *Chasing Empire across the Sea: Communications and the State in the French Atlantic, 1713–1763*. Montreal: McGill-Queen's University Press, 2002.
Banner, Stuart. *How the Indians Lost Their Land*. Cambridge, MA: Harvard University Press, 2005.
Baptist, Edward E. *The Half Has Never Been Told: Slavery and the Making of American Capitalism*. New York: Basic, 2014.
Barksdale, Kevin T. *The Lost State of Franklin: America's First Secession*. Lexington: University Press of Kentucky, 2009.
Barnett, James F. *Natchez Indians: A History to 1735*. Jackson: University Press of Mississippi, 2007.
Barr, Daniel P., ed. *The Boundaries between Us: Natives and Newcomers along the Frontiers of the Old Northwest Territory, 1750–1850*. Kent, OH: Kent State University Press, 2006.
Bean, Jonathan. "Marketing 'the Great American Commodity': Nathaniel Massie and Land Speculation on the Ohio Frontier, 1783–1813." *Ohio Valley History* 40, no. 1 (1931): 156–63.
Beckert, Sven. *Empire of Cotton: A Global History*. New York: Knopf, 2014.
Bemis, Samuel Flagg. *Jay's Treaty: A Study in Commerce and Diplomacy*. Revised ed. 1923; New Haven, CT: Yale University Press, 1962.

———. *Pinckney's Treaty: A Study of America's Advantage from Europe's Distress, 1783–1800*. Baltimore: Johns Hopkins University Press, 1926.
Bergmann, William H. *The American National State and the Early West*. Cambridge, UK: Cambridge University Press, 2012.
———. "A 'Commercial View of This Unfortunate War': Economic Roots of an American National State in the Ohio Valley, 1775–1795." *Early American Studies* 6, no. 1 (2008): 137–64.
Berry, Daina Ramey. *The Price for Their Pound of Flesh: The Value of the Enslaved, from Womb to Grave, in the Building of a Nation*. Boston: Beacon Press, 2017.
Bilder, Mary Sarah. "Without Doors: Native Nations and the Convention." *Fordham Law Review* 89, no. 5 (2021): 1707–59.
Blaakman, Michael A. *Speculation Nation: Land Mania in the Revolutionary American Republic*. Philadelphia: University of Pennsylvania Press, 2023.
Blaakman, Michael A., Emily Conroy Krutz, and Noelani Arista, eds. *The Early Imperial Republic: From the American Revolution to the U.S.-Mexican War*. Philadelphia: University of Pennsylvania Press, 2023.
Bogart, Ernest Ludlow. *Financial History of Ohio*. Urbana-Champaign: University of Illinois, 1912.
Bogert, Pen. "Sold for My Account: The Early Slave Trade between Kentucky and the Lower Mississippi Valley." *Ohio Valley History* 2, no. 1 (2002): 3–16.
Bond, Beverley W. *The Civilization of the Old Northwest*. New York: Macmillan, 1934.
Bouton, Cynthia A. "Flour for Pesos: Precarious Atlantic Financial Interdependency and the Provisioning of the Leclerc Expedition, 1802–1803." *Atlantic Studies* 15, no. 4 (2018): 504–22.
Bouton, Terry. "A Road Closed: Rural Insurgency in Post-Independence Pennsylvania." *Journal of American History* 87, no. 3 (2000): 855–87.
———. *Taming Democracy: "The People," the Founders, and the Troubled Ending of the American Revolution*. New York: Oxford University Press, 2007.
Bradburn, Douglas. "A Clamor in the Public Mind: Opposition to the Alien and Sedition Acts." *William and Mary Quarterly*, 3rd series, 65, no. 3 (2008): 565–600.
Breen, T. H. *The Marketplace of Revolution: How Consumer Politics Shaped American Independence*. New York: Oxford University Press, 2005.
———. *Tobacco Culture: The Mentality of the Great Tidewater Planters on the Eve of Revolution*. Princeton, NJ: Princeton University Press, 2001.
Bush, Robert D. *The Louisiana Purchase: A Global Context*. New York: Routledge, 2014.
Bushnell, David I., Jr. "The Virginia Frontier in History, 1778." *Virginia Magazine of History and Biography* 24, no. 1 (1916): 44–55.
Buss, James Joseph. *Winning the West with Words: Language and Conquest in the Lower Great Lakes*. Norman: University of Oklahoma Press, 2011.

Cangany, Catherine. *Frontier Seaport: Detroit's Transformation into an Atlantic Entrepôt*. Chicago: University of Chicago Press, 2014.

Caughey, John Walton. *McGillivray of the Creeks*. Columbia: University of South Carolina Press, 2007.

Cayton, Andrew R. L. *The Frontier Republic: Ideology and Politics in the Ohio Country, 1780–1825*. Kent, OH: Kent State University Press, 1986.

———. "Land, Power, and Reputation: The Cultural Dimension of Politics in the Ohio Country." *William and Mary Quarterly*, 3rd series, 47, no. 2 (1990): 266–86.

———. "'Separate Interests' and the Nation-State: The Washington Administration and the Origins of Regionalism in the Trans-Appalachian West." *Journal of American History* 79, no. 1 (1992): 39–67.

Chappell, Gordon T. "Some Patterns of Land Speculation in the Old Southwest." *Journal of Southern History* 15, no. 4 (1949): 463–77.

Claiborne, John Francis Hamtramck. *Mississippi, as a Province, Territory, and State: With Biographical Notices of Eminent Citizens*. Vol. 1. Jackson, MS: Power and Barksdale, 1880.

Clark, John Garretson. *New Orleans, 1718–1812: An Economic History*. Baton Rouge: Louisiana State University Press, 1970.

Clark, Thomas Dionysius, and John D. W. Guice. *Frontiers in Conflict: The Old Southwest, 1795–1830*. Albuquerque: University of New Mexico Press, 1989.

Clay, Floyd M., and Army Department, U.S. Department of Defense. *History of Navigation on the Lower Mississippi*. National Waterways Study 83-8, U.S. Army Engineer Water Resources Support Center, Institute for Water Resources, 1983.

Coatsworth, John H. "American Trade with European Colonies in the Caribbean and South America, 1790–1812." *William and Mary Quarterly*, 3rd series, 24, no. 2 (1967): 243–66.

Connolly, Emilie. "Panic, State Power, and Chickasaw Dispossession." *Journal of the Early Republic* 40, no. 4 (2020): 683–89.

Corbitt, D. C. "James Colbert and the Spanish Claims to the East Bank of the Mississippi." *Mississippi Valley Historical Review* 24 (1938): 457–72.

Cornell, Saul. "Aristocracy Assailed: The Ideology of Backcountry Anti-Federalism." *Journal of American History* 76, no. 4 (March 1990): 1148–72.

Cowger, Thomas A., and Mitch Caver. *Piominko, Chickasaw Leader*. Ada, OK: Chickasaw Press, 2017.

Cresswell, Nicholas. *The Journal of Nicholas Cresswell, 1774–1777*. New York: Dial Press, 1924.

Cromwell, Jesse. *The Smugglers' World: Illicit Trade and Atlantic Communities in Eighteenth-Century Venezuela*. Chapel Hill: University of North Carolina Press, 2018.

Cummins, Light Townsend. "'Her Weary Pilgrimage': The Remarkable Mississippi River Adventures of Anne McMeans, 1778–1782." *Louisiana History* 47, no. 4 (2006): 389–415.
Cutterham, Tom. "The International Dimension of the Federal Constitution." *Journal of American Studies* 48, no. 2 (2014): 501–15.
Davis, William C. *A Way through the Wilderness: The Natchez Trace and the Civilization of the Southern Frontier*. New York: HarperCollins, 1995.
Dawdy, Shannon Lee. *Building the Devil's Empire: French Colonial New Orleans*. Chicago: University of Chicago Press, 2008.
Dawson, Joseph G. *The Louisiana Governors: From Iberville to Edwards*. Baton Rouge: Louisiana State University Press, 1990.
DeConde, Alexander. *This Affair of Louisiana*. New York: Scribner, 1976.
Delo, David Michael. *Peddlers and Post Traders: The Army Sutler on the Frontier*. Salt Lake City: University of Utah Press, 1992.
Dickson, Charles Ellis. "James Monroe's Defense of Kentucky's Interests in the Confederation Congress: An Example of Early North/South Party Alignment." *Register of the Kentucky Historical Society* 74, no. 4 (1976): 261–80.
Din, Gilbert C. "Arkansas Post in the American Revolution." *Arkansas Historical Quarterly* 40, no. 1 (1981): 3–30.
———. "Spain's Immigration Policy in Louisiana and the American Penetration, 1792–1803." *Southwestern Historical Quarterly* 76, no. 3 (1973): 255–76.
Downes, Randolph C. "Trade in Frontier Ohio." *Mississippi Valley Historical Review* 16, no. 4 (1930): 467–94.
Drake, James D. *The Nation's Nature: How Continental Presumptions Gave Rise to the United States of America*. Charlottesville: University of Virginia Press, 2011.
Dupre, Daniel S. *Transforming the Cotton Frontier: Madison County, Alabama, 1800–1840*. Baton Rouge: Louisiana State University Press, 1997.
DuVal, Kathleen. *Independence Lost: Lives on the Edge of the American Revolution*. New York: Random House, 2015.
Dyson, John P. *The Early Chickasaw Homeland*. Ada, OK: Chickasaw Press, 2014.
Edelson, S. Max. *The New Map of Empire: How Britain Imagined America before Independence*. Cambridge, MA: Harvard University Press, 2017.
Edling, Max M. *A Revolution in Favor of Government: Origins of the U.S. Constitution and the Making of the American State*. New York: Oxford University Press, 2003.
Einhorn, Robin L. *American Taxation, American Slavery*. Chicago: University of Chicago Press, 2006.
Ellis, Elizabeth. *The Great Power of Small Nations: Indigenous Diplomacy in the Gulf South*. Philadelphia: University of Pennsylvania Press, 2023.

———. "The Natchez War Revisited: Violence, Multinational Settlements, and Indigenous Diplomacy in the Lower Mississippi Valley." *William and Mary Quarterly*, 3rd series, 77, no. 3 (2020): 441–72.

Eslinger, Ellen. *Citizens of Zion: The Social Origins of Camp Meeting Revivalism*. Knoxville: University of Tennessee Press, 1999.

———. "Farming on the Kentucky Frontier." *Register of the Kentucky Historical Society* 107, no. 1 (2009): 3–32.

———, ed. *Running Mad for Kentucky: Frontier Travel Accounts*. Lexington: University Press of Kentucky, 2004.

Ethridge, Robbie Franklyn. *From Chicaza to Chickasaw: The European Invasion and Transformation of the Mississippian World, 1540–1715*. Chapel Hill: University of North Carolina Press, 2010.

Feer, Robert A. "Shays's Rebellion and the Constitution: A Study in Causation." *New England Quarterly* 42, no. 3 (1969): 388–410.

Ford, Lisa. *Settler Sovereignty: Jurisdiction and Indigenous People in America and Australia, 1788–1836*. Cambridge, MA: Harvard University Press, 2010.

Fraser, Kathryn M. "Fort Jefferson: George Rogers Clark's Fort at the Mouth of the Ohio River, 1780–1781." *Register of the Kentucky Historical Society* 81, no. 1 (1983): 1–24.

Friend, Craig Thompson. *Along the Maysville Road: The Early American Republic in the Trans-Appalachian West*. Knoxville: University of Tennessee Press, 2005.

———. *Kentucke's Frontiers*. Bloomington: Indiana University Press, 2010.

Fuentes, Marisa. *Dispossessed Lives: Enslaved Women, Violence, and the Archive*. Philadelphia: University of Pennsylvania Press, 2016.

Furstenberg, François. "The Significance of the Trans-Appalachian Frontier in Atlantic History." *American Historical Review* 113, no. 3 (2008): 647–77.

Garcia, Hazel Dicken. "'A Great Deal of Money . . .': Notes on Kentucky Costs, 1786–1792." *Register of the Kentucky Historical Society* 77, no. 3 (1979): 186–200.

Garrison, Tim, and Greg O'Brien. *The Native South: New Histories and Enduring Legacies*. Omaha: University of Nebraska Press, 2017.

Gibson, Arrell Morgan. *The Chickasaws*. Norman: University of Oklahoma Press, 1981.

Gilje, Paul A. "Commerce and Conquest in Early American Foreign Relations, 1750–1850." *Journal of the Early Republic* 37, no. 4 (2017): 735–70.

Gleijeses, Piero. "Napoleon, Jefferson, and the Louisiana Purchase." *International History Review* 39, no. 2 (2017): 237–55.

Goodwin, Frank P. "The Development of the Miami Country." *Ohio History Journal* 18, no. 4 (1909): 484–503.

Gould, Eliga H. *Among the Powers of the Earth: The American Revolution and the Making of a New World Empire*. Cambridge, MA: Harvard University Press, 2012.

Griffin, Patrick. *American Leviathan: Empire, Nation, and Revolutionary Frontier*. New York: Hill and Wang, 2008.

Gruenwald, Kim M. *River of Enterprise: The Commercial Origins of Regional Identity in the Ohio Valley, 1790–1850*. Bloomington: Indiana University Press, 2002.

Guild, Josephus Conn. *Old Times in Tennessee, with Historical, Personal, and Political Scraps and Sketches*. Nashville: Tavel, Eastman, and Howell, 1878.

Hall, Nigel. "The Business Interests of Liverpool's Cotton Brokers, c. 1800–1914." *Northern History* 41, no. 2 (2004): 339–55.

———. "The Emergence of the Liverpool Raw Cotton Market, 1800–1850." *Northern History* 38, no. 1 (2001): 65–81.

Hammon, Neal O. "Initial Land Acquisition in Kentucky." Secretary of State Articles, Kentucky Secretary of State. https://www.sos.ky.gov/land/resources/articles/Documents/HammonInitialLandAcq.pdf.

———. "Settlers, Land Jobbers, and Outlyers: A Quantitative Analysis of Land Acquisition on the Kentucky Frontier." *Register of the Kentucky Historical Society* 84, no. 3 (1986): 241–62.

Hammond, John Craig. *Slavery, Freedom, and Expansion in the Early American West*. Charlottesville: University of Virginia Press, 2007.

———. "Slavery, Settlement, and Empire: The Expansion and Growth of Slavery in the Interior of the North American Continent, 1770–1820." *Journal of the Early Republic* 32, no. 2 (2012): 175–206.

Hancock, David. *Oceans of Wine: Madeira and the Emergence of American Trade and Taste*. New Haven, CT: Yale University Press, 2009.

Harper, Rob. *Unsettling the West: Violence and State Building in the Ohio Valley*. Philadelphia: University of Pennsylvania Press, 2018.

Harrison, Lowell H. *Kentucky's Road to Statehood*. Lexington: University Press of Kentucky, 1992.

Harrison, Lowell H., and James C. Klotter. *A New History of Kentucky*. Lexington: University Press of Kentucky, 1997.

Hartigan-O'Connor, Ellen. *The Ties That Buy: Women and Commerce in Revolutionary America*. Philadelphia: University of Pennsylvania Press, 2009.

Hatter, Lawrence B. A. *Citizens of Convenience: The Imperial Origins of American Nationhood on the U.S.-Canadian Border*. Charlottesville: University of Virginia Press, 2017.

Haynes, Robert V. *The Mississippi Territory and the Southwest Frontier, 1795–1817*. Lexington: University Press of Kentucky, 2010.

———. *The Natchez District and the American Revolution*. Jackson: University Press of Mississippi, 1976.

Hendrickson, David C. *Peace Pact: The Lost World of the American Founding*. Lawrence: University Press of Kansas, 2003.

Hill, Peter P. "Prologue to the Quasi-War: Stresses in Franco-American Commercial Relations, 1793–96." *Journal of Modern History* 49, no. 1 (1977): 1039–69.
Hinderaker, Eric. *Elusive Empires: Constructing Colonialism in the Ohio Valley, 1673–1800*. New York: Cambridge University Press, 1997.
Holmes, Jack D. L. "Cotton Gins in the Spanish Natchez District, 1795–1800." *Journal of Mississippi History* 31, no. 3 (1969): 159–71.
———. *Gayoso: The Life of a Spanish Governor in the Mississippi Valley, 1789–1799*. Baton Rouge: Louisiana State University Press, 1965.
Holton, Woody. "An 'Excess of Democracy': Or a Shortage? The Federalists' Earliest Adversaries." *Journal of the Early Republic* 25, no. 3 (2005): 339–82.
———. *Forced Founders: Indians, Debtors, Slaves, and the Making of the American Revolution in Virginia*. Chapel Hill: University of North Carolina Press, 1999.
———. *Unruly Americans and the Origins of the Constitution*. New York: Hill and Wang, 2007.
Hopkins, James F. *A History of the Hemp Industry in Kentucky*. Lexington: University Press of Kentucky, 1951.
Hudson, Angela Pulley. *Creek Paths and Federal Roads: Indians, Settlers, and Slaves and the Making of the American South*. Chapel Hill: University of North Carolina Press, 2010.
Hunter, Brooke. "Wheat, War, and the American Economy during the Age of Revolution." *William and Mary Quarterly*, 3rd series, 62, no. 3 (2005): 505–26.
Hurt, R. Douglas. *The Ohio Frontier: Crucible of the Old Northwest, 1720–1830*. Bloomington: Indiana University Press, 1998.
Hyde, Anne Farrar. *Empires, Nations, and Families: A History of the North American West, 1800–1860*. Lincoln: University of Nebraska Press, 2011.
Hyde, Francis E., Bradbury B. Parkinson, and Sheila Marriner. "The Cotton Broker and the Rise of the Liverpool Cotton Market." *Economic History Review* 8, no. 1 (1955): 75–83.
Inman, Natalie. *Brothers and Friends: Kinship in Early America*. Athens: University of Georgia Press, 2017.
James, D. Clayton. *Antebellum Natchez*. Baton Rouge: Louisiana State University Press, 1968.
———. "The Role of the Natchez Trace in the Development of the Nation." *Southern Quarterly* 29, no. 4 (1991): 21–34.
James, James Alton. *Oliver Pollock: The Life and Times of an Unknown Patriot*. New York: D. Appleton-Century, 1937.
Jillson, Willard Rouse. *The Kentucky Land Grants: A Systematic Index to All of the Land Grants Recorded in the State Land Office at Frankfort, Kentucky, 1782–1924*. Louisville, KY: Standard Printing, 1925.
John, Richard R. *Spreading the News: The American Postal System from Franklin to Morse*. Cambridge, MA: Harvard University Press, 1995.

Johnson, Sherry. *Climate and Catastrophe in Cuba and the Atlantic World in the Age of Revolution.* Chapel Hill: University of North Carolina Press, 2011.

———. "El Niño, Environmental Crisis, and the Emergence of Alternative Markets in the Hispanic Caribbean, 1760s–70s." *William and Mary Quarterly*, 3rd series, 62, no. XX (2005): 365–410.

Johnson, Walter. *River of Dark Dreams: Slavery and Empire in the Cotton Kingdom.* Cambridge, MA: Belknap Press of Harvard University Press, 2013.

———. *Soul by Soul: Life inside the Antebellum Slave Market.* Cambridge, MA: Harvard University Press, 1999.

Jones, Robert Francis. *The King of the Alley: William Duer, Politician, Entrepreneur, and Speculator, 1768–1799.* Philadelphia: American Philosophical Society, 1992.

Kaminski, John P. *George Clinton: Yeoman Politician of the New Republic.* Madison, WI: Madison House, 1993.

Karp, Matthew. *This Vast Southern Empire: Slaveholders at the Helm of American Foreign Policy.* Cambridge, MA: Harvard University Press, 2016.

Karras, Alan L. "'Custom Has the Force of Law': Local Officials and Contraband in the Bahamas and the Floridas, 1748–1779." *Florida Historical Quarterly* 80, no. 3 (2002): 281–311.

Kastor, Peter J. *The Nation's Crucible: The Louisiana Purchase and the Creation of America.* New Haven, CT: Yale University Press, 2004.

Kastor, Peter J., and François Weil, eds. *Empires of the Imagination: Transatlantic Histories of the Louisiana Purchase.* Charlottesville: University of Virginia Press, 2009.

Kelton, Paul. *Epidemics and Enslavement: Biological Catastrophe in the Native Southeast, 1492–1715.* Lincoln: University of Nebraska Press, 2007.

Kingston, Christopher. "Marine Insurance in Philadelphia during the Quasi-War with France, 1795–1801." *Journal of Economic History* 71, no. 1 (2011): 162–84.

Klein, Kerwin Lee. "Reclaiming the 'F' Word; or, Being and Becoming Postwestern." *Pacific Historical Review* 65, no. 2 (1996): 179–215.

Kukla, Jon. *A Wilderness So Immense: The Louisiana Purchase and the Destiny of America.* New York: Knopf, 2003.

Lakomäki, Sami. "'Our Line': The Shawnees, the United States, and Competing Borders on the Great Lakes Borderlands, 1795–1832." *Journal of the Early Republic* 34, no. 4 (2014): 597–624.

Lee, Jacob F. *Masters of the Middle Waters: Indian Nations and Colonial Ambitions along the Mississippi.* Cambridge, MA: Harvard University Press, 2019.

Lepler, Jessica M. *The Many Panics of 1837: People, Politics, and the Creation of a Transatlantic Financial Crisis.* New York: Cambridge University Press, 2013.

Levy, Jonathan. *Freaks of Fortune: The Emerging World of Capitalism and Risk in America.* Cambridge, MA: Harvard University Press, 2014.

Lewis, James A. "Anglo-American Entrepreneurs in Havana: The Background and Significance of the Expulsion of 1784–1785." In *The North American Role in the Spanish Imperial Economy, 1760–1819*, edited by Jacques A. Barbier and Allan J. Keuthe, 112–26. Manchester, UK: Manchester University Press, 1984.

Lewis, James E. *The American Union and the Problem of Neighborhood: The United States and the Collapse of the Spanish Empire, 1783–1829*. Chapel Hill: University of North Carolina Press, 1998.

Libby, David J. *Slavery and Frontier Mississippi, 1720–1835*. Jackson: University Press of Mississippi, 2004.

Limerick, Patricia Nelson. *The Legacy of Conquest: The Unbroken Past of the American West*. New York: Norton, 1987.

Link, Eugene Perry. *Democratic-Republican Societies*. New York: Columbia University Press, 1942.

Linklater, Andro. *Artist in Treason: The Extraordinary Double Life of General James Wilkinson*. New York: Walker, 2009.

Lydon, James G. *Fish and Flour for Gold, 1600–1800: Southern Europe in the Colonial Balance of Payments*. Philadelphia: Library Company of Philadelphia, 2008. https://www.librarycompany.org/Economics/PDF%20Files/lydon_web.pdf.

Mack, Dustin J. "The Chickasaws' Place-World: The Mississippi River in Chickasaw History and Geography." *Native South* 11 (2018): 1–28.

Marks, Frederick W., III. *Independence on Trial: Foreign Affairs and the Making of the Constitution*. Baton Rouge: Louisiana State University Press, 1973.

Martin, Ann Smart. *Buying into the World of Goods: Early Consumers in Backcountry Virginia*. Baltimore: Johns Hopkins University Press, 2008.

Mathews, Catharine Van Cortlandt. *Andrew Ellicott: His Life and Letters*. New York: Grafton Press, 1908.

Matson, Cathy D. "Accounting for War and Revolution: Philadelphia Merchants and Commercial Risk, 1774–1811." In *The Self-Perception of Early Modern Capitalists*, edited by Margaret Jacob and Catherine Secretan, 183–202. New York: Palgrave-McMillan, 2008.

———. *Merchants and Empire: Trading in Colonial New York*. Baltimore: Johns Hopkins University Press, 1998.

———. "Putting the Lydia to Sea: The Material Economy of Shipping in Colonial Philadelphia." *William and Mary Quarterly*, 3rd series, 74, no. 2 (2017): 303–32.

Matson, Cathy D., and Peter S. Onuf. *A Union of Interests: Political and Economic Thought in Revolutionary America*. Lawrence: University Press of Kansas, 1990.

Maul, George A. "The Annual Cycle of the Gulf Loop Current." *Journal of Marine Research* 35, no. 1 (1977): 29–47.

Maulden, Kristopher. *The Federalist Frontier: Settler Politics in the Old Northwest, 1783–1840*. Columbia: University of Missouri Press, 2019.

McCoy, Drew R. "James Madison and Visions of American Nationality in the Confederation Period: A Regional Perspective." In *Beyond Confederation: Origins of the Constitution and American National Identity*, edited by Richard R. Beeman, Stephen Botein, and Edward Carlos Carter, 226–58. Chapel Hill: University of North Carolina Press, 1987.

McMichael, F. Andrew. *Atlantic Loyalties: Americans in Spanish West Florida, 1785–1810*. Athens: University of Georgia Press, 2008.

Meacham, Jon. *American Lion: Andrew Jackson in the White House*. New York: Random House, 2008.

"Measures of Worth, Inflation Rates, Saving Calculator, Relative Value, Worth of a Dollar, Worth of a Pound, Purchasing Power, Gold Prices, GDP, History of Wages, Average Wage." Measuring Worth. http://www.measuringworth.com/datasets/exchangepound/result.php.

Merritt, Eli J. M., Thomas Green, and John Campbell. "Sectional Conflict and Secret Compromise: The Mississippi River Question and the United States Constitution." *American Journal of Legal History* 35, no. 2 (1991): 117–71.

Mihm, Stephen. "Follow the Money: The Return of Finance in the Early Republic." *Journal of the Early Republic* 36, no. 4 (2016): 783–804.

———. *A Nation of Counterfeiters: Capitalists, Con Men, and the Making of the United States*. Cambridge, MA: Harvard University Press, 2007.

Milne, George Edward. *Natchez Country: Indians, Colonists, and the Landscapes of Race in French Louisiana*. Athens: University of Georgia Press, 2015.

Mintz, Sidney Wilfred. *Sweetness and Power: The Place of Sugar in Modern History*. New York: Viking, 1985.

Morris, Christopher. *Becoming Southern: The Evolution of a Way of Life, Warren County and Vicksburg, Mississippi, 1770–1860*. New York: Oxford University Press, 1995.

———. *The Big Muddy: An Environmental History of the Mississippi and Its Peoples from Hernando de Soto to Hurricane Katrina*. New York: Oxford University Press, 2017.

Newhall, David S. "The Chickasaw." In *The Mississippi Encyclopedia*, edited by Ann Abadie, Charles Reagan Wilson, and Ted Ownby, 196–98. Jackson: University Press of Mississippi, 2017.

Nichols, David Andrew. *Red Gentlemen and White Savages: Indians, Federalists, and the Search for Order on the American Frontier*. Charlottesville: University of Virginia Press, 2008.

Norton, Marcy. *Sacred Gifts, Profane Pleasures: A History of Tobacco and Chocolate in the Atlantic World*. Ithaca, NY: Cornell University Press, 2008.

O'Brien, Greg. *Choctaws in a Revolutionary Age, 1750–1830*. Lincoln: University of Nebraska Press, 2002.

Onuf, Peter S. "Federalism, Republicanism, and the Origins of American Sectionalism." In *All Over the Map: Rethinking American Regions*, edited by Edward L. Ayers et al., 11–37. Baltimore: Johns Hopkins University Press, 1996.
———. *Jefferson's Empire: The Language of American Nationhood*. Charlottesville: University Press of Virginia, 2000.
———. *The Origins of the Federal Republic: Jurisdictional Controversies in the United States, 1775–1787*. Philadelphia: University of Pennsylvania Press, 1983.
———. *Statehood and Union: A History of the Northwest Ordinance*. Bloomington: Indiana University Press, 1987.
Orihel, Michelle. "'Mississippi Mad': The Democratic Society of Kentucky and the Sectional Politics of Navigation Rights." *Register of the Kentucky Historical Society* 114, nos. 3–4 (2016): 399–430.
Owsley, Harriet Chappell. "The Marriages of Rachel Donelson." *Tennessee Historical Quarterly* 36, no. 4 (1977): 479–92.
Pauketat, Timothy R. *Cahokia: Ancient America's Great City on the Mississippi*. New York: Penguin, 2010.
Pearce, Adrian J. *British Trade with Spanish America, 1763–1808*. Liverpool: Liverpool University Press, 2014.
Pelzer, Louis. "Economic Factors in the Acquisition of Louisiana." *Mississippi Valley Historical Association Proceedings* 6 (1912–13): 109–28.
Perdue, Theda. *Mixed Blood Indians: Racial Construction in the Early South*. Athens: University of Georgia Press, 2003.
Perkins, Elizabeth Ann. *Border Life: Experience and Perception in the Revolutionary Ohio Valley*. Chapel Hill: University of North Carolina Press, 1992.
———. "The Consumer Frontier: Household Consumption in Early Kentucky." *Journal of American History* 78, no. 2 (September 1991): 486–510.
Phelps, Dawson A. "The Natchez Trace in Tennessee History." *Tennessee Historical Quarterly* 13, no. 3 (1954): 195–203.
———. "Stands and Accommodations on the Natchez Trace." *Mississippi Journal of History* 11 (1949): 1–54.
Poovey, Mary. *Genres of the Credit Economy: Mediating Value in Eighteenth- and Nineteenth-Century Britain*. Chicago: University of Chicago Press, 2008.
Prewitt, Brad, and Brad Lieb. "A Tale of Two Cities: Chickasaw Inkana Foundation/Homecoming Series." *Journal of Chickasaw History and Culture* 18 (2016): 26–33.
Prucha, Francis Paul. *The Sword of the Republic: The United States Army on the Frontier, 1783–1846*. New York: Macmillan, 1968.
Quintero Saravia, Gonzalo M. *Bernardo de Gálvez: Spanish Hero of the American Revolution*. Chapel Hill: University of North Carolina Press, 2018.
Ramage, James A. *John Wesley Hunt, Pioneer Merchant, Manufacturer, and Financier*. Lexington: University Press of Kentucky, 1974.

Randall, James G. "George Rogers Clark's Service of Supply." *Mississippi Valley Historical Review* 8, no. 3 (1921): 250–63.
Rao, Gautham. "Thomas Worthington and the Great Transformation: Land Markets and Federal Power in the Ohio Valley, 1790–1805." *Ohio Valley History* 3, no. 4 (2003): 21–34.
Ray, Kristofer. *Middle Tennessee, 1775–1825: Progress and Popular Democracy on the Southwestern Frontier*. Knoxville: University of Tennessee Press, 2007.
Rea, Robert R. "A Naval Visitor in British West Florida." *Florida Historical Quarterly* 40, no. 2 (1961): 142–53.
Reda, John. *From Furs to Farms: The Transformation of the Mississippi Valley, 1762–1825*. DeKalb: Northern Illinois University Press, 2016.
Rees, Mark A., and Patrick C. Livingood, eds. *Plaquemine Archaeology*. Tuscaloosa: University of Alabama Press, 2007.
Remini, Robert V. "Andrew Jackson Takes an Oath of Allegiance to Spain." *Tennessee Historical Quarterly* 54, no. 1 (1995): 2–15.
Richter, Daniel K. *Facing East from Indian Country: A Native History of Early America*. Cambridge, MA: Harvard University Press, 2001.
Rockman, Seth. *Scraping By: Wage Labor, Slavery, and Survival in Early Baltimore*. Baltimore: Johns Hopkins University Press, 2009.
Rodriguez, John Eugene. *Spanish New Orleans: An Imperial City on the American Periphery, 1766–1803*. Baton Rouge: Louisiana State University Press, 2021.
Rodriguez, Junius P., ed. *The Louisiana Purchase: A Historical and Geographical Encyclopedia*. Santa Barbara, CA: Routledge, 2002.
Rohrbough, Malcolm J. *Trans-Appalachian Frontier: People, Societies, and Institutions, 1775–1850*. Bloomington: Indiana University Press, 2008.
Rosenthal, Caitlin. *Accounting for Slavery: Masters and Management*. Cambridge, MA: Harvard University Press, 2018.
Rothman, Adam. *Slave Country: American Expansion and the Origins of the Deep South*. Cambridge, MA: Harvard University Press, 2005.
Rothman, Joshua. *Flush Times and Fever Dreams: A Story of Capitalism and Slavery in the Age of Jackson*. Athens: University of Georgia Press, 2012.
———. *The Ledger and the Chain: How Domestic Slave Traders Shaped America*. New York: Basic, 2021.
Sachs, Honor. *Home Rule: Households, Manhood, and National Expansion on the Eighteenth-Century Kentucky Frontier*. New Haven, CT: Yale University Press, 2015.
Sadosky, Leonard J. *Revolutionary Negotiations: Indians, Empires, and Diplomats in the Founding of America*. Charlottesville: University of Virginia Press, 2009.
Saler, Bethel. *The Settlers' Empire: Colonialism and State Formation in America's Old Northwest*. Philadelphia: University of Pennsylvania Press, 2015.
Salvucci, Linda K. "Anglo-American Merchants and Stratagems for Success in Spanish Imperial Markets, 1783–1807." In *The North American Role in the*

Spanish Imperial Economy, 1760–1819, edited by J. A. Barbier and A. J. Kuethe, 127–33. Manchester, UK: Manchester University Press, 1984.

———. "Atlantic Intersections: Early American Commerce and the Rise of the Spanish West Indies (Cuba)." *Business History Review* 79, no. 4 (2005): 781–809.

———. "Supply, Demand, and the Making of a Market: Philadelphia and Havana at the Beginning of the Nineteenth Century." In *Atlantic Port Cities: Economy, Culture, and Society in the Atlantic World, 1650–1850*, edited by Franklin W. Knight and Peggy K. Liss, 40–57. Knoxville: University of Tennessee Press, 1991.

Saunt, Claudio. "Financing Dispossession: Stocks, Bonds, and the Deportation of Native Peoples in the Antebellum United States." *Journal of American History* 106, no. 2 (2019): 315–37.

———. *Unworthy Republic: The Dispossession of Native Americans and the Road to Indian Territory*. New York: Norton, 2020.

Scheerer, Hanno. "For Ten Years Past I Have Constantly Wished to Turn My Western Lands into Money: Speculator Frustration and Settlers' Bargaining Power in Ohio's Virginia Military District, 1795–1810." *Ohio Valley History* 14, no. 1 (2014): 3–27.

Schermerhorn, Calvin. *The Business of Slavery and the Rise of Capitalism, 1815–1860*. New Haven, CT: Yale University Press, 2015.

Schmitt, Casey S. "Virtue in Corruption: Privateers, Smugglers, and the Shape of Empire in the Eighteenth-Century Caribbean." *Early American Studies* 13, no. 1 (2015): 80–110.

Schoen, Brian. *The Fragile Fabric of Union: Cotton, Federal Politics, and the Global Origins of the Civil War*. Baltimore: Johns Hopkins University Press, 2009.

Sellers, Charles Coleman. *Mr. Peale's Museum: Charles Willson Peale and the First Popular Museum of Natural Science and Art*. New York: Norton, 1980.

Shannon, Timothy J. "The Ohio Company and the Meaning of Opportunity in the American West, 1786–1795." *New England Quarterly* 64, no. 3 (1991): 393–413.

Shepherd, William R. "Wilkinson and the Beginnings of the Spanish Conspiracy." *American Historical Review* 9, no. 3 (1904): 490–506.

Simeonov, Simeon Andonov. "'With What Right Are They Sending a Consul': Unauthorized Consulship, US Expansion, and the Transformation of the Spanish American Empire, 1795–1808." *Journal of the Early Republic* 40, no. 1 (2020): 19–44.

Sioli, Marco M. "The Democratic Republican Societies at the End of the Eighteenth Century: The Western Pennsylvania Experience." *Pennsylvania History* 60, no. 3 (1993): 288–304.

Sklansky, Jeffrey. *Sovereign of the Market: The Money Question in Early America*. Chicago: University of Chicago Press, 2017.

Snyder, Christina. *Slavery in Indian Country: The Changing Face of Captivity in Early America*. Cambridge, MA: Harvard University Press, 2010.

Swearingen, Mack. "Luxury at Natchez in 1801: A Ship's Manifest from the McDonogh Papers." *Journal of Southern History* 3, no. 2 (1937): 188–90.

Szatmary, David P. *Shays' Rebellion: The Making of an Agrarian Insurrection*. Amherst: University of Massachusetts Press, 1980.

Talbert, Charles Gano. "Kentuckians in the Virginia Convention of 1788." *Register of the Kentucky Historical Society* 58, no. 3 (July 1960): 187–93.

Tomlins, Christopher L. *Freedom Bound: Law, Labor, and Civic Identity in Colonizing English America, 1580–1865*. New York: Cambridge University Press, 2010.

Totten, Robbie J. "Security, Two Diplomacies, and the Formation of the U.S. Constitution: Review, Interpretation, and New Directions for the Study of the Early American Period." *Diplomatic History* 36, no. 1 (2012): 77–117.

Tucker, Robert W., and David C. Hendrickson. *Empire of Liberty: The Statecraft of Thomas Jefferson*. New York: Oxford University Press, 1990.

Turner, Frederick J. "The Significance of the Frontier in American History." In *Annual Report of the American Historical Association, for the Year 1893*, 197–227. Washington, DC: Government Printing Office, 1894.

U.S. Bureau of Labor Statistics. *History of Wages in the United States from Colonial Times to 1928*. Washington, DC: Government Printing Office, 1934.

U.S. Department of Commerce and Labor, Bureau of the Census. *Cotton Production*. Washington, DC: Government Printing Office, 1909.

Usner, Daniel H. *Indians, Settlers, and Slaves in a Frontier Exchange Economy: The Lower Mississippi Valley before 1783*. Chapel Hill: University of North Carolina Press, 1992.

Van Atta, John R. *Securing the West: Politics, Public Lands, and the Fate of the Old Republic, 1785–1850*. Baltimore: Johns Hopkins University Press, 2014.

Van Cleve, George. *A Slaveholders' Union: Slavery, Politics, and the Constitution in the Early American Republic*. Chicago: University of Chicago Press, 2010.

———. *We Have Not a Government: The Articles of Confederation and the Road to the Constitution*. Chicago: University of Chicago Press, 2017.

Veracini, Lorenzo. *Settler Colonialism: A Theoretical Overview*. Basingstoke, UK: Palgrave Macmillan, 2010.

Vidal, Cécile. *Caribbean New Orleans: Empire, Race, and the Making of a Slave Society*. Chapel Hill: University of North Carolina, 2019.

Washburn, Jeffrey. "Directing Their Own Change." *Native South* 13 (2020): 94–119.

Watlington, Patricia. "Discontent in Frontier Kentucky." *Register of the Kentucky Historical Society* 65, no. 2 (1967): 77–93.

———. *The Partisan Spirit: Kentucky Politics, 1779–1792*. New York: Atheneum, 1972.

Weaver, John C. *The Great Land Rush and the Making of the Modern World, 1650–1900*. Montreal: McGill-Queen's University Press, 2003.
Weeks, Charles A. "Of Rattlesnakes, Wolves, and Tigers: A Harangue at the Chickasaw Bluffs, 1796." *William and Mary Quarterly*, 3rd series, 67, no. 3 (2010): 487–518.
———. *Paths to a Middle Ground: The Diplomacy of Natchez, Boukfouka, Nogales, and San Fernando de Las Barrancas, 1791–1795*. Tuscaloosa: University of Alabama Press, 2005.
Whitaker, Arthur Preston. "The Commerce of Louisiana and the Floridas at the End of the Eighteenth Century." *Hispanic American Historical Review* 8, no. 2 (1928): 190–203.
———. *The Mississippi Question, 1795–1803: A Study in Trade, Politics and Diplomacy*. 1934. Reprint Gloucester, MA: P. Smith, 1962.
———. "Reed and Forde: Merchant Adventurers of Philadelphia: Their Trade with Spanish New Orleans." *Pennsylvania Magazine of History and Biography* 61, no. 3 (1937): 237–62.
———. *The Spanish-American Frontier, 1783–1795: The Westward Movement and the Spanish Retreat in the Mississippi Valley*. New York: Houghton Mifflin, 1927.
White, Richard. *The Middle Ground: Indians, Empires, and Republics in the Great Lakes Region, 1650–1815*. Cambridge: Cambridge University Press, 1991.
———. *The Roots of Dependency: Subsistence, Environment, and Social Change among the Choctaws, Pawnees, and Navajos*. Lincoln: University of Nebraska Press, 1983.
Wood, Gordon S. *The Creation of the American Republic, 1776–1787*. New York: Norton, 1993.
Woodward, Ralph Lee, Jr. "Spanish Commercial Policy in Louisiana, 1763–1803." *Louisiana History* 44, no. 2 (2003): 133–64.

Dissertations and Theses

Arena, Carmelo Richard. "Philadelphia–Spanish New Orleans Trade, 1789–1803." PhD diss., University of Pennsylvania, 1959.
Craig, Ronald Eugene. "The Colberts in Chickasaw History, 1783–1818: A Study in Internal Tribal Dynamics." PhD diss., University of New Mexico, 1998.
Doherty, Raymond. "The Colbert-Walker Site (22Le1048): History and Archaeology of a Chickasaw Home, Council House, and Travelers' Stand." PhD diss., University of Mississippi, 2022.
Flaherty, Daniel. "'People to Our Selves': Chickasaw Diplomacy and Political Development in the Nineteenth Century." PhD diss., University of Oklahoma, 2012.

Krichtal, Alexey. "Liverpool and the Raw Cotton Trade: A Study of the Port and Its Merchant Community, 1770–1815." MA thesis, Victoria University of Wellington, 2013.
Mack, Dustin J. "A River of Continuity, Tributaries of Change: The Chickasaws and the Mississippi River, 1735–1795." PhD diss., University of Oklahoma, 2015.
Ramage, James A. "The Hunts and Morgans: A Study of a Prominent Kentucky Family." PhD diss., University of Kentucky, 1972.
Smithey, Emily Paige. "Transformation of Early Nineteenth Century Chickasaw Leadership Patterns, 1800–1845." MA thesis, University of Mississippi, 2014.
Teute, Frederika. "Land, Liberty, and Labor in the Post-Revolutionary Era: Kentucky as the Promised Land." PhD diss., Johns Hopkins University, 1988.
Washburn, Jeffrey. "'Labor in the Field Is Much Changed': The Chickasaws and the Civilization Plan, 1790–1837." PhD diss., University of Mississippi, 2020.

INDEX

Italicized page numbers refer to illustrations.

agriculture: Chickasaw, 116–17, 120, 187, 190–91; Kentucky as veritable Eden for, 36; in Louisiana, 26; in Northwest Territory, 7; overproduction in West, 95, 238n13; payment for land with commodities and animals, 132–33. *See also* cotton; flour trade
Alabaman, 49
alcohol, federal tax on, 107. *See also* "Whiskey Rebellion"
American empire: and American Revolution, 69; beginnings of, as byproduct of obtaining commercial benefits, 257n16; and British withdrawal from posts in West, 128; cotton and enslavement as core of, 7–8; early visions of, 69–70, 93–94, 234n14; importance of Natchez Trace, 185–86; Louisiana Purchase as establishment of, 212–13; Mississippi River trade and growth of, 5, 135, 216; requirements for building, 5; and Western flour, 213
American Revolution: British along Mississippi River, 46; British colonists in lower Mississippi during, 29–30; British naval blockade during, 47; Chickasaw during, 30, 50, 52–54, 115; Choctaw during, 52; flour trade, 48, 54, 56, 57; Indigenous peoples during, 49, 50; land claims of United States, Spain, and Britain, 58; land sales to pay off debt, 7; legal title to land during, 33; Mississippi River trade during, 46, 48–49, 52–53, 55; Natchez during, 49–50; New Orleans during, 56; Ohio River during, 46; settlement of West by European Americans during, 31; Spain during, 47, 48–50, 52, 57, 58, 60–61; Treaty of Paris, 11–12, 13, 57, 59, 129; and vision of empire, 69
Amis, Thomas, 96
Annapolis Convention (1786), 69, 83
Articles of Confederation: revision of Articles, 82; treaty ratification requirements, 75, 77. *See also* U.S. government: under Articles of Confederation
Ashfield, V. Pearse, 170, 171, 172, 174
Atakapa people, 27
Atkin, Edward, 20
Atlantic trade system: arming of ships during European Wars, 173; circulation of cash in, 174; cotton, 152, 168, 212, 252n48; fur, 119; importance of, to West, 109; insurers of ships, 173; and Natchez, 195; and Natchez Trace, 186; and New Orleans, 25, 154–55, 160–62, 163–64, 195–96, 249nn6–7, 251n27; typical cargoes, 163, 168, 252n48; and value of Western land, 175; Western commodities, 149, 155
Austin, Moses, 32

Baily, Francis, 181, 184–85
Balbaha' Ásha' Okhina, 12. *See also* Mississippi River
Baldwin, Abraham, 87
Barbary States and Mediterranean trade, 71
Barbé-Marbois, François, 209–10
Barle, John, 105
Baton Rouge, 49
Battle of Fallen Timbers (1794), 102, 126, 129

Beall, Samuel, 31–32
Bemis, Samuel Flagg, 223n7
Biddle, Ann, 97
Blount, William, 85, 86, 120
Bolong, Gabriel, 4
Bradford, David, 139
Britain: and Chickasaw, 22, 25, 29, 50, 232n30; colonists in lower Mississippi during American Revolution, 29–30; flour trade in, 172, 174; fur trade, 22, 27, 129; Jay's Treaty and Northern Confederacy, 129; and land as payment for Army service, 39; land claims during American Revolution, 58; Louisiana as Spanish buffer against, 59–60; and Louisiana Purchase, 211; and maps of Mississippi River, 12; markets closed to American trade, 67–68, 71; along Mississippi River during American Revolution, 46; and Natchez people, 22; naval blockade during American Revolution, 47; Proclamation of 1763, 32, 35, 227n6; quality and price of cotton in, 171–72, 252n57; and Seven Years War, 28; shipping capacity of, 206; Spanish-French alliance against, 134; trade barred from New Orleans by Spain, 29; trade with Southeast tribes, 232n30; Treaty of Paris (1763), 28, 29; Treaty of Paris (1783), 11–12, 13, 57, 59, 129; withdrawal from western posts, 128
Broadhead, Daniel, 54
Brown, Captain John, 172, 174, 205
Brown, James, 100
Brown, John (Kentucky Senator), 205, 238n10, 252n47
Brown, Shepherd, 150, 175
Buckles, John, 25
Buckner, Philip, 184
Bullitt, Alexander, 95–96, 100
Burr, Aaron, 206

Caffery, John, 148
Cahokia, 18

Caribbean trade: and American goods in New Orleans, 154–55, 157–58, 195–96, 249n6; Cuba, 60–61, 159; and European Wars, 166, 169–70; flour, 158, 159, 169; French colonies in, 25; and Natchez Trace, 186; St. Domingue, 146, 157–58, 209; Western agricultural products in, 9
Carmichael, William, 124
Carondelet, Francisco Luis Héctor, Baron de, 65, 121, 141
cash: and bills of exchange, 105–6; and cotton, 153–54; for enslaved people, 151; Louisiana as source of, for Americans, 158–59; and market access, 45–46; and Mississippi River trade, 105, 107, 134, 155, 247n7; monetary policy during 1780s, 34; and Natchez Trace, 179, 184–86, 192, 193; necessary for tax payments, 107, 133–34; and New Orleans trade, 173, 206, 253n59; obtaining, to secure land, 32–33, 42–43, 62; and sale of federal land, 218; scarcity of, and payment in commodities and animals, 132–33; in Spanish colonial ports, 158; Spanish tobacco policy, 140, 245n9; trade and circulation of, 174; and trade with U.S. Army, 105; in West, 14, 34, 43–46, 104, 132–33, 174, 192, 193
Chakchiuma, 114–15
Charles-Maurice de, Talleyrand, 209
Cherokee: Americans on land of, 64; attacks on settlers in West by, 102; and Chickasaw, 28, 115, 118–19, 120, 122; and improvement of Natchez Trace, 186–87
Chickasaw: agriculture, 116–17, 120, 187, 190–91; American military aid, 126; during American Revolution, 30, 50, 52–54, 115; and British, 22, 25, 29, 150, 232n30; and Chakchiuma, 114; and Cherokee, 28, 115, 118–19, 120, 122; and Choctaw, 23–24, 28, 112, 116, 118; and Creek, 28, 112, 115, 118–19, 120, 122, 126; cultures membership, 254n6; dependence on European goods, 118;

economy, 116–18, 120, 179, 188, 190; and European diseases, 21–22; factions, 113–14; Fort Nogales, 64–65; and Jackson, 218; and Kickapoo, 118–19, 120; land distribution practices, 189; leadership structure of, 115–16, 188–89; lifeways of, 19, 187–88, 225n7; migration stories, 19, 225n6; and Mississippi River trade, 18, 20–21, 30, 50, 53, 61–62, 121; and Natchez people, 21, 22, 23; and Natchez Trace, 179, 186–87, 189–90, 191, 193; need for trading opportunities, 21, 113–14, 117; and Northern Confederacy, 126; peace with local Indigenous peoples, 28, 115, 116; and Pinckney's Treaty, 125; population, 25; removal of, from Mississippi, 218–19; settlers on land of, 50–51; during Seven Years War, 28; and Spain, 53, 59–60, 64–65, 113–14, 117–18, 121, 122–23, 125, 232n39, 242n7; territory of, 12–13, 20; trade in enslaved people, 21, 22, 118; Treaty of the Chickasaw Council House, 218; and United States, 53, 112, 113–14, 117–18, 121, 242n7. *See also* Colbert family

Chickasaw Trace, 21, 22, 177. *See also* Natchez Trace/Road

Chinubbee (Chickasaw Minko "king"), 117, 189

Chippewa, 63

Chitimacha, 22

Choctaw: during American Revolution, 49, 52; and Chakchiuma, 114; and Chickasaw, 23–24, 28, 112, 116, 118; and Creek, 112; Mississippi River as part of territory of, 12; and Natchez people, 23; and Natchez Trace, 186–87; and Spain, 59, 64–65, 232n39; trade with British, 232n30; and United States, 112, 121

Chokka' Falaa' (Long Town), 116, 126, 127, 177, 188, 190, 225n7

Chokkilissa' (Old Town)/Chukalissa (Big Town), 24–25, 114, 116, 127, 187–88, 225n7, 242n8

Christian, William, 95

Cincinnati, 101–2, 147

Claiborne, William C. C., 202, 212, 213

Clark, Daniel, Jr., 164, 165–66, 166–67, 168

Clark, Daniel, Sr., 248n61

Clark, George Rogers, 37, 50, 96–97

Clinkenbeard, Isaac, 38–39

Clinton, George, 203–4

codfish trade, 71–72

Colbert, George: as Chickasaw leader, 125, 189; and the cotton gin, 191; military victory against Creeks, 126; and the Natchez Trace, 189–90; as owner of enslaved persons, 191, 193; St. Clair's defeat, 120; and Treaty of the Chickasaw Council House, 218

Colbert family: and Chickasaw control over Natchez Trace, 179–80, 189–90; James, 52–53, 55, 177, 179; Levi, 189–90; as promoters of Chickasaw, 179, 254n6; William, 120, 122. *See also* Colbert, George

Common Sense (Paine), 155

Company of the West/of the Indies, 25–26

Constitution: admission of Western states, 87; and adoption of Northwest Ordinance, 84, 94; Connecticut Compromise, 87; delegates, 84–85; and Jay-Gardoqui Treaty, 90; and Mississippi Question and trade, 9, 68–69, 83, 86–89, 233n10, 236n63; ratification of, 89–91; treaty-making in, 88; and vision of American empire, 70. *See also* U.S. government: under Constitution

Continental Congress. *See also* U.S. government: under Articles of Confederation

cotton: adoption of, 135; American trade deficit and Western, 213; Atlantic trade system, 152, 168, 212, 252n48; and availability of cash, 153–54; bagging, 217; and Chickasaw, 190–91; cultivation, harvesting, and processing, 140, 146–47; and domestic slave market,

cotton (continued)
  150–51, 217; and enslavement as core of American empire, 7–8; European demand for, 152; ginners, 140, 151, 191, 247n57; importance of, 153; largest Liverpool importer of, 170; as lynchpin of interdependent global capitalist economy, 156; and Natchez, 120, 137, 149–51, 195, 248nn60–61; and Natchez Trace, 193; and New Orleans, 150, 155, 156, 195, 247n6, 248n61; profitability of, 150, 248n60; and purchase of New Orleans, 8–9; quality and price in Britain of, 171–72, 252n57; as replacement for tobacco, 140
Coxe, Daniel, 173–74
Coxe, Tench, 173
Creek: and American settlers, 64, 118; and Chickasaw, 28, 112, 115, 118–19, 120, 122, 126; and Choctaw, 112; and Spain, 59–60, 232n39; trade with British, 232n30; and United States, 112
Cruzat, Francisco, 239n25
Cruzat, Nicanora Ramos de, 53
Cuba, 60–61, 159
Cutler, Manasseh, 86

Dane, Nathan, 78, 81, 85
Davis, Caleb, 77
Davis, Thomas, 258n43
Deaderick and Foster, 148
deerskin trade. See fur trade
Delaware (Lenape), 102
Democratic-Republican Party: and Congress, 211; and improvement of Natchez Trace, 186; and western politics, 204–5
Democratic-Republican societies: and Mississippi Question and trade, 94, 106–9, 241n64; and secession from Union, 107
de Soto, Hernando, 18, 19
d'Iberville, Pierre Le Moyne, 22
diseases and Indigenous peoples, 21–22, 23
Dixon, Jeremiah, 142
Doughty, John, 116, 118, 119–20

Dunbar, William, 140, 151
Dunlap, John, 32
Dunn, Isaac, 99–100

Easterners/East: and adoption of Northwest Ordinance, 84, 86; cash from New Orleans to, 206; and closure of Mississippi River to Americans, 68, 75; fear of power of Westerners, 87; financial tools used in, 14; and Gardoqui, 76, 80–81, 82; as insurers of ships, 173; land in, 32; Louisiana Purchase as victory for merchants in, 9; and Louisiana retrocession to France, 198, 203–4; merchants' debts to British, 174; position on Americans' ability to navigate Mississippi River, 77; reaction to Jay-Gardoqui treaty proposals, 79; trade as binding West to, in American empire, 93–94
economy: and cash, 14, 34, 43–46, 104, 132–33, 174, 192, 193; Chickasaw, 116–18, 120, 188, 190; cotton as lynchpin of interdependent global capitalist, 156, 247n6; and enslaved people, 8; and Louisiana retrocession to France, 198; and Natchez Trace, 185–86, 192–93; Panic of 1797, 132; Pinckney's Treaty and creation of national, 175; recession of 1780s, 34; of United States under Articles of Confederation, 67–68, 71; Western reliance on external markets, 3, 34, 46
Ellicott, Andrew, 136, 142–43, 144, 164
Ellis, John, 201
enslaved people/enslavement: Africans imported for, 23, 26, 226n39; Chickasaw trade in, 21, 22, 118; and cotton, 7–8, 150–51; domestic trade in, 8, 138, 151, 217, 248n65; "Fancy Girls," 183, 254n19; Forks of the Road slave market, 194, 256n58; fugitive slave clause in Northwest Ordinance, 86; Indigenous peoples, 23, 226n27; in Louisiana, 26, 226n39; in Natchez, 145–46, 151, 183, 246n39, 247n41, 248n67; and Natchez

Trace, 193–94; and national economy, 8; in Northwest Territory, 86; rebellions by, 145–46; revolt of, in St. Domingue, 157–58; and Spanish policy, 138; in St. Domingue, 146

"federalist frontier," 92–93
Federalist Party: dismissal of Westerners' claims of government neglect, 110; and election of Jefferson, 205; journals of, 110, 241n76; and Louisiana Purchase, 211; and Mississippi River trade, 106–9, 241n64; in power in federal government, 106; Western animosity toward, 204–5
Ferguson, Daniel, 174
Ferguson, David, 149, 247n54
Few, William, 85, 86, 87
Fielding, John, 12
Filson, John, 36
first occupancy, right of, 38–39, 229n35
Fleming, William, 43
Floridas: during American Revolution, 30; Chickasaw and Spain, 65; under French, 207–8; trade and British residents in West, 49–50; Treaty of Paris terms, 28, 29
flour trade: and American empire, 213; and American Revolution, 48, 54, 56, 57; in Britain, 172, 174; Caribbean, 158, 159, 169; with Cuba, 60–61; in New Orleans, 24, 26, 48, 135, 155, 157, 168
Floyd, John, 43
Forks of the Road slave market, 194, 256n58
Forman, Gordon, 201
Fort Jefferson, 50–51
Fort Nogales, 64–65
Fort Rosalie, 24
Fowler, John, 100
France: alliance with Spain against Britain, 134; American Revolution peace terms, 57, 59; and Bourbon Compact, 78; embargo on American shipping, 169–70; and enslaved Africans, 23; and Floridas, 207–8; fur trade, 22, 24, 27, 55; invasion of Spain by, 124; Louisiana retroceded to, 196–99, 201–2, 258n25, 258n43; and Natchez people, 22–23; sale of Louisiana by, 209–11; settlements in Illinois, 26; settlements in lower Mississippi Valley, 23–24; and trade with Indigenous peoples, 27; trade with United States under Articles of Confederation, 67–68, 71; Treaty of Paris terms, 28–29; and warfare between Choctaw and Chickasaw, 23–24
Francisco Luis Héctor, Baron de Carondelet, 63
Franklin and Armfield, 256n58
fur trade: and Atlantic trade system, 119; and Britain, 22, 27, 129; and France, 22, 24, 27, 55; importance of, to Louisiana, 26–27; Ohio River Valley, 35–36; and Spain, 29

Gálvez, Bernardo de, 47, 48–49, 52, 56, 98
Gardoqui, Don Diego de: basic facts about, 74; on Congress's reaction to treaty proposals, 80; cultivation of Jay and Eastern members of Congress, 76; instructions given to, 74; negotiations with Jay, 74, 75, 78, 91; possible treaty with Eastern states, 80–81, 82; on reason for closing of Mississippi River to Americans, 61; on specie smuggling, 158
Garrard, James, 195, 202
Gayoso de Lemos, Don Manuel: and Chickasaw Bluffs, 122, 123; on cotton production, 140; governor of Natchez, 1, 136, 138–39; Hannon incident and Natchez Rebellion, 144–46, 147; and Pinckney's Treaty, 141–43; and separation of West from United States, 141; tax rate for American ships, 166–67; treaties made with Indigenous peoples by, 141
Georgia, 64, 87, 122, 141
Gerry, Elbridge, 88
Girault, John, 96, 157

Godoy y Álvarez de Faria, Manuel, 123, 142
Graham, John, 130
Grand Pré, Carlos de, 112, 113
Grayson, William, 79, 80, 85
"Great Southeastern Smallpox Epidemic," 21–22
Green, Thomas, 96
Grigra, 22
Grotius, Hugo, 123
Gulf of Mexico, as Spanish lake, 60

Habersham, Joseph, 176–77
Hall, James, 183
Hammond, Henry, 156
Hancock, John, 76
Hannon/Hannaw/Janan/Innan, 143–44, 147, 246n25
Harmar, Josiah, 92, 102
Hawkins, Benjamin, 84, 85, 86, 187
Hennen and Dixon, 153
Henry, Patrick, 37, 47, 90
Hopkins, Samuel, 185, 195
Houma, 49
Houston, William, 87
Hulings, William, 164, 199
Hunt, Abijah: and cotton, 149, 150, 216–17; Kentucky venture, 103–4; as New Orleans and Natchez broker/retailer, 149; Ohio merchant, 101–2, 216; as slave trader, 151; and U.S. Army, 94, 104–6, 110, 147, 148, 247n49
Hunt, Jeremiah, 101–2, 105–6, 217
Hunt, Jesse, 101–2, 105, 148
Hunt, John Wesley, 103–5, 148, 217
Hunt, Pearson, 103
Hunt, Wilson, 103
Hutchins, John, 248n60
Hutchins, Thomas, 70

Imlay, Gilbert, 13–14, 34
Indigenous land: Americans on, 50–51, 64–65; ceded after defeat of Northern Confederacy, 129; declared as "wasted" by Virginia, 38–39, 229n35; roads through, 179–80; sale of, 112, 122

Indigenous peoples: during American Revolution, 49; attacks on settlers in West by, 102; Cahokia, 18; "civilization policy" of U.S. government, 188; defeat of, west of Ohio, 106; dependence on European goods, 118; diplomatic agreements with, and Pinckney's Treaty, 128; enslavement of, 21, 22, 23, 118, 226n27; era of removal of, 218–19, 260n10; in Floridas, 208; lifeways of, 18, 27–28; Mississippian culture, 18; Mississippi River closure and American trade with, 118–19; Mississippi Valley trade structured for, 15; pan-tribal alliances of, 63–64, 65; Proclamation of 1763, 32, 35, 227n6; Spanish diplomatic and trade networks with, 59–60, 232n39; summit of largest tribes, Washington and McHenry, 126; trade with, as synonymous with maintaining political relations, 27, 59–60; treaties made by Gayoso with, 141
Innes, Harry, 100
Iroquois, 102
Irvine, William, 54–55

Jackson, Andrew: allegiance to Spain declared, 1, 2, 139; basic facts about, 1, 2, 219, 260n13; and Chickasaw, 218; on Louisiana Purchase, 211; and Memphis, 219; mental map of Mississippi River of, 13; and Rachel Robards, 139; transportation of enslaved people by, 8
Jay, John: and American right to Mississippi trade, 207; and Gardoqui, 74, 75, 76, 78, 91; negotiations with Spain, 74, 91, 234n34; treaty with Spain, 75, 78–81, 83, 85, 90, 235n43; Western animosity toward, 109, 204
Jay-Gardoqui Treaty (1786), 74, 75, 78–81, 83, 85, 90, 235n43
Jay's Treaty (1794): and British support for Northern Confederacy, 129; and British withdrawal from posts in West,

128; and reduction in U.S. Army force, 147; Spanish reaction to, 129, 142
Jefferson, Thomas: and American right to Mississippi River trade, 123–24, 207; election of, 205; on feeding Europe, 159; and Fort Jefferson, 50; on importance of New Orleans, 197; and improvement of Natchez Trace, 186–87; and Louisiana Purchase, 207–8, 259n50; and Monroe, 208; and right of preemption, 38
Johnson, William, 67
Jones, Evan, 160, 164, 181–82, 251n27

Kaskaskia (Illinois), 26, 27
Kemp, Levi, 190
Kentucky: cash shortage in, 34, 104; closure of New Orleans after retrocession to France, 202–3; consumer goods in, 104, 240n53; landless men in, 62; land speculation in, 31–33, 34, 227n11; Lord Dunmore's War in, 35; and Louisiana Purchase, 212; militia action against Spanish, 96–97, 98; and Mississippi River closure, 92; money in circulation in, 185; opposition to ratifying Constitution, 89–90; population growth, 38–39, 87, 95, 196; sentiment for secession from Union in, 100; separation from Virginia, 97, 100; statehood, 100; as veritable Eden, 36; and Virginia land policy, 39–42, 41, 229nn25–26; winter of 1779–80 in, 43–44
"Kentucky boats," 180–81
Kentucky Gazette, 103–4
Kickapoo, 63, 118–19, 120
King, Rufus, 77, 79, 80, 81
Knox, Henry, 77
Koroa, 22

La Balize (the Beacon), 160
L'Abbadie, Sylvester, 52–53
labor theory of property, 38
land: Atlantic trade system and value of Western, 175; ceded after defeat of Northern Confederacy, 129; Chickasaw, 50–51, 125, 189, 218; cost of unimproved versus improved, 150; in East, 32; forfeited by settlers, 44; of Indigenous peoples, 38–39, 50–51, 64–65, 112, 122, 129, 179–80, 229n35; legal title to, during American Revolution, 33; market access equated to, in West, 4; metes and bounds system of describing, 41–42; and Natchez Trace, 187, 193; obtaining cash to purchase, 32–33, 42–43, 62; obtaining title to, 40, 42–44; Ohio Company, 86; as payment for service in British Army, 39; policies of Spain, 1–2; right of preemption, 38–39, 229n35; sales in Northwest Territory, 72–73, 130–32; sales to pay national debt under Articles of Confederation, 67–68; Spanish policy of grants, 137–38; values in West and Mississippi River trade, 3, 4, 61. *See also* land speculation; United States: boundaries
Land Act (1796), 131–32, 133, 244n14
Land Act (1800), 133–34
land speculation: after American Revolution, 13; and Blount, 85; of Chickasaw land, 31–33, 34, 218, 227n11; and federal government, 227n11; and Land Acts (1796 and 1800), 133–34; land claims during American Revolution, 58; and Mississippi River, 95, 134; and national debt, 7; as national pastime, 31–32; and Panic of 1797, 132; Pinckney's Treaty, 4, 124, 127; after Pinckney's Treaty and defeat of Northern Confederacy, 129–32; and Proclamation of 1763, 32, 227n6; and Spanish policy, 138; and Virginia policy, 34, 39–42, 41, 44, 229nn25–26
Lanthois and Pitot, 166
Lark, William, 169
la Salle, René-Robert Cavelier, Sieur de, 18
Law, John, 25–26
LeClerc, Charles, 209
Lee, Henry, 82

Lenni Lenape, 63, 102
Lincoln, Benjamin, 77
Little Turkey (Cherokee chief), 115
Livingston, Robert, 208, 210
Lochry, Archibald, 36
Locke, John, 38
Lord Dunmore's War (1774), 35
Louisiana: agriculture in, 26; as buffer for Spain against British, 59–60; and Company of the West, 25–26; economy dominated by trade, 28; and economy of West, 198; enslaved Africans imported to, 26, 226n39; food deficit in, 157; fur trade, 26–27; profitability of colony of, 138; retrocession to France, 19, 196–99, 201–4, 205–6, 257n16, 258n25, 258n43; as source of cash for Americans, 158–59; under Spain, 55; Treaty of Paris terms, 28–29
Louisiana Purchase: area comprising West at time of, 5; British banks and, 210–11; as establishment of American empire, 212–13; and Federalist Party, 211; French reasons for selling, 208–10; and Jefferson, 207–8, 259n50; Monroe as negotiator for, 208, 210; as victory for collaboration of western farmers, southern planters, and Atlantic merchants, 9; and Westerners loyalty to federal government, 211–12, 259n65
Lynne, Edmund, 95

Madison, James: and American right to Mississippi trade, 207; Constitution and right of Westerners to navigate Mississippi River, 94; and division over Jay-Gardoqui Treaty, 82; expansion of federal authority, 83; and Louisiana retrocession to France, 198, 203; on Mississippi River trade and wealth of West, 87–88; and ratification of Constitution, 90
Manchac, 29, 49
market access: and cash, 45–46; economy of West as reliant on, 3, 46; as equal to land in West, 4; and peace terms of American Revolution, 59. *See also* Mississippi River trade
Marks, Frederick W., III, 236n63
Marshall, Thomas, 100
Martin, Joseph, 153
Martínez de Yrujo, Carlos Fernandez, 201
Mason, Charles, 142
Mason, George, 87, 88
Massachusetts, 34
Massie, Nathaniel, 132, 135
May, John, 31–32, 43–44
McClure, Robert, 132
McDonald, Thomas, 132
McDonogh, John, 162–64, 168, 172, 173, 175, 253n69
McDowell, Benjamin, 100
McGillivray, Alexander, 63, 121
McHenry, James, 105, 126
McIntosh, John, 190
McIntosh, Lachlan, 54
McMeans, Anne Jamison, 34–38, 42, 50, 51–52, 55–56, 61, 228n14
McNeill, John, 160, 168–69, 252n48
McQueen, Joshua, 11, 14, 48, 54–55, 62, 215, 216, 232n44
Memphis, 219
metes and bounds system of describing land, 41–42
Mexico, 60
Miami (Indigenous people), 63, 102
Miami Company, 130
Miami Purchase, 93
Michaux, François, 153, 154
military warrants, 39–40
Mingo, 102
Minkos (Chickasaw leaders), 115–16
Miró, Esteban: American expansion as threat to Spain, 98, 238n27; and Colbert, 53; departure of, 101; and Mississippi River as bargaining tool, 65, 98–99; proposed fort on Chickasaw Bluffs, 121; Wilkinson and, 98
Mississippian culture, 18
"Mississippi Bubble," 26

Mississippi Question: during Articles of Confederation government, 3, 4, 59, 61, 65, 83, 85, 236n63; during Constitutional government, 2–4, 68–69, 74, 75, 78–79, 107, 222n9, 223n7; control of, and Western loyalty, 19, 198, 202–4, 205–6, 257n16; and Democratic-Republican societies, 106, 107; and drafting of Constitution, 9, 68–69, 83, 86–89, 233n10, 236n63; and Pinckney's Treaty, 4, 9, 124–25, 222n9; and ratification of Constitution, 89–91; and secession from Union, 99–100, 101. *See also* Mississippi River closure

Mississippi River: during American Revolution, 46, 47; basic facts about, 17–18, 25; main shipping channel, 159–62, *161*, 251n27; maps of, 11–13, *12*, *13*, *161*; and Natchez Trace, 184; as vital to U.S. security, 70

Mississippi River closure: and American trade with Indigenous peoples, 118–19; and control of Southwest, 59, 61; and Democratic-Republican societies criticism of federal government, 94; effect on Easterners, 68; Jay-Gardoqui Treaty, 75, 78–81, 83, 85, 90, 235n43; and land values, 3, 95; Monroe on political effect of, 68; partial reopening (1788), 100, 239n37, 240n39; Pinckney's Treaty, 123–25; and slowing of American expansion, 61, 65

Mississippi River trade: during American Revolution, 48–49, 52–53, 55, 56; antebellum growth of, 215; Articles of Confederation government commitment to, 83, 91; and cash, 105, 107, 134, 155, 174, 247n7; and Chickasaw, 18, 20–21, 30, 50, 53, 61–62, 121; Colbert's attacks on, 52–53; and Constitution, 69, 90–91; and growth of American empire, 5, 135, 216; Gulf entrance procedures, 160–62, 251n27; and Indigenous peoples, 15; Jefferson and American right to, 123–24, 207; and Louisiana retrocession to France, 197–98; and Pennsylvania, 47–48, 54, 106–7; positions of political factions about, 106–9, 241n64; as positive right of Westerners, 108; skirmishes over, in Western Pennsylvania, 106–7; as tool in separation of West from United States, 65, 93, 94, 98–100, 107, 108, 237n4; Treaty of Paris (1783), 59; and wealth of West, 13–14, 45–46, 87–88; and Western land values, 3, 4, 61; and Wilkinson, 94, 99, 101, 106. *See also* Mississippi River closure; Natchez; New Orleans

Mississippi Territory: as borderlands, 222n4; closure of New Orleans after retrocession to France, 202; population growth, 196; removal of Chickasaw from, 218–19; sale of Chickasaw land in, 218

Mitchell, Samuel, 190

Monongahela Farmer, 196

Monongahela River, 35, *58*

Monroe, James: as negotiator for purchase of Floridas and New Orleans, 208, 210; on political effect of closure of Mississippi River to Americans, 68; and purchase of New Orleans, 8–9; on separate treaty between Spain and Eastern states, 81; on trade with Spain, 72

Morales, Juan, 166–67, 199, 201

Morris, Gouverneur, 86, 87

Mountain Leader's Trace. *See* Chickasaw Trace; Natchez Trace/Road

Muckleshamingo (Chickasaw war captain), 112

Muter, George, 100

Nahy. *See* Natchez people
Napoleon, 208–9
Napoleonic Wars, 251n43
Natché people. *See* Natchez people
Natchez (city and port): during American Revolution, 49–50, 52; American trade in, 135; and Atlantic trade system, 195;

Natchez (city and port) (*continued*)
attempted smuggling of American products in, 96; British trade in, 29; commodities brokers/retailers in, 149, 247n54; and cotton, 120, 140, 149–51, 195, 248nn60–61; enslaved population in, 145–46, 151, 183, 246n39, 247n41, 248n67; Forks of the Road slave market, 194, 256n58; Hannon incident and Rebellion in, 143–45; importance of, 24, 137; Natchez-under-the-Hill, 183; and Pinckney's Treaty, 7, 140–43; population, 137–38, 139, 145–46, 246n39, 247n41; prostitution in, 183, 254n19; and right of deposit, 168; road between Tennessee and, 176–77; sale of flour in, 54; slave trade in, 8, 151, 248n65; and Spain and American expansion, 64; Spanish retention of, 136; as stop to and from New Orleans, 181, 182–83; transfer of, to American sovereignty, 168; wealth of, 195

Natchez people: basic facts about, 21; and British, 22; and Chickasaw, 21, 22; and Choctaw, 23; control of Mississippi River, 18; dispersal and near destruction of, 24, 27; and European diseases, 21–22, 23; and French, 22–24

Natchez Trace/Road, *178*; and American traffic on Mississippi River, 184; basic facts about, 183–84; and Chickasaw, 179, 186–87, 189–90, 191, 193; as Chickasaw Trace, 21, 22, 177; Colberts' control of traffic on, 179–80; and enslaved people, 193–94; importance of, 192–94, 217; improvement of, under Jefferson administration, 186–87, 191; specie carried on, 184–86; and Westerners' loyalty to United States, 185–86, 192

"Natchez-under-the-Hill," 137, 245n2

Navarro, Martin, 98

New England: fish trade, 71–72, 79; loss of trade markets, 67–68; possible secession of, 77–78, 80–81. *See also* Easterners/East

New Orleans: during American Revolution, 56; and Atlantic trade system, 25, 154–55, 160–62, 163–64, 195–96, 249nn6–7, 251n27; British trade barred from, 29; and Caribbean trade, 157–58; commodities brokers/retailers in, 149; and cotton, 8–9, 150, 155, 156, 195, 247n6, 248n61; effect of European Wars on, 166, 251n43; finding buyers for Western goods in, 181; flour trade in, 24, 26, 48, 155, 157, 168; founding of, 25; and Henry, 47; importance of, 197; limited American trade allowed, 94, 99, 100, 106; ownership of ships and affordability of trading in, 165–66; port of, described, 162; and privateering, 170; and right of deposit, 154, 155, 163; road between Nashville and, 217–18; Spanish closure of, after Louisiana retrocession to France, 198–99, *200*, 201–2, 211, 258n25; Spanish imperial dominion and American trade in, 156–57; Spanish procedures in, 160–62, 163–64, 251n27, 251n35; specie as lure for using, 46, 173, 253n59; as target of attack by Kentucky militia, 98, 238n27; trade deficit and cash, 158–59; as transportation hub, 3, 26; and Treaty of Paris (1763), 28; trip back to Ohio Valley, 181–83; as U.S. port, 213; volume of American shipping in, 135, 154–55, 175, 189, 249nn6–7

New York and Northwest Territory, 72–73

North Carolina, 87, 96–97

Northern Confederacy: attacks on European American settlers, 64; and Britain, 129; defeat of, 102, 126, 129; members, 63; Piominko and attacks on, 114, 120; at summit of largest tribes, Washington, and McHenry, 125, 126

Northwest Ordinance, 84, 86, 94, 112

Northwest Territory: enslaved people in, 86; established, 84; governor of, 79; land tax, 133–34, 244n14; and

New York and Virginia land claims, 72–73; population growth, 7; sale of land, 72–73, 130–32; Virginia Military District, 131, 133
Nutt, Rush, 187–88

Odawa, 63
Ohio (state), 196, 205
Ohio Company of Associates, 86, 130
Ohio River, 45, 46, 119
Ohio River Valley: boatmen in New Orleans and trip home, 181–83; cash needs for land in, 134; economy of, 46; fur trade, 35–36; growth of settlements in, 129–32, 135; and Land Acts (1796 and 1800), 133–34; and Natchez, 137; New Orleans as nexus of trade, 155, 247nn6–7; opening of, 31; and Treaty of Greenville, 128; violence between Indigenous peoples and European Americans, 35–36
Ojibwe, 102
Old Hickory. See Jackson, Andrew
Opelousa people, 27
Ottawa, 102

Paine, Tom, 67–68, 155
Panic of 1797, 132
Panton and Leslie, 232n30
Path to the Choctaw. See Chickasaw Trace
Patterson, Joseph, 228n14
Paya Mattaha (Payamataha, Oppoia Mattaha, "Piomingo," Chickasaw war chief), 28, 115
Payne, William O., 162, 168, 173, 175, 253n69
Piankashaw, 63
Pickens, Andrew, 187
Pickering, Timothy, 169, 176
Pierce, William, 85, 86, 87
Pinckney, Charles, 79, 80, 81–82, 197–98, 207
Pinckney, Thomas, 123, 207
Pinckney's Treaty (1795), 127; and creation of national economy, 175; and diplomatic agreements with Indigenous peoples, 128; and Jefferson, 123–24; and Mississippi Question, 4, 9, 124–25, 222n9; and Natchez, 7, 140–43; and New Orleans, 155, 156; and right of deposit, 154, 155, 199; and role of West in political economy of United States, 9; as shaper of Western trade, 135; and Spain, 128; system developed to follow, 160–64, 251n27, 251n35
Piominko (Chickasaw war chief): attacks on Northern Confederacy, 114, 120; basic facts about, 114–15; on Chickasaw need for trading opportunities, 117; importance of, 117; Mississippi River as part of territory of Chickasaw, 12–13; plea for government relief by, 120–21; relations with United States, 113, 114, 120, 122, 242n7; and Spain, 123; at summit of largest tribes, Washington, and McHenry, 125, 126, 128; on U.S. failure to live up to building trading post, 117
Plaquemine peoples, 18
Pollock, Oliver, 47–48, 54, 61
Postlethwaite, Samuel, 149, 247n54
Potawatomi, 63, 102
preemption, right of, 38–39, 229n35
preemption warrants, 39–40
Proclamation of 1763, 32, 35, 227n6
Pufendorf, Samuel von, 123

Quapaw people, 27, 28

Rathbone, Hughes, and Duncan, 170–71
Rebecca, 155, 157, 163, 168–69, 170, 171–72
Reed and Forde, 169, 173, 174, 247n54
Reynolds, Benjamin, 218
right of deposit: functioning of, 154, 155, 163; and Louisiana retrocession to France, 199; and Pinckney's Treaty, 154, 155, 199; ships involved in, 165–68; Spanish procedures, 160–62, 163–64, 251n27
Road to Nashville. See Chickasaw Trace; Natchez Trace/Road

Road to Natchez. *See* Chickasaw Trace; Natchez Trace/Road
Robards, Lewis, 139
Robards, Rachel Donelson, 139
Robertson, James, 120, 121

Sakti Lhafa' (Chickasaw Bluffs), 20
Salecedo, Juan de, 201
Sargent, Winthrop, 176, 251n27
Scioto Land Company, 130
Second Treaty of San Idelfonso (1796), 134
Sedgwick, Theodore, 77, 79
Seneca people, 54
settlement warrants, 39–40, 44
settlers/settlements (European Americans): allegiance of, to Spain, 1, 2, 137–38; during American Revolution, 31, 48; attacks on by Northern Confederacy, 64; defined, 222n13; French, 23–24, 26; on Indigenous land, 50–51, 64, 118, 179–80; land forfeited by, 44; and Natchez Trace, 193; reliance on trade to sell products, 34; settlements after Pinckney's Treaty and defeat of Northern Confederacy, 129–32, 135; warfare with Indigenous peoples, 35–36, 102
Seven Years War (1756–63), 28, 39
Shane, John Dabney, 11
Shawnee, 63, 102
Shays, Daniel, 34
Shays' Rebellion, 82
Shepherd Brown and Company, 170–71, 175
Short, William, 123, 124
slavery. *See* enslaved people/enslavement; slave trade, domestic
slave trade, domestic, 8, 151, 217, 248n65
smallpox, 21–22
Smith, Daniel, 153
southern confederacy, 65, 121
Southerners/South: and adoption of Northwest Ordinance, 84; Louisiana Purchase as victory for, 9; position on Americans' ability to navigate Mississippi River, 75, 85; reaction to Jay-Gardoqui treaty proposals, 79; roads through western part of, 179–80
Southwest: defense of, from attacks, 102; Mississippi River trade closure and control of, 59, 61; warfare in West north of Ohio River versus in, 238n5
Spain: alliance with France against Britain, 134; and American expansion, 61, 64, 98, 238n27; during American Revolution, 46, 47, 48–50, 52, 57, 60–61; and American Revolution peace terms, 57, 59; British trade barred from New Orleans, 29; cash in colonial ports of, 158; and Chickasaw, 53, 59–60, 64–65, 113–14, 117–18, 121, 122–23, 125, 232n39, 242n7; and Choctaw, 59, 64–65, 232n39; closure of New Orleans after retrocession of Louisiana, 198–99, 200, 201–2, 211, 258n25; diplomatic and trade networks with Indigenous peoples, 59–60, 232n39; French invasion of, 124; fur trade, 29; imperial dominion of, and American trade in New Orleans, 156–57; Jay's negotiations with, 74, 91, 234n34; and Jay's Treaty (1794), 129, 142; Kentucky militia action against, 96–97, 98; land claims of, 58, 74; land grant policies, 1–2, 137–38; Louisiana retroceded to France, 196; Louisiana under, 55, 59–60; maps of Mississippi River, 11–12, *12*; Mississippi River trade as tool in separation of West from United States, 65, 98–100; and New England trade, 71–72; and pan-tribal alliance of Indigenous peoples, 63, 64, 65; and Pinckney's Treaty, 127, 128; procedures in New Orleans, 160–62, 163–64, 251n27, 251n35; restrictions on American trade, 67–68, 165–68, 240n39; and right of deposit in New Orleans, 154, 155, 163; settlers allegiance to, 1, 2, 137–38; tobacco policy, 139–40, 245n9; trade with Southeast tribes, 232n30; Treaty of Paris (1763), 28–29

specie. *See* cash
St. Clair, Arthur, 79, 80, 81, 102, 120, 205
St. Domingue, 146, 157–58, 209
St. Genevieve, 26
Summary View of the Rights of British America, A (Jefferson), 38
Swan, Caleb, 104, 105
Symmes, John Cleves, 93–94, 129–30, 132

Taboca (Chocktaw chief), 112
Taski Etoka (Chickasaw leader), 63–64, 65, 118
Taylor, John, 163, 168, 171, 172, 173
Taylor, William, 157, 162, 163, 171, 172–73, 174
Tchoukafala. *See* Chokka' Falaa' (Long Town)
Tennessee: animosity toward Federalist Party in, 205; closure of New Orleans after retrocession to France, 202–3; money in circulation in, 185; population growth, 196; road between Natchez and, 176–77; road between New Orleans and, 217–18
Tennessee Gazette, 148, 185, 186
Thomson, Charles, 84–85
Tiou, 22
tobacco, 139–40, 245n9
Todd, Levi, 36
Toulmin, Henry, 105
trade: American with Britain, 67–68, 71, 172; and American empire, 69–70, 93–94, 234n14; American with Chickasaw, 113–14, 117, 118–19; American with France, 67–68, 71, 169–70; American with Spain, 156–57, 164, 240n39, 251n35; American with Spanish Caribbean possessions, 60–61; by British residents in West Florida during American Revolution, 49–50; Cahokia, 18; Chickasaw, 21, 113–14, 117; Chickasaw with Spain, 59–60, 113–14, 117–18, 232n39, 242n7; commodities other than cotton, 153; and disease, 21–22; Eastern prosperity tied to Western, 206; and economy of Louisiana, 28; and Federalist view of western development, 93; fish, 71–72, 79; in guns and gunpowder, 118; importance of, to Westerners, 34, 135, 181; and Indigenous peoples, 27–28, 59–60, 118–19; information from right of deposit, 154, 155, 163; and integration of West into Union, 5, 93, 94, 237n4; modes of, 225n2; New England fish, 71–72, 79; in New Orleans, 25, 26, 154–55, 160–62, 163–64, 165–66, 195–96, 249nn6–7, 251n27; and road between Tennessee and Natchez, 176–77; role of retailers and brokers, 148–49, 170–71, 247n53; ship insurance, 173; ships involved in right of deposit, 165–68; as tied to diplomacy, 27; and U.S. Army, 102, 104–5; and writing of Constitution, 83, 236n63. *See also* Atlantic trade system; Caribbean trade; cotton; flour trade; fur trade; Mississippi River trade; slave trade, domestic
treasury warrants, 39–40
Treaty of Greenville (1795), 102, 128
Treaty of Hopewell (1785–86), 113–14, 117
Treaty of Ildefonso (1800), 196
Treaty of Paris (1763), 28, 29
Treaty of Paris (1783), 11–12, 13, 57, 59, 129
Treaty of San Lorenzo (1795). *See* Pinckney's Treaty
Treaty of the Chickasaw Council House (1816), 218
"treaty worthiness," 62
Tumbleston, Nat, 54
Tunica, 22
Turner, Frederick Jackson, 6

Ugulayacabé (Wolf's Friend), 113, 121, 122–23, 125
United States: boundaries, 2, 4, 11–12, 13, 28, 57, 58, 59, 124, 127, 128, 136; defeat of Northern Confederacy, 126; Jay's negotiations with Spain, 74, 91, 234n34; land sales, 130–32; and Mississippi Question, 2–4, 83, 108, 236n63

U.S. Army: and Abijah Hunt, 94, 104–6, 110, 147, 148, 247n49; bills of exchange, 105–6; as largest consumer in West, 102, 104–5; provisioning, 148, 247n49; redeployment of, 148, 247n48; reduction in force, 147

U.S. government:

—under Articles of Confederation: and American right to Mississippi River trade, 83, 91; and Chickasaw, 112, 113–14, 117–18, 242n7; economy of, 67–68, 71; Jay's presentation of negotiations' results, 78, 235n43; Kentucky statehood, 100; land speculation, 7, 227n11; and Mississippi Question, 3, 4, 83, 236n63; need to secure recognition of national claims, 62; perception of, as hostile to West, 97; sectional differences, 68, 233n9; Treaty of Paris (1783), 11–12, 13, 57, 59, 129; treaty with Choctaw and Chickasaw against Creek, 112

—under Constitution: and Chickasaw, 120, 121, 122, 218; and Choctaw, 121; Congress and Louisiana retrocession to France, 205, 258n43; and election of Jefferson, 205; Federalist Party in power, 106; Jay's Treaty, 129; legitimization of, in West, 5; Madison and expansion of authority of, 83; and Mississippi Question, 4, 222n9; Pinckney's Treaty (1795), 4, 123–25; policy of "civilizing" Indigenous peoples, 188; presidential power to purchase land, 211; reduction of Navy, 257n12; road building, 176–77, 179, 217–18; strength in West of, 93, 237n4; trade as principal component of western development, 93; West as shaping policy of, 93, 94, 238n5; Western Democratic-Republican societies, 94; Westerners' loyalty to, 19, 109–10, 185–86, 192, 198, 202–4, 205–6, 211–12, 257n16, 259n65; Western reliance on, 89

Vattel, Emmerich, 123
Vincennes (Illinois), 26, 27

violence. *See* warfare
Virginia: currency devaluation, 43, 44; and Henry, 47; Kentucky separation from, 97, 100; and Northwest Territory, 72–73; policy and land speculation, 34, 39–42, 41, 44, 229nn25–26; policy and Western reliance on external markets, 46; strength of government of, 62; types of land warrants, 39–42, 41, 229nn25–26; unclaimed land as "wasted" (1779), 38–39, 229n35
Virginia Military District (VMD), 131, 133
voyageurs, 22, 24

Wallace, Caleb, 100
Walnut Hill, 64
warfare: among Indigenous peoples, 23–24, 118–19, 120, 122, 126; between Indigenous peoples and European Americans, 35–36, 64, 102, 106; by Kentucky militia against Spanish merchants, 96–97; in Kentucky to open Mississippi River, 92; skirmishes over Mississippi River trade, 106–7; U.S. neutrality during, in Europe, 134–35; in West north of Ohio River versus in Southwest, 238n5. *See also* American Revolution
War of the First Coalition, 251n43
Washington, George: inauguration, 2; on land speculators, 31; and Piomunko, 122; summit with largest tribes, 126
Wayne, Anthony, 102–3, 104, 129
Wea people, 63
West, the: admission to Union, 87; and American Revolution peace terms, 57; area of, at time of Louisiana Purchase, 5; British withdrawal from posts in, 128; cotton and American trade deficit, 213; defined, 6; Democratic-Republican societies in, 106, 204; Easterners' fear of power of, 87; Eastern prosperity tied to trade with, 206; effect of Jay-Gardoqui Treaty, 81–82; expansion of, as threat to Spain, 98, 238n27; "federalist frontier,"

92–93; and Federalist Party, 204–5; flour and American empire, 213; governing structure of, 86; land sales to pay national debt, 67–68; land values, 3, 4, 175; legitimization of federal government in, 3, 5; Louisiana Purchase as victory for, 9; loyalty to United States, 19, 109–10, 141, 186, 192, 198, 202–4, 205–6, 211–12, 257n16, 259n65; and Mississippi Question, 2–4, 222n9; and Mississippi River, 2–3, 13–14, 61, 65, 87–88, 93, 94, 98–100, 101, 106–7, 108, 110, 189, 237n4; opposition to Jay in, 109; perception of Continental Congress as hostile to, 97; and Pinckney's Treaty, 9, 127, 128, 135; and ratification of Constitution, 89–90; reliance on federal government, 89; roads through southern part of, 179–80; settlements during American Revolution, 31, 48; shaping of federal policy by, 93, 94, 238n5; trade as necessary for integration of, into Union, 94; U.S. Army as consumer in, 102; and vision of American empire, 69–70, 93–94, 234n14; warfare in Southwest versus in, north of Ohio River, 238n5; "Whiskey Rebellion," 106–10. *See also* Western economy

Western economy: and agriculture, 9, 95, 238n13; and Atlantic trade system, 109, 149, 155, 175; cash in, 14, 34, 45–46, 104, 132–33, 174; and external markets, 3, 34, 46; and Louisiana retrocession to France, 198; and Natchez Trace, 185–86, 192–93; reliance on trade to sell products, 34

"Whiskey Rebellion," 106–10. *See also* Bradford, David

White, James, 82

White, Thomas, 56

Whitney, Eli, 140

Wilkinson, James: Abijah Hunt and, 104; acceptance of Louisiana from France, 213; early life, 97; and Natchez Trace, 187, 191, 192; and Spanish officials, 94, 97–100, 101, 239n25; trading privileges of, 94, 99, 101, 106; on wealth of Natchez, 195

Williamson, Hugh, 67, 73, 88–89

Willing, James, 49, 50

Wilson, Anne. See McMeans, Anne Jamison

Wilson, James, 88

Wooley, Milling, 149, 247n54

Wyandot, 63, 102

Yamasee War (1715), 22, 118

Yazoo Act (Georgia, 1795), 122

Youghiogheny River, 35, 37

Young, James, 37–38, 42

RECENT BOOKS IN THE SERIES
Jeffersonian America

Black Reason, White Feeling: The Jeffersonian Enlightenment in the African American Tradition
Hannah Spahn

Replanting a Slave Society: The Sugar and Cotton Revolutions in the Lower Mississippi Valley
Patrick Luck

The Celebrated Elizabeth Smith: Crafting Genius and Transatlantic Fame in the Romantic Era
Lucia McMahon

Rival Visions: How the Views of Jefferson and His Contemporaries Defined the Early American Republic
Dustin Gish and Andrew Bibby, editors

Revolutionary Prophecies: The Founders and America's Future
Robert M. S. McDonald and Peter S. Onuf, editors

The Founding of Thomas Jefferson's University
John A. Ragosta, Peter S. Onuf, and Andrew J. O'Shaughnessy, editors

Thomas Jefferson's Lives: Biographers and the Battle for History
Robert M. S. McDonald, editor

Jeffersonians in Power: The Rhetoric of Opposition Meets the Realities of Governing
Joanne B. Freeman and Johann N. Neem, editors

Jefferson on Display: Attire, Etiquette, and the Art of Presentation
G. S. Wilson

Jefferson's Body: A Corporeal Biography
Maurizio Valsania

Pulpit and Nation: Clergymen and the Politics of Revolutionary America
Spencer W. McBride

Blood from the Sky: Miracles and Politics in the Early American Republic
Adam Jortner

Confounding Father: Thomas Jefferson's Image in His Own Time
Robert M. S. McDonald

The Haitian Declaration of Independence: Creation, Context, and Legacy
Julia Gaffield, editor

Citizens of a Common Intellectual Homeland: The Transatlantic Origins of American Democracy and Nationhood
Armin Mattes

Between Sovereignty and Anarchy: The Politics of Violence in the American Revolutionary Era
Patrick Griffin, Robert G. Ingram, Peter S. Onuf, and Brian Schoen, editors

Patriotism and Piety: Federalist Politics and Religious Struggle in the New American Nation
Jonathan J. Den Hartog

Becoming Men of Some Consequence: Youth and Military Service in the Revolutionary War
John A. Ruddiman

Amelioration and Empire: Progress and Slavery in the Plantation Americas
Christa Dierksheide

Collegiate Republic: Cultivating an Ideal Society in Early America
Margaret Sumner

Era of Experimentation: American Political Practices in the Early Republic
Daniel Peart

Paine and Jefferson in the Age of Revolutions
Simon P. Newman and Peter S. Onuf, editors

Sons of the Father: George Washington and His Protégés
Robert M. S. McDonald, editor

Religious Freedom: Jefferson's Legacy, America's Creed
John Ragosta

Nature's Man: Thomas Jefferson's Philosophical Anthropology
Maurizio Valsania

State and Citizen: British America and the Early United States
Peter Thompson and Peter S. Onuf, editors

The Queen of America: Mary Cutts's Life of Dolley Madison
Catherine Allgor, editor

Light and Liberty: Thomas Jefferson and the Power of Knowledge
Robert M. S. McDonald, editor

"Those Who Labor for My Happiness": Slavery at Thomas Jefferson's Monticello
Lucia Stanton

www.ingramcontent.com/pod-product-compliance
Lightning Source LLC
Chambersburg PA
CBHW031758220426
43662CB00007B/449